MAKING
COMMUNICATIVE
LANGUAGE
TEACHING
HAPPEN

The McGraw-Hill Second Language Professional Series

General Editors: James F. Lee and Bill VanPatten

Directions in Second Language Learning and Teaching

Primarily for students of second language acquisition and teaching, curriculum developers, and teacher educators, *Directions in Second Language Learning* explores how languages are learned and used and how knowledge about language acquisition and use informs language teaching. The books in this strand emphasize principled approaches to language classroom instruction and management as well as to the education of foreign and second language teachers.

Making Communicative Language Teaching Happen, Second Edition
  by James F. Lee and Bill VanPatten, ISBN 0-07-365517-1

Translation Teaching: From Research to the Classroom
  by Sonia Colina, ISBN 0-07-248709-7

Gender in the Language Classroom
  by Monika Chavez, ISBN 0-07-236749-0

Tasks and Communicating in Language Classrooms
  by James F. Lee, ISBN 0-07-231054-5

Affect in Foreign Language and Second Language Learning: A Practical Guide to Creating a Low-Anxiety Classroom Atmosphere
  Edited by Dolly Jesusita Young, ISBN 0-07-038900-4

Communicative Competence: Theory and Classroom Practice, Second Edition
  by Sandra J. Savignon, ISBN 0-07-083736-8

Beyond Methods: Components of Second Language Teacher Education
  Edited by Kathleen Bardovi-Harlig and Beverly Hartford, ISBN 0-07-006106-8

Monographs in Second Language Learning and Teaching

The second strand in the series, *Monographs in Second Language Learning and Teaching,* is designed to provide brief and highly readable texts for beginners and nonspecialists that can be used as supplements to any of the books in the *Directions* strand or with other main texts. An additional goal of the *Monographs* strand is to provide an array of short texts that instructors may combine in various ways to fashion courses that suit their individual needs.

From Input to Output: A Teacher's Guide to Second Language Acquisition
  by Bill VanPatten, ISBN 0-07-282561-8

Breaking Tradition: An Exploration of the Historical Relationship between Theory and Practice in Second Language Teaching
  by Diane Musumeci, ISBN 0-07-044394-7

MAKING COMMUNICATIVE LANGUAGE TEACHING HAPPEN

SECOND EDITION

James F. Lee
Indiana University

Bill VanPatten
The University of Illinois at Chicago

Boston   Burr Ridge, IL   Dubuque, IA   Madison, WI   New York
San Francisco   St. Louis   Bangkok   Bogotá   Caracas   Kuala Lumpur
Lisbon   London   Madrid   Mexico City   Milan   Montreal   New Delhi
Santiago   Seoul   Singapore   Sydney   Taipei   Toronto

Making Communicative Language Teaching Happen, 2e

Published by McGraw-Hill, a business unit of The McGraw-Hill Companies, Inc., 1221
Avenue of the Americas, New York, NY, 10020. Copyright © 2003, 1995 by the McGraw-Hill
Companies, Inc. All rights reserved. No part of this publication may be reproduced or distributed in any
form or by any means, or stored in a database or retrieval system, without the prior written consent of The
McGraw-Hill Companies, Inc., including, but not limited to, in any network or other electronic storage or
transmission, or broadcast for distance learning.
Some ancillaries, including electronic and print components, may not be available to
customers outside the United States.

This book in printed on acid-free paper.

8 9 0 QFR/QFR 154321

ISBN-13: 978-0-07-365517-8

ISBN-10: 0-07-365517-1

Publisher: *William R. Glass*
Developmental editor: *Kate Engelberg*
Project manager: *David Sutton*
Production supervisor: *Richard DeVitto*
Designer: *Violeta Diaz*
Compositor: *Techbooks*
Typeface: *10/12 Palatino*
Printer: *QuadGraphics/Fairfield*

Library of Congress Cataloging-in-Publication Data

Lee, James F.
   Making communicative language teaching happen / James F. Lee, Bill VanPatten.-- 2nd ed.
      p. cm. -- (The McGraw-Hill foreign language professional series)
   Includes bibliographical references and index.
   ISBN 0-07-365517-1 (softcover)
    1. Language and languages--Study and teaching. 2. Communicative competence. I.
VanPatten, Bill. II. Title. III. Series.

PN53.L437 2003
418'.0071--dc21

                                                          2002045199

www.mhhe.com

DEDICATION

In the first edition of our book, we offered the following dedication:

To Lucy and Ginger, *two beautiful branches on the Lee-VanPatten family tree.*

To Tracy D. Terrell, *whose death left a tremendous void in the profession. Tracy was a role model both personally and professionally. His research in Spanish linguistics is standard reading, and his contributions to language instruction shaped the direction of communicative language teaching throughout the 1980s. From the start of our careers, Tracy encouraged us to explore and develop our ideas, to publish, to research, to make changes, and to challenge tradition.*

To Ivan A. Schulman, *under whose tenure as head of our department second language acquisition became recognized as a legitimate field of scholarly endeavor. We hope that other applied linguists and second language acquisitionists working in foreign language departments find the support, challenge, freedom, friendship, and mentoring that we found in Ivan.*

Lucy and Ginger have since passed on, and our lives have changed in a number of ways. While keeping the above we would like to add the following:

To Darlene F. Wolf, *whose career in language teaching was cut short in 1994 and never got to see our book (and her name) in print.*

To Murphy Wolf Lee VanPatten *who, being the cat that he is, has hung on a lot longer than Lucy and Ginger.*

ABOUT THE AUTHORS

JAMES F. LEE is Professor of Spanish at Indiana University, where he directs the Spanish Language Program as well as the programs in Hispanic Linguistics. With Bill VanPatten, he serves as general editor of the McGraw-Hill Second Language Professional Series. Lee is the author of *Tasks and Communicating in Language Classrooms* (2000), published by McGraw-Hill. He is also the co-author of the best-selling college text *¿Sabías que... ?* as well as the well-known college second-year text, *¿Qué te parece?* He is widely known for his research on second language reading, input processing, and the relationship between the two; his articles have appeared in *Studies in Second Language Acquisition,* the *Modern Language Journal, Applied Language Learning,* and *Spanish Applied Linguistics.* He has also co-edited a number of research volumes and has contributed chapters to numerous books. When not engaged in scholarly activities, he is busy taking care of his triplet daughters.

BILL VANPATTEN is Professor of Spanish and Second Language Acquisition at The University of Illinois at Chicago, where he directs the Spanish Basic Language Program. VanPatten is the author of *From Input to Output: A Teacher's Guide to Second Language Acquisition* (2003), published by McGraw-Hill; *Processing Instruction: Theory, Research, and Commentary* (2003), published by Erlbaum; and *Input Processing and Grammar Instruction: Theory and Research* (1996), published by Ablex. He is the co-author of the best-selling college text *¿Sabías que... ?* and is the creator and designer of the popular PBS television course *Destinos* as well as the upcoming *Sol y viento.* VanPatten is an internationally known scholar in input processing and processing instruction; his contributions appear not only in book chapters but also in journals such as *Studies in Second Language Acquisition,* the *Modern Language Journal,* and others. When not engaged in scholarly activities, he is busy writing novels and doing stand-up comedy in Chicago.

CONTENTS

When the first edition of *Making Communication Language Teaching Happen* was published, we believed we were offering a novel framework for classroom language teachers. Not only were we talking about new roles and responsibilities for instructors and students in classrooms, but we were also advocating new ways to conceptualize lesson goals and planning as well as a relatively new (at the time) approach to teaching grammar within a communicative framework.

In the course of working on this second edition, we came to understand that what for us may be old hat now (and sometimes difficult to go back to and revise!) is still very new for others. After all, a primary audience for this book is students who are taking their first course on language teaching. So we find once again that the framework outlined in this book will be novel to many. With this realization in mind, we explain here, as we did in the first edition, some of the premises on which this book is based.

WHAT IS THIS BOOK ABOUT?

Making Communicative Language Teaching Happen is intended as a guide to help language teachers develop communicative classroom environments that blend listening, speaking, reading, and writing. Starting from the perspective that communication is the expression, interpretation, and negotiation of meaning—not rote repetition, the exchange of information in the service of a grammar lesson, or simply oral expression—the book explores various topics that lead to concrete suggestions for implementing communicative language teaching. Among these topics are the following:

- A classroom dynamic in which instructor and learner take on roles and responsibilities different from those they traditionally hold
- The important role of comprehensible, meaning-bearing input in second language acquisition, and suggestions for creating such rich input

- The process of developing and building toward proficiency goals in classroom lessons
- An examination of oral communication in the classroom, and suggestions for redirecting oral communication toward information-exchange tasks
- An approach to grammar instruction based on structured input and structured output activities that help learners connect meaning to grammatical form

This book is not the product of a particular theory, method, or school of thought. Instead, it culls from second language research as well as our own experiences as researchers, classroom teachers, language program directors, teacher educators, and materials developers. Many ideas and suggestions contained in *Making Communicative Language Teaching Happen* represent our attempts to shape practice out of research and theory on second language acquisition.

We wrote this book for graduate teaching assistants and undergraduate teacher education majors who might benefit from a directed exploration of communicative language teaching. We also wrote it for practicing teachers who need a resource manual for developing tasks and materials for their classrooms. For them, as well as for instructors-in-training, there are some two hundred activities and test sections throughout the book.

WHAT'S CHANGED IN THIS EDITION?

For the second edition, we have thoroughly revised and updated the entire text. The major changes are as follows:

- The organization of the book has been substantially revised, and the grouping of chapters into units has been eliminated. Discussions of oral communication, information-based tasks, and building toward a proficiency goal now come early in the book rather than later. We think this reorganization corresponds better to the experiences of instructors, including ourselves, than did the organization of the first edition. In particular, moving the chapter on building toward a proficiency goal to an earlier position—it's now Chapter 4—places the framework of the book at the beginning, where it should be.
- We have added new information on second language acquisition that we believe is essential for understanding the nature of communicative language teaching (Chapter 1).
- We have added a new chapter on issues in grammar learning and teaching (Chapter 6) to broaden the context in which we develop our own ideas.
- We have included an Appendix that contains a sample processing instruction lesson in its entirety so students can see how this approach to grammar instruction works.
- We have added sections on the teaching of culture where appropriate and useful.

- We have included three different types of activities at the ends of chapters to support learning and application both in the classroom and beyond it.
- We have added a Prologue to orient the reader and preview the topics to be covered in the text. We also use this section to explain how we view the teaching of culture and how culture is treated in this book. The Prologue is a substantially rewritten version of the first edition's Epilogue.

The book, then, is still useful—we hope, more useful—for its intended audiences. For some, the book will service as a complete course. For others, it will direct their thinking about topics they are exploring in other readings. For still others, it will serve as a resource manual for developing communicative tasks and activities. In short, although we have updated and reorganized the book considerably, its purpose and audience remain the same.

HOW IS THE BOOK ORGANIZED?

As mentioned, the book has been substantially reorganized. Chapter titles, which are fairly self-explanatory, are listed below. For those familiar with the first edition, we also include a brief explanation of the correspondence between the new organization and the organization of the first edition.

Chapter 1 From Atlas and Audiolingualism to Acquisition. This chapter includes some material from the first-edition Chapter 1 and a great deal of new material on second language acquisition.

Chapter 2 Working with Comprehensible Input. A revised version of the first-edition Chapter 3.

Chapter 3 Communicating in the Classroom. A revised version of the first-edition Chapter 8.

Chapter 4 Building Toward a Proficiency Goal. A revised version of the first-edition Chapter 13.

Chapter 5 Suggestions for Using Information-Exchange Tasks for Oral Testing. A revised version of the first-edition Chapter 9.

Chapter 6 Issues in Learning and Testing Grammar. A new chapter, using some ideas from the first-edition Chapters 5 and 6.

Chapter 7 Processing Instruction and Structured Input. A revised version of the first-edition Chapter 5.

Chapter 8 Structured Output: A Focus on Form in Language Production. A revised version of the first-edition Chapter 6.

Chapter 9 Suggestions for Testing Grammar. A revised version of the first-edition Chapter 7.

Chapter 10 Listening Comprehension. A revised version of the first-edition Chapter 4.

Chapter 11 Comprehending Written Language. A revised version of the first-edition Chapter 10.

Chapter 12 Writing and Composing in a Second Language. A revised version of the first-edition Chapter 11.

Chapter 13 Issues in Testing Comprehension and in Evaluating Writing. A revised version of the first-edition Chapter 12.

SPECIAL FEATURES

Because we have used *Making Communicative Language Teaching Happen* with our own students, we have created a pedagogical framework to enhance the content of the chapters. *"Pause to consider . . ."* *boxes*, placed strategically throughout each chapter, invite students to stop and think about a particular issue. These boxes address such topics as classroom management, error correction, lesson planning, testing and evaluation procedures, and the components of communicative language ability, among many others. The teaching of culture is a new topic in several "Pause to consider . . ." boxes. In addition to providing students with opportunities for reflection, these boxes can be used as starting points for classroom discussion, topics for individual presentations in class, or writing assignments.

At the beginning of each chapter we have added a *list of the main topics* explored in the pages that follow ("In this chapter we explore: . . ."). This list previews the chapter for students, alerting them to the content of the chapter and providing an advance organizer.

Listings of *Key Terms, Concepts, and Issues* are included at the end of every chapter. As suggested by the title, this feature includes more than just the important terms used in the chapter; rather, it includes references to all the significant ideas presented in the chapter. Students can use this list as a review and self-test, making sure they have understood the content of the entire chapter.

New additions to the end-of-chapter materials are three different types of activities. Activities for additional discussion on selected topics from the chapter are included in *Thinking More About It: Discussion Questions.* Activities designed to promote hands-on research are included in *Getting a Closer Look: Research Activities.* And activities for the development of a language teaching portfolio are included in *Making Communicative Language Teaching Happen: Portfolio Activities.*

Many of the activities have been taken from the workbook that accompanied the first edition (though many others are new). We have elected not to revise the workbook with this edition but instead to use the best of what it offered within the text itself. We also provide a *Web site* (**www.mhhe.com/mclth2**) with this edition that includes additional exercises, assignments, and other resources. Together, all of these features provide a rich, flexible, and active learning experience for those using the book in a course on language teaching.

ACKNOWLEDGMENTS

In the first edition, we expressed thanks to a number of people who commented on the manuscript, used it in courses they taught, and reviewed it as part of the McGraw-Hill review process. We have added to their names below the names of those who offered comments and suggestions as part of our second edition review process; many of them used the first edition in courses on language teaching. Our thanks to all.

First Edition

Terry L. Ballman, University of Northern Colorado
Jane E. Berne, University of North Dakota
Frank B. Brooks, Florida State University
Paul Chandler, University of Hawaii
Jerome L. Packard, University of Illinois
Gail L. Riley, Syracuse University
Lourdes Torres, University of Kentucky
Cira Torruella, University of Illinois
Darlene Wolf, University of Alabama
Dolly J. Young, University of Tennessee
Donna Deans Binkowski, Kansas State University
William R. Glass, Pennsylvania State University
Carol Klee, University of Minnesota
H. Jay Siskin, University of Oregon
Susan Bacon, University of Cincinatti
Richard Kern, University of California, Berkeley

Second Edition

Lynne Marie Barnes, Colorado State University
Margaret Beauvois, University of Tennesse
Anna Bergström, University of Delaware
Gladys Brignoni, Old Dominion University
Robert L. Davis, University of Oregon
Carmen García, University of Virginia
Tony Houston, St. Louis University
Harry Howard, Tulane University
Jeanette Kraemer, Marquette University
Jennifer Lynn Lawrence, Colorado State University
Judith E. Liskin-Gasparro, University of Iowa
Sheri Spaine Long, University of Alabama at Birmingham
Susanne Rott, University of Illinois, Chicago

We owe continued thanks to Thalia Dorwick, Vice President and Editor in Chief of Humanities, Social Sciences, and Languages at McGraw-Hill Higher Education, who, in her previous capacity as Publisher of World Languages, got this book and the professional series rolling. We also owe thanks to William R. Glass, our new publisher, for getting this book into a second edition and to Kate Engelberg for her work as editor (a job that can never be thanked enough). Thanks are also extended to the Editorial, Production, and Design team who assisted with this book: Violeta Diaz, David Sutton, and Richard DeVitto.

Last but not least, thanks to those around us who have sustained us over the years. You know who you are, and you are loved for it.

Prologue

What is communicative language teaching? At first blush, the answer to this question may seem obvious: It is language teaching that has communication as its goal. It is the *how* that often escapes people—and this is especially true in the foreign language context. When language is being learned in a second language context, the communicative needs of learners may be obvious. Given that there are opportunities to be communicative outside of the classroom, the second language context allows the class to be an extension of the outside world. But what of the foreign language context, in which the language is not spoken outside the classroom? If we examine most contemporary textbooks and materials available on the market, we find that they are, in essence, not really communicative. As we argue later in this book, much of what passes as "communicative" these days is nothing more than communication at the service of grammar learning; that is, these materials offer added-on speaking activities that provide additional grammar practice in "a context." Communicative language teaching, as we show a number of times in this book, cannot be equated with first learning some vocabulary, then learning some grammar, and then finding something to talk about to use the grammar and vocabulary.

In short, communication is not "putting the past tense to work" or "using the subjunctive to communicate doubt," as some textbooks would have you believe. Teaching communicatively involves addressing a series of fundamental questions that every teacher needs to think about explicitly:

- What is communication? What is a good working definition for language teaching purposes?
- What do we want to communicate about and how do we want to do it?
- Although most people think of communication as speaking (that is, communication = conversation), what of listening, reading, and writing as communicative acts?

In most commercially available language teaching materials, these questions seem to be ignored. It is our goal in this book not just to explore these questions theoretically or philosophically but to provide some tools that show teachers *how* to teach communicatively. In other words, our goal is to provide a coherent framework for making communicative language teaching happen in any foreign language class.

A PREVIEW

The purpose of this prologue is to preview how we will achieve this goal. We invite you to examine the list of concepts and ideas that are touched on in this book and then, after completing your reading of the text, turn back to this list and take stock of the issues we lay out here. Perhaps, long after reading this book, when you may not even recall its title, you will remember some if not all of the following ideas:

1. Communicative language teaching involves letting go of certain roles that both teachers and students bring to the classroom as part of their implicit socialization in the educative process. Teachers often assume too much responsibility in language teaching, and students often assume too little. This pattern needs to change if communicative language teaching is to work, and it needs to be addressed not only by understanding these roles but also by changing certain behaviors.

2. Instructors need to understand some fundamental aspects of second language acquisition that apply both to the foreign language context and to the second language context. As you review these, you will see that some aspects of the roles mentioned in the previous point just cannot be supported by research.

3. Communication involves more than just speaking; it is a complex act that is context-dependent and that varies in purpose. One context is the classroom, and teachers cannot replicate the outside world in the classroom. They can, however, take advantage of one purpose of communicating and develop tasks around that purpose. That is the cognitive-informational purpose, and the type of task that encourages and promotes real communication in a classroom context is called an *information-exchange task* or an *information-based task.* The point of these tasks is not to practice language but to use the language to get information and then do something with that information.

4. Although lesson goals can be described as "learning the present tense irregular verbs" and "learning time expressions," these are not communicative goals. We explore the use of the information-exchange task as a truly communicative lesson objective. At the same time, we show how this kind of task can be broken down into its language components to create classhour communication goals as well as language goals. The idea we advocate is to build toward a proficiency goal, with the goal being the performance of a concrete task.

5. At the same time, we review how such tasks can be used for oral testing purposes. Although a variety of standardized oral tests exist, they may not be appropriate for the purposes of a particular class or curriculum. In keeping with the idea that we ought to test what we teach

and test it the same way, we advance the idea of using information tasks as tests. In addition, we explore the advantages to students of rating tests using a componential rather than a holistic analysis.

6. A thorny issue for some time has been the role of grammar instruction in communicative language teaching. Much of the debate has been couched in either/or terms—either teach grammar or do not teach grammar. We believe that the either/or approach misses the point, overlooking the processes underlying acquisition and the kinds of teaching practices informed by these processes. Here, we describe an approach that fits well not only with communicative language teaching in general but also with what we know about language acquisition. We call this approach *processing instruction,* and in accordance with this approach, we show how *structured input* activities can be used to promote the growth of grammatical competence.

7. Processing instruction, however useful it may be in supporting the development of grammatical competence, does not address how learners develop the ability to use grammar to speak. We review what we call *structured output* activities, which promote fluency and accuracy in speech. Thus, we advocate one kind of instruction for developing the underlying system (processing instruction) and another for tapping that system and promoting the development of fluency (structured output).

8. A recurring theme in this book is the importance of matching testing formats to teaching goals. To this end, we review the use of structured input activities and structured output activities as testing formats, keeping in mind the notions of economy, validity, and reliability in grammar testing.

9. Comprehension is an important part of communicative language ability. Thus, helping learners to listen for informational purposes is an important part of communicative language teaching. We review the two kinds of listening situations, collaborative and noncollaborative, and show how both can be used in the classroom to mirror what happens outside the classroom (e.g., watching a commercial on TV, listening to a weather report). Listening as a skill is different from getting comprehensible input as part of language acquisition. The latter refers to the ability to acquire grammar and vocabulary from input; the former refers to the ability to perform one side of a communicative act.

10. In addition to listening, reading should be a substantial component of any communicative classroom, because it provides additional input and content. However, this does not mean that reading should consist only of reading and answering questions, as in traditional approaches. These approaches ignore the processes involved in reading comprehension and encourage learners to read word for word or to simply look for the answers to the comprehension questions at the end of the reading. The communicative classroom uses insights from second language reading research to forge process-oriented reading lessons. We advocate prereading activities for the purposes of establishing a common base of background knowledge. We also advocate reading a text in stages, with the learner getting different kinds of information from the text at different times. This stands in direct contrast to more traditional approaches in

which learners struggle through a passage word by word. We follow up reading with a synthesis stage, in which learners pull together the information they have gathered from the text. And, because communicative classrooms are learner-centered, we also advocate a phase in which learners address the content of the reading in some personal way.

11. Writing is a fourth skill that should not be neglected in the communicative classroom, and instructors should distinguish between writing activities and composition development. Instructors should understand what it means to communicate through writing and keep in mind that composition development is not equivalent to transcription, however appropriate transcription activities may be for certain parts of a lesson. Composition involves a number of processes, including thinking, organizing, reflecting, adjusting, and later, editing. There is no reason why the development of composition ability should wait until advanced stages of language learning. Indeed, it should be present at all levels of instruction, including basic language.

12. The testing of comprehension and the evaluation of composition require that instructors make certain decisions in the communicative classroom. Using the rule of thumb to "test what and how you teach," we show how reading can be tested as content learned from a previous reading or as skills development. Each has its place; instructors can make use of both in the evaluation of learners' performance. For composition, we show that evaluation can be either componential or holistic, as in oral testing, and we again favor componential evaluation for the specificity of the information that it provides both learners and instructors.

These precepts represent what we consider essential to the framework of this book, and we believe them to be necessary to language learning from the earliest stages of classroom instruction. Each reader will no doubt develop personal approaches to the classroom using these ideas. This is to be expected, since communicative language teaching involves the personal investment of instructors in the process and the application of principles, not simply rote techniques.

CULTURE IN COMMUNICATIVE LANGUAGE TEACHING

Instructors often ask about the role of culture in communicative language teaching. The emphasis in a communicative class is on the learners and the information exchanged between them as well as between them and the instructor. How does the culture of the target language fit into the picture?

There are two ways to examine this question. The first centers on learning to communicate in culturally appropriate ways. The second centers on learning about the people, customs, and cultural artifacts associated with the language. You may be surprised to read that we do not believe that students, especially foreign language students, can be taught to communicate in culturally appropriate ways. After three years of French instruction, an eighteen-year-old will not communicate like anyone from France, Quebec, Morocco, or any other French-speaking country. The foreign language classroom is a particular context; it is not the context of those cultures. Although a student may be taught some things that make him or her sensitive to culturally appropriate communication, this information will always be but a small fragment of any culture's concept of appropriate linguistic behavior. There are many things that classrooms can do well and many things they cannot. In terms of culturally appropriate linguistic behavior, classrooms isolated from the second language speaking community will always do poorly in preparing students to conform to certain norms. Why? Because the classroom cannot duplicate the multiple cultural contexts that native speakers live and work in on a day-to-day basis (see Breen, 1985, for additional discussion). The classroom is a fixed context devoid of native-speaker cultural behavior. The best way to develop culturally appropriate behavior of any sort is to live and work in the culture in question— and to keep one's eyes open and ask lots of questions.

Culture in the second sense—culture as people, customs, and artifacts—is content and can be treated as same as any content in any course. What instructors must decide is *what* aspects of culture to teach, if any. The *how* comes out of the activities and framework developed in this book. For this reason, you will not find any chapter on the teaching of culture. Instead, you will find references to using culture as content in the various kinds of activities that can be developed for communicative language teaching. Sometimes you will be asked to pause and consider how a particular activity might incorporate a cultural focus. At other times, especially in the chapters on listening and reading, you will see how comprehension-oriented activities lend themselves particularly well to the learning of cultural information. Our point here is that culture, although sometimes referred to as the "fifth skill," is not a skill at all but informational content that can be infused into any language course. The tools for working with the information in the classroom are no different from those used to do everything else. (For more information on culture and the teaching of culture to complement what appears in this book, see Seelye, 1993.)

BEFORE MOVING ON

We recognize that what we advocate and discuss in this book is one way of looking at communicative language teaching. We believe that this approach makes the most sense for the foreign language context (although some teachers in a second language context may find activity types discussed in this book useful for their own contexts and purposes). To be sure, we focus on the informational and cognitive uses of language in communication as the basis for our activities. We do this, as you will see, because of the particular context in which students and instructors find themselves: the classroom. Classrooms consist largely of nonnatives. Thus, some aspects of communication that are important in native–native interchanges simply won't be found in this book. But as already mentioned, some aspects of communication can be developed only in a native-speaking environment. If we view the classroom as a springboard to the non-classroom world and not as a substitute for it, we can focus on the things that can be done well in classrooms and leave the rest to the outside world.

CHAPTER 1

From Atlas and Audiolingualism to Acquisition

In this chapter we explore:

- The classroom dynamic known as the "Atlas Complex," in which teachers assume all responsibility for what happens in the classroom
- A mid-twentieth-century teaching approach called audiolingualism (ALM), which embodied the Atlas complex par excellence
- Teachers' attempts to move away from ALM in the 1970s toward communicative language teaching, while at the same time carrying over the traditional roles of teachers and students in the classroom
- Some observed findings, or "givens," from second language acquisition research that call into question long-held notions about teaching and learning

THE ATLAS COMPLEX

Teaching, in all subject areas, entails *roles* and *tasks*. Both instructors and students play out roles in the classroom, but what determines these roles? The role that instructors often assume (and that students very willingly grant to them) is that of the authority, the expert, the central figure in the classroom who transmits knowledge to the students. Because instructors are authoritative knowledge transmitters, the students become their passive audience, receptive vessels into which that knowledge is poured. It is not difficult to see how such a classroom is organized; Figure 1.1 captures this dynamic in schematic form. The physical setup of many classes reflects and codifies the instructor's (I) authoritative role and the students' (S) receptive role.

Authoritative transmitter of knowledge and *receptive vessels* are the primary roles, respectively, that instructors and students play in many traditional classrooms. The tasks we most often associate with these roles are those of lecturing and notetaking. Other, secondary roles may be enacted in language classrooms. Depending on one's point of view, some of these

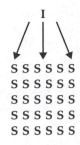

FIGURE 1.1 Knowledge transmission in a transmission-oriented class

secondary roles are neutral or positive, others negative. A partial list appears in Table 1.1.

> ## *Pause to consider . . .*
>
> whose responsibility it is to learn. If the instructor is the expert and authority, what happens when students do not carry out an assignment correctly or score poorly as a group on an exam? Would (and should) the instructor take it personally? Would (and should) the students blame the instructor for their performance?

The following description of a language class exemplifies the classroom dynamic characterized by the transmission-oriented roles of instructors and the receptacle roles of students.

1. Students were given ten minutes to complete individually a worksheet that contained a series of paragraphs. In each paragraph, various grammatical elements were deleted from sentences, with multiple choices provided for each blank. There were some twenty deletions.
2. At the end of ten minutes, students were instructed to work in groups of three. As a group they were to come to an agreement on the correct answers.
3. After about seven minutes, the instructor called for the class's attention. She began going over the correct answers, one by one, in the order in

TABLE 1.1 Secondary Roles in a Transmission-Oriented Class

Instructor	Student
Lecturer	Notetaker
Leader	Follower
Tutor	Tutee
Warden	Prisoner
Disciplinarian	Disciplinee

which they appeared on the worksheet. She did not ask for volunteers but rather called on students to respond. She read each sentence to the class, pausing at the deletion to call attention to it, and then continued reading to the end of the sentence. The student who was called on supplied the word or phrase needed to complete the sentence.

4. On the second item, although the student gave the correct answer, the instructor offered a lengthy explanation of the particular grammatical item worked on (in this instance, comparisons such as *more than* and *less than*). On the fifth item, a student gave an incorrect answer and the instructor offered a lengthy explanation of the grammar point (in this instance, conjunctions). On the tenth item, a student gave an incorrect answer and the instructor gave a lengthy explanation of passive constructions. Just as the instructor was finishing the explanation, the bell rang. Ten items were left to complete.

The language instructor depicted in this example clearly exemplifies the role of authority or expert transmitter of knowledge. All action and interaction, as well as all explanations, are dictated by the instructor. The students' role is to be taught, to receive knowledge. Like the titan Atlas of Greek mythology, who supported the heavens on his shoulders, instructors such as the one described in the preceding example

> assume full responsibility for all that goes on. They supply motivations, insight, clear explanations, even intellectual curiosity. In exchange, their students supply almost nothing but a faint imitation of the academic performance that they witness. [Instructors] so thoroughly dominate the proceedings that they are cut off from what the students know or are confused about. For their part, the students form a group of isolated individuals who have no more in common than their one-to-one relationship with the same individual. While [instructors] exercise their authority through control of the subject matter and the social encounter in the classroom, they lack the power to make things happen for their students. They are both caught in the middle of their classes by a host of mysterious forces—hidden assumptions, hidden expectations, and the results of their own isolating experiences. [This is] the Atlas Complex.
> (Finkel & Monk, 1983, p. 85)

The Atlas Complex is not discipline specific; teacher-centered, knowledge-transmitting classrooms are the norm for many subject areas. In many chemistry classes, for example, students sit and take notes while the instructor lectures (except in lab sessions). Very often in history and political science classes, students listen to instructors give descriptions and explanations that will more than likely appear on subsequent tests. It often seems that much of American educational practice reflects the Atlas Complex.

To be sure, instructors have invested much time in becoming experts in their fields. In the classroom, they often (and perhaps rightly so) seek to share that expertise. Most instructors "assume that their principal task is one of improving the ways in which they express their expertise: Clear and precise explanations can always be sharpened; penetrating questions can always be made more penetrating" (Finkel & Monk, 1983, p. 86). An implicit assumption here is that students actually *do* learn from the explanations instructors provide. Therefore, instructors think that by improving their explanations they will improve students' learning. Another assumption is that students learn by being asked questions: by improving the questions asked, instructors assume students will learn more. How valid are these assumptions for learning in general and language learning in particular? In Chapter 2, we briefly examine some major findings of language learning research that challenge these assumptions. For the moment, let's examine the Atlas Complex in language teaching in more detail.

Pause to consider . . .

the cultural appropriateness of Atlas-like behavior. Can you identify cultures in which Atlas-like behavior is culturally appropriate and even expected?

Audiolingualism

In language teaching, the instructor as central figure has always been the norm. As the profession moved from grammar and text-translation methods to a more "oral" approach, the instructor-as-authority-and-expert was codified in a teaching method called Audiolingual Methodology, commonly referred to as ALM or audiolingualism. ALM was predicated on the marriage of behaviorist psychology and then-current structural linguistics. According to behaviorist psychology, all learning—verbal and nonverbal—takes place through the process of habit formation. Habits are formed through repetition, imitation, and reinforcement. In ALM, language habits were formed by memorizing dialogues and practicing sentence patterns, usually through drills that required learners to imitate and repeat what their instructors said. Second language acquisition (SLA) was seen to be the replacement of first language habits by second language habits. Under this framework for learning and teaching, the first language (L1) was seen to interfere with the acquisition of the second (L2); that is, the first language habits got in the way of acquiring the second language habits. Maximum care was thus taken not to allow learners to make errors, because errors were evidence of bad habits. During drills, a premium was placed on error-free repetition, with no attention paid to whether or not learners understood the meaning of what they were saying.

Developed at military schools (where one did not question authority), ALM's teaching materials explicitly cast the instructor as drill leader, perhaps the ultimate manifestation of the Atlas Complex. With ALM, students were typically given a model sentence. The instructor then provided the cue that students would substitute into the sentence; some substitutions required that the sentence be altered in various ways, while other substitutions did not. The students' role has been likened to that of a parrot, since their task was to perform the substitution or transformation quickly and accurately. Note the following examples.

Activity A.   Substitution Drill

Change the model sentence, substituting the cue word for its corresponding element in the model.

MODEL: I don't want to eat anymore!

INSTRUCTOR'S CUE	STUDENT RESPONSE
1. to sleep	I don't want to sleep anymore!
2. to study	I don't want to study anymore!
3. to drink	I don't want to drink anymore!

Activity B.   Transformation Drill

Transform each sentence, substituting the past for the present.

1. I eat.	I ate.
2. He goes.	He went.
3. We sleep.	We slept.

What the ALM instructor did not usually provide was the opportunity for students to use the language in a meaningful or communicative way, one involving the exchange of messages. Nothing that happened in an ALM classroom could be construed as an exchange of information because *output* (the actual production of language) was severely restricted. In fact, many thought that students did not need to know what they were saying; they needed to know only that what they were saying was correct.

Pause to consider . . .
_____

the meaning and purpose of expressing oneself orally. Should learning be divorced from reality? Re-examine the drills in Activities A and B. Should a language learner be required to state something such as "I don't want to sleep anymore!" if it isn't true? How often in your language learning experience did you say or repeat things that had no basis in reality? Did you memorize any dialogues that you can still repeat to this day? In your experience, how often were you allowed to express real ideas, real thoughts?

Communicative Language Teaching

With the advent of *communicative language teaching* (CLT), the instructor's role changed. The instructor was no longer simply the drill leader but was also charged with providing students with opportunities for communication, that is, using the language to interpret and express real-life messages. The Atlas Complex did not, however, disappear. ALM had so rigidly institutionalized it that we find a transition period in early CLT in which the classroom dynamic could not yet be characterized as "free" communication. In early CLT, many instructors equated communication with conversation—but conversation of a particular type: the authority figure asked the questions, the students answered them. The instructor's task was no longer just to drill but also to interact. Instructors often did attempt to personalize the questions, and these questions usually did not require patterned responses from students. The contrast between the open-ended question "What did you do last night?" and the cued sentence pattern "———— went to the movies last night" illustrates the shift from ALM to early CLT. The students' task was no longer to parrot but to create an answer. (In Chapter 6 we examine drills and drill types in some detail.) In short, although CLT may have caused a major revolution in the way that some people *thought* about language teaching, no major revolution occurred in the day-to-day *practice* of most language teachers.

As language teaching began its slow evolution away from methods such as ALM, the roles played by instructors and students changed very little, if at all. As we saw previously, communication was seen merely as conversation, which took the form of a question-and-answer session with the instructor in charge. Atlas's burden was yet to be relieved or shared. An example of the Atlas Complex combined with a question-and-answer conversation can be seen in the following exchange (taken from Leemann Guthrie, 1984, p. 45). As you read, note the role assumed by the instructor and try to imagine the exchange taking place in a classroom (for example, who was standing or sitting where? What was the rest of the class doing?).

(1) INSTRUCTOR: Pensez-vous qu'il y a vraiment une personnalité française, typiquement française?
(2) Oui?
(3) STUDENTS: Non.
(4) INSTRUCTOR: Non? Pourquoi?
(Pause)
(5) Claudia?
(6) STUDENT: *Um… Je pense qu'il y a une…*
(7) INSTRUCTOR: *(Interrupting)* Qu'il y a une personnalité française?
(8) Bon, décrivez la personnalité française.
(9) STUDENT: *How do you say "pride"?*
(10) INSTRUCTOR: Oh… vous avez déjà eu deux mots.
(11) *(Writing on blackboard)* Okay, «La fierté» est comme en anglais "pride," et l'adjectif, «fier».
(12) Je suis fier. *I'm proud.*
(13) Bon, est-ce que les Français sont très fiers?
(14) Ils ont beaucoup de fierté?
(Silence)
(15) Est-ce que les Français sont nationalistes?

[translation]

(1) TEACHER: Do you think there is really one French personality, a typically French personality?
(2) Yes?
(3) STUDENTS: No.
(4) TEACHER: No? Why?
(Pause)
(5) Claudia?

(6) STUDENT: Um . . . I think that there's a . . .

(7) TEACHER: *(Interrupting)* That there's a French personality?

(8) Good, describe the French personality.

(9) STUDENT: How do you say "pride"?

(10) TEACHER: Oh . . . You've already had two words.

(11) *(Writing on blackboard)* Okay, "la fierté" is like in English "pride," and the adjective, "fier."

(12) *Je suis fier*, I'm proud.

(13) Good, are the French very proud?

(14) Do they have a lot of pride?
       (Silence)

(15) Are the French nationalistic?

The instructor as central figure and authority is clearly evidenced in line 5, where she selects the next person who will speak rather than a conversational partner. In line 7, the instructor again asserts her role as authority figure by finishing the student's sentence for her. Claudia, the student, subsequently appeals to the instructor's expert knowledge of the French language, one of the forces that binds instructors to the Atlas Complex. The instructor obliges Claudia's appeal, yet she offers a much more detailed account of the French language than Claudia requested, the assumption being that students learn from explanations. The instructor, incidentally, also assumes to know what Claudia's opinion is, since she never gives Claudia the opportunity to express her opinion before interrupting her and completing her sentence for her. This instructor imposes herself on Claudia's self-expression. In lines 13–15, rather than waiting for Claudia to use the explanation provided, the instructor continues to ask questions. The result? Silence. When silence ensues, she asks another question using an altogether different adjective. In order to maintain her role as authority, this instructor assumed the responsibility of not only asking questions but also answering them. As Leemann Guthrie (1984) points out about this exchange, "It is clear that the [instructor] defines her own role not as that of a conversational partner or facilitator, but as one responsible for telling her students how to speak" (p. 46).

Pause to consider . . .

how different the interactional dynamic and resulting discussion between Claudia and her instructor might have been. Why do you think silence resulted from the instructor's explanation of *fier* and *fierté*? How might the interaction have been different if the instructor had responded to Claudia by saying nothing more than "Fierté" in response to her question?

In the next phase of CLT, the instructor was not the only one to ask questions. In this phase, a novel classroom dynamic emerged: students were now allowed to work in pairs and to pose questions to each other. But for many, the basic assumed roles of transmitter and receptacles were played out in pair work as well. In the following exercise, aimed at fostering communication, a model is provided that clearly spells out the Atlas-like question-and-answer model of conversation, even though the instructor is not part of the exercise.

Activity C.   What Did You Eat Last Night?

With another student, ask and answer questions according to the model.

MODEL: french fries → Did you eat french fries last night?
                          → Yes, I ate them. (No, I did not eat them.)

1. tacos
2. hamburgers
3. a steak
4. tuna casserole

During this exercise students ask each other questions that they can answer truthfully, but the real intent is to practice producing direct-object pronouns. The instructor is most likely monitoring students' performance. Are they asking the questions correctly? Are they answering them in complete sentences? Is the respondent using the correct direct-object pronoun? This activity has a clear focus on form rather than on meaning or communication.

Thus, even though pair work was intended to provide speaking opportunities, the resulting speech did not necessarily entail true communication, namely, the interpretation and expression of meaning. Many paired exercises differed very little from the classic ALM pattern-substitution drills, with their rigid constraints on what could be said and how it could be said. In the evolution of language teaching, we find that practice did not keep up with theory: instructors might have wanted to take on new roles, but the classroom activities still emphasized formal correctness, not communication.

Theory and practice did begin to converge as instructors began to talk to their students. That is, in addition to providing controlled exercises such as Activities A–C, they also engaged in more open-ended conversations. In the next example (from a classroom whose instructor explicitly claimed to be teaching communicatively), the instructor is dialoging with the students. Many instructors use the technique of asking personalized questions to begin a class, perhaps incorporating grammar and vocabulary from the previous day's work. The resulting conversations have a much more natural feel than do the conversations examined previously. Does this instructor still carry an Atlas-like burden?

INSTRUCTOR: What did you do last week? Raúl.
        RAÚL: I went to Florida. To the beach. We ate in a lot of
               restaurants.
INSTRUCTOR: That sounds like a fun week. Gloria, what did you do
               last week?
      GLORIA: Not much. My husband and I read. We watched TV.
INSTRUCTOR: Did you go to Florida?
      GLORIA: No.
INSTRUCTOR: Did you go to Florida last week? John.
        JOHN: Me? No. I went to Bloomington to visit my parents.

In spite of the surface differences between this exchange and, say, the one Leemann Guthrie illustrated, the instructor is still the central figure. In a typical classroom, the instructor will call on a student to answer, probe the student's response, and let the student know when she has completed her turn by calling on another student. The students answering the question will most likely address only the instructor and not their classmates, as the instructor is controlling the interaction. The entire burden is on the instructor, who initiates, responds, follows up, keeps the interaction going, and assigns turns. We will see in the next section some alternative ways instructors can engage students in using the second language without being so Atlas-like.

Pause to consider . . .

the nature of conversations. Was the verbal interaction between the four speakers in the example a true conversation? Did any of the individual students carry on a conversation with the instructor? How conversational can the exchange be if the students merely answer questions but never ask any of either the instructor or each other?

In the activities and exercises we have examined, the instructor assumes an authoritative role and then asserts it in all situations. Both instructors and students accept the fact that instructors are language authorities or experts and ought, therefore, to be the central figures in the classroom. A central reason that instructors assume the authority role is the way in which many people view language learning. As we noted, ALM viewed language learning as the acquisition of correct habits, and correct habits were learned through repetition and reinforcement. The language instructor's role, then, was to ensure that correct habits were learned and that no one deviated from the path of accuracy. This focus on correct habit formation demanded absolute control not only over how students spoke but also over what students said. Thus, drills and pattern practices naturally became staple classroom interactional routines. As Finkel and Monk (1983) point out, hidden assumptions bind instructors and students to the Atlas Complex, among them the popular beliefs about how adults learn languages. But does language acquisition actually happen as the theorists of 1955 envisioned? What do we know about language acquisition? In the next section, we briefly review some findings from the field of second language acquisition research.

SECOND LANGUAGE ACQUISITION: SOME GIVENS

In a book of this nature, it is impossible to synthesize all of what we now know about the nature of second language acquisition; that is the job of other books (e.g., Ellis, 1994; Gass & Selinker, 2001; VanPatten, 2003a). For the purposes of our discussion, we need only to review some of the accepted findings in SLA research to see what impact they have on our notions of teaching and of peoples' roles in the classroom.

Borrowing from VanPatten (2003a), we discuss here five "givens" about SLA relevant to language teaching. These can be considered *observable facts* culled from thirty-five years of accumulated evidence in the field of SLA research and uncontested by any theoretical account of SLA. These givens are

1. SLA involves the creation of an implicit (unconscious) linguistic system.
2. SLA is complex and consists of different processes.
3. SLA is dynamic but slow.
4. Most L2 learners fall short of native-like competence.
5. Skill acquisition is different from the creation of an implicit system.

We examine each of these in turn.

SLA Involves the Creation of an Implicit (Unconscious) Linguistic System

Like first language learners, second language learners ultimately construct an *implicit linguistic system* consisting of a variety of components that interact in language use (e.g., a lexical system of words and grammatical inflections such as noun markers and verb markers, a phonological system that governs the sounds, a syntactic system that controls the structure of sentences). By *implicit* we mean an unconscious system that lies outside of awareness; we are unaware of its properties even though we use it every single second of our lives. For example, every native speaker of English knows that we can contract *want* and *to* in order to form *wanna* in everyday speech. However, every native speaker of English also knows that only one of the following sentences is a possible English sentence:

1. Who do you wanna invite to the party tonight?
2. Who do you wanna bring the potato chips tonight?

For speakers of English, (1) sounds fine, but (2) sounds awful and is generally rejected as a possible sentence. However, these same speakers would accept as possible (3) *Who do you wanta bring the potato chips tonight?* At the same time, the speakers will tell you that they have no idea why (2) is bad but (1) and (3) are acceptable. This is because the rules of syntax that govern sentence structure (of which contraction is part) lie outside their awareness in an implicit system. Likewise, they could not tell you why in English they have to use a [z] sound when pluralizing *dog* → *dogs* but have to use an [iz] sound when pluralizing *house* → *houses*.

Although second language learners may not arrive at the same implicit rules as native speakers (a point we discuss later), they do create an implicit system that functions in the same manner. In a good deal of research, investigators have given learners judgment tests like the one mentioned (i.e., Which sentence is possible and which isn't?) and the learners usually come up with the right answers. What is important about this is that researchers test them on things they could never have been taught and could never have learned from instruction or feedback. Like native speakers, if asked "Why" when giving a judgment, they either make something up (because they think they are supposed to know!) or they simply say, "I don't know. It just sounds wrong." But it is also worth pointing out that second language learners may indeed have *conscious* or *explicit rules* or knowledge about rules, especially if they have experienced any classroom language learning. They may know things and be able to express in some way rules such as verb-subject agreement, the difference between an active and a passive sentence, when to use *du* in French, that German requires case marking on articles before nouns, or the difference between the two linking verbs *ser* and *estar* in Spanish. However, this conscious knowledge of *some* rules is not the same as and, as we see later, is not the starting point for the creation of the developing system.

The finding that learners come to know things they couldn't have been taught has led the field of SLA theory and research to posit a fundamental role for what we call *input*. Input is *the language learners hear that is meant to convey a message;* that is, the learner's job is to attempt to understand what is being said. In this sense, it is language that is *meaning bearing.* To be clear, input is not explanation about language, nor is it explicit corrective feedback because the learner has made an error. We can illustrate this with the pluralization example in English. It is not input when we tell learners the rule for pluralization; it is input when learners hear pluralization in sentences that they are to attend to for meaning, for example, "So, just how many houses do you think Bill Gates owns?" or "Did you have pets while growing up?" It is not input when we stop learners and correct them by saying, "Not watch[is] but watch[izzzzzz]." It is input when we say to them, "He fixes watches? Is that what you mean?" In short, input is language embedded in some kind of communicative interchange no matter how trivial or how important. The role of the learner is to attend to the meaning in order to respond to the content or perform a task. Embedded in input are many subtle clues about the way language works, and it is only by getting lots of input that learners can build up an implicit linguistic system.

Krashen (1982 and elsewhere) has put forth the *Input Hypothesis.* His claim is very strong: Comprehensible input *causes* acquisition. He believes that as long as there is motivation and the right affective environment (e.g., low anxiety), a person cannot avoid learning a second language if there is sustained comprehensible input. Others don't make as strong a claim and suggest that language acquisition is a complex process involving social, cognitive, linguistic, and other factors. Because not all language learners are equally successful, there must be more at work than comprehensible input. Nonetheless, every scholar today believes that comprehensible input is a critical factor in language acquisition. Long (1990) puts it quite nicely when he says that comprehensible input is a necessary (but perhaps not sufficient) ingredient of language acquisition (see also Gass, 1997). What this means is that *successful language acquisition cannot happen without comprehensible input.* Classroom learners who get a steady diet of explanations and practice might appear to have some kind of language ability, but it is not the same as those who get consistent and constant exposure to comprehensible input. At the same time, learners need more than comprehensible input. As we shall see later in this book, learners also need opportunities to use the language in communicative interaction. Although input may be responsible for the evolution of the language system in the learner's head, having to use the language pushes the learner to develop what we call *communicative language ability*.

SLA Is Complex and Consists of Different Processes

It is, in a sense, misleading to talk about second language acquisition in the singular. The term suggests there is one process that accounts for how acquisition happens, which in turn leads people naively to believe that there is one theory of SLA. In actuality, we should talk about second language acquisition *processes*. At the same time, we also have to recognize that although we often concern ourselves as language teachers with such rudimentary notions as vocabulary and grammar, what the learner actually acquires over time is much more. To learn a second language, here is a partial list of what a person must acquire (depending on the language type):

- The lexicon, that is, words, including their forms and meanings. For example, the concept of a small domestic feline (the meaning) is generally expressed by the form [kaet].
- What words can do. For example, some verbs, such as *hit*, can take an object, as in "John is good at hitting home runs," and others, such as *seem*, cannot, as in the impossible sentence, "John is good at seeming home runs."
- The phonology, that is, the sound system, pronunciation. This includes such things as learning the r/l distinction in English (if you're a Japanese speaker), learning pluralization (that the use of the [s], [z], and [iz] sounds are governed by the vowel or consonant sound that immediately precedes the addition of a plural marker), or learning how to syllabify when speaking (for example, in English when we speak, we constantly create syllables that end or begin in consonants and consonant clusters. Indeed, we would normally pronounce "clusters" as *clu-sters*, whereas in Spanish the verb "estar" would be pronounced *es-tar*.)
- Inflectional morphology. This includes, for example, endings on verbs and nouns, as in *talk, talks, talked* and *dog, dogs*.
- Derivational morphology, that is, the use of prefixes and sometimes suffixes to create new words, such as *transportation* from *transport* and *misbehave* from *behave*. It also includes knowing that some formations are impossible; for example, something can be *unlawful* but not *dislawful*, and someone can be *disloyal* but not *unloyal*.
- Particles. For example, in Japanese, certain one-syllable words are tagged onto sentences to indicate a question or some other type of utterance to distinguish these from mere statements.
- Syntax, that is, the rules that govern what is a permissible sentence and what is not, such as examples (1), (2), and (3) in the previous section. Syntax includes some very abstract rules.
- Pragmatics, that is, what a speaker intends by a sentence. For example, in English, questions can be used to make a suggestion, as in "Why

don't you take a break?" or to solicit information, as in "Why is SLA so difficult?"

- Sociolinguistics, that is, what is appropriate and inappropriate use of language in particular situations, such as whether to use *tu* or *vous* in French or "Howz it goin?" instead of "Good afternoon" in English, or whether you should speak at all!
- Discourse competence, that is, what makes language cohesive and what is permissible or accepted in a language regarding cohesion across sentences. For example, these sentences are cohesive: "Mary ran down the street. John saw her, but he didn't say anything." These are not: "Mary ran down the street. He didn't say anything. John did see her." Discourse competence also includes "knowing" such things as turn-taking during conversation.

And this list is a reduction and simplification of what needs to be learned. Now, imagine that learning those things *happens all at the same time in SLA,* and you can begin to see just how complex the learning process is when it comes to the *what* of language.

As for the *how* of acquisition, that is, the processes, at least three distinct sets of processes are involved in language acquisition, all of them going on at the same time. We can outline them in the following way:

- *Input processing:* How learners make sense out of the language they hear and how they get "linguistic data" from it
- *System change.* This process involves two subprocesses:
  ○ *accommodation:* How learners actually incorporate a grammatical form or structure into the implicit system of the language they are creating
  ○ *restructuring:* How the incorporation of a form or structure can cause a ripple effect and make other things change without the learner ever knowing
- *Output processing:* How learners acquire the ability to make use of the implicit knowledge they are acquiring to produce utterances in real time, for example, during conversational interactions or while making a presentation in class

These processes in turn have subprocesses so that the learner's brain is manipulating quite a few things at once. We need not go into these processes here since they are explained and described elsewhere in detail (see VanPatten, 2003a). What we do need to point out, though, is that just because something appears in the input does not mean that learners get it right away. During input processing, for example, learners *selectively* attend to features in the input, a selectivity that is driven by internal processes and strategies about which we will see in Chapter 8. Thus, learners filter and even sometimes *alter* what they pick up in the input. And just because these linguistic data have been somehow processed in the input does not mean they are automatically accommodated into the learner's linguistic system. For reasons we do not quite understand, some linguistic forms are incorporated and others are not. These latter are literally "dumped" from working memory once a sentence is comprehended and do not receive any further attention by the learner's internal processors. Thus, the learner is constantly filtering data from the input; acquisition is slow and piecemeal, as we will see in the next section.

SLA Is Dynamic but Slow

As long as learners continue to get input, the implicit system they create over time evolves constantly. At the same time, nothing comes quickly; there is no such thing as instantaneous acquisition. For this reason we say that acquisition is *dynamic* (it evolves), but it is *slow* (it takes years for learners to build up a system that is anywhere native-like).

What does this evolution or dynamism look like? One example can be found in developmental sequences or *stages of development*. Stages of development refer to how, over time, a learner acquires a particular feature of the language or a particular structure. We might ask ourselves, "How does the learner acquire negation in English?" or "How does the learner acquire *ser* and *estar* in Spanish?" These are questions that speak directly to stages of development.

One of the classic examples of stages of development involves the acquisition of negation in English. Researchers studying both classroom and non-classroom learners have observed a general tendency to pass through four stages of development for this one grammatical feature. The errors made at each stage do not seem to be influenced by any particular L1, since learners from a wide variety of L1 backgrounds all pass through these stages. (The examples that follow are taken from Ellis, 1986, pp. 59–60).

Stage 1: no + PHRASE
No drink.
No you playing here.

Stage 2: negator moves inside phrase; *not* and *don't* added to list of negators, but *don't* is considered one word
I no can swim.
I don't see nothing mop.

Stage 3: negator attached to modals but initially may be unanalyzed as is *don't* in Stage 2
I can't play this one.
I won't tell.

Stage 4: auxiliary system of English is developed, and learner acquires correct use of *not* and contractions
He doesn't know anything.
I didn't said it.

As these patterns for the acquisition of negation in English suggest, learners make particular kinds of errors at particular stages in the acquisition of a structure. Each stage marks some kind of restructuring in the mind of the learner regarding that particular structure. That is, a structure does not just "pop into the heads" of learners; it *evolves* over time.

In a study of the acquisition of Spanish *ser* and *estar* (equivalents of *to be* in English), VanPatten also found stages of development in classroom learners.

He found a tendency for learners to pass through five stages of development in their acquisition of basic uses of the Spanish copular (linking) verbs, with Stage 2 lasting some time for English speakers learning Spanish. (The following examples are taken from VanPatten, 1987; asterisks indicate ungrammatical constructions.)

Stage 1: no copular verb
  Juan alto. (John tall.)

Stage 2: acquisition of *ser* and its overextension in contexts where *estar* would be appropriate
  María es muy simpática. (Mary is very nice.)
  Ella es estudiar. (She's studying.)
  Mis padres son a Chicago. (My parents are in Chicago.)
  Soy muy contento hoy. (I'm very happy today.)

Stage 3: acquisition of *estar* + progressive
  Está estudiando. (She's studying.)

Stage 4: acquisition of *estar* + location
  Están en Chicago. (They're in Chicago.)

Stage 5: acquisition of *estar* + adjectives of condition
  Estoy muy contento. (I'm very happy.)

Stages of development have been found for word order in German, WH-questions in English (that is, the structure of questions containing *when, who, why, where,* and so forth), tense and aspect in Romance languages and English, and case marking, among other linguistic structures. (Stages overlap; a learner may clearly be in Stage 2 of the acquisition of a structure but have residual patterns from Stage 1, for example.) Stages of development suggest that learners actively organize language in their heads independently of external influence. Something causes them to make certain kinds of errors and not others, and something produces certain universal patterns of acquisition regardless of the L1.

The slowness of acquisition is demonstrated by the fact that learners may take a number of years (even with lots of input) to go through such stages. And first language influence may cause learners to linger in one stage more than another. Such is the case with negation. Spanish-speaking learners of English tend to linger in Stage 2 more than do learners of French (in which negation is postverbal with *pas*), but both sets of speakers experience all of the stages. Likewise, English-speaking learners of Spanish may linger in Stage 2 for the acquisition of *ser* and *estar* because the stage resembles their own language's "one copula" system. Chinese speakers learning Spanish, on the other hand, do not have a copula verb and so would not linger in Stage 2 as long as English speakers do. (They would linger longer in Stage 1 because this stage resembles Chinese.) Both sets of learners, however, will eventually traverse all the stages on their way to native-like competence with these structures.

Another example of the slowness of acquisition is to be found in what are called *acquisition orders*. These orders refer to the sequential acquisition of *various* grammatical features over time without focusing on the acquisition of any particular item (as in the case of stages of development research). Certain elements of grammar are learned before others, and this progression can be observed and quantified in learners' oral production. The grammatical features studied in the 1970s were *morphemes* (pieces and parts of words, such as verb endings and noun endings) and *functors* (words such as *the, is, a,* and *an,* which have particular grammatical functions in sentences). In English, for example, it has been shown that the acquisition of verb morphemes tends to follow the following order:

1. *-ing*
2. regular past tense
3. irregular past tense
4. third-person present tense *-s*

In other words, if we studied the language produced by learners of English, we would first see the greatest accuracy in the use of *-ing* with verbs in our learners' output. The last thing we would see is accuracy in the use of third-person *-s*. This order would be apparent regardless of the learner's L1. In other words, Chinese, Spanish, and Arabic speakers of English follow the same acquisition order for verb morphemes. This order is thus believed to be universal for learners of English. To be sure, some learners might progress through the order faster than others; still others might never complete the acquisition process because they could not quite get third-person *-s* into their speech. But we would nevertheless be able to see a universal pattern of acquisition. Acquisition orders also provide empirical evidence that learners possess "internal strategies" for organizing language data and that these strategies do not necessarily obey outside influences (Corder, 1981).

Most L2 Learners Fall Short of Native-like Competence

In spite of instructors' efforts to "ensure" accuracy and in spite of some measures of performance that include a component for accuracy, most learners never become native-like in their acquisition of a second language. Either their implicit system is nonnative-like or their ability to use the implicit system is nonnative-like, or both. Second language learners often speak with an accent, no matter how fluent or accurate they are with grammar and other aspects of the language. Second language learners often have certain late stage aspects of development that are never acquired, for example, the otherwise very accurate and eloquent nonnative who still says, "She wants to know what is his name," rather than the more native "She wants to know what his name is." Second language learners may never quite get some of the lexical differences between languages, as in the case of Agatha Christie's sleuth, Hercule Poirot, who routinely uses the word *derange* when meaning "bother," as in "I'm sorry to derange you with this little matter." (In French *déranger* means "to bother;" French is Monsieur Poirot's native language.)

Learners, of course, plateau at all different kinds of levels; that is, their nonnativeness is not all at the same level of nonnativeness. The point here is that they are nonnative-like in a number of ways. Why learners seldom become native-like is still unknown. Some scholars have found evidence for a *critical period*, a time around puberty from which learning another language is difficult. Others find evidence that there is no critical period at puberty, that learning is constantly attenuated, and that it may have a lot to do with time on task (how much input you get over time). In Birdsong (1999), these diverse points of view are evident, as they are in Harley and Wang (1997).

Skill Acquisition Is Different From the Creation of an Implicit System

It is one thing to develop some kind of implicit system. Being able to use it is altogether different. Thus, we can separate out skill acquisition, especially speaking skills, from the notion of any underlying system on which speaking might draw. Learners, for example, may be quite aware of certain distinctions in a language, say the vowel contrast between the two words *kook* and *cook*, but might not be able to produce them. Learners may be able to judge a certain sentence as possible or impossible but not be at the stage where the rule on which they rely can be used in sentence generation.

The implication from this observation about SLA is that skill acquisition happens independently of the creation of the linguistic system, even though speaking must access the system in order for the learner to express meaning. In one theory, called *Processability Theory* (Pienemann, 1998), an entire developmental ordering of "output procedures" is presented and discussed, and as the author himself says, the concern of the theory is about how learners acquire the *procedures* necessary for creating novel utterances and not the acquisition of the linguistic system itself. The procedures are used to put together linguistic elements in real time (while speaking) and exist in the mind of the learner as *mechanisms* and not as *knowledge*.

Pause to consider . . .

the implications for a teacher's role after reviewing the givens of SLA research. Is the role of Atlas sustainable? Just who is in charge of acquisition? If there is a new role or new roles for the communicatively oriented teacher, what might it/they be?

SUMMARY

In this chapter, we have seen that many instructors take on the burden of ensuring learning by the roles they and their students adopt in the classroom. Very often this dynamic plays out in the Atlas Complex, in which teachers assume the role of transmitter and verifier of information while learners assume the role of knowledge recipient. Even though the profession abandoned ALM as a singular approach to language teaching as it attempted to embrace communicative methodologies, the role of the teacher did not change. We can still find an Atlas-like role played out in question-answer "conversations" that teachers carry out with students in their classrooms.

At the same time that language teaching has attempted to shift from the mechanistic approach of ALM, researchers in second language acquisition have accumulated a body of work that offers us certain observed phenomena that we must address as teachers. Apparently, the language learner is in much more control of acquisition than anyone had assumed prior to the 1970s. And ultimately we may come to the conclusion that languages are, in essence, unteachable; that is, that we cannot force or cause the creation of the learner's implicit system. We may not be able to force or cause the acquisition of speech-making procedures that are essential to skill development. Our conclusion may very well be that we can only provide opportunities in the classroom for acquisition to happen, but that these opportunities must be informed by what we know about acquisition. As such, our roles as teachers in the classroom may change—and the roles of the students may change as well.

Throughout this book, we explore ways in which instruction can work *in unison with* acquisitional processes rather than *against* them. We emphasize that what happens in language classrooms reflects the view that students are not merely recipients and instructors are not merely transmitters. Instructors must resist the constant temptation to display their knowledge of the language they teach. Instead, they must formulate tasks to maximize learners' contributions to the language-learning enterprise. To ensure that kind of result, the students who were put into groups in order to reach a consensus about the correct answer should be allowed to state their thought processes and to know that their work in groups counted for something. Likewise, Claudia (in the Leemann Guthrie example) should have been allowed to state her opinion and not have it stated for her. Similarly, learners must be provided with opportunities to express real information and not merely the information in drills. And finally, learners must be given opportunities to construct communicative interactions in the classroom as they would outside the classroom—to interpret, express, and negotiate meaning. In short, to move students beyond the role of recipient, we must give them both the responsibility and the appropriate materials. Most important, they must learn how to carry out that responsibility.

KEY TERMS, CONCEPTS, AND ISSUES

Atlas Complex
classroom dynamic
roles dictate tasks
knowledge transmission and
  receptive vessels
secondary roles for instructors
  and learners
Audiolingual Methodology
  (ALM)

habit formation
pattern practices and substitution
  drills
Communicative Language
  Teaching (CLT)
conversation
    question-and-answer only
    paired work
    classroom versus nonclassroom

implicit linguistic system
  conscious or explicit rules
  input
  meaning-bearing
  explanation is not input
  correction is not input
complex processes
  input processing
  accommodation

restructuring
  output processing
dynamic but slow
  stages of development
  acquisition orders
native-like competence
  critical period
skill acquisition versus acquisition
  of an implicit system

THINKING MORE ABOUT IT:
DISCUSSION QUESTIONS

1. Brooks (1990) has pointed out that when learners work together in pairs, one of the partners may reenact the instructor's role. Examine the following exchange (based on Brooks, pp. 158–159) between two learners who are working in pairs asking and answering questions. What do you infer the instructor's role to be in their class?

> STUDENT A: *¿Cómo es Luisa?*
> STUDENT B: *Luisa, Ahhhh, es… Luisa.*
>   *Lindas* (prosodic stress on 'as'), *lindas* (prosodic stress on 'as').
> STUDENT A: *¿Lindas o linda?* (prosodic stress on 'as' and 'a')
> STUDENT B: *Linda.* (prosodic stress on 'a')
>   You're right.
> STUDENT A: *Muy bien.* It's not plural. Okay.
> STUDENT B: Switch?
> STUDENT A: Switch.
> STUDENT B: *Por favor, señor, ¿cómo son Luisa?*
> STUDENT A: *¿Cómo son o cómo es?*
> STUDENT B: Would that be *cómo es?*
>   *¿Cómo es Luisa?*
> STUDENT A: *Luisa es muy simpática.*
> STUDENT B: *Muy simpática.*

2. Examine the list of things people must acquire as part of their implicit system on pages 17–18 and consider your own second language acquisition. In what areas do you think you are native-like? In what areas do you think you are decidedly nonnative-like? Compare this with others in your class. Then consider these well-known nonnative speakers of English and ask the same questions about their native-likeness and nonnative-likeness when not acting or singing:

   • Arnold Schwarzenegger
   • Celine Dion
   • Antonio Banderas
   • Jackie Chan

GETTING A CLOSER LOOK: RESEARCH ACTIVITIES

Observe the same instructor a total of three times, once a week for three weeks. Each time, make notes on the following: (1) physical setup of the room (rows, semicircle, groups, etc.); (2) the number of teacher-fronted (Atlas-like) exercises compared to the number of non–Atlas-like exercises; and (3) circumstances under which the instructor uses the learners' native language. Prepare a report of your findings.

MAKING COMMUNICATIVE LANGUAGE TEACHING HAPPEN: PORTFOLIO ACTIVITIES

Given what we know about learner control of acquisition, develop a list of ideas for handling learners' errors in the classroom and in written production. Would you treat all errors equally? Would you correct any and all errors? Would you ignore them altogether? Under what conditions would you correct and not correct? Is there a difference between semantic or vocabulary and grammatical errors in your mind? Is there some method of feedback other than "direct" error correction that makes sense to you?

CHAPTER 2

Working with Input

In this chapter we explore:

- The nature of input, a necessary ingredient for successful language acquisition
- The ways in which speakers simplify their speech to make their input comprehensible to both first and second language learners
- The ways in which speakers modify their input through interaction and negotiation of meaning with language learners
- Meaning-bearing input, that is, language that contains a message to which a learner needs to attend
- Ways to provide input in language classrooms

WHAT IS GOOD INPUT?

A useful way to conceive of input is to consider that input is to language acquisition what gas is to a car. An engine needs gas to run; without gas, the car would not move an inch. Likewise, *input* in language learning is what gets the "engine" of acquisition going. Without it, acquisition simply doesn't happen.

Gas itself is a refined and filtered petroleum product; you cannot simply put crude oil into your gas tank and expect the car to run. And because gas is a refined petroleum product, some gas is better than others. High-octane gas makes many cars run more smoothly and efficiently than does low-octane gas. Likewise, some input is better than others, and the kind of input that is best for language learners is a kind of refined language.

There are several general characteristics of input that make it potentially useful to the learner. First, it has to be *comprehensible*. This is perhaps the most important characteristic of input from the learner's point of view. It is also the characteristic that has received the most attention in second language acquisition theory and research. *The learner must be able to understand most of what the speaker (or writer) is saying if acquisition is to happen.* In other words, the learner must be able to figure out what the speaker is saying if he is to attach meaning to the speech stream coming at him. Why is this? Acquisition consists in large part of the building up of form-meaning connections in the learner's head. For example, the learner of French hears the word *chien* in various contexts and eventually attaches it to a particular meaning: a four-legged canine. As another example, a learner of Italian might hear *-ato* in various contexts and eventually attach it to a particular meaning: past-time reference. Features of language, be they grammar, vocabulary, pronunciation, or something else, can only make their way into the learner's mental representation of the language system if they have been linked to some kind of real-world meaning.

Second, input has to be *meaning bearing*. Stated another way, the language that the learner is listening to (or reading, if we are talking about written language) *must contain some message to which the learner is supposed to attend.* Thus, meaning-bearing input has some communicative intent; the purpose of the speaker is to communicate a message to a listener. When someone says to a learner, "I went out last night. And, boy! Did I have a good time!" the speaker is attempting to communicate a message about last night's events, and both speaker and listener understand that the learner-listener is supposed to focus on the message.

If the input is incomprehensible or if it is not meaning bearing, then these form-meaning connections just don't happen. Imagine the beginning second language learner finding herself in the middle of a café in a country where the language is spoken. What would she understand? What use would the language environment be to this beginner?

Input with Children

Return for a moment to the gas-car metaphor. What makes input "high octane"? And, given that we are concerned with getting learners *started* in acquisition, what kind of input is good for beginners? It is clear that learners cannot be spoken to in the way native-speaking adults talk to each other. Language learners—especially beginners—need input that is simplified compared to the free-flowing language that native speakers may use with each other (or what might appear on television or radio broadcasts, for instance). Most children get some kind of simplified input when learning their first language. They get this simplified input from parents, caretakers, siblings, and story books. Note, for example, the following interchange between a parent and a one-and-a-half-year-old child that is typical of interchanges during diaper changing or crib play. (Intonation and rhythm are not indicated in the interchange. You should try to imagine what this interchange would sound like.)

PARENT: Where's your nose?
CHILD: (*Touches nose.*)
PARENT: Where's your mouth?
CHILD: (*Grabs for parent's face.*)
PARENT: Come on. Show me your mouth. Your mouth. Where is it?
CHILD: (*Giggles and puts finger on mouth.*)
PARENT: That's it. That's your mouth! Oh! You're so smart! How'd I get such a smart baby, huh? Are you smart? Yes you are, aren't you? Aren't you?

Now contrast the preceding speech with the following conversation between the same parent and a friend.

PARENT: I'm pretty fed up with my job these days. I mean, I can't believe that the company thinks we will take a cut in pay and not say anything. I mean, it's just—I don't know.

FRIEND: But it's like that everywhere! Last week I read in *Newsweek*—at least I think it was *Newsweek*. We get both *Newsweek* and *Time*—but anyway I read where IBM is cutting another 500 jobs this next week. I bet those people wouldn't mind a cut in pay just to keep food on the table.

PARENT: Come on! It's not that easy and you know it. . . .

As you can see, the speech the infant heard and the speech used by that infant's parent with a friend are different in a number of ways: breadth of vocabulary, length of utterance, repetition, and clarity. And even though we have not included indications of intonation, articulation, rhythm, and pitch, these too would vary in the two communicative situations. Work on child language acquisition in the 1960s and 1970s revealed that the speech addressed to first language acquirers was generally simpler and more redundant than speech addressed to older children and adults. In arguing against many linguists' position that children receive degenerate input—input full of false starts, incomplete sentences, and even grammar mistakes—Snow (1978) summarizes her research findings by stating that

> children such as those included in [this] study do not learn language on the basis of a confusing corpus full of mistakes, garbles, and complexities. They hear, in fact, a relatively consistent, organized, simplified, and redundant set of utterances which in many ways seems quite well designed as a set of "language lessons."
>
> (Snow, 1978, p. 498)

Another important aspect of speech directed to children is that adults often rephrase what children say to them, thus providing the children with target models of what the children intend to say. Focusing on the child's message, an adult often expands the child's utterances as illustrated in the following example. [Note: Peter is the child; all others are adults.]

PATSY: What happened to it [the truck]?

PETER: (*looking under his chair*) Lose it. Dump truck! Dump truck! Fall! Fall!

LOIS: Yes, the dump truck fell down.

(Lightbown & Spada, 1999, p. 10)

In the example given, Lois expands Peter's child utterance "Fall! Fall!" to its full adult form, "The dump truck fell down." Researchers have suggested that these *expansions* provide input data that the child's internal mechanisms may use to compare the current state of his language with what a full-fledged grammatical utterance might sound like. What is important about Lois's expansions—and most expansions in adult-child interchanges—is that the adult is *not* correcting the speech of the child; the adult is merely confirming what the child says. The adult echoes the child's utterance to let him know that she understands the message. A final point to make is that adults naturally modify their speech when interacting with children. We want children to understand us.

Input with Second Language Learners

The research on input addressed to children prompted second language researchers to examine second language input in the same way. Several characteristics of simplified—or better yet, modified—second language input have been enumerated by various researchers. Larsen-Freeman (1985) summarizes the research in this way:

> Input to [nonnative speakers] is shorter and less complicated and is produced at a slower rate than speech between adult [native speakers]. This input tends to be more regular, canonical [that is, typical] word order is adhered to, and there is a high proportion of unmarked patterns. There are fewer false starts and there is less repair. High-frequency vocabulary is used. . . . There is a limited use of pronouns. . . . There are more questions. Question tags and alternative questions occur more frequently. There is less pre-verb modification, presumably so new information can be highlighted at the end of the utterance, where it is more salient. The input is higher-pitched, it shows more intonation variation in pitch, and it is louder in volume. It contains fewer reduced vowels and fewer contractions.
>
> (Larsen-Freeman, 1985, p. 436)

Pause to consider . . .

Larsen-Freeman's description of typical simplified second language input. Look at her description and then compare it to the adult-child exchanges quoted. Would you say that the input directed to child language acquirers and the input directed to second language acquirers (as described by Larsen-Freeman) undergo some of the same modifications as native-to-native adult language does?

Perhaps the most comprehensive list of the characteristics of simplified input in second language situations was made by Hatch (1983), who examines simplified input in terms of five general categories: (1) rate of speech, (2) vocabulary, (3) syntax, (4) discourse, and (5) speech setting. With these characteristics, she also suggests possible *benefits* derived from each characteristic. That is, each characteristic presumably has some impact on how the language is perceived and/or processed by the language learner. In Table 2.1 we reproduce Hatch's list. From Hatch's point of view, it is clear that simplified input provides learners with language that is, overall, easier to process: The ability to make form-meaning connections is enhanced because the language is structured in such a way as to make certain features of language *acoustically more salient*. The forms and structure of the language are more easily perceived, and the learner has a greater chance to hear

TABLE 2.1 Characteristics of Input Simplified for Second Language Learners

General Characteristic	Examples
Slower rate	1. Fewer reduced vowels and fewer contractions 2. Longer pauses 3. Extra stress on nouns; half-beat pauses following topic noun
Vocabulary	1. High-frequency vocabulary, less slang, fewer idioms 2. Fewer pronoun forms of all kinds; high use of names for "one," "they," "we" 3. Definitions are marked (e.g., "This is an X," "It's a kind of X") 4. Lexical information in definitions that provide extra information related to derivational morphology (e.g., "miracle—anything that's miraculous"), form class (e.g., "funds or money"), or semantic features (e.g., "a cathedral usually means a church that has very high ceilings") 5. Use of gestures and/or pictures (drawings)
Syntax	1. Simple propositional syntax, short sentences 2. Repetition and restatement 3. Less pre-verb modification; more modification after the verb 4. Expansion of learner's utterance
Discourse	1. Speaker gives the learner a choice of responses within a posed question (e.g., "Where did you go? Did you go to the beach or to the mountains?") 2. Speaker uses tag questions (e.g., "What did he want? A book?") 3. Speaker offers correction (e.g., "You mean he left?")
Speech setting	1. Repetition of scenarios (e.g., daily encounters in a particular place)

Source: Adapted from Hatch (1983)

and process the form-meaning connections that are contained in the input. For example, speech with fewer contractions results in the learner being able to hear whether the language has a copular verb or not or what the auxiliary verbs are. Simpler syntax reduces the burden on processing and increases the chances that the learner will hear certain forms and structures. Some modifications of input aid the acquisition of related words and their morphology (form). When someone defines a word using another word with the same root, for example, the learner receives evidence about word endings related to nouns, verbs, and adjectives.

> *Pause to consider . . .*
>
> some of Hatch's descriptions of input modifications. Reread and consider the examples related to syntax. Can you give concrete examples of each? Can you think of a specific benefit for each type of modification? What might be the specific benefit of repetition and restatement?

The idea of processing input and linguistic data has led researchers and theorists to posit another construct: *intake*. Whereas input is the language the learner is exposed to, intake is the *language that the learner actually attends to and that gets processed in working memory in some way.* Thus, not all input—no matter how comprehensible or meaningful—automatically makes its way into the learner's head. Intake, then, can be considered a subset, or a filtered version, of the input. Recall from Chapter 1 that learners possess certain internal mechanisms that operate on input and that just because a learner hears something in the input does not mean that she will automatically acquire it. Acquisition is not instantaneous! Although the source of the input is external to the learner, what happens to the input is largely in the learner's hands—or brain, to be precise. In Chapter 6 we examine in some detail the processes that learners use to derive intake from input. For now, it is sufficient to understand that comprehensible, meaning-bearing input is necessary for successful second language acquisition but that not all input becomes intake.

Modifying Input Through Interaction and Negotiation

We have been discussing input as though the learner's interlocutor is in complete charge of the language that the learner hears. The speaker makes adjustments or modifications and thus simplifies the input that the learner receives. This picture is, however, a bit one-sided. Although it is true that speakers generally modify their speech to make themselves more comprehensible to language learners, it is equally true that language learners often get the speakers to *make* specific modifications. In other words, language learners often *negotiate* the flow and quality of input directed to them when they are engaged in some kind of conversational *interaction* (Gass, 1997). Learners may ask for repetitions and clarifications, or they may use some other device to signal that comprehension is problematic. These signals cause the other interlocutors to modify their speech in an attempt to facilitate the learner's comprehension. This negotiation is clearly illustrated in the following four examples taken from another investigation by Hatch (1978a):

Example 1

NATIVE SPEAKER: Did you have a nice weekend?
RICARDO: Huh?
NATIVE SPEAKER: Friday, Saturday . . . did you have fun?

Example 2

NATIVE SPEAKER: Did you ride the mules?
RICARDO: Mules?
NATIVE SPEAKER: The horses around. The pack mules.
RICARDO: Pack mules?

Example 3

NATIVE SPEAKER: Do you wear them every day?
RICARDO: Huh?
NATIVE SPEAKER: Do you put them on every day?
RICARDO: Wear?

NATIVE SPEAKER: Yeah, do you (*Adds gesture here.*) put them on every day?
RICARDO: Ah! No!

Example 4

NATIVE SPEAKER: I see. Well, is it typed?
LEARNER: Type? Yes . . . uh . . . for the . . . I don't . . . I don't type.
NATIVE SPEAKER: Is it handwritten?
LEARNER: Uh. Pardon me? Excuse me?
NATIVE SPEAKER: Is your thesis now handwritten?
(*later*)
NATIVE SPEAKER: Is your thesis now typewritten or did you write it by hand?
LEARNER: Ah, yes, by hand.
NATIVE SPEAKER: By hand.

In each interchange, the learner caused the speaker to modify utterances. *Interaction*, then, may enhance the availability of comprehensible input, because interaction pushes the learner to indicate what he does and does not understand. This, in turn, can cause the interlocutor to modify her input in the ways suggested by Hatch in Table 2.1. Comprehensible input derived from interaction, then, may be quite different from, say, input from the radio or the TV, where the speaker *is* in absolute and complete control of both what is said and how it is said, and the learner has no opportunity to negotiate comprehension.

Pause to consider . . .

how the speaker modified her speech in the four examples given. Use Hatch's list of the characteristics of simplified input (Table 2.1) to analyze what the speaker did each time. Also, reflect on how the learner actually signaled a comprehension problem. Did all learners use the same devices to get the speakers to modify their language? What kinds of devices or phrases might you teach learners early on to help them negotiate comprehension and thus the input they receive? Make a list of at least five phrases that your learners would find useful.

INPUT AND THE CLASSROOM

Many beginning instructors (and even some experienced instructors!) who have not been in communicative classes frequently ask, "But how can you use the language with beginning learners? They can't understand anything!" Indeed, this belief is reflected in some of the research on foreign language classrooms in the United States. In one study, for example, Wing (1987) found that the average instructor used the second language about 50 percent of the time in a second-year high school class. Of that 50 percent only about half of the language was communicative in nature. That is, only about a quarter of *teacher talk* (the specialized input that instructors often use with beginners) could be considered meaning-bearing input. And much of this was language used to solicit or confirm the speech of learners in the class ("Enrique, do number 3, please." "Good." "Excellent!"). In short, it was language used to manage the classroom exercises. To the extent that Wing's subjects represent instructors in general, learners may not be getting much comprehensible meaning-bearing input during class time in the early stages. If the class period is forty minutes long, then learners are at best getting approximately ten minutes of comprehensible input a day. And given the restricted range of language functions exhibited by the instructors in Wing's study, the input may not be very broad in terms of the linguistic data it contains—not an optimal condition for language acquisition to take place.

The belief that beginning learners cannot understand anything is simply that—a belief. Imagine what life would be like if parents believed the same thing about their one-year-olds: No one would ever acquire language! There are, however, instructors for whom talking to beginning language learners is as natural as talking to a baby. These instructors may or may not be consciously aware of Hatch's and Larsen-Freeman's descriptions of simplified input; they simplify their language as a natural part of trying to make themselves understood. How do they do this? These instructors first make use of as many *nonlinguistic means* as possible to make themselves understood. They use drawings, photos, diagrams, objects, gestures, and other visual aids to accompany their speech. These nonlinguistic means serve to anchor the input in the "here and now"; that is, they provide a mechanism for making the subject of conversation *concrete rather than abstract.*

In the following example, a first-semester language instructor points, uses gestures, and draws on the blackboard. All these actions (indicated with all-capital letters) facilitate learner comprehension. Not indicated are the pauses, use of stress, slower articulation, and other strategies that would also form an important part of the spoken version of what you are about to read. As you read it over, consider what you would sound like if you were the instructor. What words would you emphasize with added stress? How long would your pauses be?

> Instructor: Let's draw a face. This is a face. [POINTS TO HER OWN FACE AND MAKES A CIRCLE AROUND IT WITH FINGER.] Let's draw a face, O.K.? [DRAWS AN OVAL ON THE BLACKBOARD.] You draw a face on your paper, too. Go ahead. Draw an oval to begin the face. [POINTS TO PAPERS AND MAKES AN OVAL MOTION WITH FINGERS.] Good. That's the first part of the face. The most important features on a face are the eyes. The eyes. [POINTS TO HER OWN EYES.] Eyes are very important. With eyes we see the world. Eyes are also the first thing someone sees on your face. What kind of eyes shall we put on this face? Big eyes? [MOTIONS BIG WITH HANDS.] Or little eyes? [GESTURES WITH HANDS.] Let's give this face two big eyes. [DRAWS EYES ON THE BOARD.] You draw two big eyes on your paper, too.

In addition to nonlinguistic means, language instructors who use a good deal of the second language in the classroom exhibit another trait: They tend to focus on topics that the learners already know something about. Such "high-input-giving" instructors tend to put learners into *familiar situations* (drawing a face, playing a card game) so that learners can make use of what they know about the real world in order to comprehend better. For example, an instructor might talk about his dog, drawing on the fact that learners already know certain things about dogs and dog behavior: They bark, wag their tails, have four feet, and so on. This instructor expects that learners' background knowledge will help them anticipate vocabulary and topics that he, the instructor, is talking about. In hearing about dogs, for example, learners would not expect the instructor to talk about milking, feeding them hay, or riding them. The instructor knows that learners will rule out a whole set of possible topics and words because of what they know about dogs. Using familiar themes and situations, good instructors allow their learners to process for language alone and do not push them to struggle with the topic itself. Imagine a first-semester Japanese course in which the instructor talked about particle physics! Just what background knowledge would the nonphysics student be able to draw on in order to comprehend the message? (In Chapter 11 we explore making use of learners' background knowledge in further detail as it relates to reading comprehension.)

In short, good high-input-giving instructors follow the advice that Brown (1977) has given to parents:

> Believe that your child can understand more than he or she can say,
> and seek, above all, to communicate. . . . There is no set of rules of
> how to talk to a child that can even approach what you unconsciously
> know. If you concentrate on communicating, everything else will follow.
> (Brown, 1977, as cited in Krashen, 1982, p. 65)

Let's turn to another example of teacher input, from an introductory Spanish lesson on vocabulary related to family. In introducing the new vocabulary, the instructor chose to tell the class about his own family. The instructor's purpose was both *didactic* and *communicative*. It was didactic because the instructor was actually presenting vocabulary related to the family, and it was communicative because he was also attempting to have his class understand as much about his own family as possible. As you read the description, note what the instructor does to make himself comprehensible. Also ask yourself at what point in the course of study this presentation might have occurred. As in the case of the face-drawing episode presented earlier, the following example is a sterilized presentation of input. False starts, stops, learner clarification requests, and other interruptions are omitted for presentation here. Note that providing learners with a lot of input is not equivalent to talking *at* them. The instructor in the following example is talking *to* and *with* the learners. First, the real-world information helps the input be meaning bearing. Second, his use of comprehension checks helps keep the learners attending to the message and, hence, processing the input. (We give an English translation here; the original teacher input was, of course, in Spanish.)

> Today we are going to talk about my family. I have a most interesting
> family. (*Displays* "My Family" *chart on board or overhead.*) Here is
> me. These are my parents. This is my father and this is my mother.
> Father . . . mother. My father's name is Bill. My mother's name is

Juanita. They are divorced. This is my stepfather, Joe. My stepfather. And this is my sister . . . my only sister. Her name is Gloria. (*Turns off the overhead or covers visual.*)

Let's see what kind of memory you have. What is my father's name—Joe or Bill? (*responses*) What is my mother's name—Juanita or Gloria? (*responses*) Right. Gloria is my sister, not my mother. And do I have any brothers? (*responses*) No. (*Shows visual again.*) All right, to summarize, my family consists of my father, Bill, my mother, Juanita, and my sister, Gloria. I have no brothers. Oh, I also have a stepfather, Joe. My parents have been divorced since 1972. (*Writes date on board.*) Now, that was easy, but here are some other family members. (*Now reveals grandparents.*)

These are my grandparents. My grandparents. These are my maternal grandparents and these are my paternal grandparents. This man here, Dick, is my paternal grandfather. And this woman, Bridgette, is my paternal grandmother. Grandfather . . . grandmother. But Bridgette passed away many years ago; Bridgette is dead. (*Points to tombstone.*) These are my maternal grandparents. Domingo is my maternal grandfather . . . and Concepción is my maternal grandmother. Domingo passed away in 1985; Domingo is dead. Just to review, Dick and Bridgette are my paternal grandparents, and Domingo and Concepción are my maternal grandparents. Grandfather . . . grandfather . . . grandmother . . . grandmother. Both Bridgette and Domingo are dead. By the way, Dick lives in Indiana and Concepción lives in California. (*Removes or covers visual.*)

Ready for a real memory test? (*Shows new overhead, or distributes photocopy.*) In the left column are names; in the right column are relationships. You have two minutes to match the name to a relationship. (*After two minutes, teacher calls time and quiz is reviewed with original drawing exposed; teacher engages in some light conversation in which students answer with one word, "yes/no" responses, such as, "Did you know that I was half Mexican? How does your family compare to mine—do you have more brothers and sisters?"*)

Now, here is the real interesting part. (*Reveals visual of extended family with aunts and uncles, some cousins, and so on. Instructor continues presentation using same format as before.*)

(VanPatten, 1991, pp. 59–60)

Many beginning instructors think that this scene must have taken place in the second semester or late in the year. Actually, this lesson on family occurred during the first week of instruction! What makes the input comprehensible? The visual display of the family tree establishes the topic, and learners then know that the instructor is talking about family. This instructor thus draws on the background knowledge of the class in order to facilitate comprehension. By locating himself first in the family tree, learners know that the other people are his relatives. Learners are thus engaged in matching names to relationships: Juanita = mother, Gloria = sister. Thus, they are engaged in the didactic aspect of the lesson as mentioned earlier, that is, vocabulary acquisition. But note at the same time that they are processing far more than vocabulary related to family. As part of their attempt to comprehend, they may be picking up certain phrases, such as "name is," "my _____," "I have _____," and they may be starting the process of acquiring gender markings on nouns and adjectives. Instructors who use the second language to teach vocabulary expose the learner to much more language—and provide richer input—than merely the vocabulary of the lesson.

Pause to consider . . .

the nature of the simplified input in this interchange. After reviewing Larsen-Freeman's and Hatch's descriptions of simplified input to language learners, determine which aspects of simplification this instructor seemed to do naturally. See if you can find the following:

1. Lack of contractions
2. Repetitions
3. Reformulations of an utterance (i.e., saying one thing in various ways)
4. Simple syntax (i.e., sentence structure)
5. Frequent and/or "concrete" vocabulary
6. Comprehension checks (e.g., "Do you follow?" "Are you with me?")

To be sure, the second language learners in the two examples given may not be understanding every word their instructors utter. It would be surprising if they were! Instead, learners are most likely catching bits and pieces of the language. In the very beginning stages, they may catch only content words and repeated chunks or formulas ("I have _____," "name is," "Draw a _____," "Who is _____?"). Most likely the learners are not attending to certain grammatical features of the language, such as articles and case endings, as they concentrate on getting the message. Some learners, however, may notice verb endings, noun endings, and other features early on, but these are the exceptional learners. Or, these learners might notice that endings vary, but they are unable to pick up on the systematic nature of the variation. With time, however, learners are able to comprehend the input with greater ease. Ease of comprehension brings with it a greater likelihood that learners will attend to grammatical features in the input that they missed previously, a topic that we discuss in Chapter 6.

Pause to consider . . .

the culture-specific dimensions of presenting a family tree. What culturally specific information is encoded in the presentation? Does this information need to be made explicit? If so, what needs to be explicit? How would you make the language you use to express the information comprehensible to the learners?

We have presented comprehensible input as it relates to language acquisition in general. That is, we have not referred to specific aspects or features of a language that learners acquire through input and interaction. In Chapters 6 and 7, we describe how learners acquire grammar through input and interaction. But to prepare the stage for those concepts, we turn now to the acquisition of vocabulary through input and interaction. Can you cite specific instances in your own language development when you acquired words from the contexts in which they were used?

Vocabulary Lists and Visuals

In at least one of your beginning language classes, you probably had a textbook with vocabulary lists. The vocabulary may have been presented in bilingual lists, as in the following example from a French book:

la maison	the house
la pièce	the room
la cuisine	the kitchen
la chambre	the bedroom
la salle de bain	the bathroom
les meubles	furniture
la chaise	the chair
le lit	the bed

Very often such lists suggest to learners that vocabulary acquisition is a matter of memorizing second language equivalents of first language words. Some textbooks even have study hints for learning vocabulary and recommend that learners make flashcards with the second language word on one side and the first language word on the other. Other study hints include covering the first language side of the list with a piece of paper and giving the first language equivalent of each second language word. Or, it is suggested that one cover the second language side of the list and give the second language equivalent of each first language word. Although these study hints can be helpful for the specific purpose of studying for a test in which one may have to give first or second language equivalencies, these types of practice are no substitute for meaning-bearing comprehensible input in learning vocabulary.

We saw in the previous section a vocabulary lesson that was built around an attempt to communicate about one person's family. The vocabulary was initially presented and practiced with significant comprehensible input. Learners actively attended to the teacher's input for its meaning and were learning words during the process. Many professionals advocate the introduction and learning of vocabulary via comprehensible input whether they call it "vocabulary learning" or not. Krashen and Terrell (1983), for example, advocate the use of topics around which input activities can be developed. The following list of selected topics form natural vocabulary groups; you can think of others as you read the list:

description of students
clothing
colors
objects in the classroom
favorite activities
sports and games
climate and seasons
weather
seasonal activities
holiday activities
family and relatives
physical states
emotional states
daily activities
holiday and vacation activities
pets

(Adapted from Krashen & Terrell, 1983, pp. 67–68)

Most textbooks have similar vocabulary groups. Some still make use of bilingual lists, but others have moved toward the use of visuals (drawings, photographs, cartoons) to present vocabulary. In Figure 2.1, German vocabulary words related to clothing are accompanied not by English translations but by drawings. As learners study vocabulary in this way, they are encouraged to make direct form-meaning connections similar to those that they would make if the vocabulary were presented within the context of comprehensible, meaning-bearing input. Terrell refers to the process of making direct form-meaning connections as *binding*.

FIGURE 2.1 Presentation of German clothing vocabulary in a contemporary German textbook

Binding is the term I propose to describe the cognitive and affective mental process of linking a meaning to a form. The concept of binding is what language teachers refer to when they insist that a new word ultimately be associated directly with its meaning and not with a translation.

(Terrell, 1986, p. 214)

How can we encourage binding during vocabulary acquisition? We have already explored the nature of simplified or modified input and the use of visuals as means by which instructors can make input comprehensible. These can also be used to encourage binding of vocabulary: We saw how visuals such as photos and drawings "anchor" the input in the here-and-now, making the idea and references to it more concrete. As one more example of binding new vocabulary, the instructor in the following classroom excerpt uses photos to introduce vocabulary related to clothing. Her speech is anchored in the here-and-now because both she and the learners have the concrete reference of the photo before them; this photo serves as the common ground between them. The italicized information in brackets represents the instructor's or students' actions, and the nonitalicized information represents what learners say.

Look at this picture. What do you see? A woman? [Yes.] Yes, that's right. There is a woman in the picture. [*The instructor points to the hat.*] What is this? [*Learners shake heads, indicating they don't know.*] This is a hat. This picture of the woman who is wearing the hat is for Yvonne. O.K.? Now, who has the picture of the woman who is wearing the hat? [Yvonne.] Good. Now here is another picture. Is this a man or a woman in the picture? [A man.] Right. Yvonne has a picture of a woman with a hat, but this is a picture of a man. Is he wearing a hat? [No.] Right. He's not wearing a hat. What is he wearing? Well, he's wearing a suit. [*Instructor points to suit.*] This is a grey suit. And he's also wearing a tie. [*Instructor points.*] So, this man is wearing a suit and a tie. Let's give this photo to Dave. Now, who has the picture of the man in the suit and tie? [Dave.] And who has the picture of the woman with the hat? [Yvonne.] Does the man with the suit also have on a hat? [No.] Does the woman have on a tie? [No.] Here's another photo. This woman is wearing a blouse and pants. . . .

(Adapted from Terrell, 1991)

But anchoring input is not limited to visuals. In the remainder of this chapter, we examine some other ways in which instructors can anchor their speech in the here-and-now to promote vocabulary acquisition.

Pause to consider . . .

including information about culturally appropriate attire. Would you include this information when you are first presenting vocabulary or would you develop an activity for later in the lesson?

Using Learners and the Classroom

The classroom is rich in resources for teaching common vocabulary. Indeed, instructors can make use of learners, their features, and their belongings to teach vocabulary. Involving learners heightens attention and adds a personal element to the class as learners become active participants in the teaching process. The following is an example of an instructor using learners in the classroom to teach the vocabulary associated with physical descriptions.

> [*Instructor points to a learner.*] What is your name? [Barbara.] Barbara, come here please. [*Gestures to Barbara to approach.*] That's right, come here. [*Barbara approaches.*] Good. Thank you. Class, look at Barbara. She has long brown hair. [*Instructor points and gestures to assist comprehension.*] Her hair is long and brown. Her hair is not short. It is long. What is the name of the person with long brown hair? [Barbara.] Now, let's see. What's your name? [Sharon.] O.K. Sharon, please come here. [*Sharon approaches.*] Class, look at Sharon. She has short blond hair. Her hair is not long. It is short. [*Gestures "long" and "short" with palms facing each other as he moves them close to each other or away from each other.*] It is not brown. It is blond. What is the name of the person with short blond hair? [Sharon.] Right. And what is the name of the person with long brown hair? [Barbara.] Right again. Now, what's your name? [Steve.] Come here, please. Class, this is Steve. Look at Steve's hair. Is it blond? [No.] Is it brown? [Yes.] Then Steve has hair like Barbara's. But is it long? [No.] Is it short? [Yes.] Then Steve has hair like Sharon's. He has the same color hair as Barbara. But he has the same length [*gestures in an up and down motion with palms facing each other*] of hair as Sharon. The color is brown. The length is short.
>
> (Adapted and expanded from Krashen & Terrell, 1983, p. 76)

Pause to consider . . .

the roles of instructor and learners in the classroom during these initial input activities. At first glance, the presentations may seem Atlas-like since the teacher is shouldering the burden of communication and is doing all the work. But is this so? Are the learners mere receptacles? What are the instructors doing to keep the learners active and attentive during the lesson? What distinguishes what learners are doing during these activities from what they would do during a drill?

Total Physical Response

Another technique for providing input that has been formalized as a method is *Total Physical Response*, generally referred to by practitioners as TPR. Although no longer used as a method, many instructors find TPR a useful instructional technique or activity, especially in early stages of language development, when learners can comprehend much more than they can say. Developed by James Asher of San Jose (California) State University, TPR in its simplest terms refers to learners carrying out the actions commanded by the instructor. The instructor first performs the actions while learners listen and watch. Then the learners perform the same actions with the instructor. The instructor subsequently "tests" the binding of the commands by stopping her simultaneous performance of the command and allowing learners to do it as a group on their own. For example, on the very first day of class an instructor might begin with the following. (Italicized words are in the second language; nonitalicized words are in the native language. The information in parentheses indicates the physical actions occurring.)

> In this class, you are going to learn language by performing actions based on my commands. To help you learn the commands, I will say them and demonstrate each one. You will then act out the action with me. Ready?
>
> *Stand up.* (Instructor stands up.)
> *Sit down.* (Instructor sits down.)
> *Stand up.* (Instructor stands up.)
> *Sit down.* (Instructor sits down.)
> Now do it with me. *Stand up.* (Instructor and class stand up.)
> *Sit down.* (Instructor and class sit down.)
> *Stand up.* (Instructor and class stand up.)
> *Sit down.* (Instructor and class sit down.)
> Watch and listen again.
> *Stand up. Walk to the blackboard. Walk to your seat. Sit down.* (Instructor acts each out as she says it.)
> *Stand up. Walk to the blackboard. Walk to your seat. Sit down.* (Instructor acts each out as she says it.)
> Now do it with me. *Stand up. Walk to the blackboard. Walk to your seat. Sit down.* (Instructor and learners act each out as she says it.)
> *Stand up. Walk to the blackboard. Walk to your seat. Sit down.* (Instructor and learners act each out as she says it.)
> Robert, you try it. *Stand up.* (Robert stands up while teacher simply stands to the side.) *Sit down.* (Robert sits down.) *Stand up.* (Robert stands up.) *Walk to the blackboard.* (Robert walks to the blackboard.) *Walk to your seat.* (Robert walks to his seat.)
> *Sit down.* (Robert sits down.)
> *Excellent.* Who else wants to try? (Instructor does this again with another learner.)
> Now, watch and listen again. *Stand up. Walk to the blackboard. Touch the blackboard. Walk to your seat. Touch your seat. Sit down.* (Instructor acts each out as she says it.)
> [The activity may continue.]

Correct performance of the actions demonstrates learners' comprehension. If a learner makes an error (performs the wrong action) or hesitates, the instructor simply repeats the command, acts it out again, or gives some other clue to the learner. Note that TPR qualifies as both meaning bearing and comprehensible. It is meaning bearing because the input contains a message and comprehensible because the instructor demonstrates the actions. The instructor's own actions, then, serve a similar function to the drawings, photos, and other visual aids mentioned previously. Very quickly, learners begin to make the connections between what is said and what they are supposed to do. Note, too, that TPR contains many of the characteristics of simplified input discussed earlier in this chapter: shorter sentences, pauses, concrete vocabulary. Many instructors find TPR an ideal way to introduce vocabulary once learners know the commands "show," "take," "touch," "hide," "draw," "give," and "pick up." A great deal of vocabulary can be introduced during the course of thirty minutes! As instructors introduce vocabulary with objects and/or visuals, they can instruct learners to carry out the following actions:

Hide the picture of the house.

Walk to the drawing of an apartment.

Give the brown dog to Emily.

Draw a tree on the board.

Pick up the history book and give it to Robert.

Pick up the math book and show it to the class.

In a lesson on body parts, an instructor might ask learners to manipulate photos of various body parts. With the photos arranged in the chalktray and on his desk, he could call learners to the front of the class and give them commands such as these:

Put the photo of the nose on top of the photo of the mouth.

Take the two ears and put them on top of the eyebrows.

The instructor might subsequently have the class "build a face" on the blackboard. With tape added to the back of the visuals, he might tell learners:

Robert, put a nose on the board.

Now, Jane, put a mouth on the board.

Stan, select an ear and place it on the board.

and so on until the class completed a Picasso-like face and head.

Pause to consider . . .

the importance of visuals in language instruction. Why is it a good idea for beginning instructors to start a "picture file"? (A picture file is a file of photos from magazines that have been cut and mounted onto construction paper.) What are the qualities of "good" visuals for the language classroom? How large should a picture be? Should it be simple and straightforward or contain a complex scene? Why do some consider the overhead projector to be a language instructor's best friend?

Inexperienced instructors often see TPR as consisting of only simple commands. But as learners progress, the instructor can combine commands and declarative statements, thus increasing the quality of the input that learners receive. For example, after several days of TPR, instructors can push their learners into comprehending "if-then" statements by simply giving the second language equivalents for *if, but,* and *then* and giving commands of the following type: "If Susan walks to the blackboard, then stand up. But if she walks to the door, just raise your hand."

Vocabulary Activities

Specific input-oriented activities and quizzes can be developed once vocabulary is introduced. One activity type that serves as both a classroom activity and a quizzing activity is to have learners mark up a photocopied visual according to what their instructor says. Once again using body parts, imagine that the learners have at their desks a photocopied line drawing of a human being. The instructor uses already known vocabulary (shapes, numbers, letters) to test the learner's comprehension of body parts in context.

1. Draw a circle around the nose.
2. Write the number 15 on the left eye and the number 14 on the right eye.
3. Place an X over the mouth.

If learners already know colors, then they could be given crayons or colored pencils and told to

1. Color the eyes red.
2. Color the left ear blue and the right ear green.

Learners could play games such as Bingo, using cards with body parts rather than numbers (each card would be slightly different). The instructor would reach into a bag and pull out the name of a body part and read it. Students would place a marker on each body part, and the first learner to obtain a row of body parts vertically, horizontally, or diagonally would win.

Another type of input activity requires visualization. Learners are given crayons and colored pencils for drawing. They then close their eyes and listen to a brief description that uses current vocabulary. As they listen, they should develop a mental picture of what is described. Once the description is complete, they open their eyes and draw. Visualization activities could be used for vocabulary such as physical descriptions, clothing, weather, family members and relatives, physical states, and emotional states. Following is an example of one such visualizing activity used as an end-of-class quiz. It uses vocabulary related to rooms and furniture.

I am going to describe a room in a house. I want you to close your eyes and listen. Try to picture the house in your mind. Visualize it as I describe it. After I complete the description, you will draw it! Ready? O.K., close your eyes. Now listen carefully—and visualize the room. (*The instructor lowers her voice and speaks slowly and dramatically, using many pauses.*) This is a living room. Not a kitchen, not a bedroom, and not a dining room, but a living room. This room has two large windows. Through the windows you can see some trees. Between the two windows is a small green sofa. Above the small green sofa is a painting. It is a painting of a woman. To the left of the sofa is a chair. It is a large chair. The chair is blue and green. Next to the chair is a small round table. The small round table is made of wood.

Some textbooks have begun to incorporate input-oriented work as part of the initial vocabulary presentation, making the first-time instructor's task a bit easier if her goal is to provide as much input as possible. Activities include matching (vocabulary-visuals, vocabulary-statements, vocabulary-definitions), true/false (likely/unlikely, possible/impossible), and others. As an example, the following textbook activity uses vocabulary related to moods and feelings (*happy, sad, bored, tired*). Learners first glance over the expressions in their textbooks as the instructor pronounces them. Then they complete the subsequent matching activity.

Following is a list of thoughts that Claudia [the person in the visual display of emotions and feelings] had during the three days previously described. Match each feeling your instructor mentions to one of Claudia's thoughts.

MODEL: INSTRUCTOR: She's nervous.
            CLASS: That goes with number 2.

1. "I would like to sleep ten hours tonight!"
2. "Gee whiz! I only have four hours left to study. I'm gonna fail!"
3. "They are going to think I'm dumb."
4. "Didn't this prof learn about public speaking? How monotonous."
5. "Yippee! I got an A! I got an A!"

[*Instructor reads:*
She's very happy.
She feels embarrassed.
She's nervous.
She's tired.
She's bored.]

A related input-oriented activity would be the following, in which the instructor states a mood or emotion about typical students and the learners select the reason for that mood.

Your instructor will read some moods that are common among students. Choose the activity that might cause that mood in the typical student.

1. **a.** He is studying in the library.
   b. He has three exams today.
   c. He slept fine last night.
2. **a.** She has to study but a roommate is playing the stereo loud.
   b. She received a letter from a good friend this morning.
   c. She is going shopping after class.
3. **a.** He is attending classes.
   b. He is going to the cafeteria to eat.
   c. He won $1,000,000 in the lottery.

4. **a.** She is going to a party with some friends.
   b. She ate in a great restaurant last night.
   c. She got an F on a test.

[*Instructor reads:* 1. The student is very tense. 2. The student is upset. 3. The student is happy. 4. The student is depressed.]

Pause to consider . . .

using the previous examples of activities as tasks on a short vocabulary quiz. Are they equal in difficulty? For example, how does the task of coloring body parts compare in difficulty to the activity in which a learner has to visualize and then draw a room? How do both compare, say, to the activity about students' moods and their possible causes? If these tasks are not equal in difficulty, how would you determine point value and assign a grade to each?

SUMMARY

We have explored a number of issues related to input and second language teaching. First, we saw that the necessary characteristics of good input are that it be (1) comprehensible and (2) meaning bearing (it carries a message that the learner attends to).

In both first and second language acquisition, people who speak to learners modify their speech in certain ways to facilitate learner comprehension. Learners, when actively engaged in attempting to comprehend, can get their interlocutors to make modifications in what they said. These modifications include simplification of vocabulary and syntax, reduction of speed, increased use of pauses, shorter sentences, repetition and rephrasing, and others. These modifications enable learners to attend to form-meaning connections in the input, which in turn translates into better acquisition. In short, it is not native-like discourse that fuels acquisition in the early stages but rather discourse that is tailored to the learner. This tailoring may adjust over time as the learner builds up a linguistic system and becomes increasingly skilled in comprehension.

We also explored examples of teacher talk in classrooms, showing how some instructors provide comprehensible input in large doses to their learners. Focusing on the here-and-now, anchoring the input in topics with which learners are familiar, using visuals, and drawing on the board, these instructors provide classroom learners with the kind of high-octane input their internal mechanisms need in order to succeed in language acquisition. These instructors are providing opportunities for binding to take place.

Finally, we examined some specific uses of comprehensible, meaning-bearing input in the teaching of vocabulary: visuals, Total Physical Response, visualization techniques, and matching activities. These activities are also easily adaptable for quizzing in an input format, thus linking instructional techniques with testing techniques.

Remember that vocabulary acquisition is not the only critical use of input. In this chapter, we have seen various examples of input useful for vocabulary acquisition, and it would be easy to infer that input provision equals vocabulary acquisition. But it should be clear that comprehensible, meaning-bearing input is crucial for *all* domains of language: syntax, verbal morphology, nominal morphology, pronunciation, and semantics, in addition to vocabulary. In Chapters 6 and 7, we explore in detail the relationship of input to the acquisition of grammar. For now, you should understand that, although learners are reaping the benefits of vocabulary acquisition from the input they are exposed to, they are also acquiring grammar.

KEY TERMS, CONCEPTS, AND ISSUES

input
  comprehensible
  meaning bearing
  simplified
  modified
expansions in adult-child
  interactions
simplified input in second language
  acquisition
    linguistic characteristics
intake
learner negotiation of input
  interaction
how to make input comprehensible
  in the classroom
    nonlinguistic aids
      concrete versus abstract
        referent

familiar topics
  familiar situations
binding in vocabulary acquisition
form-meaning connections
  direct versus indirect
    bilingual lists
    visuals
TPR
activities and quizzes
  drawing
  games
  visualization
  matching

THINKING MORE ABOUT IT: DISCUSSION QUESTIONS

1. Imagine that you are the native-speaking instructor participating in the following interchanges. What would your natural expansions of the learner's utterances be like? What would you say next? (NS = Native Speaker, L = Learner)

   (1) NS: Do you ride a bike to school?

   L: No bike.

   NS: _____

(2)   L: (who is telling how he turned down an invitation to go out with friends last night): So, I stay. No go. Stay and study.

NS: _____

Now recast these interchanges into the language you teach. How would you expand on the learner's utterances in the L2?

2. As mentioned in the chapter, learners may often signal a lack of comprehension, thereby causing a modification in the native speaker's speech. How would you modify the question or statement in each of the following situations? (As in the interchanges in the preceding activity, do this first in English and then in the language you teach.)

(1)   NS: At what time did you get home?

L: Sorry?

NS: _____

(2)   NS: And so they lived happily ever after.

L: After?

NS: _____

(3)   NS: With lobsters I only eat the tails and claws.

L: Cl-cl . . .

NS: _____

3. Review the following conversation between two adults (presented earlier in the chapter). Then modify the second person's (the friend's) speech, so that a beginning learner could more easily understand it.

PARENT: I'm pretty fed up with my job these days. I mean, I can't believe that the company thinks we will take a cut in pay and not say anything. I mean, it's just—I don't know.

FRIEND: But it's like that everywhere! Last week I read in *Newsweek*—at least I think it was *Newsweek*. We get both *Newsweek* and *Time*—but anyway I read where IBM is cutting another 500 jobs this next week. I bet those people wouldn't mind a cut in pay just to keep food on the table.

PARENT: Come on! It's not that easy and you know it. . . .

GETTING A CLOSER LOOK: RESEARCH ACTIVITIES

Record on either audio- or videotape two language instructors who are native speakers of the language they teach. First, record them talking to each other. Transcribe ten minutes of their speech. Then observe and record one or both of these instructors teaching, and transcribe ten minutes of that recording.

Prepare a report detailing the most outstanding differences between how they speak to each other and how they speak to language learners. Be sure to provide specific examples of techniques they use to make themselves understood.

MAKING COMMUNICATIVE LANGUAGE TEACHING HAPPEN: PORTFOLIO ACTIVITIES

Using the family tree presentation as a guide, make a visual of your weekly (Monday–Friday) schedule and write a detailed script for how you would present it to your class. Remember: Your goal is to have your learners know what your schedule is. Keep in mind the kinds of true/false or other questions you might "quiz" them with that do not require production on their part. Prepare a quiz to give them as a final task. Imagine that you would present this in the second or third week of instruction.

CHAPTER 3

Communicating in the Classroom

In this chapter we explore:

- The process of learning to communicate in a second language
- The nature of communication—defined as the expression, interpretation, *and* negotiation of meaning—and communicative language ability
- The informational-cognitive purpose of communication as suited to classroom communication
- The characteristics of the discourse that results from using communicative drills, teacher-fronted activities, and paired or group interaction
- Suggestions for developing information-exchange tasks
- Non–Atlas roles for instructors that result from using information-exchange tasks for communicating in classrooms

LEARNING TO COMMUNICATE

Studies of the acquisition of grammar were not the only research to undermine theories of habit formation and ALM. According to these theories, communicating with the language was something that would happen as a result of internalizing grammatical habits: The learner had to learn habits before using them. In 1972, Savignon published a study that would have a major impact on the way in which professionals perceived the ALM classroom and its effect on developing communicative language abilities. In her study, she compared three groups learning French in a first-semester college classroom. The first group received classical ALM training with four classroom days and one lab day per week. The second received the same ALM training, but on the fifth day lab practice was replaced by cultural studies: Students saw films and slide shows, had discussions about their impressions of France, and participated in informal discussions with French students studying in the United States, among other activities. The third group received ALM training, but lab day was devoted to training in communication: Students first discussed what it meant to communicate and how nonverbal communication played a role in face-to-face interactions. They then engaged in activities that focused on doing things in French: greeting, departing, information gathering, information sharing. Savignon subsequently gave students from all three groups a test of communicative competence that involved four different kinds of activities: (1) discussion with a native speaker of French; (2) information gathering with a native speaker of French (that is, the students interviewed a French person); (3) a monologue on a topic, with the learner alone in a room with a tape recorder; (4) narration (describing the activities of an actor who performed a nonspeaking series of actions).

Native speakers of French were trained to evaluate the first two tasks based on the effort to communicate and the amount of communication, and the second two tasks based on fluency and comprehensibility. In addition, all students were given the College Entrance Examination Board (CEEB) tests for listening and reading in French. The results from Savignon's study were quite clear; they are displayed in Table 3.1. The learners in the third group, the "communication" group, scored significantly higher than the others on the tests of communicative competence. More important, the control ALM group scored quite low on the tests of communicative competence, suggesting that drill and practice were not effective in promoting communicative language ability. The communication group also scored as well if not slightly higher than the others on the CEEB tests. (Independent measures of aptitude and scholastic ability were used before the study began to be sure that all groups were of the same general language learning ability.)

Savignon's study was the first empirically based research to suggest a very important aspect of language acquisition: One learns to communicate by practicing communication. As savignon states, "Those students who had been given the opportunity to use their linguistic knowledge for real communication were able to speak French. The others were not" (1983, pp. 78–79). Since Savignon's seminal study, others have gone on to study various aspects of both classroom and nonclassroom communication with similar findings. Some researchers have gone so far as to claim that learners actually learn language through communicating. Hatch (1978a), for example, suggests that during communication, learners "negotiate" and even "regulate" the kind of input they receive so that they obtain input suited to their individual needs. Swain (1985) argues that commu-

TABLE 3.1 Comparative Study of Communicative Competence in Three Groups

		Group Means			
Group	N	CEEB Listening	CEEB Reading	Instructor's Evaluation of Oral Skills	Test of Communicative Competence
ALM only	15	6.67	6.00	14.80	34.27
Culture	15	6.20	6.67	15.87	44.27
Comm.	12	9.00	8.08	19.92	66.00
F-ratio		1.11	0.56	3.98*	8.54**

*$p < .05$
**$p < .001$

Source: Adapted from Savignon (1998)

nicative production encourages learners to attend to input better since they themselves need to use language they are hearing around them. Others, however, suggest that some aspects of grammar and syntax cannot be acquired through simple acts of everyday communication (see, e.g., Sato, 1986). While research continues on the relationship between communication and acquisition, one thing remains clear: Communicative language ability—the ability to express one's self *and* to understand others—develops as learners engage in communication and not as a result of habit formation with grammatical items.

Pause to consider . . .

what Savignon's study suggests about a lament often heard from classroom learners of a language. It is not uncommon to hear "I took four years of high school French and can't speak a word," or "I was really good in Spanish and got A's, but I can't understand a thing when someone talks to me." What would you ask these people about their language classrooms? In what ways do these comments argue against habit-formation theory in language learning?

COMMUNICATION AND COMMUNICATIVE LANGUAGE ABILITY

The act of communication in most settings involves the expression, interpretation, and negotiation of meaning (Savignon, 1998). That is, a person wishes to express an idea (opinion, wish, request, demand) to someone else and does so. The other person must understand both the message and the intent of the message. Sometimes interpretation is partial, and some negotiation is needed. How many times have you heard the following expressions?

I'm sorry. Did you say . . . ?

I'm not sure what you mean.

I don't get what you're telling me.

What are you getting at?

Say what?

Are you kidding?

It's hard for me to put in words, but . . .

What I mean is . . .

No way!

Do you know what I'm saying?

As you will see throughout this chapter, communication always happens in some sort of context. In many second language contexts, communication breakdowns are likely. With underdeveloped second language knowledge and ability, learners might not have the resources to express themselves easily or to interpret a speaker of the second language. This could be due either to underdeveloped cultural knowledge or to underdeveloped linguistic knowledge. In the latter case, learners simply cannot express themselves easily because of missing vocabulary ("Geez, how do you say 'screwdriver' in this language?") or missing grammar ("How do you say 'If it hadn't have been for John' in Italian?"), or because pronunciation is a problem (the Asian early stage ESL speaker in the supermarket who asks for lettuce and is shown where the radishes are).

Leemann Guthrie (1984) provides an excellent example of an exchange between a classroom learner and his instructor in which a problem in communicating an idea leads to negotiating the meaning. One of the important points to glean from this example is that *both* the instructor and the learner are negotiating meaning. The instructor needs to understand Roger's message just as much as Roger needs to express his intent in a comprehensible manner. The instructor has been discussing the idea of "the typical French person" with the class, and Roger has just met a French person.

INSTRUCTOR: Roger, vous venez de faire la connaissance d'un Français. Quelles sont vos impressions?
ROGER: Ah... c'est... c'est ne Français typique.
INSTRUCTOR: Il n'était pas typique?
ROGER: Ne personne est typique.
INSTRUCTOR: Personne n'est typique? C'est à dire qu'il n'est pas possible de généraliser, c'est ça?
ROGER: Oui.

[Translation]

INSTRUCTOR: *Roger, you have just met a French person. What are your impressions?*
ROGER: *Ah . . . it is . . . it is no typical French.*
INSTRUCTOR: *He wasn't typical?*
ROGER: *No person is typical.*
INSTRUCTOR: *Nobody is typical? That is to say that it isn't possible to generalize, is that so?*
ROGER: *Yes.*

(Adapted from Leemann Guthrie, 1984, p. 49)

In this exchange, Roger attempts to say, "There is no such thing as a typical French person," and does so by translating, in part, from English. The instructor interprets his utterance as meaning the person whom Roger just met was not typical. Roger realizes from the instructor's response that he must reformulate his utterance, say it in another way, and eventually the *two* work out what Roger means to say. Both Roger and the instructor demonstrate a certain *strategic competence:* Instead of abandoning the idea, they attempt to get it across in another way.

Although negotiation occurs as a result of partial interpretation and incomplete comprehension, it can also be a natural part of a communicative exchange. There is a natural give and take when two people decide what to do on a Friday night—selecting a movie of joint interest, choosing a time (the early show or a late one), and deciding whether to have dinner together or separately. The game of 20 Questions is another example of negotiation to close a gap in knowledge. The question askers are trying to fill in the gap, to gain useful information by asking a series of questions, and finally to guess the answer correctly. When people make plane reservations using a travel agent, they engage in negotiation, discussing the most convenient departure and return times, the lowest price in relation to departure and return dates, and airline preferences. There are many other everyday scenarios during which we negotiate meaning—getting the best price when trading in a car, consulting a sales clerk when buying new shoes (comfort, style, price), persuading a reluctant instructor to hold class outside on a warm sunny day, interacting with telemarketers on the phone, and so on.

Pause to consider . . .

what *communicative competence* is. Savignon (1998) says that communicative competence consists of four underlying competences: *grammatical competence* (knowledge of the structure and form of language), *discourse competence* (knowledge of the rules of cohesion and coherence across sentences and utterances), *sociolinguistic competence* (knowledge of the rules of interaction: turn taking, appropriate use of first names, appropriate formulae for apologizing, appropriate greetings), and *strategic competence* (knowing how to make the most of the language that you have, especially when it is "deficient"). Do you think that one underlying competence is more important than another? Do they interact in some way, balancing each other out? Which competences are more important than others to the beginning, intermediate, or advanced language learner?

PURPOSES OF COMMUNICATION

In the nonclassroom world, people engage in oral communication for a variety of reasons. However, the two most common purposes of communication can be described as *psycho-social* and *informational-cognitive*. The psycho-social purpose of language involves using language to bond socially or psychologically with someone or some group or to engage in social behavior in some way. Thus, asking someone "How's it going?" might be less a desire to know the actual details of someone's life than a means of exchanging pleasantries or letting someone know that "you care." The informational-cognitive use of language involves communication for the purpose of obtaining information, generally for some other task. Stopping and asking someone "Do you have the time?" if we think we are running late is generally an informational activity rather than a psycho-social behavior; we ask because we really want to know the time so that we can decide if we need to walk faster, run, or catch a cab.

In a different context, the very same question ("Do you have the time?") could have a psycho-social function as a pickup line. Telling someone that you will not be in the office tomorrow but working at home and can be reached there is not a psycho-social behavior: Its purpose is to inform that person of your whereabouts because the information is necessary.

To be sure, psycho-social and informational-cognitive uses of language can and often do co-occur. A director of a movie might tell actors where to stand, whether or not they should underplay or play up a line, and so on. Information is exchanged: The actor needs the information to perform the job. At the same time, the director might use language in a particular way to let the actors know his feelings: "I trust you. You will do well" or "Don't screw this up. We're behind schedule and it's your fault." In this way, the director not only instructs and informs but also reminds all participants of their relationship to the project.

> ## *Pause to consider . . .*
>
> the two broad categories of purposes for language use. Observe some daily interactions between native speakers. What psycho-social uses of language do you see? Informational-cognitive uses? For the average person traveling abroad, which language purpose do you think is more important? For the business person abroad? For the learner spending a year in France, Germany, or Japan?

What of the language classroom? Although the instructor may use language for both psycho-social and informational-cognitive purposes, it is doubtful that the learner, especially in the beginning and intermediate stages, would use language for many psycho-social purposes. The classroom context typically does not promote the kind of interaction that requires language to be used psycho-socially. However, the classroom does lend itself exceptionally well to the use of communicative language for informational-cognitive purposes. The classroom is ideally suited to the development and implementation of activities in which learners exchange information for a common purpose. Before we examine these kinds of activities, let's review some very typical interactional patterns between instructors and learners.

CLASSROOM DISCOURSE

Communicative Drills

In Chapter 6, we discuss Paulston's traditional hierarchy of mechanical, meaningful, and communicative drills or practices as they relate to grammar teaching. For now, you should be aware that the drills differ in terms of who controls the response and what types of messages they contain. For communicative drills, the learner controls the response and provides new information; the

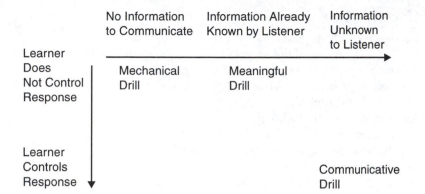

FIGURE 3.1 Factors determining practice or drill type

differences are summarized in Figure 3.1. So, in response to the question "What did you eat last night?" during a communicative drill or practice, the learner gives new and real information unknown to the listener ("I ate a tuna sandwich"). Although communicative drills might have the semblance of real communication, they fall short of providing learners with opportunities that allow them to work at expressing, interpreting, and negotiating meaning with another person. Such drills fall short of providing an extended exchange between two or more people because once an answer is given, the learners simply move on to the next question.

To examine how short drills fall, let's return to Leemann Guthrie's research. In the following example, the instructor is leading the class through a question-and-answer communicative drill in which learners practice the interrogative pronoun *lequel* ("which one") and its variants. The exercise calls for two learners to interact, but they do so without the kind of success the instructor hopes for. The learners continually circumvent the obvious linguistic intent of the activity because they are conforming to the rules of everyday conversation. That is, they attempt to exchange real information, but the instructor, who has a different purpose in mind, constantly brings the learners back to the linguistic point of the exercise. There is thus very little negotiation happening in the exchanges.

INSTRUCTOR: Okay, bon.
Demandez à... Carol... si elle connaît des chanteurs et lesquels. Ask her if she knows any singers and which ones.
LEARNER A: Uh... connas-tu des chanteurs?
LEARNER B: Je connais... Mick Jagger.
(laughter)
LEARNER A: xxx *[inaudible]*
INSTRUCTOR: Elle connaît Mick Jagger.
INSTRUCTOR: Susan, est-ce que tu connais des acteurs?
LEARNER C: Oui, je connais...
INSTRUCTOR: *(interrupting)* Lesquelles?
Oui, lesquelles?
LEARNER C: Oh, je connais... um... Shirley MacLaine, Jane Fonda...

[Translation]

INSTRUCTOR: *Okay, good.*
            Ask . . . Carol . . . if she knows any singers, and which ones she knows.
LEARNER A: *Uh . . . do you know any singers?*
LEARNER B: *I know . . . Mick Jagger.*
           (laughter)
LEARNER A: xxx [inaudible]
INSTRUCTOR: *She knows Mick Jagger.*
INSTRUCTOR: *Susan, do you know any actors?*
LEARNER C: *Yes, I know . . .*
INSTRUCTOR: (interrupting) *Which ones? Yes, which ones?*
LEARNER C: *Oh, I know . . . um . . . Shirley MacLaine, Jane Fonda . . .*

(Adapted from Leemann Guthrie, 1984, p. 47)

In another revealing study, Brooks (1990) found that learners reproduce in pairs those behaviors that the instructor uses at the whole-class level. He states that

> rather than use the exercise to participate in a communication simulation activity, as originally intended by the teacher, the students seem to have turned the activity into another chance to reinforce the rules of Spanish grammar, thereby getting ready for the subsequent quiz. . . . It appears as though the two students have learned through imitation and inference, rather than explicit instruction, an acceptable manner for doing this type of activity.
>
> (Brooks, 1990, p. 162)

The following two exchanges (adapted from Brooks's study) demonstrate his point. Note the pattern of interaction between instructor and learner in A that is subsequently played out between two learners in B.

A. Teacher-Fronted Activity

INSTRUCTOR: ¿Es antipática?
  LEARNERS: *(several together)* No.
INSTRUCTOR: No es antipática.
  LEARNER: Es muy simpático.
INSTRUCTOR: ¿Simpático? *(said loudly with rising intonation)*
  LEARNER: Simpática.
INSTRUCTOR: Sí, es muy simpática.

[Translation]

INSTRUCTOR: *Is she mean?*
  LEARNERS: (several together) *No.*
INSTRUCTOR: *She isn't mean.*
  LEARNER: *He is nice.*
INSTRUCTOR: *Nice?**
  LEARNER: *She is nice.*
INSTRUCTOR: *Yes, she is very nice.*

---

*Translator's note: The Spanish adjective is inflected for gender as well as for number. The instructor is vocally drawing attention to the inflection, which cannot be rendered in the translation.

A: Ah, ¿cómo son Carolina y Luz?
B: Carolina y Luz es
no
son rubiøs. (*final vowel inaudible*)
A: Son (*voice in holding tone*)
rubi…
a…
rubias
B: ¿«a» o «as»?
A: «as».
B: «as», sí. Rubias (*prosodic stress on "as"*)

[Translation]

A: *Ah, what are Carolina and Luz like?*
B: *Carolina and Luz is*
no
are blonde.
A: *are . . .*
blo . . .
n . . .
d
B: *«a» or «as»?*
A: *«as».*
B: *«as», yes. Blonde.*

Leemann Guthrie and Brooks provide just two examples of what is often the typical discourse pattern in language classrooms. They demonstrate that as far as communicative drills go, whether led by an instructor or carried out by pairs of learners, communication and negotiation of meaning may well not be taking place.

> *Pause to consider . . .*
>
> what message the instructor sends the learners about communicating in the target language. Reexamine the exchange between instructor and learners that focuses on *lequel,* noting that the instructor translated her directions to the class. What effect does translating one's utterances have on the classroom dynamic? On the type of interactions one can expect? On creating a classroom environment conducive to communication?

Teacher-Fronted versus Paired or Group Interaction

In addition to the kinds of discourse and observational research noted earlier, there is quantitative research on interactional patterns and communication in the language classroom. Like the research conducted by Leemann Guthrie and

Brooks, this research reveals that teacher-fronted activities provide few opportunities for the expression and negotiation of meaning among participants (perhaps because there are too many potential participants). Rulon and McCreary (1986) report on the findings of one investigation in which they compared small-group activities and teacher-fronted activities. Their conclusion was that small-group work produced twice the number of content confirmation checks (indications that a person has understood, such as "I got it. Then what?") and thirty-six times the number of content clarification requests ("Right?" "Do you follow?" "So, you mean . . . ?") as did the teacher-fronted tasks. Learners did much more of the talking when given the opportunity to work in groups. In the words of the researchers, "Very little negotiation of either content or meaning was actually taking place in these [teacher-fronted] classes" (p. 194). At the same time, these researchers found no statistical difference between group and teacher-fronted activities in terms of the amount of informational content covered. So there seems to be more communication occurring in paired work than in teacher-fronted activities, with just as much content covered.

Porter (1986) also found that learner-to-learner interactions in the classroom resulted in increased opportunities for self-expression for the learner. But she also found that uneven proficiency resulted in yet more interactions. In other words, advanced-intermediate pairings resulted in increased negotiation for both learners compared to intermediate-intermediate and advanced-advanced pairings. In terms of quality of interaction, Porter reports only one "negative" finding: that sociolinguistic competence is not something that can be developed in the absence of native-speaking interlocutors.

Pause to consider . . .

Porter's "negative" finding. Why would sociolinguistic competence not develop in most classroom situations? On what does the development of sociolinguistic competence depend? Is sociolinguistic competence linked to psycho-social or informational-cognitive uses of language? Is it linked to both?

Lee (2000) conducted an experiment comparing the participation and content remembered by different groups of learners enrolled in four language classes. Two classes participated in a teacher-fronted discussion, answering questions, and two others performed group work developed from the discussion questions. Lee's findings support Porter's and Rulon and McCreary's findings. Only 11 of 42 learners spoke during the question-and-answer discussion, whereas 46 of 46 learners spoke during the group work. Thirty-one learners did not verbalize their thoughts during the discussion. The learners who participated in the group work recalled almost twice as many ideas as did those who participated in the discussion. This finding was true immediately after the learners did the discussion or activity and one week later.

Examine the following two activities that Lee used in his research on communication. As you compare the two activities, you can easily imagine that very few learners participated in Activity A and that the instructor spoke more during the activity than any of the eleven learners did (transcripts are provided in the research report for those interested in consulting them). You can also easily imagine that when they were working in groups, all the learners participated in Activity B. The instructor managed the interaction and, in particular, gathered the information learners generated in each step for all in the class to evaluate. While completing the task, all learners were actively engaged in constructing the discourse about the topic.

Activity A.   Guiding Discussion Questions

Phase 1. Associations

What do you associate with the term *bilingual?*
What do you associate with the term *bicultural?*

Phase 2. Becoming bilingual/bicultural

How can you become bilingual?
How can you become bicultural?

Phase 3. Conclusions

Do you become bilingual and bicultural in the same way?
Are they two different processes?
Can you be bicultural without being bilingual?
Can you be bilingual without being bicultural?
Is it possible to appreciate another culture without knowing its language?

Activity B.   Bilingual and Bicultural

Phase 1. Associations

Step 1. In groups of four, prepare a list of everything you associate with the terms *bilingual* and *bicultural.*

BILINGUAL	BICULTURAL
1.	1.
2.	2.
3.	3.
4.	4.
5.	5.

Phase 2. Becoming bilingual/bicultural

Step 2. In groups, first respond to the question, "How can you become bilingual?" Propose various ideas.

   1.
   2.
   3.
   4.

Other ideas?

Step 3. Now, in groups, respond to the question, "How do you become bicultural?" Propose various ideas.

1.

2.

3.

4.

Other ideas?

Phase 3. Conclusions

What do you think? Do you become bilingual and bicultural in the same way? Are they two different processes? Can you be bicultural without being bilingual? Can you be bilingual without being bicultural? Is it possible to appreciate another culture without knowing its language?

(Adapted from Lee, 2000, pp. 46–47)

We can conclude that teacher-fronted activities may not be optimal for providing opportunities to develop communicative language ability. Paired and group work, on the other hand, do seem to provide these opportunities. In order to bring communication (expression, interpretation, and negotiation of meaning) into the classroom, instructors have to look beyond communicative drills and teacher-fronted questions.

Pause to consider . . .
_____

the difference between teacher-fronted and teacher-assisted activities. What does the instructor need to do to assist learners in carrying out the steps in Activity B?

CLASSROOM COMMUNICATION AS INFORMATION EXCHANGE

As we have seen, communication involves the expression, interpretation, and negotiation of meaning in a given context. The context most relevant to instructors and learners is, of course, the classroom. We focus now on creating classroom activities that allow for communication within the context of the language classroom. We call these activities "information-based" tasks or "information-exchange" tasks. These activities require learners to obtain information from each other that is then put to use in some way. The schematic display in Figure 3.2 shows what is involved in developing activities that foster communication in the classroom.

Identifying the Topic

We see in Figure 3.2 that information-exchange tasks do not occur in a vacuum. They are generally part of some larger informational unit or are relevant to current events surrounding the learners. Many language courses, for example, build syllabi around vocabulary groups or themes. Thus, courses (and text-

Identify the topic or subtopic to be addressed

↓ ↑

Design an appropriate immediate purpose

↓ ↑

Identify the information sources

FIGURE 3.2 Construction of information-exchange tasks

books) have a food chapter, a family chapter, a jobs and professions chapter, among others. Identifying a topic or subtopic for a task is best achieved when a concrete question can be asked. In other words, the topic can be explored by questions that learners will eventually answer with the information they obtain.

Taking the example of food, we can immediately generate a list of questions that explore various topics and subtopics:

1. What are a typical student's eating habits?
   a. What does a student eat for breakfast? Lunch? Dinner?
   b. What does a student eat for snacks?
   c. Where do students eat?
   d. When do students eat?
   e. How do student eating habits compare with those of nonstudents?
2. What is the nutritional content of the foods we eat?
   a. Is meat good for you?
   b. Do you need fat in your diet? How much?
   c. What is the difference between carbohydrates and proteins?
   d. Why does everyone talk about cholesterol levels?
3. What do people from other cultures eat?
   a. How are nutritional needs met in the various diets?
   b. How does our diet compare with theirs?
4. How do you prepare certain foods?
   a. What ingredients do you need?
   b. How much time is involved?
   c. Who is responsible for food preparation in your household?
5. Does what you eat affect your frame of mind?
   a. Can you be addicted to food?
   b. Is chocolate an aphrodisiac?

Needless to say, this list of questions is far from exhaustive; we could generate a great number of other questions. A glance at the list reveals that some questions are broader than others; some have a much more narrow focus. Certain questions rely on personal experience, whereas others involve the world outside our own. Some are concrete and others more abstract. Some can be explored using the learners' own experiences and knowledge, and others require consulting an outside information source. What needs to be kept in mind is lesson planning, that is, time and material management. When moving their classes toward communication through information exchange, instructors need to ask themselves such questions as "What topics can be treated in a 50-minute class period?" and "What topics can be treated in a 10–15 minute activity?"

Designing an Appropriate Purpose

Once a topic or subtopic is selected and a question is developed, an appropriate immediate purpose needs to be designed. The immediate purpose can take the form of a task that learners must complete. Such tasks include:

- Filling in a grid, chart, or table
- Writing a paragraph
- Making an oral report
- Answering questions
- Sharing information with others for comparative purposes
- Creating an outline
- Creating a list of questions
- Creating a survey
- Drawing something (a picture, a graph, a diagram)
- Creating a photo montage

In constructing an information-exchange task, it is important *not* to mistake "getting or exchanging information" as the purpose of the task. Getting and exchanging information are the *means* to some other *end* or *purpose*. Learners will not only get and exchange information—they will *do something with it*. What they *do* with the information is, in essence, the true purpose of the task. Instructors must be able to identify the purpose, not only for themselves but for the learners as well. We can see the importance of this by comparing the following two versions of the same activity. In the first version, even though learners exchange information, the activity lacks an end: The learner is not given a purpose for obtaining and exchanging the information. In the second version of the activity, the learner is asked to fill in a chart and make a comparison. The learner now has a reason for getting information and knows what to do with it.

Activity C.   Compare Your Birthday Experiences

Working with a classmate, compare how you have celebrated your birthdays by asking and answering the following questions:

> How did you celebrate your birthday two years ago? Five years ago? Ten years ago? Where did you spend the day and with whom did you spend it? Was it fun? Were a lot of people present? What kind of food was served?

Activity D.   Compare Your Birthday Experiences

Step 1. Fill in the following chart as you interview a classmate.

Birthday	Where?	With whom?	Food?	Fun?
2 years ago				
5 years ago				
10 years ago				

Step 2. Now write a paragraph in which you compare and contrast your own birthdays with the three birthdays your classmate just described.

The information-exchange task structures the interaction between the learners, accomplishing several things. First, if two learners were given the list of questions in Activity C to ask and answer, they might fall into perpetuating the teacher-fronted dynamic described by Brooks. Would the learners conceive of the activity as an opportunity for information exchange? Would they simply try to get through the list of questions? Would they imitate their instructor? Second, if we restructure the interaction as in Activity D, the learners become task-oriented; they must work together to fill in the chart. Filling in the chart gives each learner an information base to work from, either to write the paragraph, as suggested in Step 2, or to keep for testing purposes (as we will see later). Activity D is more "free form," with the learners more likely to move on to topics other than birthday celebrations and to use their native language to discuss these other topics.

---

*P*ause *to consider . . .*

the classroom dynamic that Activities C and D generate. How will pairs of learners know when they have completed the activity? What happens when they do?

Identifying Information Sources

Whatever the task selected, it must fit with the topic and guide the learners' oral interaction. Task selection is tied to the information source necessary to carry out the interaction; the nature of the topic will indicate what the information source should be. There is no need to limit information exchanges to personal information or information generated from personal experiences, such as the class's sleeping habits or their likes and dislikes. The learners' experiences are a rich source and certainly ought to be exploited, but learners also know things about the world beyond their own experience. They know, for example, who certain famous people are, what these people did, what many principles of science are, and how to add and subtract. What they know beyond their own personal experience, therefore, is also a rich source to be exploited for information-exchange activities. A reading or listening text is another source of information for classroom communication. Learners can consult either an oral or written text that provides information related to the task. (We explore the use of readings and texts in Chapter 11.) Thus, rather than ask and answer questions of each other, learners can get information from a text for the purpose of completing a task.

The purpose of the task will often clarify if not dictate the information source required. If the purpose is to fill in a chart *about a classmate's eating habits,* it will be clear that the information source is the learners' personal experience. If the purpose is to create a list of questions they would like to ask *a Brazilian about the disappearing rain forests,* then the information source could very well be outside the learners' personal experiences and might be provided by a reading or by a guest speaker to the class. In the following example, learners' world knowledge is the source of information needed to complete the activity.

Activity E.   What Else Was Going On Then?

Step 1. Complete the following with accurate information.

1. When John F. Kennedy was assassinated . . .
    a.
    b.
    c.
2. When Nixon resigned the presidency . . .
    a.
    b.
    c.
3. When Columbus landed in the Caribbean . . .
    a.
    b.
    c.

Step 2. Compare your answers to a classmate's. Is your information correct? What information did your classmate think of that you did not?

Step 3. Compare your items to those of the rest of the class, adding any new items to your list.

Step 4. Select one of the preceding episodes and prepare a brief oral presentation. Remember to use connectors (such as *also, but, at the same time*) to make your presentation flow.

Pause to consider . . .

the options for using texts as information sources. In order for authentic information exchange based on written texts to occur, the learners should not all have read the same texts. Why would Learner A ask Learner B questions about a text that A herself has just read? Pairs of learners can instead be given two different texts to read. Together, they then must fill out a chart, complete an outline, or write a paragraph based on the information they provide each other. Can you think of other options? What about having only one person read a text?

NEGOTIATING MEANING

Lee (2000) identifies six reasons, from theory to classroom practice, for the emphasis on negotiation as an important element in communicative language ability by second language acquisition researchers and language teaching experts. We saw negotiation happen on page 52 when the learner Roger attempted to comment on someone he had recently met. And as discussed earlier, negotiation takes place in various everyday contexts. Lee offers the following definition of negotiation that is meant to address a wide variety of contexts in which negotiation takes place:

> Negotiation consists of interactions during which speakers come to terms, reach an agreement, make arrangements, resolve a problem, or settle an issue by conferring or discussing; the purpose of language use is to accomplish some task rather than to practice any particular language forms.
>
> (Lee, 2000, p. 9)

The group tasks in Activity B certainly get learners to speak; they might not get speakers specifically to negotiate meaning. In the following two sections, we will highlight information-gap and group decision activities as two types of activities that require negotiation.

Information-Gap Activities

One type of activity that promotes negotiation is the *information-gap* task. The *gap* refers to information that one person possesses but others do not. Gaps, therefore, create the absolute need to communicate as well as the need to cooperate. Information-gap tasks were briefly described with reference to the use of texts as information sources in communication activities (see the Pause to consider . . . on p. 64). The example described two learners working cooperatively to fill out a chart, each learner contributing information from a text the other has not read. Activity F is a fully developed version of such a task. The person who has done the reading is the "expert" who will answer others' questions about his or her province.

Activity F. Compare Provinces

Step 1. Each person in the group reads a different short text produced by the national travel bureau. Each text describes the desirable features of a province in order to generate tourism to that region. As you read your own text, think about how you might describe or explain the content of the reading to the other members of your group.

Step 2. Working together, the group completes the following chart. Remember to try not to use English if you must use a new word from your text that the others might not know.

Province:	A	B	C
Terrain			
Festivals			
Sporting			
Climate			

Step 3. Weighing all the information, the group must plan a travel itinerary to visit each of the three provinces. First plan one for a two-week stay and then one for a one-week stay.

Information-gap activities may be based on sources of information other than texts. For example, the following activity is based on a visual.

Activity G.   The Garden

Step 1. Each person in the group except one will receive part of a picture of a garden. No one is to show his or her picture to anyone else.

Step 2. Each person in the group then describes his or her picture to the others using only the target language.

Step 3. As a group, describe what the original garden looked like in such a way that the person who did not receive a picture can draw the garden.

Pause to consider . . .

the teaching and learning of negotiation devices such as clarification checks, indications of lack of comprehension, and so on. For example, negotiation devices include expressions such as:

"Sorry. What did you say?"
"Pardon me? I didn't catch that."
"Could you say that again, please?"
"Say what?"

What examples of such devices can you think of for the language you teach? Can you think of how these might be taught in class? What kinds of activities could you develop for them?

Group Decision Activities

Activities can also encourage learners to collaborate in solving a problem, reaching a consensus, or making some other kind of decision. Step 3 of Activity F is an example of an activity that requires learners to reach a consensus. Perhaps the best-known set of group decision activities is the *Non-Stop Discussion Book* (Rooks, 1981), which also is available in several languages other than English. The following activity has been developed from one originated by Rooks, Scholberg, and Scholberg (1982). Note as you examine it that learners must negotiate the contents of the time capsule, contents that are limited to ten items. The activity is structured so that each person in the group, and then the class as a whole, will have a particular point of view to express and defend. However, consensus marks the conclusion of the two phases of the activity.

Activity H.   The Time Capsule

Step 1. Your university wants to place a time capsule in the new library being constructed. The capsule will be opened in the year 2200, and in it will be ten items that represent the last part of the twentieth century. What will those ten items be?

Step 2. The capsule is only two cubic feet in size, so anything you choose must be small. Also, the items selected should reflect not only the achievements of our society but also our values.

Step 3. Work in groups of five or six to come to a consensus about the contents of the time capsule. You can use the following list to guide your discussion, but you must choose at least three of the ten from items not on this list.

a book	a computer
a movie	a credit card
a gun	a VCR
running shoes	a miniature TV
a cell phone	a pair of jeans
a brochure for Disney World	a baseball

Step 4. Present and explain your list to the rest of the class. Listen and take notes as the other groups present and explain their lists. Finally, as a class, come to a consensus on what to include in the capsule.

Step 5. Optional. Can you reduce the contents to only five items?

Pause to consider . . .

feedback that instructors provide on learners' output. How would you treat errors when learners are engaged in communicative language tasks? What kind of feedback do children receive? Here are some possibilities:

1. Direct correction (pointing out the error)
2. Indirect correction (rephrasing the learner's utterance to look like a confirmation check and, thus, to model correct grammar)
3. Delayed feedback (noting learners' common errors and then pointing them out at the end of class or on a special "review" day)
4. No special feedback

As you ponder these possibilities, keep in mind the following: What kind of errors would you give feedback on (if at all)? Do all errors need some kind of treatment?

RELIEVING ATLAS: WHEN TASKS DICTATE ROLES

Communicative language teaching has been evolving since its inception. Roles other than those of linguistic disciplinarian, authority figure, expert, and parent have become available to instructors based on what we have learned about language acquisition and on changes in instructional materials. When instructors shift their roles, so do their students. As we saw earlier, under ALM and early CLT the role of the instructor dictated the tasks given to students. Since the instructor's role was that of central authority, the fundamental task for all students was to respond to the instructor. However, the contemporary communicative era is now incorporating tasks that encourage communicative language development. In a reversal of direction, the tasks now determine the roles that instructors and learners may take. The major roles that instructors are beginning to assume are those of *resource person* and *architect.* In order for an instructor to be a resource person, there must be a fundamental change in the conversational dynamic of the classroom, something we see in Activity J (p. 69). As architects, instructors provide activities and tasks that allow for a distribution of teaching functions between instructors and students. As a consequence, when the instructor gives up the role of Atlas, the students are no longer mere receptive vessels; they must become more active, more responsible for their own learning.

Instructor as Resource Person

What is a resource person? The best way to describe this role is with an example. In the nonclassroom world, when you ask someone for directions, you assume responsibility for understanding those directions. The person giving directions makes no assumptions concerning what you did or did not understand. Rather, the person assumes you will ask if you have a question. The person giving directions actually responds to your specific needs; he or she will give you additional information, clarifying whatever you did not understand. This kind of give-and-take characterizes nonclassroom interaction.

But what happens in the classroom? Let's examine another example. The following listening activity is a fairly common one for practicing vocabulary. In essence, the instructor describes a visual and the students respond with the appropriate vocabulary word. In reading the activities, be sure to think about the roles that the instructor and the students play.

Activity I.   What Food Is It?

Look over the food chart, getting a sense of serving size, weight, and calories for the various foods listed. Your instructor will read a description twice. Listen carefully and then identify the food being described.

MODEL: *(you hear)* A cup of this dairy product contains 125 calories.
　　　　　(you say) Yogurt.

Although this activity might seem quite simple, it reflects the assumption that the instructor is responsible for teaching and learning. In Activity I, assumptions are made about what students will and will not comprehend. It is assumed that they will not comprehend the first time. The instructor should, therefore, automatically repeat all information. Is the assumption correct? Perhaps only a handful of students will be able to identify the items the first time; perhaps everyone will. Since either case is possible, the issue becomes one of responsibility. Whose responsibility is it to indicate a lack of comprehension? In the nonclassroom setting, those who receive information generally carry the burden of indicating a lack of comprehension and must ask for repetition, clarification, and so on. If instructors automatically repeat themselves, they have assumed a responsibility that typically would not be theirs in the nonclassroom setting. Automatic repetition is one sign of the Atlas Complex.

We know that the Atlas Complex is a difficult mindset to alter because both instructors and students are generally willing to allow this type of dynamic in the classroom. But in order to share responsibility with the instructor or to shift it entirely, students must be given certain tools, such as the questions in Activity J. This activity is a version of Activity I in which the instructor acts as a resource person, not an authoritative Atlas figure. The instructor has the information and is willing to supply it—but only when asked. The instructor does not assume that everyone requires every item to be repeated. Thus, those who need repetition are responsible not only for asking for it but also for identifying that part of the item they did not comprehend. Students take on the burden of responsibility the instructor assumed in Activity I.

Activity J.   What Food Is It?

Look over the food chart, getting a sense of food groups, serving size, weight, and calories for the various foods listed. Your instructor will read a description of a food item. Listen carefully and try to identify the food.

MODEL: *(you hear)* A cup of this dairy product contains 125 calories.
  (you say) Yogurt.

If you cannot identify the item, then you should ask any or all of the following questions, depending on what you did not understand.

  What quantity did you say?
  How many calories, please?
  What was the food group?

When instructors' roles change, so do those of students. The students negotiated meaning for themselves in Activity J: They initiated part of the interaction. When the instructor's role is that of a resource person, the student's role is that of information gatherer and negotiator of meaning. Her task is no longer simply to listen and respond but to signal if and where comprehension has not taken place.

---

*P*ause to consider . . .

the nature of responsibility. How attentive will students be if they know that instructors will repeat each item verbatim? Which of the two sets of directions favors students being passive, receptive vessels? Which favors them being actively engaged in processing the language?

Instructor as Architect

In a nonclassroom setting, conversations are not directed by an individual. That is, one person does not choose who the next speaker will be. When three or four people talk, they talk among themselves. There is give-and-take as contributions to the topic are made from all sides. Information is gathered, checked, and built up among the participants.

In order to examine these issues within the context of the language class, let's compare and contrast the following two versions of the same activity. The first version, Activity K, resembles the traditional open-ended discussion question during which the instructor's tasks are to ask questions, select participants, and keep the interaction moving. The students' task is no more than to answer the question asked. The second version, Activity L, contains the same content as K, but the structure of the interaction has been radically altered. Activity L sets up a series of intermediate steps, each of which contains concrete tasks for students to perform: make lists, compare them, and discuss the information they generate. The end result of both versions is that students address the question, but the *process* is not the same for each. As you read, try to picture the interactions between instructors and students as well as those among students that result from each version of the activity.

Activity K.   Changing Roles

Contrast the traditional roles men and women played in the family structure with their contemporary ones. In what ways have their roles in the family changed?

Activity L.   Changing Roles

Step 1. With a classmate, make a list of the actions, attitudes, or qualities that characterize the traditional role played by men in the family structure.

Step 2. Compare your list with those prepared by the rest of the class. Do you all have the same ideas? Do you wish to modify your list?

Step 3. Make a list of actions, attitudes, or qualities that characterize the traditional role played by women in the family structure.

Step 4. Compare your list with those prepared by the rest of the class. Do you all have the same ideas? Do you wish to modify your list?

Step 5. Now, contrast the traditional roles men and women played in the family structure with their contemporary ones. In what ways have their roles in the family changed?

If you have observed many language classes, particularly more traditional ones, you may have seen an example of the first version of the activity, namely, the open-ended discussion question. We can picture an instructor standing in front of the class. After the question is posed, silence would most likely ensue as students would not readily and eagerly volunteer. The instructor would then break the silence either by calling on a student or by restating the question. If a discussion of changing family structure ever got off the ground, the instructor would gather bits and pieces of the answer from those students willing to speak. One student might say something about male roles, the next about female roles. A cohesive response to the question would probably not result from this kind of teacher-fronted interaction (as was the case with the discussion Leemann Guthrie observed about the French personality). If asked, many language instructors will say that the purpose of Activity K is simply to get students to talk in the second language, to display what they already know about the topic, or even to practice vocabulary and grammar. In short, the open-ended discussion question format is not really designed for students to learn about the topic or from each other; it is simply a speaking exercise.

Pause to consider . . .

speaking for speaking's sake. Is it sufficient to have students speak just for the sake of having them produce language orally? Is such discussion meaningful in a communicative way? Should there be a greater purpose to language use in the classroom?

The second version, Activity L, attempts to circumvent some of the short-comings of the first by acknowledging that a discussion is a *multilayered communicative event,* that is, an interaction requiring various steps and tasks. Dividing the activity literally into steps is one way to bring out the layers and to assist the learners in tackling the topic. The instructor is the central figure only in Step 5 of the activity, but because all class members will have dealt with the prerequisite information, many more will likely participate in the discussion than would have in Activity K.

Pause to consider . . .

the specific classroom procedures involved in Activity L, which divide the discussion into steps. If you were carrying out this activity in class as an instructor, what would you be doing during each step? In other words, project yourself into the classroom. How would you enact Steps 2 and 4? Step 5?

When the instructor takes on the role of *architect,* the one who designs and plans but is not responsible for the final product, then students become *builders* or *coworkers,* who put it together. Just as discussions in nonclassroom settings allow for all participants to contribute to the construction of a message, so can discussions in a classroom setting. In order to achieve this goal, the instructor must make a decision about how to structure the interaction. In so doing, the instructor must relinquish the authority figure role during class time. When roles depend on tasks, the instructor no longer assumes the sole, Atlas-like responsibility for all that happens in the classroom. Students begin to share some of the teaching functions that instructors ordinarily assume for themselves and that students typically concede to them.

SUMMARY

In this chapter, we discussed the important role of meaningful communication in learning a second language. Communication involves the expression, interpretation, and, most important, negotiation of meaning within a particular context. People communicate with each other for a variety of purposes, but underlying all communication is some exchange of meaning or information. In the classroom, information-exchange tasks work best at giving learners a purpose for using their developing language abilities as well as further developing these abilities. As non-teacher-fronted (but, certainly, teacher-assisted) tasks, there must be some clear communicative or informational end in information-exchange tasks. Although free conversation between instructor and learners can often serve as an interesting and useful oral communication activity, we have seen that pair and group tasks that involve the sharing of information and the negotiation of meaning or information provide many more opportunities for learners to develop communicative skills. These tasks need to be carefully constructed, with attention paid to the level of the learners and the linguistic demands that can be placed on them. As they engage in these kinds of tasks, learners come to understand that activity in language classrooms can be much more than the practicing of subcomponents of communicative ability. Classrooms can become places where learners talk about real things and learn about each other. In moving away from teacher-fronted to teacher-assisted interactions, instructors will necessarily behave in less Atlas-like ways. The tasks themselves will dictate the roles instructors and learners take on in the classroom, in general, and during communicative interactions, in particular.

KEY TERMS, CONCEPTS, AND ISSUES

learning to communicate
communication
   expression, interpretation, and
     negotiation of meaning
     breakdowns
purposes of communication
   psycho-social
   informational-cognitive
contexts of communication
communicative language ability
communicative competence
   grammatical competence
   discourse competence
   sociolinguistic competence
   strategic competence
classroom discourse
   teacher-fronted
   paired or group interactions

information-exchange tasks
   steps for construction
     identify topic or subtopic
     design immediate purpose
     identify information sources
importance of negotiation
information-gap tasks
group decision activities
   tasks dictate roles
   distributing teaching functions
   responsibility for learning
   instructor = architect, resource
    person
   students = builders, negotiators,
    information gatherers
   participation and contribution
    to the classroom

THINKING MORE ABOUT IT: DISCUSSION QUESTIONS

1. Different cultures may expect different things from speakers. For example, in the United States, we tend to accept accented English and nonnative varieties of English. The popular belief about the French, however, is that they expect more precision in their language from nonnatives. What has been your experience with the languages that you have learned? Do these expectations reflect a given culture's perceptions of what it means to be "communicatively competent" in its language?
2. What are the advantages of group work from both a learner's and an instructor's perspective? What are the disadvantages? Be sure you consider the idea of an instructor keeping or losing "control" of the classroom.

GETTING A CLOSER LOOK: RESEARCH ACTIVITIES

Record two or three learners as they carry out a decision-making activity. Identify the number of times you find the learners negotiating meaning. Prepare a report on how this activity contributes to learners' communicative language ability.

MAKING COMMUNICATIVE LANGUAGE TEACHING HAPPEN: PORTFOLIO ACTIVITIES

Create an information-gap task or a decision-making activity using two or three short texts as the information base. Be sure that the interaction among the learners is purposeful.

CHAPTER 4

Building Toward a Proficiency Goal

In this chapter we explore:

- The problem inherent in equating a communicative goal with a grammar goal such that "describing daily routines" means "mastering reflexive verbs"
- The use of information-exchange tasks as lesson-end goals, thereby providing a concrete and identifiable lesson objective
- The identification of subgoals in information-exchange tasks to make lesson goals more concrete and to pinpoint the linguistic tools (specific grammar and vocabulary) learners need to complete the task
- The use of subgoals as classhour goals to represent steps on the way to the lesson-final task
- The use of certain kinds of work outside of class

ON LESSON GOALS

Imagine that you have decided to build a gazebo in your backyard. You have lumber, screws, braces, tools, and some kind of plan for constructing the gazebo. You may work very hard and, depending on your skill and knowledge of building, spend one week, two weeks, various weekends, or some other amount of time on the construction of your gazebo. How do you know when you have finished? The answer is simple. You know you have finished when you have completed the gazebo. You can look at it, touch it, point to it, and say, "I'm done." In essence, the gazebo itself was your goal, and when the gazebo is up and standing, you know you have reached your goal.

Now let's compare the building of a gazebo with a typical lesson in communicative or proficiency-oriented textbooks. Following are goal statements from various textbooks currently in use.

- In this lesson you will learn to talk about daily routines.
- Language function: describing one's daily routine.

- In this chapter you will learn to make plans with someone, talk about your daily schedule, and tell time.
- After studying this chapter, you will know how to discuss daily routines.

Although they are the staple of lesson objective lists in textbooks, these statements are vague at best. As an instructor or as a student, how do you know when you have reached the chapter objective? What does it mean to "describe" or "discuss" a routine, and how does one perform either action in a basic language class? What can you point to and say, "This is it. Now I know I'm finished"? In short, what is your "gazebo" for the lesson? There is little in the materials that tells the learner or the instructor when a goal has been reached. In most cases, a lesson is completed when learners and instructors get to the last page of the chapter in the textbook.

Perhaps the reason for the vagueness of these stated proficiency goals becomes evident if we ponder the tools provided in lessons on "daily routines." What vocabulary, grammar, and interactional patterns are part of the lesson on daily routines? Before looking at what textbooks have to offer, consider the typical daily routine of a university student. We requested that a group of students describe their daily routines, asking them to mention at least three things about their mornings, three things about their afternoons, and three things about their evenings. Following is a composite of what a typical student's day might look like, based on this group of students.

> I get up in the morning around 9:00. I sometimes eat breakfast but usually I just go to my first class. In the afternoon, I have classes and often go to the library to study. I eat a quick snack when I can. In the evening I work until 11:00 at night. I study a little when I get home, but sometimes I just watch "Nick at Night," then go to bed.

Compare this real-life routine with what is found in typical textbooks. As one example, let's look at daily routines in a university-level Spanish text published as recently as 2002. On the chapter/lesson opening page is the list of "communicative goals" under which is found "discussing daily routines." A search through the chapter uncovers a section with the heading "Discussing Daily Routines." The first thing we encounter is a grammar explanation of reflexive verbs and reflexive pronouns. Also included is a list of "common" reflexive verbs (a total of twenty that includes such items as "to shave, to take a bath, to brush (one's teeth), to go away, to put on makeup, to comb one's hair, to put on clothes, to take off clothes, to dry off, to sit down, to feel, and to get dressed").

The activities that follow the list are the following:

a. You are describing the routines of several people. Complete the following descriptions, changing the reflexive pronoun to agree with the subjects.
   1. I/to shower with hot water.
   2. you/to get up late.
   3. the boys/to put on hats.
   and so on
b. Work with a partner and ask each other questions following the model.

   MODEL: Are you going to shave tomorrow?
   Yes, I'm going to shave tomorrow.

c. What does Phillip do on a typical day? Look at the pictures and decide in which order Phillip would do the following activities. Number the activities in a logical order, then write a sentence to describe each action. Use reflexive verbs.

[The drawings are of Phillip brushing his teeth, combing his hair, drying himself after a shower, putting on his shirt, getting out of bed, going to bed, taking a shower, waking up.]

If we examine this example—which, we can guarantee, is not unique—we see that the focus of daily routines is limited to the use of reflexive verbs. Although reflexive verbs are an important grammatical concept, how important are they for talking about daily routines? Recall the typical student routine described at the outset of this section, and note that students did not mention such actions as combing their hair, brushing their teeth, taking a shower, shaving, putting on clothes, taking off their clothes, falling asleep, or the kind of water they shower with. Undoubtedly there is some variation here; some people might say, "I got up and took a shower, then I ate breakfast." However, most people spare us the details of their personal hygiene and the minute-by-minute account of their morning preparatory habits. In other words, in normal conversational situations, only a few reflexive verbs seem necessary to talk about daily routines *from the learner's point of view.*

The point, then, is that *topicalized* or *contextualized* grammar is not equivalent to a communicative or proficiency orientation. True communicative- and proficiency-oriented instruction cannot be grammar driven. Moreover, in many cases a communicative goal cannot be equated with (or reduced to) a particular grammatical item. In those textbooks in which communicative goals are apparently equated with grammar, the linguistic tools provided might not be what is needed to realize the stated communicative goals. What is evident from the preceding examples on daily routines is that the stated communicative goal is actually window dressing for a predetermined grammatical point; communication is at the service of grammar rather than the other way around.

Pause to consider . . .

why daily routines look the way they do in many current textbooks. Why do you think textbook authors and their publishers have equated "daily routines" with so-called reflexive verbs? As you think about this, you may wish to review some of the ideas and observations from Chapter 1.

RETHINKING LESSON GOALS: INFORMATION-EXCHANGE TASKS AS LESSON OBJECTIVES

The problem with many proficiency goals in commercial materials is not so much the goal statement but what happens in the lesson itself. As we saw in the previous section, a good communicative goal, such as describing one's daily routine, turns out not really to be the goal at all. What is needed in language lessons is a "gazebo," something that signals to learners and instructors that a goal has been reached.

We start by exploring the idea of a proficiency goal as some kind of information-exchange task, a task requiring students to exchange information and use it in some way. We introduced these types of tasks in Chapter 3, and we are now ready to situate them in a more focused context: achieving a lesson-wide proficiency goal. For example, to teach toward a goal such as "talking about everyday events and actions," we suggest that *instructors adopt an information-exchange task as a lesson objective.* The stated proficiency goal of a lesson would then correspond to a particular task. Having a task that represents the lesson's communicative objective, instructors and learners can point to it and say, "When we can do this task, we have reached the goal for this lesson."

In addition, instructors and learners can more easily see how the vocabulary, grammar, and other language features of a lesson fit together to realize a concrete objective. How is this so? An interactive information-exchange task implies a lesson blueprint that suggests what learners need to know and what they need to be able to do in order to complete the task. More specifically, once a task is identified we can ask questions such as the following:

- What vocabulary do learners need to have under control to complete this task?
- What grammar or pieces of grammar do the learners need to be able to comprehend or produce to complete this task?
- What functions of language will they need to perform (e.g., asking questions, making declarative statements, listing items, narrating with connective devices)?
- What content (information on a given topic) needs to be included?

These questions suggest that lessons have divisible parts or sections that can be thought of as smaller goals—lesson subgoals—along the way. In short, a lesson goal that is represented by an interactive information-exchange task allows an instructor to map out the lesson, specifying subgoals along the way. This is illustrated in Figure 4.1.

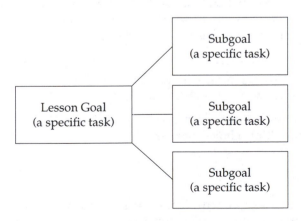

FIGURE 4.1 Lesson goals imply lesson subgoals

We can illustrate this concept with a concrete idea. Returning to our proficiency goal of talking about daily routines or everyday events, let's imagine an interactive information-exchange task such as the following. It can be used in just about any language.

Activity Z

In this lesson-final activity, you will prepare a series of quiz items for your instructor to use. In order to do so, you will need to interview someone about his or her daily routine as well as offer examples about your own daily routine in order to make contrastive and comparative statements.

Step 1. Using the chart below, fill in at least three things that you tend to do each morning, three things that you tend to do every afternoon, and three things that you tend to do every night. Include when you get up and when you go to bed. Be sure to use proper verb forms to talk about yourself.

	I . . .	My classmate . . .
Morning		
Afternoon		
Evening		

Step 2. Now interview someone in the class with whom you have not worked much during this lesson. Ask your partner specific questions to find out if he or she does the same things. For example, if you wrote for yourself, *I study for 2 hours,* in the afternoon box, ask your partner, "When do you study?" and "How long do you tend to study?" The idea here is to get information so that you can write a series of contrastive and comparative statements. (Be sure to frame your questions correctly and jot down your partner's information.)

Step 3. Using the information that you have obtained in Steps 1 and 2, write three true/false questions and three multiple choice questions comparing and contrasting you and your partner. Here are some samples:

EXAMPLE: True   False   1. I get up early, but David gets up late.

EXAMPLE: David works in the evening. In the evening I . . .
            a. work too. **b.** watch TV. **c.** study.

Step 4. Turn in to your instructor a neat copy of your chart and your list of true/false and multiple choice questions.

Vocabulary

As we examine this task we can ask ourselves, What vocabulary does the learner need to know in order to complete this task? Although we can't foresee every single lexical item a learner might need, common sense and experience in communication suggest to us that learners need vocabulary such as *get up, go to bed, eat, take a nap, watch TV, go to class, study, work, go the gym, exercise,* and so on. In addition, they need time expressions such as *in the morning, in the afternoon, in the evening, for* _____ *hours.* They may also need to know how to express a particular time *(at 10:00, at 12:30).* They will probably need to express days of the week *(Monday, Tuesday),* since schedules and routines may vary depending on the day. They also need connectors such as *but, and,* and *however* in order to make the comparative and contrastive statements in Step 3 of the task.

Thus, we see that several lesson subgoals might include work with these lexical items. One subgoal could be a short task that works with just the actions and events (introduced and practiced first using third-person verb forms).

Activity A

Make a list of eight statements about a typical student's day. Scramble the list and read it to your classmates. They should write down your statements and see if they can put the daily actions in the order in which the typical student would most likely do them. Did everyone match your order?

An alternative might be something like the following.

Activity A (alternative)

Step 1. Make a list of three daily activities a student does that you don't think your instructor does. Also make a list of three daily activities a student does that you think your instructor does as well.

Step 2. A volunteer should read his or her statements to the class, and someone should write them on the board in two columns, one for students, the other for the instructor. After the volunteer finishes, classmates should continue reading *new* statements aloud in order to make the two lists on the board as complete as possible. In the end, your instructor will tell you if you are correct about your statements.

Either of the two activities could serve as a lesson subgoal task. Thus, as learners and instructor work through vocabulary activities with daily actions, they are actually working toward one of the two tasks mentioned. When they get to the task and complete it, they have completed a lesson subgoal for talking about daily routines. That is, *they can make statements about another person's daily routine, an ability necessary to perform Step 3 of the lesson-final task, Activity Z.*

Pause to consider . . .

why actions and events for daily routines might be introduced and practiced via third-person verb forms. There are two advantages in doing this. The first is that the vocabulary practice also serves as a grammar practice. Although learners are learning vocabulary related to daily routines, they are getting exposure to and practice with third-person

(continued)

(continued)

singular verb forms at the same time. In this way, the subgoal task, Activity A, serves double duty; it represents both a vocabulary subgoal and a grammar subgoal. (We examine grammar in the next section.) The second advantage to introducing verb-related vocabulary via third-person forms is a practical one. Recall from Chapter 2 that we advocate the use of visuals to help make input comprehensible. When using such visuals with people in them we are naturally speaking in the third person. For example, "See this lady? She is a doctor. We are going to talk about her daily routine. She gets up early. She drinks coffee and reads the newspaper," and so on. What would happen if you didn't start with the third person? In what ways would introducing the vocabulary be more difficult?

Subgoal tasks for days of the week, time expressions, and specific times of the day could be developed as well, as in the following examples.

Activity B

Step 1. Write a series of statements about how many classes you have on each day of the week. Leave a blank after each one.

EXAMPLE: I have three classes on Monday. _____

Step 2. Now go about the room telling different people about your classes and asking them if their day is the same. If it is, get that person's signature in the blank. If not, move on to someone else. You must try to obtain five different signatures for the five different days of the week. Be prepared to answer questions that your instructor will ask when you are finished obtaining signatures.

EXAMPLE: *(you say)* I have three classes on Monday. Do you?
                (other person) Uh-huh. *(or)* Nope, I don't.
                        (you) Sign here, please! *(or)* Oh, well. Thanks.

Activity C

Step 1. Using the time expressions you have been learning in this lesson, indicate when you do the following activities on a particular day of the week. The last items indicate that you should come up with two activities not on the list.

EXAMPLE: On Saturday, I watch TV in the afternoon.

    watch TV
    study
    have your first class
    get up
    go to bed
    work (if you have a job)
    _____?_____
    _____?_____

Step 2. Break into groups of three and present your statements to the two other people. They should indicate whether they do the same or not. When you have finished, they should add any activities that they do that you did not mention. Are your schedules fairly similar?

EXAMPLE: *(you say)* I watch TV on Saturday, but usually in the morning.
        (other person) Me, too.
                or
        (other person) Not me. I only watch TV at night.

Activity D

Step 1. Select the day of the week that is your busiest and make a schedule of that day. Write in things such as "Chemistry class," "exercise," "I get up," and so forth.

Day of the week: _____

6:00 _____

7:00 _____

8:00 _____

9:00 _____

10:00 _____

11:00 _____

12:00 (noon) _____

1:00 _____

2:00 _____

3:00 _____

4:00 _____

5:00 _____

and so on

Step 2. Now interview a partner, asking questions to find out what his or her day is like. Jot down the information next to your schedule so that you can compare later.

EXAMPLE: What time do you get up?
              When is your first class? What is it?
              Do you eat breakfast or lunch? When?

Step 3. Comparing the two schedules, decide which of the following statements are true for you and your partner.

1. We are both equally busy on that day.
2. I have more classes than _____.
3. _____ gets up later than I do.

4. I study at night and so does _____.

5. I have more free time than _____ does.

6. _____ does not have any back-to-back classes.

In each of the activities, we see that the tasks require learners to use language in ways similar to those they will need for the lesson-final task. In Activity B, they are using days of the week to make statements about themselves and to get information from someone else. In Activity C, they must choose time expressions to make statements about themselves. In Activity D, they must use specific times of day to obtain information. These tasks, then, suggest that learners have completed a particular subgoal of the lesson: the ability to use certain vocabulary items to exchange information related to daily routines.

Grammar

We turn now to grammar. What grammatical structures and forms do learners need in order to complete the lesson-final information-exchange task in Activity Z? Here we must be careful, for if we say, "Present-tense verb forms," this is only partly true. A close examination of the lesson-final task reveals that learners actually *need* only first-person singular forms *(I get up)*, second-person singular forms *(You get up)*, and third-person singular forms *(He/She gets up)*. They need only these three forms of the verb for the task since the task requires only that they make statements about themselves (first-person singular), ask someone else about his or her schedule (second-person singular), and make contrastive statements about themselves and their partners (first-person singular and third-person singular). You might think that learners need first-person plural to make statements in Step 3 of Activity Z ("David and I both get up late"). But note that the task doesn't really require this. If you examine the examples in Activity Z again, you will note that in Step 3 learners need to be able to say only the equivalents of "and so do I," "but not me," "and David does, too," and so forth. In short, learners do not need the full paradigm of verb forms in a language to complete this task.

Do learners need reflexive verbs, as in the textbook examples we saw earlier? Again, the answer is incorrect if we say Yes. In actuality, learners *need* to use only several common reflexive verbs; full explanation of, and work with, reflexive verbs is not required. Learners can learn the two or three verbs as "special lexical items" that need special pronouns to accompany them. In other words, learners can learn these verbs as lexical items, and as they learn the different forms for first-person singular, second-person singular, and third-person singular, they can simply learn the corresponding pronoun for each form. Following are four activities, the two versions of Activity A that we saw earlier and two new activities, E and F. (Remember that Activity A does double duty as a vocabulary and a grammar subtask, so we are merely recalling here that learners have already worked with third-person singular verb forms.) Activities E and F represent work with first-person and second-person, respectively.

Activity A (original version)

Make a list of eight statements about a typical student's day. Scramble the list and read it to your classmates. They should write down your statements and see if they can put the daily actions in the order in which the typical student would most likely do them. Did everyone match your order?

Activity A (alternative)

Step 1. Make a list of three daily activities a student does that you don't think your instructor does. Also make a list of three daily activities a student does that you think your instructor does as well.

Step 2. A volunteer should read his or her statements to the class, and someone should write them on the board in two columns, one for students, the other for the instructor. After the volunteer finishes, classmates should continue reading *new* statements aloud in order to make the two lists on the board as complete as possible. In the end, your instructor will tell you if you are correct about your statements.

Activity E

Here are three words to describe how regularly you might do something:

> always
> sometimes
> never

Tell the class how regularly you do the following, and see if others say the same about themselves. Is there a pattern in the class?

get up *very* early	read the newspaper
study all night long	study at a friend's house
sleep during a class	study and watch TV at the same time
skip a class	read a novel for fun
take a nap	eat dinner out
walk to campus	watch soap operas

Activity F

Step 1. Read the following paragraph. (*Note:* Instructor would have only half the class read the paragraph. The other half would be given a comparable but different paragraph to work with.)

> Mary is a typical student at the University of _____. She gets up early and takes the bus to campus. She has three classes in the morning: Chemistry I, English Literature II, and Japanese I. She eats lunch with a friend and then goes to the library, where she studies for three hours. Then she goes to work at a photocopy shop. She normally works only four hours each day. When she gets home, she eats a light meal and reads a little. She goes to bed early so that she can sleep at least eight hours.

If you were to interview someone in class, what kinds of questions would you ask to find out if that person does the same things as Mary does in a typical day? Remember that the other person will not have the paragraph to refer to, so you will have to ask some very specific questions to get all the information you need.

Step 2. Now interview one of your classmates to find out if that person's day is like Mary's. Jot down all information, since you may need it later if your instructor asks you to report to the class what you found out. (*Note:* Here the instructor pairs learners based on who prepared one paragraph in Step 1 and who prepared the other. Partners take turns interviewing each other in Step 2.)

These grammar tasks, like their vocabulary counterparts that we saw earlier, represent subgoals within the lesson. These tasks are like way stations; completion of each signals that a particular objective has been fulfilled as learners work their way toward the lesson-final goal (which is represented by an information-exchange task). Thus, in Activity A, learners demonstrate that they can make simple statements using third-person singular verb forms, an ability necessary for Step 3 of the final task. In Activity E, they show that they can make simple statements to talk about what their daily routines are like, which they will need to do in Steps 1 and 3 of the lesson-final task. In Activity F, learners ask questions using second-person singular verb forms, which are required in Step 2 of the lesson-final task.

*P***ause to consider . . .**

the ordering of the subgoals and tasks presented so far. The lettering A–F suggests that the subgoals fall into this order, but in reality they may not. One subgoal task can incorporate vocabulary or grammar from a previous subgoal, thus requiring a particular sequencing. Study Activities A–F again carefully and see what sequence they actually represent as currently formulated.

We emphasize here that these tasks are to be preceded by vocabulary presentations and practice (see Chapter 2) and/or grammar activities (see Chapters 7 and 8). These tasks do not appear out of thin air; like lesson-final information-exchange tasks, these subgoal tasks represent something toward which learners have been working. We explore this in greater detail a bit later.

Functions

In terms of functions, it is clear from the lesson-final task that learners need to be able to make simple statements and ask each other questions. They do not need to string together sentences to create a narrative or produce an elaborate description. The question that arises here is, What do learners need to know— or know how to do—to ask the questions that they need to ask? Do they need all the question words of the target language? It seems that for the lesson-final task of Activity Z, learners actually need only *when, for how long, at what time,* and possibly one or two other time-related question phrases. In addition, they need to know the structure of questions (subject-verb inversion if the second language requires this in question formation, do-support in English, interrogative particle attachment in languages such as Japanese). Although these are typically learned early in language courses, the subgoal tasks frequently require

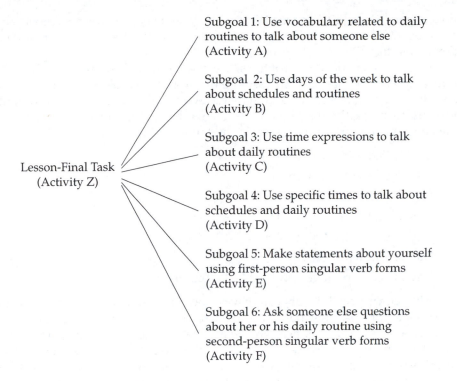

FIGURE 4.2 Suggested subgoal tasks for the lesson-final task, Activity Z

question formation by having learners interview each other and ask questions. In this way, a language function that requires certain vocabulary and syntax is systematically recycled before learners arrive at the final task.

We can now develop Figure 4.1 to make it more concrete. In Figure 4.2, we show how a lesson-final information-based task suggests certain subgoals, and we map this out using the activities in this chapter. For the sake of the present discussion, we assume that the numbers 1–30, question words and question formation, and such words as *but, and,* and *too (also)* were learned in a previous lesson. (Note: As is suggested in the last "Pause to consider" box, the ordering of Subgoals 1–6 and Activities A–F is not necessarily the order in which you would actually map out the lesson.)

ACTIVITIES AND CLASSHOUR GOALS

The discussion of lesson-final goals and lesson subgoals leads us to the question of mapping out both lessons and classhours. It should now be evident that the lesson goal is something to be attained over some period of time (a week, two weeks, ten days). It implies an accumulated set of abilities with grammar, vocabulary, language functions, interactional patterns, and so forth. It is also clear that a lesson subgoal is a stepping stone on the way to the lesson goal. Upon completion of a subgoal task, instructors and learners know that they have completed an important part of a set of materials that is moving toward a concrete end. But how, exactly, does this happen? What is the relationship between subgoals and classhours? What is the relationship between the entire lesson and actual days devoted to the lesson?

In our lesson on daily routines, we have established Activity Z as the information-exchange task representing our lesson-final objective. In turn, we specified six subgoals realized as Activities A through F. It might seem straightforward to suggest that each of these subgoal tasks could be a classhour goal. We could then map out the lesson in the following manner.

Day 1: End with Activity A

Day 2: End with Activity B

Day 3: End with Activity C

Day 4: End with Activity D

Day 5: End with Activity E

Day 6: End with Activity F

Day 7: Learners do lesson-final task, Activity Z

Although in principle subgoals may be good classhour goals, in practice some subgoals encompass material that cannot be learned in just one classhour. In Activity A, for example, learners work with isolated statements in the third-person singular forms in order to use the new vocabulary to talk about classmates and/or their instructor. Considering the basic vocabulary we need to talk about everyday events and activities, the amount of new vocabulary can seem daunting. Here is a list of vocabulary that might need to be introduced *just to get started:*

get up

exercise/run/go to the gym/do aerobics

eat breakfast/lunch/dinner

cook/prepare (a meal)

drink coffee

go to class

skip class

take the bus/walk/drive

read

work

return home

write

watch TV

listen to music

call on the phone/talk on the phone

go out

play (*e.g.,* softball, frisbee)

go to bed

sleep/fall asleep

In addition to this necessarily abbreviated list are adverbs such as *early, late, for _____ hours, for a while;* places such as *library, laboratory, restaurant, home, dormitory room, cafeteria, bar* (and the prepositions or case markings they take); objects and things such as *newspaper, novel, magazine, CD;* and other words associated with the activities in the list. You may recall from Chapter 2 that vocabulary is best introduced via comprehensible input so that learners can make form-word-meaning connections in the second language. Learners will obviously need to hear novel words and expressions dozens of times in the input before being asked to produce such words and expressions themselves with any degree of confidence. Thus, one suggestion would be to spend two days on the initial vocabulary for talking about daily routines, *making the goal of the first day the ability to comprehend the vocabulary in context and the goal of the second day to produce it as in Activity A.* What an instructor will need, then, is a comprehension- or input-based activity with which to conclude the first day. The following activity is one possibility.

Activity A1

Listen as your instructor describes a typical day for a German university student. Then, decide what inferences you can make and mark each sentence as P (Possible) or I (Impossible).

_____ **1.** He likes to get up early.
_____ **2.** He doesn't have a car.
_____ **3.** He lives alone.
_____ **4.** He's a science student.
_____ **5.** He's not very social.

[*Instructor's script:* Uwe gets up early and eats breakfast. He has a history class in the morning, and then he goes to the library where he works for an hour and a half. Afterward, he eats lunch in the cafeteria with his friend Anja. After lunch, Uwe returns to the cooperative (the place where he lives) and attends a meeting. After the meeting, he goes back to campus and attends a literature class. After this class, Uwe meets his friends Jörg and Andrea and has an espresso with them at the Cafe Eulenspiegel. When he returns home, he helps prepare dinner. After dinner, he goes out with several friends for a beer. He returns rather late and reads a little before falling asleep.]

We see, then, that our lesson mapping will require two days for the first subgoal, and our new schedule looks something like the following:

Day 1: End with Activity A1

Day 2: End with Activity A

Day 3: End with Activity B

Day 4: End with Activity C

Day 5: End with Activity D

Day 6: End with Activity E

Day 7: End with Activity F

Day 8: Learners do lesson-final task, Activity Z

Only experience will help instructors determine what is a lot of material for one day and what is not. Novice instructors and instructors-in-training will want to consult with other instructors on such matters.

Pause to consider . . .

how certain activities in a lesson might reflect cultural information. Note that activity A1 was built around a typical German student's schedule. After completing this activity, what might you do to stop and have students note some cultural differences before proceeding? Would you ask them some questions? Would you read the description again, but this time have them jot down at least one thing that seems different from a student's routine in the United States (or whatever country)? Would you come back to this later, after students have developed their own descriptions of their routines, to conduct a compare and contrast?

We have just seen that, with the basic vocabulary, we might need to spend two days to get students to the point where they can successfully complete Activity A. On the other hand, there may be cases in which two subgoals could be accomplished during the same classhour. Take, for instance, the subgoals represented by Activities C and D: being able to use time expressions (e.g., *in the morning, in the afternoon*) and specific time (e.g., *at 1:00, at 2:30*). Neither of these subgoals is nearly as demanding as that of Activity A. The amount of new vocabulary is minimal, and it might be possible to get to both Activities C and D in one classhour. Likewise, the amount of material to cover in teaching first- and second-person singular might be achievable in one classhour. Our schedule, then, would be altered to look like the following:

    Day 1: End with Activity A1

    Day 2: End with Activity A

    Day 3: End with Activity B

    Day 4: Activity C midway, end with Activity D

    Day 5: Activity E midway, end with Activity F

    Day 6: Learners do lesson-final task, Activity Z

Attaining a Subgoal

How do we reach a subgoal? Another way to phrase this question is, What do classhours look like? Although not all classhours would be the same, we can use Day 1 and Day 2 of our hypothetical schedule to suggest what a classhour might look like. Remember that language acquisition always begins with input. So, regardless of whether vocabulary, grammar, or some other aspect of language is the focus, we will want to start with input. Following, then, is a suggested classhour plan for Day 1, the object of which is completing Activity A1 as a subgoal.

Day 1

Instructor introduces the new vocabulary via visuals and comprehensible input (see Chapter 2). This will probably last 15–20 minutes.

Activity 1

Instructor makes statements and students tell where the activity might take place.

EXAMPLE: (*instructor*) A student eats lunch.
(*learner, looking at a list on the overhead*) Cafeteria.
(*instructor*) Right. A student eats lunch in the cafeteria. But is that the only place?
(*another learner*) Home.
(*instructor*) Right. A student eats lunch in the cafeteria or at home. Anywhere else?
(*and so on*)

Activity 2

Instructor makes statements about a fictitious student, and learners give their opinion as to whether the statement is typical or not for students at their school.

EXAMPLE: (*instructor*) Robert gets up very early.
(*learners*) Not typical!!!
(*instructor*) He studies at least five hours a day.
(*and so on*)

Activity A1 (See p. 87)

The next day, the instructor will probably want to review vocabulary in a comprehension- or input-based manner before leading students into output activities. The following, then, is one possible classhour plan.

Day 2

Instructor reviews vocabulary with visuals by holding up two visuals and making a statement. Learners indicate whether the statement goes with visual A or visual B.

EXAMPLE: (*instructor*) This person takes a nap every day.
(*learners*) Picture A.

Activity 1

Using the same visuals as in the review, the instructor holds up a visual and asks learners to name the activity by saying that the person in the picture does the activity regularly.

EXAMPLE: (*Instructor holds up a picture of someone reading a newspaper*)
(*learner*) That man reads the newspaper every day.

Activity 2

Instructor provides learners with two columns on the overhead. Column A contains activities listed in infinitive form. Column B contains adverbs, places, objects, and so forth. Using items from both columns, learners must make as many sentences about the typical student at their school as they can in five minutes. Instructor encourages them to agree or disagree.

Activity 3

Instructor gives learners a short text to read, similar to (but not the same as) the one they *heard* in Activity A1. Instructor puts learners into groups of three. Learners have two minutes to read the text. They then turn it over and, without looking, make as many statements about the person's daily routine as they can remember. After four minutes, the instructor calls time and sees which group recalled the most. That group then presents its recalls aloud for the class to judge their truth-value.

Activity A (See p. 79)

> ## *Pause to consider . . .*
>
> the homework assignment that learners might have received before coming to class on Day 2. Which do you think would be a better assignment: one that reviewed the vocabulary via comprehension or one that required the learners to produce the vocabulary? What is your rationale?

As you reflect on the sample classhour plans for Day 1 and Day 2, note that activities are not merely designed to practice the vocabulary and the grammar of a given lesson. Nor are they a simple collection of tasks designed to help fill a classhour. What we see is that *activities are a purposeful endeavor.* They *build toward something.* Activities are completed because the learner needs to know something and be able to do something later in the lesson or later in the class. Activities act as the lumber, screws, sawing, and piecing together that eventually lead to our gazebo, the lesson-final task.

Moving from Input to Output

Implicit in the preceding discussion, and worth making explicit, is that as we discuss subgoals and classhour goals, we are suggesting a cycling of input to output activities. What this means is that learners will always have chances to work through input activities before being asked to produce. Although we discuss this in more detail in Chapters 6 and 7 when we examine grammar-oriented activities, it should be clear why: Acquisition happens by way of input. By moving from input to output in repeated cycles, you offer learners the opportunities to bind (connect) lexical items or grammatical forms with their meanings before you ask them to produce them. Again, this input → output approach of sequencing activities is discussed later in this book. For now, it is important that you consider it as you think about how to reach a lesson subgoal.

Language learning and learning to use language are not confined to the activities completed during class time. An important question to ask is what the learners are doing outside of class as part of their language-learning endeavors. What kind of homework do they have? What kind of laboratory and computer software materials are available to them? It would seem obvious that work done outside of class should somehow be tied to the proficiency objectives of a lesson. Nevertheless, much of what is found in workbook and laboratory assignments reflects the preoccupation with mastery of grammar characteristic of ALM. These materials contain drills, fill-in-the-blank exercises, sentence dictations, and other activities often viewed by learners as busywork. What should learners be doing outside of class?

Continuing our work with the lesson on daily routines, we can ask ourselves a series of questions about outside work that can contribute to a lesson-final goal.

1. Are there opportunities for learners to hear daily routines described? Are there laboratory activities that require learners to focus on comprehending someone else's description of everyday activities? Do these listening activities work at a variety of levels: word, utterance, "extended" narrative, conversational discourse? Do the activities ask learners to compare their own routines with those of the speakers on the tape?

2. Do grammar and vocabulary practices move from input to output? Is mechanical drilling avoided, so that learners are always working with mapping form and meaning or form and function? Are learners invited to "try out" some of the things they will need to do in class (by making sentences about themselves)? Are learners engaged affectively with the materials (e.g., comparing their own lives and interests with those of others, making opinions, inferences, and so on)?

3. Do the outside materials themselves contain goals and subgoals defined as tasks? Is there a listening task toward which students work by completing a set of activities? Is there a form-focused output task that requires that learners have completed previous activities?

4. Are the materials as engaging and as varied as in-class activities? Do they contain surveys, polls, "quizzes," visual materials, short readings, or culturally authentic ads to work with? Do learners check boxes, agree/disagree, fill in names, write out questions, prepare statements, listen for main ideas, or scan for specific information?

Instructors have various opinions and preferences about what learners do outside of class. "Students should complete grammar activities before coming to class so that we don't have to spend time on that." "Students should practice and practice in the lab so that we can spend time on communication in class." "Students should read, read, read outside of class." It seems that many instructors want learners to do things outside of class that they (the instructors) think is a waste of class time. This position is partly due to the fact that instructors have not been able to envision grammar and vocabulary tasks that are meaning based—that is, the kinds of activities that we have examined in this and previous chapters.

Our position is that homework should be an *extension of the class,* not necessarily something different or unenjoyable. Outside assignments should be consistent not only with the lesson objectives but also with the general philosophy of communicative classrooms presented in this book. As one example, recall that comprehension of a short narrative about someone's daily routine could be the basis of the classhour goal for Day 1 of our lesson plan. What kinds of activities might extend this kind of practice outside of class? Homework could be a series of activities that reinforce comprehension related to daily routines. And just as in the classroom, these activities could help learners move from comprehending statements to comprehending a short narrative or dialogue. Following are three activities that would be natural extensions of Day 1 in our lesson on daily routines.

Activity 1

[Learner has a set of black and white drawings depicting the daily routines of two distinct people, Genevieve and Josephine.]

Looking at the drawings that depict typical days for Genevieve and Josephine, listen to the speaker on the tape make a statement. Tell whether the statement describes Genevieve's day or Josephine's day.

EXAMPLE: (*speaker*) She gets up late.
(*you say*) That's Josephine.

If you really want to challenge your memory, study the drawings for about five minutes and then listen to the statements. How many can you get right without looking at the drawings?

Activity 2

Listen to the speaker on the tape make a series of statements about a typical day in the life of a dog. After you hear each one, indicate whether or not you do the same thing by selecting one of the alternative responses below. How much do you and the pooch have in common?

Me, too.
Not me.

[Learner hears eight statements such as "He sleeps most of the day" and "He eats two meals."]

Activity 3

Listen to the speaker describe the schedules of two people, Mary Ziebart and John Hausserman. You might wish to take notes as you listen. Afterward, indicate to whom each statement refers. In some cases, the statement could refer to both people.

1. This person works at the science lab.
2. This person reads the newspaper every day.
3. This person studies in the library almost every day.

   4. This person has a class in the morning.
   5. This person doesn't eat lunch.

Now see if you can fill in the missing information without listening again.

   6. Mary runs _____ miles every day.
   7. John drinks _____ when he reads the newspaper.
   8. Mary has _____ classes in the afternoon.
   9. John teaches _____ classes in the afternoon.

[*Tapescript:* Mary Ziebart is a student at South Central College. Every morning she gets up early, runs three miles, then eats breakfast. She goes to class at 10:00. At noon she goes to the library and studies. She has two afternoon classes and then goes to the science laboratory where she works twenty hours per week.

John Hausserman is a professor at South Central College. Every morning he gets up, drinks coffee, and reads the newspaper. He never eats breakfast. He goes to his office and reads or prepares his classes. At noon, he eats lunch with a friend who is also a professor. John teaches two classes from 2:00 until 5:00. After class, he goes to the gym and exercises.]

Pause to consider . . .

which learning activities are better done outside of class rather than in. Consider also the converse: Which learning activities are better done in class rather than outside? Make a list of as many things as you can think of that a learner could do on his or her own. Does your list reveal a pattern?

In our experience, there are some things that learners can do on their own to help move an instructor's "communicative agenda" forward more quickly than if the same things were done in class. The first is work on extended listening comprehension. Listening to narratives, extended conversations, and other discourse-level texts is something that learners can do in a laboratory or even at home, given the popularity of tape and CD players of all kinds. By working alone, learners can move through these activities at their own individual paces. In simple terms, some learners are faster listeners than others, and a teacher-led listening comprehension activity does not allow for individual differences. Two requirements of outside listening, though, are that learners be able to perform the task on their own regardless of level (that is, the task should not be too difficult for them) and that they bring questions and comments to class to ask about what they listened to ("I couldn't quite get the word after the guy said _____" or "Gee! Where was that woman from who spoke on the tape? She spoke so fast!").

Another thing that learners can do on their own is work through input (and some types of output) activities that focus on vocabulary or grammar. Some instructors think that grammar must be explained in class because it is too difficult for students to understand without help. "They can't possibly understand the complexity of the subjunctive if they read all that stuff on their own." Such observations might be correct if one is working with a traditional give-it-all-to-them grammar focus. However, a recent study suggests that learners can indeed work through many traditional grammar explanations and practices on their own. Scott and Randall (1992) demonstrate that learners of French in a first-semester university course can easily learn meaning-related grammar points and syntax outside of class (in this case, negation formation with *ne... personne/personne... ne* and comparatives *plus... que, moins que..., aussi... que*). Nonmeaning-related grammar points seemed to be harder for their subjects to learn on their own (in this case, the relative pronouns *que* and *qui*). In their study, Scott and Randall found that learners could work on their own and come to class "ready to go" with the meaning-related grammar points but that the nonmeaning-related grammar points caused them some difficulty. They conclude that "since proficiency-oriented instruction is based primarily on devoting class time to meaningful and communicative activities, teachers can designate the linguistic structures which can be learned outside of class so that class time is not wasted on needless explicit grammar rule presentation" (page 361).

In another study, Doughty (1991) found that learners of English as a second language *could* learn the nonmeaningful elements on their own. In her study, subjects worked with computer-based materials in a laboratory. After the treatment period, Doughty found that the subjects had internalized rules for the use of relative clauses. Unlike the instruction in the Scott and Randall study, however, the grammar instruction in Doughty's computer-based materials was input and meaning oriented; learners did not practice output and did not work with drills or fill-in-the-blank exercises.

Another example of how learners can work through material on their own is provided by the "Spanish Project" at the University of Illinois at Urbana-Champaign, a model for instruction that has been adopted elsewhere. For some classes, class time is reduced from four hours per week to two. During this class time, instructors and students are engaged in meaning-oriented tasks that represent lesson subgoals and lesson-end goals. To make up for the two days they do not have class, students work on all vocabulary and grammar via online lessons (that is, via the computer). On their own, students log in to a special set of materials and work through them. The research conducted on the project has shown that these students score just as well on standardized tests as their predecessors if not better, even though their predecessors were in class four days a week and participated in classroom vocabulary and grammar activities. (Part of the reason for the success may be the nature of the materials, something we will see in Chapter 6.)

The significance of our reference at the start of this section to traditional grammar explanations and practices is now clearer. If we envision grammar learning differently, then the "problem" of working through traditional materials on one's own is obviated. In Chapters 7 and 8, we review one approach to explicit work on grammar that avoids the pitfalls and problems of a more traditional approach.

Pause to consider . . .

the possible practical problems of assigning obligatory grammar and vocabulary work outside of class. How realistic do you think it is to have learners do *all* the preparatory work *before* coming to class? What happens if your classhour becomes too dependent on learners "coming prepared" and then at least five people in class have not done the homework? What is the middle ground here?

A FINAL POINT

To be sure, not every minute of the class needs to be spent on activities that build toward the lesson goal. Classes would be boring if they were nothing but a plodding march toward "The Final Task." Like any human endeavor, classroom language learning needs its little detours, its roadstops that give the instructor and learners some breathing room. Brief cultural notes, an interesting advertisement or short blurb from a magazine, five minutes spent watching a commercial—these all can add spice to the routine. When such detours are topically related (a commercial for detergent if everyday events include doing the laundry), they make sense. And although not moving the learner toward the proficiency objective per se, they at least fit the flow of the lesson. In short, a lesson-final goal spelled out as some kind of task might imply a blueprint for organizing the pieces and parts of a lesson, but even when building a gazebo, people stop to eat lunch or take breaks.

SUMMARY

In this chapter, we explored the concept of using an information-exchange task as a communicative lesson goal. We suggested that an actual task gives instructors and learners a concrete objective, and we have shown how a concrete objective can help instructors determine what linguistic tools need to be developed to be successful with the task at the end of the lesson. We then examined how the lesson-final task suggests subgoals for the lesson and how these subgoals can be represented by smaller tasks. In addition, we explored how subgoals might or might not be used as classhour objectives. We saw how at times one subgoal could take two days to reach; in other cases, subgoals might be small enough that two could be reached in a single classhour.

It should be clear, however, that stating a communicative goal as a particular task does not necessarily mean that at the end of a lesson a learner can talk about (or write, or comprehend) a topic in all of its situations or contexts. Given what a language classroom is, instructors and learners cannot possibly cover all the linguistic ground needed to perform in all possible contexts or in all possible situations. As such, the task as lesson goal is an instructional device to help instructors and learners manage their time together. Like much of classroom language learning, it is a small piece of a complex and dynamic endeavor.

KEY TERMS, CONCEPTS, AND ISSUES

communicative goal as statement

linguistic tools and traditional goals

communicative goal versus
  grammatical goal

communicative goal as task

task as blueprint
  subgoals
  classhour goals

out-of-class work
  homework as an extension
    of class
  listening
  grammar

THINKING MORE ABOUT IT: DISCUSSION QUESTIONS

1. **Part 1.** The following is a task for describing and talking about families.

   You are going to draw the family tree of someone in the class. You must interview that person to get specific information:

   - The names of parents, siblings, grandparents, and pets
   - Ages (and whether grandparents are alive or not)
   - Eye color and hair color of the human family members

   Step 1. Sit and think about the questions you will ask before interviewing your classmate. Can you say everything you need to say? How will you express things that you cannot say?

   Step 2. Interview your classmate and jot down the information he or she gives you.

   Step 3. Using the information, draw the family tree and place all of the requested information (e.g., name and age) under each family member's head.

   Step 4. Prepare a series of summary statements for the class as you show everyone your partner's family tree. Be sure to include in your summary statements whether there is a family trait in terms of hair or eye color.

   (*Instructor note:* For Step 4, you might have one or two volunteers present their partner's family tree to the entire class, and then afterward have students work in groups of four, presenting to the others in the group the family trees they drew.)

   With several other people in class, decide what linguistic tools learners need in order to complete this task. Be as specific as possible.

   Part 2. State as many subgoal tasks as you think necessary that build toward the final task presented in Part 1.

2. As a class, argue the pros and cons of the following statement: "I expect my students to come prepared. If they don't, they just suffer the consequences." List at least three pros and three cons.

GETTING A CLOSER LOOK:
RESEARCH ACTIVITIES

Interview an experienced teacher and ask her about the following:

a. How she develops a lesson plan
b. How she knows how long a lesson will take
c. If she establishes any goals for her learners
d. In what way her materials are meeting any proficiency goals

What did you learn about how some teachers plan their lessons? What personal and intellectual reactions do you have to this teacher's responses?

MAKING COMMUNICATIVE LANGUAGE
TEACHING HAPPEN: PORTFOLIO ACTIVITIES

Take a chapter in the text that you (will) teach from. If the chapter does not have a lesson-final task that represents a goal, create one for it. Then work through the various sections of the lesson to see if you can create subgoal and classhour tasks that represent realistic proficiency goals for the materials you have. If you cannot do this or the materials do not lend themselves to easy adaptation, then review the activity under Thinking More About It. Map out a lesson in as much detail as possible, showing how you would get from the beginning of the lesson to the lesson-final goal or task. Be sure to include all the tasks that represent "stopping points along the way." You need not include every single activity for every minute of every class.

Suggestions for Using Information-Exchange Tasks for Oral Testing

In this chapter we explore:

- Four general criteria for designing language tests that can be applied to the design of oral tests
- Washback effects, the indirect influence that decisions about testing may have on teaching
- Suggestions for developing oral tests from information-exchange tasks, thereby bringing testing into consonance with classroom practices
- Evaluation criteria for oral tests, including componential rating scales that identify various components of oral language

FOUR CRITERIA FOR DESIGNING A GOOD TEST

Carroll (1980) identifies four general criteria in foreign language testing: economy, relevance, acceptability, and comparability. By *economy*, Carroll means obtaining the greatest amount of information about the learners' language in as little time as possible and with a minimum of energy expended by either the instructor or learners. For a test to be economic, we suggest that it merely sample the material covered, not exhaust it. Sampling is part of everyday life. For example, we often read opinion polls about what America thinks. The pollsters do not ask every single American what he or she thinks; rather, they sample a group of Americans and infer or project from the sample to all Americans. So it can be with testing language in general and grammar in particular. An instructor can select from among the many items covered and infer or project something about the learner's overall knowledge or ability.

Relevance refers to the match between the course and curriculum goals and the tests. For example, if you teach a course called "Reading German for Graduate Students," you would not give an oral exam at the end of the course.

If you teach a course in conversational use of Italian, you would not want to give a formal composition as the final exam. Creating formal written discourse is not relevant to a course emphasizing informal oral discourse. For a test to be relevant, we suggest that it reflect not simply what is taught but, more important, how it is taught. And of course, how we teach influences the types of tests we should give.

Acceptability is a concept that takes the learners' point of view into consideration. It implies learners' willingness to participate in the testing and their satisfaction that the test evaluates their progress. Learners should not perceive themselves as the victims of the test. For many learners, acceptability is tied to familiarity. If they are not familiar with a testing format or procedure, they may view it as unacceptable. For example, if free spontaneous recall ("Write down everything that you remember reading without looking back at the passage") was not an activity type used in class, the learners might not accept it as a valid way to test their reading comprehension. Likewise, if an instructor uses the target language only 50 percent of the time in class, the learners might not accept a test of listening comprehension.

Comparability is a concept that takes the institution's point of view into consideration. It means that we should obtain similar test scores across different groups of learners taking the test at the same time, as well as similar scores across different tests at different times for the same group of learners. In other words, test scores for learners who are taught the same material by the same method should be similar. Also, different tests—whether they examine the same material or different material—should yield similar results. For example, those enrolled in the 9 A.M. section of Portuguese 102 should have test scores similar to the scores of learners enrolled in the 2 P.M. section if the two sections have common goals, materials, syllabi, and methods. The same test should also yield similar results if it is offered a year later. Finally, two different tests examining the same content should yield similar results. If one is harder or easier than the other, the results will not be comparable.

WASHBACK EFFECTS

Krashen and Terrell (1983) made the following statement regarding classroom testing—a statement that addresses the acceptability of a test.

> [Testing] can be done in a way that will have a positive effect on the student's progress. The key to effective testing is the realization that testing has a profound effect on what goes on in the classroom. Teachers are motivated to teach and students are motivated to study material which will be covered on tests. Quite simply, if we want students to acquire a second language, we should give tests that promote the use of acquisition activities [in and out of the classroom]. In other words, our tests should motivate students to prepare for the tests by obtaining more comprehensible input and motivate teachers to supply it.
>
> (Krashen & Terrell, 1983, p. 165)

100

CHAPTER 5
*Suggestions for
Using Information-
Exchange Tasks for
Oral Testing*

Krashen and Terrell point out what is generally referred to as a *washback effect*. What and how you test has ramifications for what instructors do in the classroom, what learners *expect* instructors to do in the classroom, and what learners do *outside* the classroom. In other words, testing cannot be viewed as an isolated event; it must be an integral part of the teaching and learning enterprise.

Krashen and Terrell go on to make the following statement regarding the relevance of a test, the match between course goals and materials and testing practices.

> Using an approach in the classroom which emphasizes the ability to exchange messages, and at the same time testing only the ability to apply grammar rules correctly, is an invitation to disaster.
>
> (Krashen & Terrell, 1983, p. 165)

Because we advocate the use of information-exchange tasks for developing communicative language ability, we now offer suggestions for adapting information-exchange tasks for use as oral tests to *evaluate* communicative language ability.

ORAL TESTING IN CLASSROOMS: ADAPTING INFORMATION-EXCHANGE TASKS FOR USE AS ORAL TESTS AND QUIZZES

There are many differences between a one-on-one interview between instructor and learner and a trio of learners carrying out an information-exchange task. One of these differences is the *communicative burden* an individual learner carries. We define "communicative burden" as the responsibility of an individual test taker to initiate, respond, manage, and negotiate an oral event. The communicative burden of a group discussion is less than the communicative burden of an oral interview. In a discussion, multiple participants share the communicative burden, each one assuming the responsibilities of initiating, responding, managing, and negotiating the event. In contrast, most of these responsibilities are the test taker's during a one-on-one interview. The test taker alone must respond to the interviewer and manage the interaction. During classroom testing, an instructor must consider the communicative burden of a test format and decide if it is an appropriate burden based on the level of the learner and on the classroom practices leading up to the test.

The communicative burden of a test format becomes an issue when the teacher is considering whether to give an oral quiz or an oral test. Most people distinguish quizzes from tests in terms of length and comprehensiveness. Quizzes are shorter and less comprehensive than tests (daily quizzes, pop quizzes, and lesson quizzes versus unit tests and end-of-semester tests, for example). One might decide that an oral quiz at the end of a lesson in the first semester should have a low communicative burden, whereas a quiz at the end of a lesson in the fourth semester should have a greater one. Moreover, one might decide to quiz spoken language in the first year of language instruction but to test it only in the second year. In short, there are a number of instructional decisions to make regarding oral testing, and these decisions depend on a variety of pedagogical and practical factors (including experience of the instructor, time available, and the goals of the curriculum).

These decisions may well have a washback effect on instruction. By knowing and being familiar with the characteristics of the test (any kind of test, not just one of spoken language), instructors may incorporate activities into the classroom that they feel will lead to success on the test. That is, the type of test can influence both *what* instructors emphasize and the *way* in which they emphasize it. For example, if learners must take a test of communicative language ability at the end of a course, then the instructor would probably carry out activities during the semester that would allow learners to develop their communicative language ability. Most, if not all, instructors would make a concerted effort to speak the target language in class and to do listening comprehension activities throughout the course if 25 percent of the points on the final exam were determined by learners' performance on listening comprehension exercises.

The content of the oral test or quiz can have another kind of washback effect on instruction. If the content of the oral test is overtly tied to classroom activities, then learners are provided a stronger motivation for participating in the activities. The following examples of test sections illustrate this point. We recommend that instructors adhere to the principle that they *test what and how they teach.* Testing and teaching should be interrelated so that learners are responsible for what happens in class.

To demonstrate how we interrelate teaching and testing, we convert four of the information-exchange tasks presented in Chapter 3 into test sections. Recall the following activity from Chapter 3.

Activity D.   Compare Your Birthday Experiences

Step 1. Fill in the following chart as you interview a classmate.

Birthday	Where?	With whom?	Food?	Fun?
2 years ago				
5 years ago				
10 years ago				

Step 2. Now write a paragraph in which you compare and contrast your own birthdays with the three birthdays your classmate just described.

Here is a test section based on Activity D.

Section A

Phase 1. *Warm-up.* Make the test taker feel comfortable.

Phase 2. *Initial questioning.* Who was your partner? When is that person's birthday? When is your birthday?

102

CHAPTER 5
*Suggestions for
Using Information-
Exchange Tasks for
Oral Testing*

Phase 3. *Activity-related questions.* Referring to the chart you made in class, tell me whether you and [name of partner] have celebrated your birthdays in similar or different ways.

[*Procedural note to tester:* Let the test taker talk from the chart but do not look at it yourself. If you read the chart, then the test taker will not be exchanging real information with you; he or she will be telling you what you already know. Be sure to ask for clarification when you don't understand. Be conscious of whatever time limits there are on the test so that you move the interaction along with probe questions such as, "What about five years ago?" and "What about ten years ago?"]

Here is an information-gap task from another activity in Chapter 3.

Activity F. Compare Provinces

Step 1. Each person in the group reads a different short text produced by the national travel bureau. Each text describes the desirable features of a particular province in order to generate tourism to that region.

Step 2. Working together, the group completes the following chart:

Province:	A	B	C
Terrain			
Festivals			
Sporting			
Climate			

Step 3. Weighing all the information, the group must plan a travel itinerary to visit each of the three provinces. First plan one for a two-week stay and then one for a one-week stay.

The following test section proceeds logically from Activity F.

Section B

Phase 1. *Make the test taker feel comfortable.*

Phase 2. *Initial questioning.* [*Test taker should not need to refer to the chart.*] What province did you read about? Tell me what you remember about it. Who else did you work with? What provinces did they read about?

Phase 3. *Activity-related questions.* [*Allow the test taker to use the chart.*] Where did you as a group decide to go first? Why did you pick that one?

How long are you staying there? Province B is also very beautiful; why didn't the group choose it? Did you agree with the group choice or did you prefer another location?

Phase 4. *Beyond the activity.* Have you ever been anywhere like the provinces described? Where was that? *or* Did these descriptions remind you of any place in the United States? *or* If you had to describe your hometown [*or some other place such as where the school is located*], what would you say?

Recall that consensus building was the focus of Activity H.

Activity H. The Time Capsule

Step 1. Your university wants to place a time capsule in the new library being constructed. The capsule will be opened in the year 2200, and in it will be ten items that represent the last part of the twentieth century. What will those ten items be?

Step 2. The capsule is only two cubic feet in size, so anything you choose must be small. Also, the items selected should reflect not only the achievements of our society but also our values.

Step 3. Work in groups of five or six to come to a consensus about the contents of the time capsule. You can use the following list to guide your discussion, but you must choose at least three of the ten from items not on this list.

a book	a computer
a movie	a credit card
a gun	a VCR
running shoes	a miniature TV
a cell phone	a pair of jeans
a brochure for Disney World	a baseball

Step 4. Present and explain your list to the rest of the class. Listen and take notes as the other groups present and explain their lists. Finally, as a class, come to a consensus on what to include in the capsule.

Two test sections could be based on Activity H.

Section C

Phase 1. *Make the learner feel comfortable.*

Phase 2. *Initial questioning.* Whom did you work with? What items did you and your group select? Was it easy to reach a consensus?

Phase 3. *Activity-related questions.* Compare and contrast the list of items your group chose and those the class chose. Why did your group choose something that is not on the final list?

Phase 4. *Beyond the activity.* Our class selected ten items for the time capsule. Would you reduce the list to five items only?

104

CHAPTER 5
Suggestions for
Using Information-
Exchange Tasks for
Oral Testing

Section D

If you did not do the Time Capsule as an in-class activity, you could have a pair or group of learners do it as a quiz or part of a test. In order to reduce the amount of time required to carry out the activity, you could (a) reduce the number of items they have to decide on and (b) eliminate Step 4, the presentation of the list.

Pause to consider . . .

a nontraditional alternative. We have cautioned against the simple question-and-answer approach to communicative language teaching and have promoted the communication-as-information-exchange paradigm. Even though the test versions suggested for Activities D, F, and H promote information exchange, they still have the flavor of a question-and-answer exercise. Can any oral test be a truly communicative exchange? What would happen if the test giver were truly a participant in the communicative event? Consider the possibility, as Lee (2000) elaborates, of *doing* a communicative activity *with* the test taker instead of having the test taker report on a previous experience with the activity. How different would the interaction between test taker and test giver be in those circumstances? What would you, the test giver, learn about the test taker's communicative language ability that the traditional format would not reveal?

TWO TESTS FOR EVALUATING SPOKEN LANGUAGE

In this section, we review two oral proficiency tests. The first is the Oral Proficiency Interview (often called the "OPI"), which was developed by the American Council on the Teaching of Foreign Languages (ACTFL) in conjunction with the Educational Testing Service and several government agencies. The other test is the Israeli National Oral Proficiency Test developed by Elana Shohamy and her colleagues for the purpose of determining the ability of Israeli secondary students to use English prior to admission to university.

Elicitation Procedures

The Oral Proficiency Interview

The ACTFL Oral Proficiency Interview has been likened to a face-to-face conversation because an interviewer "converses" with an interviewee. But like many other oral testing situations in which one of the participants in the conversation evaluates the other's language abilities and purposefully elicits certain kinds of language, the interaction can be said to be only "conversation-like."

The goal of the OPI is to obtain a sample of speech that can be rated using the ACTFL Proficiency Guidelines as the measure. These guidelines comprise level-by-level (from Novice to Superior) descriptions of learner performance specifying the *content* that a learner at a particular level might dominate (such as simple greetings, health matters, family, daily routines, work, and politics), the *functions* the learner dominates (such as expressing agreement or disagreement, narrating in the past, present, and future, and hypothesizing and supporting opinions), and the *accuracy* present in the learner's speech (such as systematic errors that interfere with communication and sporadic errors that do not interfere with communication). The levels from Novice to Superior are described in the next section on evaluation criteria. For now, we would like to concentrate on the OPI itself.

The procedures used to elicit learner language during the OPI are termed *phases*—Phase 1: Warm-up; Phase 2: Level Check; Phase 3: Probes; and Phase 4: Wind-down. Omaggio Hadley (1993, pp. 456–58) describes each phase as follows:

> *Phase 1: Warm-up.* The warm-up portion of the interview is very brief and consists of greeting the interviewee, making him or her feel comfortable, and exchanging the social amenities that are normally used in everyday conversations. Typically, the warm-up lasts less than three minutes, but it serves a variety of purposes. First, on the psychological plane, it allows the interviewee to begin thinking in the language and sets him or her at ease. On the linguistic plane, it reorients the person being tested to hearing and using the language while giving the tester an opportunity to determine where the next phase of the interview should begin. This relates to the evaluative function of the warm-up, which is to allow the tester to get a preliminary idea of the rating that will eventually be assigned. Once the warm-up is completed, the tester moves on to Phase 2.
>
> *Phase 2: Level Check.* This phase consists of establishing the highest level of proficiency at which the interviewee can sustain speaking performance—that is, the level at which he or she can perform the functions and speak about the content areas designated by the ACTFL Guidelines with the greatest degree of accuracy. On the psychological plane, this phase of the interview allows the person being tested to demonstrate his or her strengths and converse at the level that is most comfortable for him or her. Linguistically, the level check is designed to elicit a speech sample that is adequate to prove that the person can indeed function accurately at the level hypothesized by the interviewer during the warm-up phase. If during the level check, the interviewer can see that his or her hypothesis was incorrect, the level of questions is adjusted upward or downward accordingly. On the evaluative plane, the level check allows the interviewer to get a better idea of the actual proficiency level of the interviewee, establishing the floor of his or her performance beyond a reasonable doubt. This phase of the interview is repeated several times throughout the entire testing process and alternates with the probe phase, described next.

106

CHAPTER 5
*Suggestions for
Using Information-
Exchange Tasks for
Oral Testing*

Phase 3: Probes. Probes are questions or tasks designed to elicit a language sample at one level of proficiency higher than the hypothesized level in order to establish a ceiling on the interviewee's performance. Psychologically, this allows the tester to show the person being tested what he or she is not yet able to do with the language, verifying the rating that will eventually be assigned to the speech sample. On the linguistic plane, the probes may result in *linguistic breakdown*—the point at which the interviewee ceases to function accurately or cogently because the task is too difficult. If a probe is successfully carried out, the interviewer may begin level checking at this higher level to see if his or her hypothesis about the true proficiency level is wrong. If the interviewee does demonstrate during the probe phase that he or she does not have the language to carry out the task, then the probe can be considered a valid indicator that the hypothesized level is correct. Several probes should be used during the interview, alternated with level checks, to establish beyond any question the appropriate rating.

Phase 4: Wind-down. When a ratable sample has been obtained, the tester brings the interviewee back to the level at which he or she functions most comfortably for the last few minutes of the interview. This serves to make individuals feel successful and allows them to leave the test with the echo of their own voice still in their ears, reminding them that they functioned well in the language. Linguistically, the wind-down portion of the interview represents the most accurate use of the language of which the person is capable. On the evaluative plane, this last phase gives the tester one more opportunity to verify that his or her rating is indeed correct. The tester may end the interview by thanking the person who was interviewed, saying what a pleasure it has been talking with him or her, and wishing the person a pleasant day. Again, the termination of the conversation should resemble as much as possible the way in which conversations normally end in authentic language-use situations.

An OPI can take anywhere from fifteen to thirty minutes depending on the level of the learner and the experience of the interviewer. From the perspective of an elicitation procedure, the OPI is well described. Each test giver follows the standard, prescribed phases. OPI training ensures that raters carry out the interview uniformly and apply the ratings consistently: OPI testers can be certified by ACTFL only after a rigorous training session with follow-up practice interviews. The OPI is referred to as a "single-format test," for it consists of only one task (an interview) and there are no other components to the test. On the basis of this one format, a holistic rating such as Novice-High, Intermediate-Mid, or Advanced is assigned.

There are two important concepts that emerge from a consideration of testing, namely, bias and inter-rater reliability. *Bias* refers to situations in which elicitation and evaluation procedures are not the same for all test takers. The test giver is the variable in this scenario. He or she might ask harder (or easier) questions of certain test takers or might evaluate one person differently from the way another is evaluated. *Inter-rater reliability* refers to the desire to have all raters evaluate a test the same way. An OPI evaluation, for example, should not vary depending on who the tester was; given a set of criteria, all raters should apply them the same way. If they do, there is inter-rater reliability. ACTFL training serves the purpose of working toward bias-free and reliable testing.

Although useful for a variety of reasons, the OPI has been questioned because of its single-format nature. Shohamy, for example, has questioned to what extent an oral interview can provide a representative sample of language proficiency. She states that

> viewing oral language as constituting a multiple of different speech styles and functions (e.g., discussing, arguing, apologizing, interviewing, conversing, being interviewed, reporting, etc.) means that being interviewed, the speech style and function tapped in an oral interview, represents only a single type of oral interaction. No doubt that it is an important speech style, but clearly, there are also other oral interactions which are equally important in real life situations.
>
> (Shohamy, 1987, p. 52)

The Israeli National Oral Proficiency Test

In a series of studies, Shohamy and her colleagues (Reyes, 1982; Shohamy, Reyes, & Bejerano, 1986) found that a learner's performance on an oral interview was not a valid predictor of that learner's performance on other oral tasks. Given those findings, Shohamy has recommended a multiple-format approach to testing oral proficiency. This test was introduced in Israel in 1986 as the national examination for students at the end of the twelfth grade. The decision to accept students into university is based on this test. The Israeli National Oral Proficiency Test in English as a Foreign Language (INOPT), in contrast to the OPI, is multicomponential by design and, therefore, more comprehensive. In addition to the oral interview, three other tasks are also used to evaluate test takers' oral proficiency: role play, a reporting task, and group discussion.

Shohamy, Reves, and Bejerano (1986) justify the four formats on several grounds. First, each format elicits a different speech style, so that the test as a whole comprises a range of speech styles that reflect communicative language use in authentic situations. Second, their research demonstrated that the test did discriminate well among various levels of oral proficiency. Third, their statistical analyses on the test (i.e., correlations of performance across each format and an analysis of shared variance) allowed them to conclude that each section of the test was indeed different from the other sections. Finally, they concluded that if the goal was to test various speech styles, then each would need to be tested via separate oral tests, for no one format could be used as a valid measure of overall oral proficiency and performance on no single format reliably predicted performance on another.

Shohamy and her fellow researchers offer the following descriptions of the four formats used in the INOPT. Each lasted about ten minutes, and different testers were assigned to administer the separate test formats. You will undoubtedly notice that their Oral Interview and the ACTFL OPI are quite similar.

108

CHAPTER 5
*Suggestions for
Using Information-
Exchange Tasks for
Oral Testing*

Test 1: Oral Interview. The rationale underlying this test was to guide the test-taker into a dialogue with the tester. The test elicits answers to questions asked by the tester on different topics at different levels of proficiency. The test followed the model of the Foreign Service Institute Oral Interview (Lowe, 1982). It included the following four phases.

1. *Warm-up:* In this phase the test-taker was put at ease and the tester derived a preliminary indication of the test-taker's level of proficiency in speech and understanding.
2. *Level-check:* During this phase the tester checked the functions and content where the test-taker's performance was most accurate.
3. *Probing:* In this phase the tester assessed the highest level at which the candidate could function.
4. *Wind-up:* In this phase the test-taker was returned to the level at which he or she could function most comfortably, and thus was left with a feeling of accomplishment. The scoring of the test-taker's performance on the oral interview was done on the basis of the rating scale used for all tests . . . [included in the following section on evaluation criteria]

Test 2: Role Play. The rationale behind this test was to stimulate the test-taker to produce spontaneous speech-behavior within given roles eliciting specific speech functions. In it the test-taker had to play one role, with the tester playing another, both partners in a dialogue. The test-taker was given a card describing a situation and his or her expected role in it. . . . The card was written in the test-taker's mother tongue (Hebrew), so that the interference of reading comprehension in the foreign language could be avoided. The tester then engaged in a simulated conversation derived from the situation described on the card. A score was assigned by an assessor who was not involved in the [role play], on the basis of the same rating-scale used for the other tests.

Test 3: Reporting Test. The rationale underlying this test was to stimulate the test-taker into a monologue in the foreign language, based on authentic input in Hebrew. The student was given a newspaper article in Hebrew. He or she was asked to read it silently and report its general content to the tester in his or her own words, in English. The test-taker was specifically asked not to translate the text, but rather to report freely, referring back to the text only if necessary. This test was also scored on the basis of the rating scale used to rate oral proficiency for all the other experimental tests.

Test 4: Group Discussion. The rationale underlying this test was to stimulate the test-takers into a spontaneous discussion of a controversial issue, in which they could express views about topical matters, debate and argue about them, defend their opinions and try to persuade the other participants to accept them. Four students were asked to discuss a topical subject or issue controversial enough to lead to a lively discussion. Members of the group picked a card at random from among the twenty cards on the table. The card provided information regarding the topic of discussion they were about to hold, and some cues for discussion, such as guiding questions with relevant lexical items. . . . They were given a few minutes to read the card and plan the procedure for their discussion among themselves in the mother tongue, before they were to start the actual discussion in English (Reves, 1982). The tester listened to the discussion without participating in it or interfering with it, and scored the performance of each of the four participant test-takers on the basis of the rating scale used for all the other tests in this study.

(Shohamy et al., 1986, pp. 215–216)

Pause to consider . . .

the relative economy of the OPI and INOPT. For the OPI we have a 15–30-minute single-format test. For the INOPT we have a four-format test, each format lasting ten minutes. Carroll's suggestion for economy in testing encourages us to test only a sample of the test taker's abilities. How are both the OPI and INOPT economical approaches to testing oral language?

Evaluation Criteria for Tests of Spoken Language

The speech sample elicited via the OPI is judged against the ACTFL Proficiency Guidelines. Four basic proficiency levels are identified (Novice, Intermediate, Advanced, and Superior), with three ratings (Low, Mid, and High) for Novice and Intermediate levels and only two ratings within Advanced (Advanced and Advanced-High). The following level descriptions are taken from Omaggio Hadley (1993, pp. 502–504). Because of space constraints, we include only one within-level rating, Intermediate-Mid, as an illustrative example.

Novice   The Novice level is characterized by the ability to communicate minimally with learned material.

Intermediate   The Intermediate level is characterized by the speaker's ability to:

- Create with the language by combining and recombining learned elements, though primarily in a reactive mode;
- Initiate, minimally sustain, and close in a simple way basic communicative tasks; and
- Ask and answer questions.

Intermediate-Mid   Able to handle successfully a variety of uncomplicated, basic communicative tasks and social situations. Can talk simply about self and family members. Can ask and answer questions and participate in simple conversations on topics beyond the most immediate needs; e.g., personal history and leisure time activities. Utterance length increases slightly, but speech may continue

110

CHAPTER 5
Suggestions for
Using Information-
Exchange Tasks for
Oral Testing

to be characterized by frequent long pauses, since the smooth incorporation of even basic conversational strategies is often hindered as the speaker struggles to create appropriate language forms. Pronunciation may continue to be strongly influenced by first language and fluency may still be strained. Although misunderstandings still arise, the Intermediate-Mid speaker can generally be understood by sympathetic interlocutors.

Advanced The Advanced level is characterized by the speaker's ability to:

- Converse in a clearly participatory fashion;
- Initiate, sustain, and bring to closure a wide variety of communicative tasks, including those that require an increased ability to convey meaning with diverse language strategies due to a complication or an unforeseen turn of events;
- Satisfy the requirements of school and work situations; and
- Narrate and describe with paragraph-length connected discourse.

Superior The Superior level is characterized by the speaker's ability to:

- Participate effectively in most formal and informal conversations on practical, social, professional, and abstract topics; and
- Support opinions and hypothesize using native-like discourse strategies.

The four speech samples elicited by the INOPT are each judged separately according to the following scale. Scores from each section are added together to yield a final score.

4: Unintelligible
No language produced
No interaction possible
5: Hardly intelligible
Very poor language produced
Only simplest, fragmentary interaction possible
6: Clearly intelligible
Simple language produced
Interaction possible
Not articulate
7: Responsive in interaction
Slightly more sophisticated language produced
Consistent errors: but do not interfere with fluency
Strong MT [mother tongue] interference (translated patterns, etc.)

8: Almost effortless in expression
   Adequate in interaction
   Errors: not consistent
9: Facility of expression
   Comfortable initiating in interaction
   Sporadic mistakes
10: No limitation whatsoever
   Near-native

(Shohamy et al., 1986, p. 219)

As indicated earlier, the OPI and the INOPT are similar because each contains some type of interview. Here we would like to point out that the two tests overlap in another significant way: Each uses holistic ratings (that is, a single final "score" for the entire test). As Bachman (1990, p. 328) points out, using holistic scores implies that "language proficiency is viewed as a unitary ability, with scores 'expressed in a single global rating of general language ability' (Lowe, 1988, p. 12)." Bachman goes on to argue that proficiency is *not* a unitary ability but, rather, a componential one because we can identify the pieces and constituent parts of oral proficiency. (See, for example, the four underlying competences discussed in Savignon, 1998, that were briefly mentioned on page 53.) The distinction between unitary and componential is not only an important theoretical distinction but also a practical one. On the practical level, instructors must decide how to score a test of spoken language and what kind of feedback they wish to give to learners about their performance.

Pause to consider . . .

the diagnostic uses of classroom tests. One of the important functions of classroom testing is its diagnostic function: By examining learners' performance on a test, we can provide them feedback on their strengths and weaknesses. Does a global, holistic score provide an instructor the capability of giving diagnostic feedback? Think about what you would want to know about your own oral proficiency in the second language. Would a high score on an oral proficiency test mean that you did not have weaknesses you could work on? Would a low score indicate what specific things you could do to improve?

COMPONENTIAL RATING SCALES

If oral proficiency is not a unitary ability, then it should not be tested as such (Shohamy et al., 1986), and, just as important, it should not be scored as such (Bachman, 1990). Bachman proposes, therefore, that tests of oral proficiency be evaluated using componential scoring criteria and provides the following criteria used in a test of oral proficiency he developed with a colleague (Bachman & Palmer, 1983). The three scales assess grammatical, pragmatic, and

112

CHAPTER 5
Suggestions for
Using Information-
Exchange Tasks for
Oral Testing

sociolinguistic competence, as shown in Table 5.1. (Pragmatic competence is similar to discourse competence and refers to cohesion across utterances.) Each component contributes a different amount to the total final score; thus, the points listed under "Rating" vary from component to component with differing ranges (for example, 0–6 for Grammatical Competence but 0–4 for Pragmatic Competence). The more important component is weighted more heavily.

Because the Bachman-Palmer criteria are designed to separate a language learner's communicative language ability into its component parts, the criteria can be adapted according to several principles. In adapting such rating scales for classroom use, an instructor might alter the weight of a scale (adding or subtracting how many points it is worth) or vary the components according to the elicitation procedures. Even though Shohamy's group used the same criteria to evaluate the speech samples in each of the four test formats, it is possible to vary the criteria depending on the type of elicitation procedure.

Pause to consider . . .

whether the grade assigned at the end of a language course is unitary or componential. What would it mean to you, to the instructor, and/or to your parents that you earned a B in Russian 101?

TABLE 5.1 Scales for Evaluating Grammatical Competence, Pragmatic Competence, and Sociolinguistic Competence

	Grammatical Competence	
Rating	Range	Accuracy
0	No systematic evidence of morphologic and syntactic structures	Control of few or no structures; errors of all or most possible types
1	Limited range of both morphologic and syntactic structures, but with some systematic evidence	Control of few or no structures; errors of all or most possible types
2	Limited range of both morphologic and syntactic structures, but with some systematic evidence	Control of some structures used, but with many error types
3	Large, but not complete, range of both morphologic and syntactic structures	Control of some structures used, but with many error types
4	Large, but not complete, range of both morphologic and syntactic structures	Control of most structures used, with few error types
5	Complete range of morphologic and syntactic structures	Control of most structures used, with few error types
6	Complete range of morphologic and syntactic structures	No systematic errors

Pragmatic Competence			
Rating	Vocabulary	Rating	Cohesion
0	*Extremely limited vocabulary* (A few words and formulaic phrases. Not possible to discuss any topic, due to limited vocabulary.)	0	*No cohesion* (Utterances completely disjointed, or discourse too short to judge.)
1	*Small vocabulary* (Difficulty in talking with examinee because of vocabulary limitations.)	1	*Very little cohesion* (Relationships between utterances not adequately marked; frequent confusing relationships among ideas.)
2	*Vocabulary of moderate size* (Frequently misses or searches for words.)	2	*Moderate cohesion* (Relationships between utterances generally marked; sometimes confusing relationships among ideas.)
3	*Large vocabulary* (Seldom misses or searches for words.)	3	*Good cohesion* (Relationships between utterances well-marked.)
4	*Extensive vocabulary* (Rarely, if ever, misses or searches for words. Almost always uses appropriate word.)	4	*Excellent cohesion* (Uses a variety of appropriate devices; hardly ever confusing relationships among ideas.)

Sociolinguistic Competence					
R	Distinguishing of Registers	R	Nativeness	R	Use of Cultural References
0	Evidence of only one register	1	*Frequent* nonnative but grammatical structures or impossible to judge because of interference from other factors	0.5	No evidence of ability to use cultural references
1	Evidence of two registers			2.5	Some evidence of ability to use cultural references
2	Evidence of two registers *and* control of either formal or informal register			4	Full control of appropriate cultural references
3.5	Control of *both* formal and informal registers	3	*Rare* nonnative but grammatical structures		
		4	*No* nonnative but grammatical structures		

Source: Bachman and Palmer (1983)

114

CHAPTER 5
Suggestions for
Using Information-
Exchange Tasks for
Oral Testing

Pause to consider . . .

sociolinguistic and pragmatic competences in the learners' native culture and the second language culture. How different are these cultures? Are these cultural differences teachable?

SUMMARY

In this chapter we adapted classroom activities for testing situations. Some formats place a greater communicative burden on the test taker than do others; the degree of communicative burden should guide an instructor's testing procedures, especially with early stage learners. Testing learners' communicative language ability can have a positive washback effect on instruction. If there is to be an oral test with content related to classroom activities, learners will have additional motivation not only to participate in the class but to strive to improve their communicative language ability.

We also examined two tests for evaluating spoken language, the ACTFL Oral Proficiency Interview and the Israeli National Oral Proficiency Test. Both tests prescribe very specific elicitation procedures and utilize specific evaluation criteria, thereby addressing two important issues in testing: bias and inter-rater reliability. We suggested the use of tests that examine a variety of speech styles and functions via multiple formats.

Test taker performance on both the OPI and INOPT is measured using holistic (single score) ratings. Following Bachman (1990), we advocated instead the use of analytic criteria in recognition of the componential nature of language proficiency. We presented several componential rating scales, which allow a more precise evaluation of the speech sample as well as a more detailed diagnosis of the learner's language. We suggested that the choice of rating scales should depend on the types of oral interactions elicited and whether the interaction involves just a test giver or other learners.

KEY TERMS, CONCEPTS, AND ISSUES

communicative burden
  level of learner
  classroom practices
quiz versus test
washback effects on instruction
elicitation procedures
  Oral Proficiency Interview
    phases
  Israeli National Oral Proficiency
   Test
    components
evaluation criteria

training of test givers
  absence of bias
  inter-rater reliability
speech styles and functions
  (discussing, arguing, apologizing,
  interviewing, being interviewed,
  conversing, reporting, and so forth)
unitary ability versus componential
  ability
single holistic score versus
  component weighting scales
diagnostic feedback

115

*Making
Communicative
Language Teaching
Happen: Portfolio
Activities*

THINKING MORE ABOUT IT:
DISCUSSION QUESTIONS

1. Make a list of the advantages and disadvantages you see with using the OPI, INOPT, and an adaptation of a classroom information-exchange task as an oral test (you can refer specifically to Test Section A on pp. 101–102). Be sure you include in your list some reference to the tests' relevance, acceptability, economy, and comparability.
2. What rating scales and language components would you select for use with an oral test that was adapted from a classroom information-exchange activity?
3. Consider the advantages and disadvantages of having three language learners perform an information-exchange task as an oral test or quiz. What rating scales would you use?

GETTING A CLOSER LOOK:
RESEARCH ACTIVITIES

Record an oral interview of an average student. Then record this person performing an information-exchange task with two other learners. Compare the speech samples for similiarities and differences in communicative language ability. Do the two testing formats elicit different speech styles and functions?

MAKING COMMUNICATIVE LANGUAGE
TEACHING HAPPEN: PORTFOLIO ACTIVITIES

Adapt an information-exchange task for oral testing purposes. Be sure to write explicit directions for both test givers and test takers. Either select an activity from the textbook you (will) teach from or use the bilingual/bicultural activity presented in Chapter 3. You should also develop the grading criteria you will use.

CHAPTER 6

Issues in Learning and Teaching Grammar

In this chapter, we explore:

- The idea that people learned languages before institutionalized education existed
- Five common ideas about learning grammar held by language teachers (and students) that, in the end, are misconceptions
- Research findings revealing that natural learning processes always assert themselves over outside intervention (i.e., grammar instruction)
- The fundamental problem inherent in traditional approaches to grammar instruction

In Chapter 1, we reviewed some givens from second language research that undermine much of pre-1970s theory about how second language acquisition happens. You may remember that we briefly explored five observations about second language acquisition:

1. SLA involves the creation of an implicit (unconscious) linguistic system.
2. SLA is complex and consists of different processes.
3. SLA is dynamic but slow.
4. Most L2 learners fall short of native-like competence.
5. Skill acquisition is different from the creation of an implicit system.

Although for scholars and researchers in second language acquisition these are accepted findings that have caused a radical shift in perspective from that of the 1950s, many instructors (and students, as well) still labor under certain unstated assumptions about how grammar (or language in general) is acquired by adolescents and adults. In this chapter we explore some of these (mis)conceptions and discuss why traditional approaches to grammar instruction are not effective in promoting acquisition. Even though it might be useful to reread the relevant sections of Chapter 1 to refresh your memory, that will not be necessary for this chapter. You should keep in the back of your mind as we continue a major point accepted by all researchers in second language acquisition: *There is no acquisition without input,* defined as communicative or meaning-bearing language that learners hear.

A FIRST THOUGHT

Have you ever asked yourself how people acquired second languages before there was schooling or universities? How did people who never had a written version acquire their second languages? Think about the following scenarios:

- Trade between ancient cultures
- American Indian tribes engaged in negotiation about land
- Spanish missionaries working with indigenous populations in Latin America
- Bilingual households resulting from the marriage of two people from different cultures

You may remember the movie *Dances with Wolves,* in which Kevin Costner plays a Civil War veteran who strikes out on his own in the Old West (what is now the Dakotas region of the northern Great Plains). In this movie, he becomes sympathetic to the Lakota tribes and, bit by bit, adopts their ways. The character learns the local dialect of Lakota and, for all intents and purposes, is integrated into their culture. Although a work of fiction, *Dances with Wolves* suggests that people must have learned languages outside of a school setting in the past and may have been quite successful in doing so.

What then of all our treasured notions of teaching language, especially our insistence that people have to "master the grammar"? One possible conclusion is that our ideas about language teaching, especially the teaching of grammar as a necessary part of language acquisition, may be artifacts of the culture of institutionalized education. As Musumeci (1997) has shown, many of our current conceptions about how languages are acquired and how they should be taught have not always been staples of education; perhaps much of our methodology is a result not of what we know about acquisition but of poor translation between theory and research and the classroom.

SOME (MIS)CONCEPTIONS

In this section, we review some often-unstated beliefs that people have about learning grammar. As you read, you may want to ask to what extent you hold these beliefs or to what extent you think previous (and perhaps current) instructors you have worked with share them.

Belief 1: That's the Way I Learned, So . . .

It is not uncommon for people to generalize from their experiences. As a human trait, we tend to put ourselves at the center of the universe as we compare and contrast what we see around us. Without disconfirming evidence, we may believe that something that happened to us is typical or that the way we learned to do something is the best way. Another aspect of human thought is how people arrive at conclusions about cause and effect. It is not atypical (nor completely unrealistic) to think that because A preceded B, A must have *caused* B. John Doe was drinking in a bar (A). On the way home he had an accident (B). Thus, his drinking (A) caused the accident (B). Although many times such logic may be true, it is not always the case. For example, Mary Smith took her "lucky shirt" with her to Las Vegas (A). While in Vegas, she won a $100,000 jackpot (B). Thus, she believes that wearing her shirt (A) caused her win (B). In this scenario, we really cannot ascribe any causative attributes to Mary's shirt. She won the jackpot because she happened to be in the right place at the right time.

In each of the examples, the individual might generalize his or her experience. If John tells people, "Don't drink and drive," he would not be far off the mark. There is abundant evidence of the relationship between drinking and accidents. However, if Mary said, "Be sure to take something lucky with you when you gamble," we could question her advice; there is no corroborating evidence that this will help others. Her experience does not generalize.

In the case of language teaching and learning, those of us who work with instructors often hear something like, "Well, I learned it this way . . .," with the implication that the way the person *thinks* he or she learned language is the way that language is learned in general. These instructors genuinely believe that what they did as learners in classrooms when they first started studying French, Spanish, German, or Russian caused their acquisition. It is difficult for them to accept the some thirty-five years of accumulated research in second language acquisition based on hundreds if not thousands of learners from different contexts. What such instructors are experiencing is A-before-B logic. Because they got explanations, because they practiced drills, and because they wrote out exercises, they think this is how they came to be advanced speakers of another language. Again, it is a human trait to think this way. But in the context of language learning, there are two fundamental flaws in this line of reasoning.

The first flaw is to overlook what else happened to them over the course of the years they were learning the language. Here are some experiences that most advanced speakers of another language have probably had:

- Extensive reading (magazines, literature, newspapers, comic strips)
- Study abroad or immersion
- Conversations and interactions with natives or more advanced speakers (while abroad, on the job where they teach, with professors while they were students, with people they may have met at the university or college)
- Watching TV or movies (while abroad or at home)

In addition, if we add to this the fact that the typical language teacher has the desire to commit time to continue beyond basic language courses, then affective reasons come into play in how far that person gets in language learning. In short, there is much more to what makes a person an advanced speaker of another language than what happened early on in his or her language courses. What is common to all advanced learners of a language is exposure to lots of communicative or meaning-bearing input (Larsen-Freeman & Long, 1991). In addition, these persons were probably engaged in quite a bit of conversational interaction with others. Such interaction, it has been suggested (Gass, 1997), is conducive to language acquisition because learners help manage the conversation by their participation. Negotiation leads to better input by other speakers as rephrasing and repetition bring linguistic data into focus. In the following example, Bob and Tom are having a conversation in a tennis locker room. Bob is a native speaker of English, and Tom's first language is Chinese.

BOB: So where's Dave [Tom's tennis partner]?
TOM: He vacation.
BOB: He's on vacation?
TOM: Yes. On vacation.
BOB: Lucky guy.

In this brief interaction, Bob made what is called a "confirmation check" with his question, "He's on vacation?" He was surprised that Dave would be on vacation and wanted to make sure he understood. Notice how in Tom's first statement he omitted the preposition *on*. But because he was participating actively and no new information was being conveyed, he was able to notice the preposition used with the word *vacation* in Bob's question. He thus subsequently used it in his own confirming statement, revealing that he got some kind of linguistic data out of the interaction.

Such interactions are discussed widely in the literature, and it has been suggested more than once that input plus interaction is the most optimal context for language acquisition. The point here, however, is that advanced nonnative speakers have most likely been involved in lots of interactions that have helped them get linguistic data from the input they might not otherwise have gotten (or might have gotten more slowly over time). These advanced nonnatives were not limited to basic language courses. Thus, based on what we know now, a more reasonable conclusion would be this: Language teachers who are advanced speakers of another language acquired their ability *in spite of the instruction* or *independently of the instruction* they received early on.

The second major flaw in the A-before-B logic is that B is often left unexamined. What does it mean to have learned something? To have acquired language? You may remember from Chapter 1 the idea that advanced learners come to know much more about language than they could have been taught or could have learned "on purpose." That is, the implicit system contains greater and richer information than what can be found in any set of instructional materials. To take a concrete example, let's look at some research presented in the late 1990s on learners of Spanish. These learners were in the initial stages of acquisition. The research (VanPatten & Mandell, 1999) reported on the grammaticality judgments of learners who were fourth-semester students of Spanish. They were asked whether certain sentences were possible or not in Spanish. If the sentence was impossible, they had to correct it. At the same time, they had to indicate whether their judgments were based on a rule they had learned (or something they were corrected on) or whether they judged by feel (e.g., "Not sure why. It just seems right/wrong."). Some of the sentences contained structures they had learned and practiced as part of their materials, such as the distinction between the two copular verbs *ser* and *estar* in Spanish.

Others contained structures they were not taught and were not corrected on (because they would never have produced such things). Examples include the placement of adverbs between verbs and objects, which is possible in Spanish but not in English (e.g., *Juan ve a menudo televisión* but not *John watches often television*), and "verb deletion," which is possible in English but not in Spanish (e.g., *John has visited Spain but Mary has not* is possible, but *Juan ha visitado España pero María no ha* is not). The researchers found that learners were overwhelmingly correct about the learned rules and also generally reported them as something they learned and for which they could offer a rule. For the other examples, learners were also overwhelmingly correct in their judgments but tended to report that they judged by feel. (In the cases where they claimed to know a rule, they made one up.) How did these learners come to know (so early) about these properties of grammar when they were never taught them? How did they come to this knowledge when these structures are not the kinds of things learners attempt to produce and get feedback on in the early stages? Clearly, something was happening that occurred independently of instruction.

Again, to be sure, this does not mean that everyone arrives at a native-like competence, but it does indicate that acquisition is not the result of instruction plus practice. It is also worth noting that most learners fall short of native-like abilities. The flip side of the issue just addressed is the following: Why do most learners never become native-like when they get instruction?

The point we wish to make here, then, is that acquisition cannot be reduced to what we did in the early stages of learning—at least not the kind of teaching-learning practices that are still prevalent in most classrooms. We must be cautious in projecting our experiences onto acquisition in general, and we must not ignore the findings of all the research we have so far.

Pause to consider . . .

how a traditional approach in instruction perpetuates itself. What does a novice teacher do when confronted with the classroom for the first time? What do novice teachers find in textbooks? How do these textbooks influence the teacher's belief system?

Belief 2: Drills Are Effective Tools for Learning Grammar

Drills, sometimes called "exercises," are found in almost all textbooks today, even those that are touted as "communicative" or "proficiency oriented." These books tend to follow a particular sequencing of practice types after a grammar point is explained. That sequence is the following:

Mechanical drills → Meaningful drills → Communicative drills

The classification of drills as *mechanical, meaningful,* or *communicative* is based on the degree of learner control over the response: whether or not there is one right answer, and whether or not the answer is already known to those participating in the interaction (see Paulston, 1972, for the origin of this classification). The classification is based also on whether or not learners need to understand either what is said to them or what they themselves are saying in order to complete the drill successfully.

Mechanical Drills

Mechanical drills are those during which the student need not attend to meaning and for which there is only one correct response. A classic example of a mechanical drill is the following, which is the first exercise in a series to practice object pronouns.

Change the sentence, substituting object pronouns for the direct object.

> *Juan pone los vasos en la mesa.* → *Juan los pone en la mesa.*
> (*las copas, la comida, el plato, la cafetera, las tortillas*)
>
> John puts the glasses on the table. → John puts *them* on the table.
> (the wine glasses, the food, the plate, the coffee pot, the tortillas)

As you read over the drill, it should become clear that the learner need not understand what she is saying in order to complete the drill. You can test this idea by substituting nonsense words for any content word in the drill. For example, if you substitute the fictitious Spanish words *gaga, momos,* and *posa* for *pone, vasos,* and *mesa,* respectively, you can still perform the drill: *Juan gaga los momos en la posa* → *Juan los gaga en la posa.* (The learner *may* understand what is being said; the point is that the learner *does not have to*.) In addition to an absence of meaning in this drill, there is one and only one response; anything other than making the correct substitution with an object pronoun is simply wrong.

Meaningful Drills

The difference between mechanical and meaningful drills is that the learner must attend to the meaning of both the stimulus and her own answer in order to complete the meaningful drill successfully. Yet there is still only one right answer, and the answer is already known to the participants. For example, in the following meaningful drill, the learner must understand what is being said to him in order to respond to the instructor, but everyone knows what the answer will be since there is no new information contained in it.

Answer each question using an object pronoun.

> 1. *¿Dónde pone Juan sus libros al entrar en la clase?*
>   (Instructor points to where Juan's books are.)
> 2. *¿Dónde pone María su chaqueta?* (Points to chair.)
> 3. *¿Dónde pongo yo mis cosas al entrar?*
>
> 1. Where does John put his books when he arrives in class?
> 2. Where does Mary put her jacket?
> 3. Where do I put my things when I come in?

Although there is a focus on meaning in this type of practice, the actual message contained in the learner's utterance is restricted to one response; everyone can see where John's books are as the teacher points to them, so the only possible answer to the question "Where does John put his books when he arrives in class?" is "He puts them on the floor." Note that the quality and quantity of meaning are not considered in these classifications. Although there is meaning involved in meaningful drills, we can question just how "meaningful" they really are, given these constraints on learner responses.

Communicative Drills

Unlike the previous two drill types, communicative drills require attention to meaning, and the information contained in the learner's answer is new and unknown to the person asking the question. Thus, the answer cannot be deemed right or wrong in terms of meaning conveyed. Here is an example of a communicative drill to practice object pronouns.

Working with a partner, ask and answer "Yes/No" questions using the cues as guides. If you are answering a question, use an object pronoun in your answer.

MODELO: *tocar/el piano*
        A: *¿Tocas el piano?*
        B: *No, no* lo *toco.*

1. *padres/llamar por teléfono*
2. *hacer/la tarea*
3. *ver/al profesor*

MODEL: to play/the piano
        A: Do you play the piano?
        B: No, I don't play *it.*

1. parents/call on the phone
2. to do/the homework
3. to see/the professor

As you can see in this example, a learner cannot complete the practice without understanding the message in the stimulus questions. He must know what *¿Tocas el piano?* means in order to answer the question. In addition, his response is not anticipated; although we are expecting a "Yes" or "No" as an answer, we do not know which it will be because the answer is presumably based on his own life.

Pause to consider . . .

just how communicative most communicative drills really are. Do learners always pay attention to the meaning of utterances in these drill types? Examine the items listed for the partner activity just described. How much communication is really taking place? Rate the activity on a scale of 1 to 5 with 1 being not very communicative and 5 being very communicative. Explain your rating.

We summarize this section by noting that, although learners are always speaking or writing when engaged in traditional grammar practice, a great deal of grammar instruction is neither meaningful nor communicative. Traditional grammar practice is largely mechanical, with the focus exclusively on using a grammatical feature to *produce* some sort of utterance. A focus on message and a focus on input are simply absent when it comes to grammar.

The question we must ask ourselves is whether such practices—especially mechanical drills—are effective for second language acquisition. The answer is No. In one important study, Lightbown (1983) demonstrated that not only was intensive drilling ineffective, it actually delayed the acquisition of the structures and forms that were drilled. The students she observed were drilled intensively on certain rules of English, only to have the natural orders of acquisition (Chapter 1) reassert themselves within one year. Research conducted since the late 1980s suggests that learners who are engaged in meaningful or meaning-based approaches to grammar (called *focus on form*) do as well as or better than those who are engaged in activities that are nonmeaningful or not part of some communicative intent. In a widely cited book (Doughty & Williams, 1998), several focus on form approaches are discussed and the research is evaluated. What is common to all the approaches, however, is that a focus on form was never divorced from meaning; the last sentence of the book is very important:

> Finally, and most important of all, we have proposed that, whatever the pedagogical decision at hand, the primary concern of the teacher should always be the question of how to *integrate* attention to form and meaning, either simultaneously or in some interconnected sequence of tasks and techniques that are implemented throughout the curriculum.
>
> (Doughty & Williams, 1998, p. 261)

In Chapter 7, we outline an approach to focus on form that integrates form and meaning. We also summarize a body of research that clearly shows how focus on form is superior to traditional instruction that relies on mechanical drills and the sequencing of drills as described earlier. And later in the present chapter, we outline the major problem with a traditional approach to grammar in the classroom.

Belief 3: Explicit Explanation Is Necessary

Almost all grammar instruction begins with some kind of presentation or explanation of the form or structure about to be practiced. Learners may be given verb charts and receive information on how the verbs "work." They may be given lists of rules on how to use the subjunctive. They may receive explanations that contrast subject and object pronouns or the accusative and dative cases. Teachers expect to see these in textbooks, and learners expect to see them as well—and very often teachers are evaluated on how well they are able to explain grammatical points.

That adolescents and adults want to know how something works before they engage in some activity is to be expected. How many times have you been told something like "Put out your hands, palms up" or "Pull out your wallet" only to respond "Why?" In learning languages, this behavior is carried over. More often than not, it is made necessary by the type of instruction. If we know that the point of a lesson is to learn the past tense or object pronouns, and we also know that we are going to be tested explicitly on the past tense or the object pronouns, we want to know as much as we can to increase our chances of being successful. But is taking a test on the past tense or object pronouns some manifestation of language acquisition? If not, is the explicit information we are given about what we are learning still necessary?

By now you may guess that such paper-and-pencil tests are not tests of acquisition. They are tests of what we have explicitly learned and explicitly practiced. In second language acquisition, the relationship between explicit knowledge (and by extension explicit practice such as that described in the previous section) has been the cause of much debate, but the evidence is indicating that explicit information—although we may like it and it makes us feel good about what we're doing—is not necessary for successful acquisition.

Let's return to the idea that we often know more about language than we could possibly have been taught. Many of these aspects of the grammar are based on very abstract notions of linguistic theory, none of which are translatable to pedagogical grammars (the kinds of grammars we use in textbooks). As an example, recall the sentences with *wanna* from Chapter 1, repeated here, and also consider the contractions with *'ve* shown in (4) and (6).

1. Who do you wanna invite to the party?
2. Who do you wanna bring the potato chips to the party?
3. Who do you wanta bring the potato chips to the party?
4. You've done it!
5. Should you have done it?
6. Should you've done it?

All are perfectly fine sentences except for (2) and (6), as long as we pronounce *you've* as [yuv] and not as *you of*. *You of* represents a reduction of *you have* that retains some kind of vowel quality for the auxiliary verb, whereas *'ve* represents a complete deletion of the vowel and the attachment of the remaining consonant to the preceding word. The question is, What are the rules for contraction? They are far more abstract and complex than can be explained here. For example, contractions, though on the surface dissimilar, are all constrained by an aspect of syntax (sentence structure) called *trace theory*. The idea of trace theory is that languages do not allow contractions across traces. So what is a trace? To define *trace*, we have to talk about movement rules. What's a movement rule? To talk about movement rules, we have to talk about surface word order and underlying word order. We begin to see the problem; there is no simple explanation of the rules that permit or disallow contraction.

Aside from the knowledge of abstract rules that we all develop without any explicit instruction, research on nontraditional approaches to grammar strongly suggests that explicit information (explanation of forms and rules) is not necessary. In VanPatten and Oikennon (1996), for example, three groups of learners were compared on their learning of object pronouns and word order rules in Spanish: a processing instruction group (described in Chapter 7), a structured input only group (also described in Chapter 7) that received no explanation, and an explanation-only group. On a pretest/posttest experiment, the first two groups made significant improvements and were not different from each other. The explanation-only group made no improvements. The conclusion was that the activities alone (the structured input activities) constituted the necessary and sufficient aspect of the instruction that would lead to learners' improvement.

Since the publication of VanPatten and Oikennon (1996), other studies have emerged that support the findings that explanation is not necessary for acquisition. An excellent replication study of VanPatten's and Oikennon's research is one conducted by Sanz and Morgan-Short (2003), in which all instruction happened via computer with no instructor. The researchers found that not only is explanation unnecessary, but with carefully constructed activities, even feedback seems to be unnecessary (and unhelpful, for that matter). Benati (2003) has replicated the same results in Italian with the teaching and learning of the future tense; Farley (2003) has shown that the Spanish subjunctive can be learned without explanation; and Wong (2003) has shown that two structures in French were learnable without explanation: the causative with the verb *faire* and the *de* versus *du / de la / des* distinction with *avoir*.

To be sure, some research has shown that explanation may be beneficial early on to help learners get into acquisition more quickly (see, for example, some of the papers in Schmidt, 1995). However, no research that we know of has demonstrated that explanation or explicit information is *necessary* for acquisition. As for the few studies that suggest explicit information is useful, the results may be due to the type of instruction used.

Pause to consider . . .

what role explicit information plays if it is not integral to acquisition. Many researchers believe that explicit information resides in some kind of conscious knowledge store (like any other "facts" we know) and can be used as a monitoring device to "repair" utterances as learners generate them. Learners can actually perform beyond their competence because they can consult this conscious knowledge to make their sentences sound more grammatical. What is your reaction to this position? How useful do you think this knowledge is in real-time conversation? Does level of proficiency make a difference?

Belief 4: The First Language Is the Source of All Errors

As we saw in Chapter 1 when we discussed the Atlas Complex and behaviorism, it was believed prior to the 1960s that second language acquisition consisted of establishing new habits and suppressing the old ones (those of the first language). Thus, the first language was viewed as the "problem" to be overcome or combated or eradicated during instruction and learning. And great care was taken not to let learners make errors, since this would lead to prolonged interference from the first language.

This notion of acquisition still prevails in many teachers' minds, largely because of the kinds of tasks learners face. Whenever learners have to perform beyond their current (implicit) competence, they have no choice but to use their first language to generate sentences or utterances that they then "dress up" in second language words. The result is language that is filled with first language–like errors. However, the research that emerged in the 1970s suggested something quite different. The first analysis of learner spontaneous speech suggested that first language–like errors did not even constitute one-half of the errors they made. LoCoco (1975), for example, found that only 23 percent of the errors made by learners of German (English as the first language) were traceable to the first language. In another study (LoCoco, 1976), just over 13 percent of the errors made by learners of Spanish (again English as the first language) were L1-like in nature. In a 1977 study, White found that 20.6 percent of the errors her Spanish-speaking subjects learning English made were L1-like. In short, more "naturalistic data," that is, data collected using techniques other than those teachers often use to examine student progress, revealed a much different picture than was believed to be the case.

Since then, L1 transfer (or interference) has been examined from a variety of perspectives, and although there is still debate about its role in second language acquisition (see, for example, the discussion in White, 2000, and the edited volumes by Gass & Selinker, 1983/1992), no one in theory or research perceives it to be the linguistic "bogeyman" that seemed to prevail in the days of behaviorism and audiolingualism. First language influence in SLA is seen to be natural and a part of the process that learners must undergo as they slowly and in piecemeal fashion construct an implicit mental representation of the language. The fact that instructors may still believe that the L1 is the source of all problems in acquisition and that textbooks often make contrasts between the learners' L1 and the second language being learned suggests that crucial research has not trickled down to teaching practice; perhaps what teachers "see" is a result of the way in which language is taught, practiced, and tested.

Belief 5: Acquisition Involves the Learning of Paradigms

In linguistics, a *paradigm* is a representation that displays the various forms of a given grammatical structure. Although we often think of paradigms as verb paradigms, the concept of a paradigm is readily applied to nouns, articles, relative pronouns, and other grammatical features. Following are sample paragraphs from Spanish, French, and German, respectively, that illustrate the various uses of paradigms.

127

Some (Mis)conceptions

paradigms from Spanish, French, and German, respectively, that illustrate the various uses of paradigms.

Spanish Verbs That Take -g

hacer *(to do; to make)*		poner *(to put; to place)*		salir *(to leave; to go out)*	
hago	hacemos	pongo	ponemos	salgo	salimos
haces	hacéis	pones	ponéis	sales	salís
hace	hacen	pone	ponen	sale	salen

French Contractions of à *and* de *with the Definite Articles* le *and* les

à + le = **au**	de + le = **du**
à + les = **aux**	de + les = **des**

German Personal Pronouns in the Accusative

Singular		**Plural**	
mich	*me*	uns	*us*
Sie	*you*	Sie	*you*
dich	*you*	ihr	*you*
ihn	*him, it*		
sie	*her, it*	sie	*them*
es	*it*		

Paradigms, it should be noted, are abstractions and generalizations. They are tools to organize information and present data, but they do not correspond to the way knowledge is structured in the brain. What is especially important is that paradigms represent neither the way morphological forms are acquired nor the order in which they are acquired. As argued by a number of linguists and psycholinguists (see, for example, Bybee, 1991), paradigms do not exist in native speakers' heads unless put there by teachers or books. The child who enters elementary school in Argentina is perfectly capable of using most verb forms in Spanish and has not memorized a grid explicitly marked with categories such as "singular/plural" and "first/second/third person." That child already possesses a complex network of form-meaning connections in which the form *pienso* ("I think") is connected not only to the concept of "present tense" but also to *pensé* (preterit tense, "I thought"), *pensamiento* (the noun, "thought"), and so on.

Likewise, the second language learner develops an equally complex, albeit in most cases incomplete, network of lexical items that does not resemble any paradigm in a textbook. Bybee, for example, uses the type of diagram shown in Figure 6.1 to illustrate how morphological information can be connected in the mind. (Note: *saber* = to know, *cantar* = to sing, *comer* = to eat, *sabio* = wise, *canción* = song, *comida* = meal, food.)

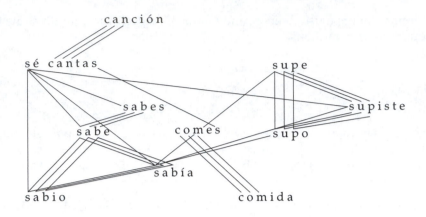

FIGURE 6.1 Mental network of verb associations in Spanish
Source: Adapted from Bybee, 1991, pp. 82–83

What Bybee suggests is that the psychological status of inflections and forms might come about only as learners *internalize whole words that contain those inflections.* Thus, a learner might internalize the verb *sé* first and then *sabe.* The *restructuring process* (the process that accommodates new linguistic data into the developing system) makes a connection between their common verb roots since their meanings are obviously connected (both involve the process of "knowing"). The learner might then internalize *sabes, cantas,* and *comes,* and still other connections begin to form in the mind (again, due to unconscious *restructuring*), this time related to verb endings. Learners might then get input data about the preterit (simple past) tense, and other connections begin to be made. The process continues, the connections becoming more and more complex and intertwined. Note that as learners acquire nouns and other words, these will also become connected to verbs if they share a root representing overlapping meanings *(comes, comida).* A paradigm, then, is actually a shorthand for a particular set of connections; paradigms have no psycholinguistic validity for acquisition.

The last idea, that such paradigms lack any psycholinguistic validity, is an interesting one. Children, for example, acquire a first language quite well without the use of paradigms. Bilinguals from birth or from an early age also acquire languages without paradigms. And if we think back to our "first thought" in this chapter, that there was language learning before there was institutionalized education, we realize that nonclassroom learners have acquired a good deal of language without paradigms. Why then do teachers and learners think they need them?

If the goal of a lesson is to learn the grammar and to be tested on the grammar, then it makes perfect sense to use such shorthand devices. They represent neat summaries from which to teach and to study and review. However, if the goal of a lesson is to learn how to perform particular tasks (see Chapters 3 and 4), then paradigms lose their immediacy in the class. You may recall from Chapter 4 that as we examine any information-exchange task and ask ourselves, "What exactly do learners need to know in order to perform this task?" we often conclude that they only need to know part of a rule or only parts of a

paragigm. In such cases, then, paradigms not only reveal their lack of psycholinguistic validity, they tend to lose their classroom immediacy as well. We
will touch upon this again in Chapter 7.

THE LIMITED EFFECTS OF INSTRUCTION

In the previous section, we reviewed and discussed some commonly held ideas
about the acquisition of language, especially grammar. We turn now to some
important research that also pushes us to question many of our long-held
notions. As the evidence on acquisition accumulated, researchers began to turn
their attention to the following question: Does instruction make a difference?
That is, does *explicit instruction* in grammar, together with practice, error correction, and so forth, have any significant effect on how learners acquire a language? The findings have stirred quite a debate in the profession, for they
delighted some theorists and bothered some instructors.

Research Findings on Instruction

One of the first findings to emerge was that acquisition orders do not match
instructional orders. That is, the emergence of verb inflections, noun endings,
functors, and even syntactic patterns did not necessarily match the order in which
they were taught and practiced. English third-person -*s,* for example, is a verb
morpheme taught early in most ESL programs. Yet, as we saw in the previous
section, it is one of the last verb morphemes to be acquired in speech. In one
study mentioned earlier, Lightbown (1983) reports that intense practice in the
language forms she investigated resulted in *overlearning* (use in linguistic contexts where the item should not be used) but that this overlearning disappeared
and the learners went right back to following the natural orders of acquisition.
And Pica (1983) found almost the same orders of acquisition in three very distinct sets of learners of English: foreign language learners in Mexico, classroom
learners in Philadelphia, and nonclassroom learners in Pennsylvania. These and
other investigations all yielded the same results: Explicit instruction and practice
did very little, if anything, to alter acquisition orders. Learners seemed to follow
a particular path on their way to developing the second language system, regardless of the order in which grammatical features were taught.

A second finding of classroom-based research is that explicit grammar
instruction does not circumvent "natural" stages of development. That is,
explicit grammar instruction does not seem to affect stages of development.
Learners still tend to pass through stages, make overgeneralizations (for
example, generalize regular past tense endings to irregular verbs), and so
forth, regardless of instruction. In a particularly notable study, Ellis (1984)
found that learners of English in the classroom who were exposed to instruction and practice nonetheless exhibited the same stages of development in
the acquisition of negation and other structures as did nonclassroom learners. In a later study, Ellis (1989) examined the acquisition of German word
order in foreign language learners in Great Britain. He found that even though
they received explicit instruction and practice, their stages of development
matched those observed in nonclassroom learners (of various L1s) who

learned German "naturally" in Germany. Kaplan (1987) found that foreign language learners of French in the United States exhibited patterns of development in the acquisition of the *passé composé* and the *imparfait* that were strikingly similar to those of nonclassroom learners (with a different L1) in France. And if you recall VanPatten's findings on the acquisition of *ser* and *estar* (pp. 19–20), it is notable that the very first stage of acquisition is the absence of copular (linking) verbs altogether. How could this be when the instructors clearly did not teach or practice with their students the erroneous omission of linking verbs? These studies and others all suggest that the learner is guided by some internal mechanisms and that instruction simply cannot override what these mechanisms do.

Pause to consider . . .

what other learning situations might or might not be affected by explicit instruction. In which of the following do you think instruction might make a difference? In which might the effects of instruction not significantly affect the stages that a person needs to go through to master the skill and internalize the intricacies of the behavior?

playing tennis	sewing
playing poker	writing a good term paper
riding a bike	jumping rope with children

In any of these learning situations, do you think that instruction might be a *hindrance?* In which of them do you think lots of input (seeing how others do it, watching the activity in real-life contexts) might be the most critical ingredient in learning?

A third finding of classroom-based research is that language produced by learners on grammar-focused tests does not necessarily match that found in communicative speech. On tests, learners of English might be able to supply third-person *-s* correctly on fill-in-the-blank and short-answer tests, although they omit this verb inflection when using the language to communicate information outside (and often inside!) the classroom. Likewise, learners of Spanish might correctly write on a test *tuve* ("I had") only to use later in conversation **tení* (an overgeneralization of the regular past tense forms) or even **tuví*. In one study of classroom learners of Spanish in Southern California, Terrell, Baycroft, and Perrone (1987) investigated what classroom learners could do with the subjunctive. Their subjects did quite well on the paper-and-pencil tests of the subjunctive that they gave, scoring an average of 23 out of 25 when asked to complete sentences such as *Juan José quiere que su hermana _____ en casa esta tarde (quedarse)* "John Joseph wants his sister _____ at home this afternoon (to stay)." But when given a communicative task, namely, to talk about topics such as "Who would you like to marry?" and "What are your plans for this summer?" the subjects produced utterances such as **Quiero que mi esposo a tener buen sentido de humor* ("I want my husband to have a good sense of humor"),

Mi padre me quiere ir a la escuela ("My father wants me to go to school"), and *El no quiere que yo trabajo* ("He doesn't want me to work"). In fact, the scores on the communicative task revealed that only 12 percent of the utterances produced by the learners contained any uses of the subjunctive that were correct in both verb form and sentence structure. Why was there such a discrepancy between tests and speech?

Krashen (1982) has suggested that learners receiving explicit grammar instruction may develop a conscious *Monitor*, a kind of "grammar police" that can edit for correct use of grammar and syntax only under certain conditions. These conditions are (1) when the learner needs to produce a correct sentence and (2) when there is time to do it (such as on a written test as opposed to in naturally occurring conversation). Krashen posits the Monitor as responsible for the difference between the language produced on form-focused tests and other kinds of language production. Krashen has further suggested that the system used during communicative interaction is a system independent of the Monitor. This other system he calls the *acquired system*, which is built up over time from exposure to comprehensible input. It is now widely accepted that learners' grammatical accuracy depends on the kinds of tasks they are engaged in.

To be sure, the overall picture of instruction is not completely negative. Classroom learners have been found to approximate normative (that is, native-like) use of grammar more than have nonclassroom learners. Thus, those who receive instruction seem to go further in terms of acquiring more of the grammar of the language. And the rate of acquisition of grammar seems to be sped up by instruction. But we should examine just why classroom learners might do better in the long run compared to nonclassroom learners.

Is Classroom Learning Superior?

Currently, three reasons may account for the so-called superiority of classroom learners. First, classroom learners tend to be exposed to a wider range of language data than are nonclassroom learners. The latter have often been immigrants of lower socioeconomic classes who move to another country for economic or political reasons, and their exposure to language in the new country is frequently limited to conversational language. Classroom language learners, on the other hand, get exposure not only to conversational language but also to the language of written texts, speeches, and other types of *planned discourse*. Planned discourse tends to contain more complex syntax (more clauses, conjunctions, passives), broader vocabulary, and a wider range of grammatical structures. In the following newspaper excerpt, note the generally more complex sentences and broader vocabulary than would normally be found in conversational language:

> COLUMBUS, Ohio—Proponents of the intelligent-design movement, which challenges Darwin's primacy in the science classroom, argued on Monday for equal footing in the state's new teaching curriculum, while critics warned that speculative theories of some ultimate agent underpinning evolution were the antithesis of true science. . . .
> [Professor Lawrence] Krauss argued that while much remained to be

discovered about natural selection, Darwin's theory had only grown in strength through decades of experimentation and discovery that intelligent design had not been subjected to.

(From the New York Times News Service as published in the *Chicago Tribune*, March 12, 2002, p. 10)

The second reason suggested for the apparent superiority of classroom learning is that instruction heightens learners' awareness of grammatical form and structure, perhaps making forms more salient in the input. In this way, learners are simply more apt to notice grammatical forms and pay attention to them in the language they hear and see. Sharwood Smith (1993) has coined a term for grammar instruction, suggesting that it be thought of as *input enhancement*. Grammar instruction might thus help learners to perceive what is in the input. This term makes great sense given the critical role of comprehensible input. In Chapter 7 we examine grammar instruction and input in more detail as we rethink explicit instruction as *structured input*.

A final reason for classroom learners going further and learning more in the long run may be that they "self-select." Those classroom learners who keep studying languages might simply be a special subset of learners with certain characteristics. Most people in the United States study languages because they have to, completing only those requirements that allow them to earn a degree or certificate. However, those who venture beyond the basic requirements could have motivation and an affinity for language learning that spurs them on. They continue to elect language classes, study more and more grammar, and even major in the language or study abroad. At this latter stage, it becomes hard to tell what happens to these learners: As we noted before, are they better now because they have had so much explicit instruction? Or are they better because they have been exposed to so much input and have had a natural disposition to process more of it?

To summarize, instruction does not seem to have the effect many instructors think it does. Learners evidently go about doing what they need to do anyway to build an implicit linguistic system. Before concluding this chapter, let's look at the typical kind of instruction that has been the focus of our attention and ask ourselves why it does not make the difference we thought it might.

INPUT AND TRADITIONAL INSTRUCTION

As we have said since Chapter 1, acquisition involves the creation of an implicit linguistic system, one that exists outside of awareness. As we discussed how this system comes to be, we outlined certain processes involved in acquisition: input processing, accommodation, restructuring, and output processing. Let us now put these ideas together in a schematic form. Again, learners build an implicit mental representation of the language they are learning. They access this system to create utterances, that is, to speak. We can depict this in the following way:

Developing System $\rightarrow$ Output

Recall that comprehensible, meaning-bearing input is a necessary ingredient for successful acquisition. To put this in other terms, input is the raw data that learners use to construct their systems. Using input data, learners make "form-meaning" connections that become part of the developing system.

$$\text{Input} \rightarrow \text{Developing System} \rightarrow \text{Output}$$

We know, however, that learners process input as they attempt to comprehend the messages contained in it. Processing the input involves "filtering" it in various ways. What learners actually wind up with after processing the input is a reduced, sometimes slightly altered set of input data that theorists call *intake*. The brain uses intake, and not raw input data, to create a linguistic system.

$$\text{Input} \rightarrow \text{Intake} \rightarrow \text{Developing System} \rightarrow \text{Output}$$

What intake data actually look like may or may not resemble what we, as language instructors and advanced speakers of the language, think that learners are "perceiving" in the input. We will return to the concept of intake shortly, for it is an important one.

Note the contradiction between traditional grammar practice and our model of acquisition. The development of an internal system is input dependent; it happens when learners receive and process meaning-bearing input. Traditional grammar practice, on the other hand, is exclusively output oriented. That is, learners get an explanation and are then led through output practices; all of the drill types reviewed in the previous section require learners to produce the language. Under this traditional scenario, how is the developing system provided with relevant input data that is both comprehensible and meaningful? Because it focuses on output, traditional grammar instruction engages those processes involved in *accessing* a developing system rather than those involved in forming the system. (We return to the topic of access and output in Chapter 8 when we discuss structured output activities.) The development of an internal system does not happen because learners practice output. Although practice with output may help with fluency and accuracy in production, it is not "responsible" for getting the grammar into the learner's head to begin with. In short, traditional grammar instruction, which is intended to cause a change in the developing system, is akin to putting the cart before the horse as it relates to acquisition; the learner is asked to produce when the developing system has not yet had a chance to build up a representation of the language based on input data. In Figure 6.2, we see the

FIGURE 6.2 Traditional practice in grammar

point at which traditional grammar practice has its effect: It acts on output, not on input.

Clearly, there are processes earlier in the sequence of events that should be addressed by instruction. It is reasonable to wonder whether grammar instruction focusing on input is more appropriate than traditional approaches to grammar instruction, in which learners are immediately engaged in production. What would happen if explicit instruction in grammar involved the manipulation of both input and input processing in some way? What if the input were structured to encourage richer grammatical intake? These questions are addressed in Chapter 7.

Pause to consider . . .

the output-based nature of traditional grammar instruction, especially the use of mechanical drills. Why do you think drilling and output are so entrenched in the minds of many language instructors and materials developers? (*Hint:* Think about the theoretical underpinnings of Audiolingual Methodology from Chapter 1.)

SUMMARY

In this chapter, we have reviewed a number of teachers' (and students') ideas about how languages are learned. In all cases, we have found these ideas to be questionable at best. We have also reviewed some important research that suggests that instructional efforts do not have the effect we thought they had and that the internal processes learners take to the task of acquisition always seem to assert themselves. Traditional approaches to instruction, then, that involve explanation plus practice in making sentences (usually involving some sequencing of drilling or exercises) are simply not effective.

These conclusions do not necessarily mean, however, that no instructional intervention can be effective or that learners can indeed do it all on their own. What the conclusions do lead us to is a rethinking of what that instructional intervention might be. In Doughty and Williams (1998), a variety of such nontraditional interventions are reviewed, but some are speculative and some result in less than stellar results in terms of the research conducted on them. In Chapter 7 we review a type of grammar instruction that does not succumb to these pitfalls. Indeed, not only does it enjoy a strong theoretical base but it also is supported by a good deal of research. This is good: Rather than rely on speculative ideas or old ways of working with grammar in the classroom, as a profession we would much prefer to say that we are working with methods and techniques that have strong empirical support. In this way, we can say that we are attempting to blend both art and science in the classroom.

institutionalized education

misconceptions about grammar in
  teaching and learning
    that's the way I learned
      cause and effect
      input and interaction
      knowing more than what is
        taught
    drills are effective
      mechanical versus meaningful
        versus communicative drills
      delaying acquisition
      form integrated with meaning
    explicit information is necessary
      some things are unexplainable
      research on explicit
        information
    the first language is the source of
      errors

being forced to produce
  beyond your competence
  research on L1-like errors
learners acquire paradigms
  network of lexical items
  psycholinguistic validity
limited effects of instruction
  acquisition orders versus
    instructional orders
  stages of development versus
    instruction
  the "superiority" of classroom
    learning
    planned discourse
    input enhancement
    the nature of the learner who
      continues language learning
input and traditional instruction

THINKING MORE ABOUT IT: DISCUSSION QUESTIONS

1. Bring textbooks to class for review. Using the criteria that distinguish mechanical from meaningful from communicative drills, identify examples of each type of exercise. Then, review five grammar sections to determine the underlying belief of the authors and thus the instructors who use the textbook. What is the role of drills in language learning for these people? Can you find any textbooks that don't contain drills?

2. Much of the early research in SLA that has debunked previous ideas about how languages are learned used learner spontaneous speech or something close to it as the data source. In that research, learners were taped engaging in interactions, describing pictures, telling stories, and so on. In what way are classroom paper-and-pencil tests different from the data-gathering methods used by SLA researchers? Do you think our conclusions about SLA would be different if researchers used paper-and-pencil tests like those used in typical classrooms to gather their data? How would they be different?

GETTING A CLOSER LOOK: RESEARCH ACTIVITIES

It is claimed that the comprehensible meaning-bearing input a learner is exposed to is the data upon which the learner's internal mechanisms operate in order to create a linguistic system. Sit in on a language class for two or three periods and, if possible, tape-record the class. Then transcribe only the instructor's speech. Analyze it for the following:

a. Breadth of vocabulary
b. Topics talked about (e.g., concrete vs. abstract, here and now vs. displaced situations)
c. Ratio of declarative to interrogative utterances
d. Ratio of present, past, and future tenses used
e. Frequency of one or two other grammatical features that you think are important in your language

What observations can you make about "the raw data" that learners are exposed to? Can you see or predict any possible relationship between either frequency of occurrence in teacher talk or quality of teacher talk and the development of the learner's internal grammatical system?

MAKING COMMUNICATIVE LANGUAGE TEACHING HAPPEN: PORTFOLIO ACTIVITIES

Select three grammar sections in a text that represent each of the following: instruction on verb forms (e.g., present tense, past tense); instruction on pronouns (e.g., object pronouns, indirect object pronouns, reflexives); instruction on word order. Recreate the sections by deleting the mechanical drills you find and adding other meaningful or communicatively oriented practices in their place.

CHAPTER 7

Processing Instruction and Structured Input

In this chapter we explore:

- The nature of input processing, that is, how learners attend to and process grammatical form in the input they hear
- Processing instruction, a grammar instruction based on the insights from input processing that has *structured input* at its core
- Research on processing instruction that demonstrates its effectiveness (compared with traditional instruction) and shows its application to various languages and structures
- A set of guidelines for developing structured input activities and an outline of activity types

INPUT PROCESSING

As we saw in Chapter 6, traditional instruction consisting of drills in which learner output is manipulated and the instruction is divorced from meaning or communication is not an effective method for enhancing language acquisition. In fact, in some cases such instruction has been shown to delay acquisition. What is needed, then, is a new pedagogy of grammar instruction that takes as its point of departure what we know about how grammatical forms and structures are acquired. This pedagogy needs to work with input and with the processes learners use to get data from that input. In Chapter 1 we listed four processes involved in the acquisition of an implicit linguistic system. Of concern here is *input processing*, how learners initially perceive and process linguistic data in the language they hear. It is here, in input processing, that learners might encounter their first problems in dealing with the properties and features of the new language. So, to develop our new pedagogy, we must come to some understanding of what input processing looks like.

Input processing is concerned with those psycholinguistic strategies and mechanisms by which learners derive intake from input. *Intake* refers to the linguistic data in the input that learners attend to and hold in working memory during online (real-time) comprehension. As such, research on input processing attempts to explain how learners get form from input while their primary attention is on meaning. *Form* here is defined as surface features of language (e.g., inflections, articles, particles), although input processing is also relevant to syntax (i.e., sentential word order).

VanPatten (1996, 2003b) presents the most complete model of input processing in SLA. This model contains a set of principles and corollaries that interact in complex ways in working memory. The role of working memory is important in this model since some of the principles are predicated on a limited capacity for processing. Limited capacity models of attention posit that humans have a finite set of attentional resources available at any given moment to perceive and take in the auditory and visual information that surrounds them. As such, humans develop mechanisms (or are born with them—we are not sure) that allow them to selectively attend to incoming stimuli. Without such mechanisms there would be informational overload and the brain might short-circuit. In terms of SLA, the same is true. Learners can only process and hold so much in their working memory before attentional resources are depleted and working memory is forced to dump information to make room for more (incoming) information.

VanPatten's principles are listed in Table 7.1. The model takes as its point of departure that during the act of comprehension learners will do whatever is necessary to grasp whatever meaning they can from the input. This is captured in VanPatten's Principle 1 (P1).

That learners are driven to get meaning from input (P1) has a set of consequences, the first being that content words (i.e., the "big" words) are searched out first. Unlike child first language learners, L2 learners know that words exist. For them—as for any fluent speaker or listener—words are the principal source or building blocks of referential meaning (P1a). This principle in turn has an effect on the processing of grammatical form in the input. If learners search first for content words, what happens when *both* a content word and a grammatical form encode the same referential meaning? VanPatten thus posits P1b, in which content words are preferred over grammatical items when both encode essentially the same information. Following are examples from Spanish and French:

1. *Ayer mis padres me llamaron para decirme algo importante.* ("Yesterday my parents called me to tell me something important.") Here, both the lexical item *ayer* and the verb inflection *-aron* encode pastness. The learner does not have to allocate attentional resources to a verb form to grasp that the action took place before the present. At the same time, both *mis padres* and *-aron* encode plurality, and again the learner does not have to allocate attentional resources to an inflection to grasp that the subject is plural.
2. *Je ne crois pas que vous parliez de lui comme ça.* ("I don't believe you talk about him like that.") In this example, both *ne crois pas* and the verb form *parliez* (instead of the indicative *parlez*) are related to mood (what textbooks call "the subjunctive of doubt" and what linguists might call "nonaffirmation"). The presence of *ne crois pas* mitigates against the processing of *-iez*, since the latter adds no information to the sentence that the learner cannot get from the former.

TABLE 7.1 Principles of Input Processing   **139**

Input Processing

Principle 1 (P1). The Primacy of Meaning Principle. Learners process input for meaning before they process it for form.

P1a. The Primacy of Content Words Principle. Learners process content words in the input before anything else.

P1b. The Lexical Preference Principle. Learners will tend to rely on lexical items as opposed to grammatical form to get meaning when both encode the same semantic information.

P1c. The Preference for Nonredundancy Principle. Learners are more likely to process nonredundant meaningful grammatical form before they process redundant meaningful forms.

P1d. The Meaning-before-Nonmeaning Principle. Learners are more likely to process meaningful grammatical forms before nonmeaningful forms irrespective of redundancy.

P1e. The Availability of Resources Principle. For learners to process either redundant meaningful grammatical forms or nonmeaningful forms, the processing of overall sentential meaning must not drain available processing resources.

P1f. The Sentence Location Principle. Learners tend to process items in sentence initial position before those in final position and those in medial position.

Principle 2 (P2). The First Noun Principle. Learners tend to process the first noun or pronoun they encounter in a sentence as the subject or agent.

P2a. The Lexical Semantics Principle. Learners may rely on lexical semantics, where possible, instead of word order to interpret sentences.

P2b. The Event Probabilities Principle. Learners may rely on event probabilities, where possible, instead of word order to interpret sentences.

P2c. The Contextual Constraint Principle. Learners may rely less on the First Noun Principle if preceding context constrains the possible interpretation of a clause or sentence.

Source: Based on VanPatten (2003b)

3. *Dicen que Julieta está enferma y que no viene a clase.* ("They say Julie is ill and she's not coming to class.") In this example, the presence of *enferma* and the context of not coming to class will give the learner the concept of perfection ("temporariness" in layperson's terms) and mitigate against the processing of *está*. Likewise, it is *Julieta* from which the learner grasps gender, and not the *-a* of *enferma*.

What these examples help to illustrate is that a great deal of form that is meaning-oriented or has referential meaning (i.e., is related to some semantic concept in the real world) may also be expressed by a lexical item or phrase elsewhere in the sentence or the discourse. This observation led to the creation of the construct *communicative value* (VanPatten, 1985b). Communicative value refers to the meaning that a form contributes to overall sentence meaning and is based on two features: [+/− inherent semantic value] and [+/− redundancy]. A given form can have [+ semantic value and − redundancy], [+ semantic value and + redundancy], [− semantic value and + redundancy], and finally

[− semantic value and − redundancy]. In general, a form's communicative value is greater if it has the characteristics [+ semantic value / − redundancy] than if it has the characteristics [+ semantic value / + redundancy]. In short, *if meaning can be retrieved elsewhere and not just from the form itself, then the communicative value of the form is diminished.* Forms with [− semantic value], regardless of redundancy, contain no communicative value. In examples 1–3, the preterit inflection *-aron,* the subjunctive marker *-iez,* and the copular verb *está* are all [+ redundant] in that their semantic value is present lexically somewhere else. One should note, however, that redundancy is not absolute; the preterit (or any other tense marker) does not always co-occur with a temporal expression in an utterance. One might also hear in the input utterances such as *¿Dónde estudiaste?* "Where did you study?" in which no lexical item provides clues to tense (or to person or number). But one rarely hears the subjunctive without a main clause that triggers it, and one rarely hears copular verbs without a predicate of some kind. In short, some forms are more redundant than others.

The nature of communicative value, then, is important for input processing: The more communicative value a form has, the more likely it is to get processed and made available in the intake data for acquisition (P1d). Conversely, the less communicative value a form has, the more likely learners are to "skip" it in the input. Of course, low frequency in the input and other aspects of language may be factors that, along with communicative value, doom a form never to get picked up by a learner. Likewise, the intersection of high communicative value and frequency may have a favorable effect on acquisition. Frequency notwithstanding, for learners to process forms of little or no communicative value in the input, they must be able to comprehend an utterance such that the act of comprehension does not tie up all their attentional resources. As learners get better at comprehension, they can process things they skipped over earlier. Thus, we posit P1 as a means of explaining how learners eventually, but not necessarily, come to process forms of little or no communicative value.

From P1f it is clear that learners perceive and process items in one position better than another. This means, for example, that learners are much more likely to pick up question words and their syntax than, say, object pronouns or the subjunctive, which tend to occur inside the sentence. Learners may not need to be told that Spanish inverts subject and verb in Yes/No questions because this is immediately evident in simple questions that learners hear from the first day of exposure.

Input processing is also concerned with word order. P2, the first noun principle, may have important effects on the acquisition of a language that does not follow strict subject-verb-object (SVO) word order. In each of the following sentences in Spanish, the first noun phrase the learner encounters is not a subject, but the learner may very well attempt to encode it as such:

4. *A Juan no le gusta esta clase mucho.* (literally, "To Juan is not very pleasing this class," meaning, "This class is not very pleasing to Juan.")
5. *La vi yo en la fiesta anoche.* (literally, "Her saw I at the party last night," meaning, "I saw her at the party last night.")
6. *Se levanta temprano.* (literally, "Raises herself early," meaning, "She gets up early.")
7. *Nos faltan varios libros.* (literally, "To us are missing several books," meaning, "We are missing several books.")

Research has shown that learners do indeed encode such pronouns and noun phrases as subjects (e.g., they think that *Juan* is the subject of 4, *la* is the subject of 5, and so on), thus delivering erroneous intake to their developing linguistic systems. In this case, it is not that meaning is gotten elsewhere; it is that meaning is not gotten at all or is gotten wrong. The form-meaning connections are not only filtered, they are altered.

An example of the same principle affecting a structure in French involves the causative with *faire*. This structure appears in 8 below:

8. *Jean fait promener le chien à Marie.*
   (literally, "John makes to walk the dog to Mary.")
   "John makes Mary walk the dog."

In 8, there are two verbs and two nouns. The first verb is *fait* with its obligatorily preposed subject *Jean*. The second verb is *promener* with its underlying subject, *Marie*, obligatorily placed in postverbal position and marked by the preposition *à*. It is the underlying subject of the second verb that is the problem for learners of French. When asked "Who walks the dog?" learners overwhelmingly say "Jean," since he is the first noun that appears before the verb, thus demonstrating their reliance on P2. When asked to give a rough translation, learners will say the sentence means something like "John walks the dog for Mary" or "John walks the dog to Mary" (VanPatten & Wong, 2003).

To summarize, research on input processing attempts to describe what linguistic data learners attend to during comprehension, which ones they do not attend to, what grammatical roles learners assign to nouns, and how position in an utterance influences what gets processed. Intake is that subset of filtered input that the learner actually processes and holds in working memory during online comprehension. Intake is thus grammatical information as it relates to the meaning that learners have comprehended (or think they have comprehended). As a reminder, input processing is but one set of processes related to acquisition; that learners derive some kind of intake from the input does not mean that the data contained in the intake automatically make their way into the developing mental representation of the L2 in the learner's head (i.e., intake ≠ acquisition). As we have seen previously, accommodation of intake and restructuring are processes separate from input processing—and how learners access their developing system to make output is also a distinct set of processes.

The presentation of input processing in this chapter has been necessarily brief and without details. Future research will no doubt add to the current model or instigate alterations in it. Nonetheless, the overview provided here is sufficient for discussion of a psycholinguistically motivated approach to grammar in the classroom. We turn to that type of instruction now.

Pause to consider . . .

to what extent learners are aware of their input processing. Do learners know what they are doing? Or do they do it automatically and without any conscious thought? On what do you base your thoughts?

RETHINKING GRAMMAR INSTRUCTION: STRUCTURED INPUT

We now have some idea of what learners are doing with input when they are asked to comprehend it. With this knowledge, we can begin to develop a new kind of grammar instruction—one that will guide and focus learners' attention when they process input. Figure 7.1 visually captures our new conceptualization of grammar instruction. We suggest that grammar instruction should *first* occur at the level of processing input. It should be directed to the following questions: (1) Are forms being processed in the input? Are learners attending to grammatical information? (2) Are learners making correct form-meaning connections when attending to input data?

The result is what VanPatten (1996) has termed *processing instruction.* Processing instruction consists of three basic components:

- Learners are given information about a linguistic structure or form.
- Learners are informed about a particular processing strategy that may negatively affect their picking up of the form or structure during comprehension.
- Learners are pushed to process the form or structure during activities with *structured input*—input that is manipulated in particular ways to push learners to become dependent on form and structure to get meaning and/or to privilege the form or structure in the input so that learners have a better chance of attending to it (i.e., learners are pulled away from their natural processing tendencies toward more optimal tendencies).

In the rest of this chapter, we concentrate on structured input activities because, as we will see when we review the research on processing instruction, structured input activities are the most important aspect of this instructional approach to grammar.

An Example of Relating Processing Strategies to Instruction: Verb Morphology

We turn our attention now to activities that focus learners' attention on verb endings; the goal is for learners to use these morphological endings to com-

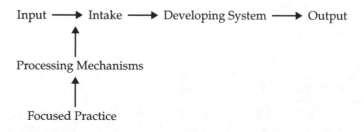

FIGURE 7.1 Processing-oriented grammar instruction

prehend tense rather than rely solely on lexical items. After learners receive a brief explanation of how past-tense endings work, they might first practice attaching the concept of past time to verb forms in an activity such as the following. The purpose is to circumvent the strategy described in P1b in Table 7.1: Learners prefer processing lexical items to processing grammatical items for the same semantic information.

Activity A.   Listening for Time Reference

Listen to each sentence. Indicate whether the action occurred last week or is part of a set of actions oriented toward the present.

> (SENTENCES READ BY INSTRUCTOR OR HEARD ON TAPE)
> **1.** John talked on the phone.
> **2.** Mary helped her mother.
> **3.** Robert studies for two hours.
> **4.** Sam watched TV.
> **5.** Lori visits her parents.

Learners might then be given sentences and told to match each to a particular adverbial.

Activity B.   Matching

Once again, listen to each sentence. Select the appropriate time-related adverbials that can be added to the sentence you hear.

MODEL: *(you hear)* John deposited money in the bank.
               (you select from)
                    a. last Monday
                    b. right now
                    c. later this week
               (you say) Last Monday

Further activities could be developed that involve what the learners themselves did or didn't do at a particular time.

Activity C.   Did You Do It, Too?

Listen to the speaker make a statement. Indicate whether you did that same thing last night.

MODEL: *(you hear)* I studied for a test.
               (you say) Me too.
          or   I didn't.

Note that, in each of these activities, only the verb ending encodes tense in the input sentence. Lexical items and discourse that would indicate a time frame are not present, thereby encouraging learners to attend to the grammatical markers for tense. Thus, we have *structured* the input so that grammatical form carries meaning and learners must attend to the form in order to complete the task.

Another Example of Relating Processing Strategies to Instruction: Adjective Agreement

Let's examine another of VanPatten's processing strategies and develop some structured input activities that would encourage learners to get better intake from the input. This time, we focus on the following strategy:

> P1d. Learners are more likely to process meaningful grammatical forms before nonmeaningful forms, irrespective of redundancy.

Some features of language do not have inherent semantic or communicative value. Quite simply, they are meaningless. In the Romance languages, for example, adjectives must agree in number and gender with the nouns they modify, but this feature of grammar contributes little or nothing to the meaning of the utterance in most cases (which is why mistakes in gender agreement rarely yield breakdowns in communication). In the following Spanish-language activity, learners' attention is directed toward proper adjective form by a task in which the adjective endings *must be attended to.* At the same time, the entire sentence must be processed for its meaning, for the learners need to know what is said in order to agree or disagree. These sentences are focused on gender agreement only, because the subject pronoun is not obligatory in Spanish (unlike French and English).

Activity D.   Who Is It?

Listen to each sentence in which a person is described. First, determine which person is being described. Then indicate whether you agree or disagree with the statement.

1. a. ❏ David Letterman   ❏ Madonna
   b. ❏ agree   ❏ disagree
2. a. ❏ David Letterman   ❏ Madonna
   b. ❏ agree   ❏ disagree
3. a. ❏ David Letterman   ❏ Madonna
   b. ❏ agree   ❏ disagree

   (*Sentences heard by learner*)
1. *Es dinámica.* (She's dynamic.)
2. *Es comprensivo.* (He's understanding.)
3. *Es reservada.* (She's reserved.)

Although grammatical gender in Activity D is restricted to humans and thus is confounded with sexual gender, it is an activity in which grammatical gender must nevertheless be processed for meaning. Note that the same kind of activity can be developed for inanimate objects such as skyscrapers versus suburban homes, or ideas such as country versus city living. Simply select any pair of items that have different grammatical gender and create statements that must be applied on the basis of processing the grammatical marker. Instead of having learners agree or disagree with the statement, you might have them indicate true/false or likely/unlikely.

> ## *Pause to consider . . .*
>
> what would happen if the sentences in Activity D contained subject pronouns. Spanish, for example, does not require *él* (he) or *ella* (she) in a sentence the way English, French, and other languages do. It is enough to say *Es dinámica*. What would happen in terms of processing for the form of the adjective if each sentence began with a pronoun: *Ella es dinámica; El es comprensivo?* Would learners need to attend to the adjective ending to complete the task? Explain.

A Third Example of Relating Processing Strategies to Instruction: The French Causative

Remember that learners apply a first-noun strategy to determine subjects and objects of sentences ("who did what to whom"). As we saw with the French causative, this leads to misinterpretation and nonacquisition. An effective processing-oriented approach to the problem might be something like Activity E. In this activity, learners are pushed to process correctly; to be sure this happens, sentences with noncausative *faire* (e.g., *faire du ski*, "to ski," and *faire les valises*, "to pack") that involve two people are also included. Thus, learners cannot slip into some mechanistic approach to answering each question; they actually have to listen to and process each sentence.

Activity E

Listen to each sentence. Then indicate who is performing the action by answering each question.

    1. Who cleans the room? _____

    2. Who packs the bags? _____

    3. Who watches the movie? _____

    4. Who sings? _____

    5. Who does the chores? _____

6. Who looks for the dog? _____

7. Who watches the show? _____

8. Who reads the instructions? _____

Teacher's Script

Read each sentence ONCE. After each sentence, ask for an answer. Do not wait until the end to review answers. Students do not repeat or otherwise produce the structure.

> **1.** *Claude fait nettoyer la chambre à Richard.*
> **2.** *Marc fait les valises pour Jean.*
> **3.** *Sandra fait voir le film à Pierre.*
> **4.** *Louis fait chanter une chanson de noël à Suzanne.*
> **5.** *Simon fait les devoirs au lieu d' Henri.*
> **6.** *Louise fait chercher le chien à Diane.*
> **7.** *Ma mère fait regarder le spectacle à mon père.*
> **8.** *Sally fait lire les instructions à Jean Luc.*

Research on Processing Instruction

For just about ten years, there has been ongoing research regarding the effectiveness of processing instruction; an important part of this research has examined the relative effects of processing instruction versus those of traditional instruction. The study that launched this research agenda is VanPatten and Cadierno (1993). We review this study here in some detail because it is the most frequently cited study and has been the impetus for a number of replication studies. VanPatten and Cadierno sought to answer the following research questions:

1. Does altering the way in which learners process input have an effect on their developing systems?
2. If there is an effect, is it limited solely to processing more input or does instruction in input processing also have an effect on output?
3. If there is an effect, is it the same effect that traditional instruction has (assuming an effect for the latter)?

VanPatten and Cadierno compared three groups of learners: a processing instruction group (number = 27), a traditional instruction group (number = 26), and a control group (number = 27). The processing group received instruction along the lines presented earlier. The focus was word order and object pronouns in Spanish. Recall that previous research (summarized in VanPatten, 1996) had demonstrated that learners of Spanish misinterpret object-verb-subject and object-verb structures as subject-verb-object and subject-verb structures, respectively. In Spanish, object pronouns precede finite verbs, and subjects may be optionally deleted or may appear postverbally. Thus, learners misinterpret structures such as *Lo ve María* as "He sees Mary" rather than the correct "Mary sees him." In the processing treatment, learners first received activities with right or wrong answers (e.g., "Select the picture that best goes with what you hear") followed by activities in which they offered opinions or personal answers. At no point did the learners in this group produce the structure and forms in question.

In the traditional group, learners received a treatment based on the most popular Spanish college-level text at the time. The treatment involved a typical explanation of object pronouns and the complete paradigm of the forms; these were followed by mechanical, then meaningful, then communicative practices as described in Chapter 6. At no time did this group engage in any interpretation or processing activities. The control group did not receive instruction on the target structure and instead read an essay and discussed it in class.

Both experimental treatments were balanced for activity items, vocabulary, and other factors that could affect the outcome. In addition, all instruction was performed by one instructor and lasted two days. This instructor believed that there would be differential outcomes—that the processing group would learn to interpret better and the traditional group would be better at production (an important point, given the results).

Assessment consisted of two tests: a sentence-level interpretation test and a sentence-level production test. These were administered as a pretest, an immediate posttest, a two-week delayed posttest, and a four-week delayed posttest, with various versions used in a split block design (e.g., if a subject received version A as the pretest, he would receive B as the first posttest, C as the second posttest, and D as the final posttest, whereas another subject might receive D as the pretest, C as the first posttest, and so on). The interpretation test consisted of ten target items and ten distracters; the production test consisted of five items with five distracters. The interpretation test was based on an activity performed by the processing group (e.g., "Select the picture that best goes with what you hear"), while the production test was based on an activity the ·traditional group performed during its treatment phase (e.g., "Complete the sentence based on the pictures you see"). The interpretation test was scored as a right or wrong answer for one point each (total = 10 points), and the production test was scored as two points each (2 points if correct use of object pronoun with correct word order, 0 points for no object pronoun, 1 point for incorrect use of object pronoun or problem with word order).

The results were clear. The pretests yielded no differences among the groups on the two tests prior to treatment. In the posttesting phase, the processing group made significant gains on the interpretation test whereas the traditional and control groups did not. The gain was maintained for the month that posttesting was conducted. On the production test, both the traditional and processing groups made significant gains but were not significantly different from each other. These gains were maintained during the month posttesting phase. The control group did not make significant gains.

In terms of their research questions, VanPatten and Cadierno drew the following conclusions. First, altering the way learners process input could alter their developing systems. The processing group showed evidence of this change on both interpretation and production tests. Second, the effects of processing instruction are not limited to processing but also show up on production measures. Finally, the effects of processing instruction are different from those of traditional instruction. With processing instruction, learners get two for one: By being pushed to process form and meaning simultaneously, they not only could process better but also could access their newfound knowledge to produce a structure they never produced during the treatment phase. The traditional group made gains only on production and did not make gains in the ability to correctly process form and meaning in the input. VanPatten and Cadierno took these latter results to mean that the members of the traditional group learned to do a task, while the members of the processing group actually experienced a change in their underlying knowledge that allowed them to perform on different kinds of tasks.

Pause to consider . . .

some other researchers' conclusions about this early research. In several other studies, researchers attempted to replicate the results of VanPatten and Cadierno but failed (DeKeyser & Solkaski, 1996; Salaberry, 1997). As Sanz and VanPatten (1998) and VanPatten (2002) have argued, part of the problem comes from the fact that these researchers equated processing instruction with comprehension practice and traditional instruction with output practice. Although it is true that learners do not produce during processing instruction and that learners do not comprehend anything during traditional instruction, why is it erroneous to equate processing with comprehension (or drills with output, for that matter)?

Areas for Future Research

Like any empirical study, the VanPatten and Cadierno study contains limitations that suggest areas for future research. These suggestions can be articulated in a series of questions that VanPatten and his colleagues have addressed over the years. These questions are as follows:

- Are the effects of processing instruction (PI) generalizable to other structures?
- Are the effects of PI due to different explicit information?
- Are the effects of PI observable with different assessment tasks?
- Are the effects of PI different from the effects of other types of instruction?
- Do the effects of PI hold over time?

We turn now to a discussion of each of these questions.

Are the Effects of PI Generalizable to Other Structures?

Cadierno (1995) replicated the VanPatten and Cadierno study using the Spanish preterit (past) tense as the target structure. This structure is morphologically complex and creates problems for learners more in terms of form rather than in terms of use. Again, contrasting a control group, a traditional instruction (TI) group, and a processing instruction (PI) group, Cadierno measured the effects of treatment via two measures: (1) an interpretation test (e.g., "Is the sentence you're hearing present, past, or future?"—note that only the verb encoded temporality; no adverbs were used) and (2) a production test (e.g., participants had to write sentences in the past to describe a situation). Cadierno's results matched those of VanPatten and Cadierno exactly: On the interpretation test, the PI group improved significantly, but the other two groups did not. On the production test, both the PI and TI groups improved significantly but were not different from each other. The control group did not improve.

In her dissertation, Cheng (1995) conducted a study with *ser* and *estar*, the two major copular verbs in Spanish. She compared a control, a processing, and a traditional group in the use of the copular verbs with adjectives as the target. Her assessments included an interpretation and production test as in VanPatten and Cadierno, but she also added a more complex test, a written composition based on pictures. In her final analysis, Cheng focused on improvement with the verb *estar* since students tend to use *ser* as the default (see VanPatten, 1987, and others). Her results mirrored those of the original VanPatten and Cadierno study. On the interpretation test, only the processing group improved. On the production test, only the processing and traditional groups improved and were not significantly different from each other. On the composition task, all groups improved significantly, but the processing and traditional groups' posttest scores were significantly better than those of the control group. (It is not clear why the control group improved at all, but its gains were minimal albeit enough to be different from its pretest score.) There was no difference between the processing and traditional groups.

In another study, Farley (2001a) demonstrated the effects of PI on the Spanish subjunctive with noun clauses. In his study he showed that participants who received PI made significant gains in both interpretation and production abilities with the subjunctive both in form and use.

In another dissertation, Buck (2000) investigated the relative effects of PI and TI in the acquisition of the present continuous (versus the present progressive) in English by native speakers of Spanish. Her assessment tests included the ability to correctly interpret sentences such as "Bill is smoking a pipe" and "Bill smokes a pipe" as well as the ability to produce the correct structure in a given context (e.g., "I _____ to music every day [listen]" and "We _____ the new schedule this week [prepare]"). Her results indicated greater gains for the processing group that were maintained over time on the interpretation test; initial gains made by the traditional group were not maintained. On the production test, both groups made similar gains, and gains were maintained over time.

In one other study, VanPatten and Wong (2003) demonstrated that PI was superior to TI with the French causative. Replicating VanPatten and Cadierno as closely as possible, they compared a control, a processing, and a traditional group and measured outcomes with an interpretation and a production test. Their results were the same as the results of the original study: On the interpretation test, the processing group was superior to the traditional group; the control group did not improve. On the production test, the processing and traditional groups both improved significantly but were not different from each other. The control group did not improve. Important to point out here is that the gains made by the processing group on the interpretation task were not maintained over time. This is due not to a decline in performance but to absenteeism on the final posttest. Several participants who had made the maximum possible gains on the immediate posttest were absent on the final posttest. Given the small population sizes of this study, the "decline" was due to sampling problems in the final posttest.

In another study involving the acquisition of verbal morphology, Benati (2001) compared PI, TI, and a control group using the Italian future tense as the target structure. He included a pretest, an immediate posttest, and a three-week delayed posttest. The test consisted of an interpretation task similar to Cadierno's and a two-part production task. The latter contained a written sentence-level task in which participants had to provide future-tense forms and an oral task in which they saw pictures and narrated a sequence of events in the future. His results were similar to but not the same as those of the original VanPatten and Cadierno study. On the interpretation task, the PI group improved significantly, the TI group did as well, and the control group did not. However, the gains made by the PI group were significantly greater than those of the TI group, such that the results on the interpretation task were PI > TI > C (with > indicating "better than"). On the two production tasks, the PI and TI groups both improved with no difference between them; the control group did not improve. The improvement of the TI group on the interpretation task is traceable to the types of activities they engaged in. Benati points out that, unlike VanPatten and Cadierno, he minimized the use of mechanical or purely form-oriented activities.

The work summarized here, then, does suggest that the beneficial effects of processing instruction are generalizable to other structures and different languages. We now turn our attention to another issue.

Are the Effects of PI Due to Different Explicit Information?

Another limitation of the original VanPatten and Cadierno study is that the processing and traditional groups received different explicit information before doing practice activities. The processing group followed the guidelines for the PI as presented earlier: Paradigms were broken up, and participants were warned about wrong processing strategies. The traditional group received a traditional explanation, and no mention of processing strategies was made. Perhaps this difference in explicit information contributed to the outcome of the study.

In VanPatten and Oikennon (1996), the researchers compared three groups: one that received PI exactly as in the original VanPatten and Cadierno study; another that received the structured input activities only, *with no prior explicit information and no explanation during the activities;* and another that received explicit information only, with no structured input activities. For this latter group, the explanation was given on one day and repeated on the second day (recall that treatment in the original study lasted two days), but the group engaged in reading activities unrelated to the structure.

The researchers used the same assessment tests as in the original study. The results were clear. Both the regular processing group and the structured input-only group improved significantly but were not different from each other.

The explanation-only group showed no improvement at all. The conclusion to be drawn was that the effects of PI are due not to the explicit information provided to learners but to the particular nature of the structured input activities and how these push learners to make form-meaning connections because the input sentences have been manipulated in particular ways.

A recent study using computer-assisted language learning (CALL) found similar results. Sanz and Morgan-Short (2003) set out to test whether explicit feedback—a component of CALL that is often championed by advocates of technology in language teaching—is necessary or helpful to learners. They chose PI as the method of instruction and used the same materials as VanPatten and Cadierno, VanPatten and Sanz, and VanPatten and Oikennon, but they transferred the materials to digital media and updated the drawings used in the activities and testing sections. Computer delivery of treatment and testing allowed for randomization and control of all variables involved. They tested four groups using the variables [+/− explanation] and [+/− explicit feedback]. (Note: All groups, regardless of the combination of these variables, received the same structured input as practice.) The first group was [+ explanation] (i.e., explicit information about the language and how to process it in the input) and [+ explicit feedback] (defined as telling learners not only whether an answer is correct or not but what the problem is if the answer is not correct). The second group was [− explanation] and [− explicit feedback], that is, learners received structured input only, with indications only of whether their answers were right or wrong. The third group was [+ explanation] but [− explicit feedback]. The fourth group was [− explanation] but [+ explicit feedback]. The results showed that all groups improved significantly on the three assessment tasks (interpretation and two production tasks—a sentence-completion task and a video-retelling task) from pre- to posttests (there were three posttests, as in the original VanPatten and Cadierno study). What is more, the researchers found that no group was better than any other on any task. In short, neither explicit information nor explicit feedback seemed to be crucial for a change in performance; practice in decoding structured input alone (as in the second group) seemed to be sufficient.

In one other recent study, Benati (2003) reported similar findings with the Italian future tense. He compared a regular PI group with a structured input-only group and an explicit information-only group. His results show that the explicit information-only group improved slightly from pre- to posttest measures, but that both PI and structured input-only groups improved much more, and their improvement was not significantly different from each other. However, both treatments were significantly better than the explicit information-only group. These findings were true for both interpretation and production tasks. These results suggest a major if not causative role for the structured input activities of PI and only a minor role, if any, for explicit information.

For this section we can conclude that structured input appears to be *the causative variable* in processing instruction. This means that explicit information is not important if the types of activities learners are engaged in actually push them to alter their processing strategies and make more or better form-meaning connections.

Two additional studies, one by Farley (2003) and one by Wong (2003), provide further support for the primary role of structured input. In Farley's study, the target item was the subjunctive in noun clauses in Spanish. Wong's study focused on negation of indefinite articles and partitives with *avoir* in French. In both studies the learners who received structured input only, without any prior explanation of the rule, made significant gains.

Are the Effects of PI Observable with Different Assessment Tasks?

Another limitation of the original VanPatten and Cadierno study is the use of sentence-level tests only. Cheng (1995) showed some effects for PI (as well as TI) on a composition task (reviewed earlier). In VanPatten and Sanz (1995) the researchers investigated the effects of PI as measured by three kinds of output tests. In this study they compared a PI group to a control group, using the same materials as in VanPatten and Cadierno with the target once again object pronouns and word order. Although they also used the interpretation test from VanPatten and Cadierno, their output tests included not only a sentence-level test but also a question-answer test (based on pictures) and a video-narration test. They administered the output tests in two modes: written and oral. Of special interest is the video narration, because of the complex cognitive task it represents. In this kind of task participants must provide all vocabulary, all syntax, and all grammatical features on their own, without any prompts. VanPatten and Sanz found that the control group did not improve on any tests. The PI group improved significantly on the interpretation test and on the sentence-level test in both modes. For some reason, the participants did not attempt to produce many object pronouns with the question-answer test, opting instead to simply repeat full nouns in their answers (e.g., "What's he going to do with the banana?" "He wants to eat the banana.") However, on the video-narration test participants did attempt to produce object pronouns. Their gains were significant in the written mode but just missed significance in the oral mode, and on all tests, the PI participants performed better on the written tests than the oral.

We discussed Sanz and Morgan-Short (2003) in terms of the role of explicit information. Relevant here is that they included in their computer-oriented study the same assessment tasks used in VanPatten's and Sanz's study. Again, the participants improved on all tasks, even the video retelling. Thus, it appears that the effects of PI are observable in a variety of output tests and are not limited to sentence-level tests.

Are the Effects of PI Different from the Effects of Other Types of Instruction?

Farley (2001a) compared the relative effects of PI with the effects of "meaning-based output" instruction (MOI). As in previous research, the PI group only interpreted sentences (via structured input activities) and did not produce any sentences with the subjunctive. Farley based the PI materials on P1b of VanPatten's model. A pilot study revealed that learners of Spanish do not pay attention to mood markers on verbs for any semantic information and rely instead on the lexical information contained in the main clause. Thus, Farley's initial activities pushed learners to attend to subordinate clauses without main clauses and had them indicate what the possible main clause could have been (or vice versa). Farley's other activities had learners combine main and subordinate clauses to express doubt and belief about various people, places, events, and so on, or to have the participants check off beliefs, doubts, and so on from lists.

Unlike TI, MOI contains no mechanical drills and is based on the tenets of structured output activities (see Chapter 8) that were first mentioned in VanPatten and Cadierno (1993). In Farley's MOI materials, participants created subordinate clauses using subjunctive or indicative forms based on the main clause triggers they heard (or read). For example, participants might have heard (translated from the Spanish), "I don't think that dogs . . .," and on a sheet of paper would see "(to be) intelligent." They would then have to indicate what the person must be saying by using the correct verb form. Other activities had them expressing their own beliefs or doubts, putting them in more control of the subordinate clause.

Both the PI and the MOI groups had two days of instruction on the Spanish subjunctive with noun clauses and expressions of doubt and negation. Farley assessed outcomes using a pretest and posttest design, with one posttest administered one month after treatment. The tests consisted of an interpretation test based on the PI materials (e.g., "Can you determine what the speaker must have said initially if all you hear is this second part of the sentence?") and a production test based on the MOI materials (e.g., "Complete the sentence . . .").

Farley's results differed from the results of the previous studies comparing PI with TI. His results showed that the PI and MOI groups improved significantly on both the interpretation and the production tests, with no difference between them. Thus, PI was not superior to MOI, and neither was MOI superior to PI. These results also differ from another study conducted by Farley. In Farley (2001b), he used the same design, procedure, and target structure as in his 2001a study. His results, however, were a bit different. Although both groups improved on the interpretation task, only the PI group maintained its performance on a delayed task. The MOI group declined in performance, and the decline was not traceable to a sampling problem like that found in the VanPatten and Wong study. Thus, PI did prove to be superior to TI in the long run.

Do the Effects of PI Hold Over Time?

In the studies reported so far, the longest delay time in administering a posttest in any one study was four weeks. As we saw with Lightbown's 1983 study, after one year the effects of instruction wore off and learners were back where they had been at the beginning. In VanPatten and Fernández (2003), the long-term effects of PI were studied in a partial replication of VanPatten and Cadierno's study. They provided PI from the VanPatten and Cadierno study (object pronouns and word order) to all available sections of a third-semester Spanish class at the college level. An immediate posttest was given after instruction, and another one was given eight months later to the students who had continued on to the next semester and who had completed all phases of the study. When VanPatten and Fernández compared the posttest results to the pretest results, they found that, as in all other studies, the students improved significantly on both measures (interpretation and production) and even though the scores dropped somewhat on the eight-month delayed test, the students were still significantly better at performing the tests than they were prior to treatment. VanPatten and Fernández concluded that at least in this one study, the observed effects of PI seem to be durable.

GUIDELINES FOR DEVELOPING STRUCTURED INPUT ACTIVITIES

It is appropriate now to establish some guidelines for the construction of structured input activities and provide examples of the many different types of activities that can be utilized in presenting structured input. What is presented here is suggestive; many readers would like to see an entire lesson that uses processing instruction. Farley (in press) contains a number of structured input activities and some entire lessons. In Appendix A of this book, we provide an entire lesson on the French causative used by VanPatten and Wong in their research. Beyond these, instructors will need to develop their own input activities as part of their grammar lessons, since most textbooks and commercial materials do not contain this type of activity.

Our guidelines, discussed in turn, are as follows:

- Present one thing at a time.
- Keep meaning in focus.
- Move from sentences to connected discourse.
- Use both oral and written input.
- Have the learner do something with the input.
- Keep the learner's processing strategies in mind.

Present One Thing at a Time

Structured input must be delivered to the learner's developing system in an efficient way. Maximum efficiency is achieved when one function and one form are the focus at any given time. This involves breaking up verb and noun-adjective paradigms or focusing on only one rule of usage at a time. Breaking up paradigms and lists of rules is useful for two reasons. First, it allows the explicit presentation and explanation of the grammatical structure to be kept to a minimum. The learner is not mired in a complex presentation and explanation of the grammatical item, as all forms and all functions are not being presented at once. Second, breaking up a paradigm is more likely to result in attention *directed* toward the targeted item. In other words, because there is less to pay attention to, it is easier to pay attention. Learners can be made aware of the rest of the paradigm and can be told that they will learn it over several days. The same is true for functions and uses of a grammar item. One possibility is to create overhead transparencies illustrating the paradigm or list of functions and to highlight (by circling and boxing) what is in focus during the lesson. As each new piece is presented, a different part of the transparency is highlighted.

Pause to consider . . .

the teaching of past tense. Does the language you teach have a different past-tense form for each person (first-person singular, second-person singular, and so on)? What does this mean for the principle "Present one thing at a time"? With which form do you think you might begin instruction? Would you have to provide instruction for all the forms, or would instruction in only some of them serve to heighten learners' awareness sufficiently?

Focus on just one form, say third-person, and develop an explanation for it as part of the "first day on past tense." "How much would you really have to say before launching into some structured input activities? Can you keep your explanation short and concise—one minute or less?

Keep Meaning in Focus

Learners should not engage in the mechanical input activities of traditional grammar instruction. Remember that input should be attended to for its message so that learners can see how grammar assists in the "delivery" of that message. In the adjective-agreement example presented earlier ("David Letterman and Madonna" in Activity D), meaning was kept in focus by having learners identify the person to whom the propositional content of the sentence referred and by asking them to give an opinion. Read the following two activities that attempt to teach -*ing* complements with the English verb *enjoy*. Which of the two keeps meaning in focus? Which does not?

Activity F.   Looking for Verb Endings

In the following paragraph circle all the uses of -*ing*. With what verb does it occur?

> Barnard Smith is an instructor who enjoys only certain aspects of his job. On the one hand, he enjoys teaching. He especially likes to teach Portuguese 101. He really enjoys preparing new and innovative tasks for learners to do in class. On the other hand, he does not enjoy correcting essays. He finds it tedious.

Activity G.   Looking for Verb Endings

Check off the statements you think are true based on what you know about your instructor.

- ❏   He/She enjoys teaching.
- ❏   He/She enjoys watching the news at night.
- ❏   He/She enjoys preparing exams.
- ❏   He/She enjoys correcting exams.
- ❏   He/She does not enjoy reading student essays.

If you said that Activity F does not follow the principle of keeping meaning in focus but Activity G does, then you are correct. Note that in the first activity, the learner can perform the task of circling verb endings and noting that *enjoy* is the co-occurring verb without understanding the meaning of the sentences. If you need to prove this to yourself, then substitute the following nonsense words for the *-ing* verbs: *fract, croder, slarg*. The activity can still be performed, and it would be performed without making any form-meaning connections. In Activity G, on the other hand, the task cannot be performed without the learner making the form-meaning connections. In order to indicate whether or not the sentence is applicable to the instructor, the learner must know what the sentence means and how the grammar encodes meaning in each.

Move from Sentences to Connected Discourse

When we teach grammar via structured input activities, it is important to begin with sentences first, the shorter the better. Short, isolated sentences give learners processing time, whereas in longer stretches of speech, grammatical form can get lost if the demands to process meaning overwhelm the learner. The principle is exemplified in the following set of four activities (H to K) on the use of third-person singular verb forms. Note the progression of activities from isolated (but related) sentences to connected discourse (short narration).

Activity H.   Alice and Ray

Look at the drawings of events from a typical day in the lives of Alice and Ray. Listen as your instructor reads a sentence. Say whether that activity is part of Alice's routine or Ray's.

MODEL: *(you hear)* This person eats lunch with friends.
          (you say) That is Ray.

Activity I.   In What Order?

Without referring to the drawings about Ray's day, put the following activities in the correct order in which he does them.

_____ **a.** He goes to bed late.
_____ **b.** He sleeps in his math class.
_____ **c.** He works at the pizzeria.
_____ **d.** He goes to music class.
_____ **e.** He gets up late.
_____ **f.** He watches some TV.
_____ **g.** He eats lunch with friends.
_____ **h.** He tries to study.

Now compare with the drawings. Did you get them all in the right order?

Activity J.   The Typical Student

Read the following sentences. Are they true for a typical student at your school?

The typical student . . .	TRUE	NOT TRUE
1. gets up at 6:30 A.M.	❑	❑
2. skips breakfast.	❑	❑
3. drives to school.	❑	❑
4. sleeps in at least one class.	❑	❑
5. studies in the library, not at home.	❑	❑
6. works part-time.	❑	❑
7. eats a microwaved dinner.	❑	❑
8. watches David Letterman at night.	❑	❑
9. goes to bed after midnight.	❑	❑

Your instructor will now read each statement and then ask you to raise your hand if you marked it as true. Someone should keep track of the responses on the board. In the end, how did the class respond to each statement?

Activity K.   John's Day

Step 1. Break into groups of three and listen as your instructor reads a short narration.

Step 2. With your group members, give as many details as you can remember by completing the following sentences. The group with the most details wins. You have three minutes.

1. John gets up at _____.
2. He requires at least _____ to wake up fully.
3. He prefers not to _____ in the morning.

(*The list continues.*)

Step 3. Look over the details that you have recalled. Read a sentence to the class and then say whether or not you do the same thing.

MODEL: John gets up at 8:00, and so do I.
John gets up at 8:00, but I don't.

[*Part of narration read by instructor:*
"John is a student at X university. On most days, he gets up at 8:00. But the mornings are very difficult for him since he just isn't a morning person. He needs to drink at least three cups of strong coffee to wake up. And more often than not he reads the newspaper in silence since he prefers not talking to anyone until he is fully awake. . . ."]

Use Both Oral and Written Input

In activities, the learner should be provided with opportunities to hear and see the input. In the progression of activities exemplified, you saw both oral and written input. Note, however, that it is not just a matter of one activity being oral and one being written. In at least two activities, learners were exposed to both oral and written structured input. In Activity J, learners read sentences that they subsequently heard their instructor speak. In Activity K, learners heard structured input and then received structured written input on verb forms as they completed their sentences with other kinds of information. In short, any combination of oral and written input within a single activity is fine.

Suggesting that structured input be both oral and written is not just a matter of calling for variety in the activities. The issue here is individual variation. Although all learners need oral input, some learners benefit from "seeing" the language and even claim they need to see it in order to learn it. Using oral input only would place these learners in uncomfortable—and ineffective—learning situations.

Have the Learner Do Something with the Input

Learners cannot be passive recipients of language. Instructors should not simply talk *at* the learners or ask learners to simply read something. The learner must be actively engaged in attending to the input to encourage the processing of grammar. In the examples that we have seen, the learner always responds to the input in some way: saying Yes/No, agreeing/disagreeing, checking off things that apply, matching, ordering, and so on. Note that the learner *does not respond by producing the targeted structure*. In those cases where production does occur, it does not involve the structure contained in the input. For example, in Step 2 of Activity K (in which learners in groups of three attempted to recall details of the narration), the structured input contained third-person singular verb forms, but the information that learners produced did not require verb forms. Instead, they recalled time of day, food items, and other features. In order to provide the requested information, they needed to process the verb forms in each sentence in Step 2 (they had to know, for example, what *gets up* means in order to recall the requested information). Learners will certainly be given opportunities to produce the forms in subsequent activities, but at this point in the day's lesson we are concentrating on providing learners with structured input and having them actively process it.

Keep the Learner's Processing Strategies in Mind

Learners should focus attention during processing on the relevant grammatical items and not on other elements of the sentence. Return to Activity B on past tense (p. 143). Do you recall that temporal adverbials such as *right now* and *later* were not used in the structured input activities? This is because we were keeping in mind the processing strategies that learners use, and we wanted them to focus on the verb endings rather than on the lexical items. Here are two additional examples: If one is teaching person-number endings, it does little good to have each and every input sentence contain an explicit subject noun or pronoun because the learner is more likely to attend to this for person number information than to the verb ending. Or, if one is teaching object pronouns in Spanish, it does little good to have each sentence begin with an explicit subject. Rather, "target" input sentences should begin with object pronouns, and subjects should be implied or positioned after the verb.

Pause to consider . . .

what to do if your language, like English, requires subject nouns and pronouns. French, for example, requires explicit subjects. One must say *Il se lève;* one cannot say *Se lève* (at least under standard and typical conditions). How does the following input activity "keep in mind the processing strategy" of word order and lexical items versus grammatical form? (The activity is part of a series that focuses on third-person object pronouns.)

> **Activité.** Select a female relative or friend and then indicate which sentences apply to you.
>
> Nom: _____
>
> Relation: _____
>
> Je ...
>
> ❏ **1.** la déteste.
> ❏ **2.** la respecte.
> ❏ **3.** la connais (plus que les autres).
> ❏ **4.** la vois les fins de semaine.
> ❏ **5.** l'admire.

TYPES OF ACTIVITIES FOR STRUCTURED INPUT

Structured input activities consist of two broad types: referential and affective. Referential activities are those for which there is a right or wrong answer and for which the learner must rely on the targeted grammatical form to get meaning. Activities A and B (p. 143) are referential in that there is a right or wrong answer, and by this answer the instructor knows whether learners are attending to the verb inflection for the meaning (temporal reference) it encodes. Normally, a sequence of structured input activities would begin with two or three referential activities.

Following referential activities, learners are engaged in *affective* structured input activities. These are activities in which learners express an opinion, belief, or some other affective response and are engaged in processing information about the real world. In the Madonna and Letterman activity (Activity D), the learners indicate whether they agree or disagree with the statement. This is an affective response. Note, however, that this particular activity also has a referential element: Learners must first decide to whom the statement refers by relying on the adjective ending (a right or wrong response). Thus, an activity may be either referential or affective, or it may have elements of both.

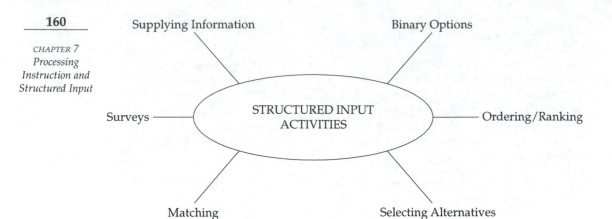

FIGURE 7.2 Major types of structured input activities

In addition to these two broad activity types, what learners do with input can be classified by response type, as depicted in Figure 7.2. Variations in content and technique within each of these activity types can help to create a variety of activities. For example, within the category of binary options (that is, giving learners two possible answers), one can answer true or false, yes or no, agree or disagree, Mom or Dad, instructor or student, dog or cat, good or bad, or any other two-option answer.

Binary Options

Let's take an activity based on a binary option and demonstrate how it can be altered using a different binary option. Recall that Activity J required learners to indicate what is true for the typical student at their school. This activity can be recast as (or even followed up by) a likely/unlikely selection task.

Activity L. The Typical Student (alternative version of Activity J)

Based on your experience, determine whether the following statements are likely or unlikely.

LIKELY	UNLIKELY	
❏	❏	1. A student who works part-time takes more morning classes.
❏	❏	2. An engineering student studies more than an art student.
		(and so forth)

Matching

In matching activities, the learner indicates the correspondence between an input sentence and something else: matching a picture to an input sentence, matching a name to an input sentence, matching an event to its cause (both could be input sentences), matching an event to its logical consequence (both could be input sentences), matching a name to an action, matching days of the week to an activity. Returning to our example of the use of third-person present tense, in Activities H and I you saw how learners matched an input sentence to a person (Alice or Ray). In the following activity, learners match events to other events in order to make logical connections.

Activity M.   Associations

For each sentence in Column A, indicate to which activity in Column B it is most logically connected.

Column A	Column B
Alice . . .	She . . .
1. works part-time.	**a.** goes to the gym.
2. exercises five times a week.	**b.** studies every night.
3. gets good grades.	**c.** earns $5.00 an hour.

Supplying Information

In Activity K, learners supplied missing information. The input was structured around third-person verb forms used to talk about people's routines. The information that the learners supplied did not require them to produce the targeted verb forms; the verbs were already supplied. For example, "He prefers not to _____ in the morning." Thus, in information-supplying activities that provide structured input, learners don't produce the grammatical item that is being taught but something else.

For another example, read the following activity, in which learners are getting structured doses of a particular English modal in the input (but it could just as well be the morphological conditional tense in Romance languages). What kind of information are they supplying?

Activity N.   Would He or Would He Not?

Step 1. Break into two groups. Select someone from the class whom you all think you know well. That person should sit by himself during the first part of this activity.

Step 2. Write that person's name in the blank as indicated. Then complete each statement with information that you believe to be true.

Unless he had to, _____
                                  (name)

1. would never eat _____.

2. would never watch _____.

3. would never go to _____.

4. would never spend money on _____.

5. would never _____.

On the other hand, _____

(name)

6. would probably eat _____ without reservation.

7. would go to _____ on vacation.

8. would study _____, time permitting.

9. would gladly spend money on _____.

10. would _____.

Step 3. Each group should give its completed statements to the instructor, who will read each statement aloud. If the selected person says, "That's true," then the group will receive a point. Which group knows him the best?

Selecting Alternatives

In this category is included any type of activity in which learners are given a stimulus and are asked to select from three or more alternatives. Either the stimulus or the alternatives contain the targeted grammatical items that are being practiced in the activity. Selecting alternatives is illustrated in the following structured input activity, which focuses learner attention on third-person present tense.

Activity O. How Well Do You Know Your Instructor?

Select the phrase that best completes each statement about your instructor. Afterward, your instructor will tell you if you are correct or not.

1. As soon as he gets home, my instructor . . .
   a. reads the mail. **b.** has a cocktail.
   c. plays with his children/dog/cat. **d.** does something else.
2. When it's time for dinner, he . . .
   a. prepares the meal. **b.** helps with the meal.
   c. waits for the meal. **d.** orders a pizza.

[The activity continues in similar fashion.]

Surveys

One of the more engaging activities providing structured input is the survey. The survey is interesting to learners because they interact with a variety of classmates and the focus is, of course, on them. In a survey, one or both of the following can happen: (1) The learner responds to a survey item; (2) the learner elicits survey information from someone else. Surveys can use a variety of the response formats already discussed (binary options, supplying information, selecting from alternatives, and matching) with typical survey tasks including the following:

- Indicating agreement with a statement
- Indicating frequency of an activity
- Answering Yes or No to particular questions
- Finding a certain number of people who respond to an item in the same way

In the following survey, learners first indicate their own degree of agreement with each statement. The statements are structured to target the grammatical concept of object pronouns, concentrating on first-person plural.

Activity P.   Attitudes Toward the Government

Step 1. Indicate the extent to which you agree with each statement.

> 5: Strongly agree
> 4: Agree
> 3: Somewhat in agreement
> 2: Disagree
> 1: Strongly disagree

The government . . .	5	4	3	2	1
1. understands us.	❑	❑	❑	❑	❑
2. helps us.	❑	❑	❑	❑	❑
3. controls us.	❑	❑	❑	❑	❑
4. ignores us.	❑	❑	❑	❑	❑
5. taxes us too much.	❑	❑	❑	❑	❑
6. doesn't represent us.	❑	❑	❑	❑	❑
7. guides us.	❑	❑	❑	❑	❑

Step 2. Share your responses with the class. Someone should tabulate the scores and calculate a class average for each item.

Step 3. Overall, does the class have a positive, negative, or mixed attitude toward the government?

Pause to consider . . .

the effect of converting Step 1 of Activity P to a paired activity with one learner interviewing the other. Does the underlying purpose of the activity change? Will both learners still be exposed to structured input if one interviews the other?

Signature searches are a type of survey activity in which learners mill around the room attempting to find people who can answer affirmatively to a particular statement. In the following signature search, learners gather information related to their classmates' moods and states of being. (In many Romance languages, as in this example from a Spanish class, the verbs all would require reflexive pronouns; the English version requires the verb *get* to indicate change of state.)

Activity Q.   State of Mind

Find people in the class who answer "Yes" to the following questions. Rules: (1) You may not use anything but Spanish; (2) you may not ask a person more than one question in a row; (3) if you find someone who answers "Yes" to a question, ask for that person's signature on the line next to the question; (4) when being asked a question, listen carefully and do not look at your paper; (5) do not sign your name unless you have been asked a complete question.

1. Do you get tense when speaking in Spanish?_____
2. Do you get nervous before taking a big exam?_____
3. Do you get angry easily?_____
4. Do you get depressed during the holidays?_____
5. Do you get bored when you're not in school?_____

As a follow up, the instructor can ask learners to report on their findings: "Robert, who said that he gets angry easily? *(David)* Dave? Is this true? Do you get angry easily? At people or at things? When you get angry with a person, do you normally tell that person?"

Some might find it confusing that we classify signature searches as structured input. After all, aren't the learners talking? Aren't they producing the structure that you are trying to embed in the input? The answer is that they aren't. In Activity Q, the learners are not creating structures or forms; they are reading aloud. Everything they need is right there on paper; in other words, output is not generated from the developing system. Learners who ask the questions get input because they must read the questions and know what they mean. The learner who responds "Yes" or "No" receives oral input from a classmate. No original language is created or produced during the task. Signature searches, as well as other surveys and activities in which students do not create language, serve another function: They place input in the hands of the learner. Note that, during the signature search (and a survey), the person asking the question or reading the statement provides input to the person listening. In this way, learners share in the work of providing input. This is why it is important to tell learners to *listen* to the other person and not read from the page at the same time when being asked a question.

Ordering and Ranking

Another type of activity for structured input involves having learners order items either in terms of importance or likelihood or in terms of chronology. For example, in the following affective activity (adapted from a Spanish activity in a lesson on the past tense), students first indicate what they think their instructor did last night and then put the activities in chronological order.

Activity R. What Did Your Instructor Do Last Night?

Step 1. Following is a list of things your instructor might have done last night. Check off those that you think he or she did.

Our instructor . . .

_____ had a cocktail.
_____ read the newspaper.
_____ walked the dog.

_____ prepared dinner.
_____ watched TV.
_____ went out with a friend.
_____ called a student.
_____ slept for eight hours.
_____ exercised.
_____ cleaned a closet.

Step 2. A volunteer will read the statements from Step 1 to the rest of the class. Indicate whether you agree or disagree with each statement. In the end, your instructor will tell you and the class if you are right.

Step 3. Now that you know what your instructor did, put his or her activities in the order in which you think they occurred. Afterward, two students will volunteer their results.

As this activity also clearly demonstrates, an affective activity can have multiple steps that work through the structured input a number of times. In Activity R, students read the structured input items in Step 1. In Step 2, they hear and read some of them again. In Step 3, they once again hear and read some of the items. Thus, they are engaged in processing and reprocessing the verb forms, all the time connecting them to meaning as they work through the task of this activity.

SUMMARY

In this chapter we have viewed in as much detail as possible the nature of processing instruction. We examined in particular the nature of structured input activities and how they push learners toward more optimal processing of language data. We cannot emphasize this last point enough: Structured input activities have to work on particular processing problems. This point is underscored in the sixth guideline for developing such activities, namely, "Keep the learner's processing strategies in mind." The bottom line for developing effective structured input activities is this: *If you have not addressed a processing problem in the activities and are not attempting to push learners away from it, then you have not developed effective structured input activities and you do not have processing instruction* (VanPatten, 2002). We reviewed research on processing instruction that demonstrates its effectiveness, an effectiveness that comes essentially from carefully constructed activities.

Missing from this chapter is a discussion of output. We are not suggesting that learners should never produce the grammatical items and that they should get only structured input. Nothing could be further from the truth. In the next chapter, we explore meaning-based grammar activities, which we call "structured output." For now, we stress that getting grammar into learners' heads requires them to process meaning-bearing input first. Our contention is that input can be structured to highlight a particular grammatical feature and to aid in its acquisition.

KEY TERMS, CONCEPTS, AND ISSUES

relationship of instruction to
  language acquisition
input processing
input versus intake
principles of input processing
communicative value
structured input guidelines for the
  construction of structured input
  activities
    present one thing at a time
    keep meaning in focus
    move from sentences to connected
      discourse
    use both oral and written input

have the learner do something
  with the input
keep the learner's processing
  strategies in mind
processing instruction
referential versus affective activities
activity types for structured input
  binary options
  matching
  supplying information
  selecting alternatives
  surveys
  ordering and ranking
vocabulary and structured input

THINKING MORE ABOUT IT: DISCUSSION QUESTIONS

1. Examine the following sentences and apply VanPatten's principles to determine how a learner of English would process each.

   1. I spoke to the builder yesterday.

      _____

   2. I purchased several magazines while I was abroad.

      _____

   3. Professor Jones requires that we turn in drafts of our papers a month before the paper is due.

      _____

   4. Evelyn was devastated by the news.

      _____

2. **Step 1.** Explain in your own words the concept of communicative value. (Remember, the term refers to input processing, not production.)

   _____

   _____

   _____

   _____

   Step 2. Now, identify three grammatical items in the language you teach that are of low communicative value and three that are of high communicative value. Justify your choices. How will learners ever acquire those items of low communicative value?

LOW COMMUNICATIVE VALUE	HIGH COMMUNICATIVE VALUE
a. _____	a. _____
b. _____	b. _____
c. _____	c. _____

3. Explain in your own words the concept of *structured input* to an instructor who is not familiar with it. Report back to the class the following:

   - Was it easy to explain the concept?
   - Did you have to also explain input processing to that person?
   - What questions did the person have? Where did your explanation get hung up, if at all?

GETTING A CLOSER LOOK: RESEARCH ACTIVITIES

Explore the concept of communicative value by having language learners tell you how they comprehend. Create two lists of eight to ten nearly identical sentences. Use a temporal adverb in one set, but omit it from the other. Read one set of sentences to a learner at a time, and ask him or her to tell you whether the sentences refer to the past, present, or future. Also ask the learner how he or she decided this. Be sure to record the interaction. (Getting learners to talk about how they process is referred to as *introspection,* and the resulting transcription is a *think-aloud protocol.*) Some sample sentences follow; you might use these as models to create your own sentences.

A.
I will go to the store.
I went to the Union.
I am going to the bank.

B.
I will go to the store tomorrow.
I went to the Union yesterday.
I am going to the bank shortly.

MAKING COMMUNICATIVE LANGUAGE TEACHING HAPPEN: PORTFOLIO ACTIVITIES

Return to the activities you worked on for Chapter 4 as you thought about the sequencing of activities to reach a goal. Examine your grammar activities. More than likely they were not structured input activities. Rework them so that you have a lesson that uses processing instruction as its approach to grammar instruction.

Structured Output: A Focus on Form in Language Production

In this chapter we explore:

- The importance of opportunities to make output in second language learning and the role of output in the development of fluency and accuracy
- The use of drills for promoting fluency and accuracy in speech after learners have begun to internalize a form or structure
- *Structured output,* a special type of form-focused activity that is communicative in nature
- The use of paradigms to preview or summarize
- Ways in which output activities can be used with vocabulary

WHY "OUTPUT"?

As you read Chapter 7 and reviewed the activities that focus on structured input, you might have said to yourself that input is not enough, that learners must eventually use a form or structure in their output. We agree with this position. Although input is *necessary* for creating a system, input is not *sufficient* for developing the ability to use language in a communicative context. Recall that the processes involved in producing language, or what might be called "making output," can be distinguished from those used in getting language into the developing system. Production of the foreign language (be it writing or speaking) involves those processes that operate at point III in Figure 8.1. These processes include *access* (retrieval of correct forms), *monitoring* (editing one's speech when one realizes "something is wrong"), and *production strategies* (stringing forms and words together to make sentences) and are affected by a variety of factors (see also Pienemann, 1998).

For the purposes of our discussion of output and focus on form, we concentrate on the concept of *access* in this chapter. *Access* is a term coined by Terrell (1986, 1991), the second major component of his *binding/access framework*. According to Terrell, producing an utterance in a language minimally involves

$$\text{Input} \xrightarrow{\quad\text{I}\quad} \text{Intake} \xrightarrow{\quad\text{II}\quad} \text{Developing System} \xrightarrow{\quad\text{III}\quad} \text{Output}$$

FIGURE 8.1 Outline of processes in second language acquisition

two processes or abilities: (1) the ability to express a particular meaning via a particular form or structure; (2) the ability to string forms and structures together in appropriate ways. The first ability Terrell calls *access;* the second he refers to as *production strategies.* An example of access would be coming up with the word *went* when attempting to express the concept of "having gone somewhere," as opposed to *will go* when talking about some projected or intended going.

As Terrell points out, access does not follow automatically from acquisition. Just because a learner has incorporated a particular form or structure in the developing system does not mean that it can be accessed easily (and thus produced automatically). In fact, learners can acquire a great deal of grammatical information but not be able to use it in communicative situations, as in the case of learners in courses such as "German for Reading Knowledge." In these kinds of reading-based courses, learners build up a system, but their experience with the language does not include opportunities to create output. In one informal experiment that he conducted, Terrell (personal communication) noted certain positive effects of providing opportunities for making output. In the first session of a German-as-a-foreign-language class, learners received a Total Physical Response lesson. All learners listened to and then carried out particular commands. During the second session, half the learners gave the same commands to the other half. The result was that half the learners received input only while the other half received input *and* were required to access and make output. Each student in the class was subsequently tested on the ability to access the forms, that is, his ability to produce the correct command. The test revealed that all learners could access but that those who had to give the commands after listening to them and acting them out could access faster (see Table 8.1).

Pause to consider . . .

the factors that might influence the ability to access grammatical forms and structures from the developing system. Terrell mentions the "strength of binding," namely, the frequency of the form in the input so that its presence in the developing system is reinforced. Can you think of other factors? What about phonological (sound) shape? Relationship to other forms and structures? Number of functions attached to one form and vice versa (number of forms attached to one function)?

In short, while input processing is linked to acquiring form and structure, access is linked to *accuracy* (correctness) and *fluency* (ease and speed) in output. The implication for language instruction is that learners need not only

170

CHAPTER 8
Structured Output:
A Focus on Form
in Language
Production

TABLE 8.1. Results of Terrell's Informal Experiment on Access

Learners	Average Access Time
Those who received commands (received input only)	2.23 seconds
Those who gave commands after receiving input	1.68 seconds

Source: Terrell (personal communication)

input to build a developing system but also opportunities to create output in order to work on fluency and accuracy. Focusing on fluency and accuracy, however, does not necessarily entail a return to mechanical drills and meaningless practice. A focus on output in language instruction should make every attempt to have learners produce language that communicates something—has meaning—to someone else.

TRADITIONAL APPROACHES TO FORM-FOCUSED OUTPUT

A survey of introductory language textbooks reveals an almost exclusive focus on production. As soon as vocabulary is presented, there are exercises for producing it. When pronunciation is taught, it is via production. And when grammar is presented, every textbook has hundreds of manipulative and controlled practices that have the learner "creating" output with particular forms or structures. In Chapter 6, we questioned the utility of these practices for getting linguistic information *into* the developing system. But one could also ask if these output-oriented drills actually have any utility for building accuracy and fluency in output. Before answering this question, we briefly review the nature of such exercises.

In Chapter 6, we saw that traditional approaches to grammar instruction focusing on output very often involve what Paulston (1972) noted as a progression from mechanical to meaningful to communicative drills. These drills are distinguished according to two criteria: (1) focus on meaning and (2) range of possible student responses. Recall that a mechanical drill is an exercise in which learners do not have to understand the stimulus or even understand what they are saying in order to complete the exercise: there is no focus on meaning. The substitution of nonsense words was used to demonstrate this. In addition, there is always one—and only one—learner response possible in a mechanical drill. With meaningful drills, learners must understand the meaning of both the stimulus and their answer; it is not possible to substitute nonsense words in the practice and still reach the desired effect. As in mechanical drills, in meaningful drills there is only one response possible and that response is known by instructor and other learners alike. Communicative drills are also meaning focused, but, unlike mechanical drills and meaningful drills, the range of learner responses is open since there is no single correct response. In short, there is some kind of exchange of unknown information in communicative drills.

The original purpose of mechanical drills was to instill good habits in language learners and to help them internalize correct forms and structures. As we have seen, research in second language acquisition has demonstrated the importance of input and input processing in developing an internal system and led to the realization that mechanical drills do not fulfill this function. Do mechanical drills serve some other purpose? Do they serve to increase fluency or accuracy? Following Lamendella (1977), we can question the use of pattern practice and mechanical drills for this purpose as well. According to him, mechanical drills do not make use of the same brain processes (or *neural networks*) involved in accessing language during communicative language use. Mechanical drills bypass deeper levels of processing where form-meaning connections are involved. Viewed in another way, the learner "switches off" the mechanisms and processes used in relating form to meaning and performs the drill without thinking very much. Recall that the definition of *access* is "being able to express a particular meaning via a particular form or structure." The learner generally performs mechanical drills in such a way that the processes needed to develop more fluent and accurate access are bypassed. Whatever has potential for being learned is not processed deeply enough to make a difference.

Schmidt (1992) has also questioned the utility of mechanical drilling and practice based on his review of possible psychological mechanisms underlying the development of fluency. After reviewing five major models of skill development from the field of cognitive psychology, Schmidt concludes that there is no theoretical support for the belief that fluency is simply a matter of increasingly skillful application of rules: learning a rule and then practicing it until it becomes automatic.

> As commonly practiced, the technique of pattern practice rests on the assumption that short training sessions with a small number of exemplars, each of which is typically practiced once, will lead to fluency based on automatic rule application. The theories reviewed in this paper suggest that unless such practice is very extensive (introducing the boredom factor), neither the specific examples practiced nor the general rule will be available subsequently for fluent use.
>
> (Schmidt, 1992, p. 381)

Even if one were to accept the belief that practice makes perfect (or fluent, in this case), Schmidt rightfully points out that the psychological literature that *could* be used to support this position has nothing to do with language. Studies on practice and training effects involve such nonlinguistic issues as typing, target-letter detection, and alphabet arithmetic. It is difficult to conceive of the same psychological mechanisms responsible for rapid performance in those studies underlying the much more complex and cognitively challenging tasks of first or second language speaking as well.

In short, we do not see much utility in mechanical practice for the development of fluency and accuracy in production. Mechanical practice is obsolete, based on shaky theoretical constructs tied to habit-formation theory. In terms of communicative language teaching, mechanical practice is of dubious value.

172

CHAPTER 8
Structured Output:
A Focus on Form
in Language
Production

But isn't it nevertheless true that meaningful and communicative drills involve form-meaning connections, so aren't they consistent with the broader philosophies and aims of communicative language teaching? Although this is true in principle, in practice researchers have found that meaningful drills are not the best use of class or homework time. Given the limitations in both class and outside work, communicating already known information has been shown to be a poor way to facilitate the development of the processes underlying access. The reasoning is simple: Why spend time creating messages that your listener or reader already knows?

Several researchers have investigated what learners do with communicative drills in class. (We presented detailed discussion of this research in Chapter 3, so we will touch upon only the major issues here.) Because learners understand quickly that the purpose of meaningful and communicative drills is to practice a grammar point, they very often abandon the informational message in the utterances and convert the practice into a mechanical drill (Brooks, 1990; Kinginger, 1990). That is, focus on meaning is minimal if not nonexistent, and learners instead concentrate on getting the form or structure correct. This is particularly true when the learners encounter such drills outside of any larger communicative purpose. Kinginger's findings point to learners focusing on the *drill* and not the *communicative* part of a communicative drill.

For example, in the following communicative drill (which does require the exchange of unknown information), the two learners must use the present perfect to communicate. The activity's grammatical focus does not escape either instructors or learners. Yet, as the practice unfolds, being accurate with the grammar becomes more important than exchanging information because the latter aspect of the activity is rather incomplete. Each sentence is disconnected from the others.

Use the following verbs to describe what you have or have not done this weekend.

MODEL: study → I have not studied chemistry this week.

1. open
2. write
3. leave
4. break
5. speak

In addition, in the materials from which this practice was taken, several mechanical drills precede it. Thus, the communicative practice is actually preceded by a series of activities in which informational exchange is either tenuous or nonexistent. The communicative drill does not form part of a cohesive series of activities based on information exchange. As a result, learners may very well perform this activity by simply "going through the motions." The crucial question that emerges from this discussion is the following: Can classroom output activities that focus on form also be activities that focus on information exchange? The answer is Yes, and we turn our attention now to these types of activities.

In this section we explore *structured output activities*. These activities have two major characteristics.

1. They involve the exchange of previously unknown information.
2. They require learners to access a particular form or structure in order to express meaning.

Structured output activities share most of the same guidelines for construction that we developed in Chapter 7 for structured input activities. The obvious exception is that the guidelines refer to production, not input. The guidelines for developing structured output activities are as follows:

- Present one thing at a time.
- Keep meaning in focus.
- Move from sentences to connected discourse.
- Use both written and oral output.
- Others must respond to the content of the output.
- The learner must have some knowledge of the form or structure.

We review these guidelines by examining three different activities.

Applying the Guidelines to Create Structured Output Activities

Presenting "one thing at a time" once again refers to focusing on only one form and one function of a particular grammatical device or structure. Remember that most traditional output drills have learners manipulate a variety of forms in one activity; they also generally attempt to cover all functions of a form or structure within several activities. With structured output, the focus is on one form and/or one function at a time. In the following French-language activity, "Present one thing at a time" means the following: (1) only the second-person singular of (2) the past tense (imperfective aspect) within the context of talking about (3) habitual actions. In other words, the activity does not include all person-number manipulations mixing imperfective and perfective aspect.

Activity A.   What You Used to Do

Step 1. You are attempting to find out if a fellow classmate was a model student in high school. Think of questions that you can ask about what he or she used to do or about events that used to happen involving your partner that would help you gather the information. You should come up with about eight good questions.

MODÈLE: *Est-ce que tu faisais des questions quand tu ne comprenais pas quelque chose?* (Did you usually ask questions when you didn't understand something?)

Step 2. Now, interview the person of your choice. Be sure to jot down your partner's responses because you will need them later.

174

CHAPTER *8*
Structured Output:
A Focus on Form
in Language
Production

Activity A satisfies the requirement "Present one thing at a time" because the learner focuses on producing *tu* (second-person singular) forms, and each question formulated concerns a past habitual action or event. In addition, the activity follows the second guideline, "Keep meaning in focus." Each and every question created by the learner is for the purpose of obtaining information from someone else. Thus, both questioner and respondent must attend to meaning.

---

*P*ause to consider . . .
_____

the nature of the communication in Activity A. Would the interviewee have to respond with complete sentences? Keep in mind the purpose of the activity as you respond. Is the purpose for the interviewer to practice making output or for the interviewee to practice making output?

The guideline "Move from sentences to connected discourse" points to the importance of allowing learners to access forms and structure at the sentence level before proceeding to connected sentences. This does not mean that output for beginners should be restricted to sentences only and that discourse-level output should be reserved for more advanced learners. It merely suggests that, within a given lesson or series of activities, learners should not be forced to string utterances together at the outset. In the following sequence of activities focusing on first-person object pronouns (*me* in Italian), notice how the learner moves from output with simple sentences to output involving connected sentences.

Activity B. My Friends

Step 1. Write at least five statements about what your friends do for you—or to you—that makes you appreciate them.

ESEMPIO: *Me ascoltano.* (They listen to me.)

Step 2. Now write at least five statements about what your friends do to or for you that sometimes gets on your nerves.

ESEMPIO: *Non me renderono di soldi.* (They don't return money to me.)

Step 3. Now present your sentences to a partner. Your partner will subsequently present his or her sentences to you. How much similarity is there?

Activity C. My Parents

Step 1. Now think about your parents. What do they do to or for you? Repeat Steps 1 and 2 from Activity B, this time substituting your parents for your friends.

Step 2. Compare and contrast your friends and parents by sharing your statements with the class. Use connectors like *anche* and *ma* as well as topic starters like *Per cominciare* to make your presentation flow.

[*Instructor notes:* Tell students to jot down things they hear. Afterward, have the class explore the question, Is there a pattern to our relationships with friends and parents that we can see based on this information?]

You may also notice that the string of Activities B and C, as well as the steps within the activities, demonstrates another guideline for structured output: "Use both written and oral output." The actual roles of written and oral output in activities depend on purpose and topic. Overall, however, structured output activities should not favor one of these modalities over the other. One might include both written and oral output within the same activity, or some activities might be oral and others written. Again, choice depends on purpose and topic.

The guideline "Others must respond to the content of the output" indicates that the output created by the learner is purposeful: Because it contains a message, someone in some way must respond to the content of the message. As exemplified in the activities, a response might be any of the following:

- Comparing with something else
- Taking notes, then writing a paragraph about what was said
- Making a list of follow-up questions and interviewing a partner to get the new information
- Filling out a grid or chart based on what was said
- Signing something
- Indicating agreement or disagreement
- Determining veracity of the statement
- Responding using any of several scales
- Drawing something
- Answering a question

(You might wish to review the types of responses to structured input given in Chapter 7, since many overlap.) The point here is that the respondent must indicate in some way that he or she has attended to the meaning of the other's output.

> *Pause to consider . . .*
>
> why it is important to ensure that the meaning of a learner's output is attended to. What might happen if it were not?

The final guideline, that "the learner must have some knowledge of the form or structure," simply means that structured output activities flow from previous work. They are not starting points but part of a continuum of work with a particular grammatical feature. This brings us to a question: What is the relationship of structured output to structured input? In the communicative approach we favor, structured output follows structured input. Structured input encourages form-meaning connections during input processing so that intake is created for the developing system. Because structured output activities work at accessing existing or developing linguistic knowledge, they should thus follow structured input activities rather than precede them when both types of activities focus on the same grammatical form or structure.

Structured Output as Input

If you think about Activities A, B, and C, it might occur to you that learners are producing language that, although communicative, looks very much like the kind of language an instructor would use in a structured *input* activity. That is, in something like Activity A, the learner will produce a string of questions with very similar structure, all using the second-person singular of the imperfect. This is because we focus on one thing at a time, the same way we do in structured input activities. It very well may be, then, that one learner's structured output could serve as another learner's structured input. Is this possible?

Not only is this scenario possible, it is probably likely. You may recall the Farley studies we reviewed in Chapter 7 (Farley, 2001a and b). In those studies, Farley compared the results of processing instruction and meaning-based output instruction, or MOI. The MOI activities were essentially fashioned out of the guidelines for structured output presented here (but based on the first edition of this book). The focus of his study was the subjunctive with matrix clauses of doubt and nonbelief. One group received PI for two days while the other group received MOI. Both were pretested on their ability to perceive and interpret subjunctive forms as well as their ability to produce them in a sentence-level task. What Farley found after treatment was that both groups improved on both tasks. Although we can understand the results for the PI group based on the theory presented in Chapter 7, the results were somewhat surprising for the MOI group. Looking at what happened in the classrooms during the treatment phase, however, Farley argues that learners in the MOI group got concentrated doses of input as their partners and classmates worked through structured input activities. It would seem that even though the students did not get a structured input lesson, they accidentally got something that was close enough to it to allow them to improve as much as the PI group.

You might ask, then, Why bother with structured input if we can just give learners structured output knowing that they'll get some input as a byproduct? The problem with relying only on structured output is this: With structured input, you are assured of getting something (review all the research in Chapter 7), but with structured output, you are not similarly assured. In fact, in one of Farley's studies, the MOI group's ability to perform the interpretation task dropped significantly after treatment, whereas the PI group maintained its ability on both tasks. It may be that the byproduct input of MOI is not sufficient enough to have long-lasting effects; the special structured input of PI is.

Structured Output versus Information-Based Communication Tasks

As you reflect on structured output tasks, you may say to yourself, "These tasks and the information-based tasks in Chapter 3 are very similar. What's the difference?" On the surface the two types of activities do look alike, since unknown information is exchanged in each. But a closer inspection of the information-exchange or information-based communication tasks reveals that these activities do not focus on a particular form or structure; structured output activities always do. If you review the sample tasks in Chapter 3 you will see that information-exchange tasks require a variety of forms or structures, a range of vocabulary, and certain discourse devices. Structured output activities, on the other hand, are focused on what the learner needs in order to create a message. In short, whereas information-exchange tasks are explicitly communication-centered, structured output tasks are form-centered.

PARADIGMS REVISITED

You will recall from Chapter 6 that the psycholinguistic validity of paradigms is questionable. We noted that speakers do not have paradigms as part of the mental representation of language in their implicit systems. What speakers, both first and second language learners, have is a vast network of lexical items and forms that are drawn upon during communication.

Yet some learners report a need or desire for paradigms, and many instructors feel a need to provide them. Our interpretation of this situation is that paradigms can serve an *affective* function: Although lacking any immediate psycholinguistic usefulness, paradigms may satisfy some psychological or emotional need to summarize or keep track of the grammar. A learner might feel anxious or mystified without the "big picture" that a paradigm can provide. Paradigms and lists can be used to show learners where they are headed, with the feature that is under immediate attention highlighted. In our experience, however, paradigms can thwart the acquisition of grammar if used to preview what is being learned. Instructors and learners alike might become so preoccupied with "mastering" the paradigm that they lose sight of the importance of developing form-meaning connections and the need to communicate real information in the classroom. They lose sight of the value of "one thing at a time," as learners struggle to cope with all the forms of a verb. In such cases, the presentation or use of the paradigm at the outset has lost its function as a previewing device and has become, instead, the goal.

This will become even more likely if the lesson goal is a formal test on the grammar feature. After all, if learners know or believe that a good grade depends on success in conjugating verbs and displaying knowledge of rules, they will use a paradigm to help themselves memorize the material to be tested. Although this is probably a fine strategy for particular kinds of test preparation, the issue under discussion here is learning to speak and gaining fluency. If learners memorize from paradigms, then they will generally grope for verb forms and even tick off verb conjugations in their mind as they attempt to speak: "Ellos no . . . *uh* . . . no voy . . . *I mean* . . . *uh* . . . voy, vas, va, vamos, van . . . van! Ellos no van." In cases such as this one, learners vocalize their thoughts and actually run through the paradigm orally. The result is halting and disfluent speech.

Another possibility, of course, is to present paradigms *after* some success with a set of forms or structures, to let students know what they have been learning. In this way, a paradigm can serve as a review, summarizing what has been learned or practiced.

The issues of teaching one thing at a time and using or not using paradigms are related to another issue, namely, the purpose of grammar instruction. When

178

CHAPTER 8
Structured Output:
A Focus on Form
in Language
Production

grammar instruction serves the need of communication, then teaching one thing at a time makes special sense. Suppose, for example, that we have a lesson on "Talking About Your Weekend." The grammar item implied in this topic is the need for past tense to talk about what happened. However, "Talking About Your Weekend" is a broad topic. What aspects of the weekend are we talking about? What activities do we want to discuss? Is there some cognitive-informational purpose (for example, comparing what we did last weekend to what some other group did)? And, most important, *whom* do we want to talk about? We explored the nature of lesson goals and lesson structure in Chapter 4, but here we point out that a lesson on "Talking About Your Weekend" may require that only certain verb forms be used (not comprehended) by students. For example, the lesson may require only first-person singular (for talking about yourself), second-person singular (for asking a classmate questions), and/or third-person singular (to report on a fellow classmate). Thus, parts of a paradigm may be more important in one lesson than in another. Or, parts of a paradigm may be more important in one part of a lesson than in another part of that same lesson.

Here is one illustrative example. Returning to the topic "Talking About Your Weekend," we can imagine a scenario in which the lesson begins with talking about a typical student. Appropriate structured input and output activities would explore what the student probably did over the weekend, and the learners would practice third-person singular past tense. The final structured output activity in the sequence might be the following.

Activity D.   A Description

Based on all the activities and discussion that have taken place so far, create a short description (seven or eight sentences) of what the typical student on your campus did over the weekend. Remember to use such connectors as *also, but, on Saturday,* and any others you think of to give your description some flow and to connect the ideas smoothly.

Next, learners could work on first-person singular, again with appropriate structured input and output activities, with the final activity possibly the following.

Activity E.   Last Weekend, I . . .

With a partner, make statements about what you did over the weekend. Each time you make a statement your partner will respond with "I did, too" or "I didn't." When you and your partner have five activities in common, raise your hands. You will then share them with the class. (Note: Do not make simple statements like "I slept" or "I got up." Everyone sleeps and everyone gets up! Make statements such as "I slept ten hours Saturday night" or "I got up really late on Sunday—at noon.")

Finally, learners could work on second-person singular using structured input and output activities, with the final activity being some sort of interview.

Looking again at the sequence of activities presented for teaching past-tense verb forms, we see that if grammar is at the service of topics and communication, then the relevance of paradigms decreases. Because the immediate communicative goal of each part of the lesson is specifically delineated (talking about someone else's weekend, talking about your own weekend, asking questions of another person), only one piece of the paradigm is needed at each point of the lesson. One reason, then, that some instructors might question the guideline "Present one thing at a time" is that they do not see grammar at the service of communication. Indeed, they see communication at the service of grammar and look for ways to "practice the preterit in a communicative context." In this case, it is understandable why some instructors are eager to have their students learn the "big picture."

VOCABULARY AND OUTPUT

The focus of this chapter has been grammar, namely, linguistic form and structure. However, Terrell's concept of access applies just as well to lexical items as it does to grammar; learners must develop fluency in vocabulary and must learn to access it easily and accurately during communicative interchanges. Thus, "structured output" is a concept that can be applied to the development of activities that encourage learners to use newly learned vocabulary in a productive manner. (Note: Vocabulary and input were discussed in Chapter 2.)

Because the very nature of vocabulary encompasses meaning (words represent concepts), it is difficult to imagine vocabulary activities that are mechanical in nature. Although textbook materials generally use meaningful vocabulary practices before learners move on to communicative practices, many textbooks also follow another sequence in vocabulary learning and practice: from producing isolated words to producing phrases to producing utterances. Although this sequence is not always observed rigidly, textbooks and instructional materials nevertheless tend to have students work first with single words and then with those words used in sentences. In one textbook, for example, the following activity is the first used to practice vocabulary useful for describing student rooms. Note how the learner need only respond with one word from the vocabulary list that precedes the activity. (The vocabulary list is embedded within a visual display contrasting two students' rooms.)

Activity F.   Two Rooms

Describe the two rooms. What is there . . .

> **1.** on Mary's desk? on Jacqueline's desk?
> **2.** next to Mary's bed? next to Jacqueline's bed?
> **3.** under Mary's table? under Jacqueline's table?

Pause to consider . . .

how Activity F is meaningful but neither mechanical nor communicative. In what way do the criteria of (1) meaningfulness and (2) freedom of response determine that this is a "meaningful" practice? Next, reflect on the topic of this activity and the kind of speaking the learners produce. How meaningful is this meaningful practice?

180

CHAPTER 8
Structured Output:
A Focus on Form
in Language
Production

Later, in the fourth activity in vocabulary used to describe rooms, the learner must string together utterances. Thus, the learner has moved from isolated words to connected sentences (discourse) with the new vocabulary.

Activity G.   Rooms and Personalities

A room reveals an occupant's personality. Describe the room in the photo. What is in the room? What adjectives and words describe the room the best? Give as many details as you can.

Moving from isolated words to words used in sentences does not seem unreasonable to us during structured output activities. However, as we recommended in the previous section, work with vocabulary does not have to be a series of unconnected activities. Nor should the work be divorced from the student's own world. Instead, the activities can form a series of connected pieces that build toward something: the learning of vocabulary has a purpose. In the following, note how we reconceptualize the activities described so that they form part of some connected train of thought.

Activity H.   On the Floor

Step 1. Name the items that are on the floor in Mary's room.

Step 2. Now name the items that are on the floor in Jacqueline's room.

Step 3. Who leaves more items on the floor? Who would you say is neater?

Activity I.   Compared to Your Room . . .

Step 1. Look at the photo. Describe the room and tell where the objects can be found.

Step 2. Now compare the room in the photo to your own room. Are they similar or different? Who is neater, you or the occupant of the room in the photo?

Step 3. Present your case to the class to see if they agree. You might need phrases such as "I never leave . . ." or "I always put _____ away." Feel free to ask your instructor how you say other related phrases.

Pause to consider . . .

the teaching and learning of vocabulary in communicative language teaching. Do you see any need to introduce and work with vocabulary any differently than you introduce and work with grammar? In what ways is the acquisition of grammar similar to the acquisition of vocabulary?

SUMMARY

In this chapter, we advocated the development and use of the output analog to structured input. Structured output activities enable learners to access forms and structures in their developing system to communicate an idea. (The actual development of the linguistic system was the focus of Chapter 7.) As with structured input activities, the creation of one's own structured output activities follows a series of guidelines. In terms of sequencing, structured output activities should *follow* structured input activities. Thus, a coherent grammar lesson is one that takes the student from processing a grammatical feature in the input to accessing the feature from her developing system to create output. As with structured input activities, structured output activities are never divorced from meaning. During these kinds of activities learners make output that encodes a message.

We touched again upon the use of paradigms in teaching, suggesting that they could be used as preview or *post hoc* summaries. The suggestion that paradigms could be used as preview devices was accompanied by a note of caution, for they can undermine grammar instruction in the communicative classroom by becoming a list of things to master.

We ended the chapter with a brief discussion of vocabulary and output. It is clear that, as with grammar, learners need opportunities to use vocabulary to communicate information. Only in this way can they work on those processes responsible for the development of fluency and accuracy in second language speech.

KEY TERMS, CONCEPTS, AND ISSUES

input is necessary but not sufficient
output
access
   accuracy
   fluency
monitoring
production strategies
sequence of drills
   mechanical
   meaningful
   communicative
structured output
guidelines for creating structured
  output activities
   present one thing at a time
   keep meaning in focus

move from sentences to
  connected discourse
use both written and oral output
others must respond to the
  content of the output
learner must have some
  knowledge of the form or
  structure
paradigms
  instructional uses
   affective considerations
   preview
   summary
vocabulary and structured output
  words → sentences → discourse

182

CHAPTER 8
Structured Output:
A Focus on Form
in Language
Production

THINKING MORE ABOUT IT: DISCUSSION QUESTIONS

1. Define and explain in your own words the processes involved in making output.
2. What are the characteristics of *structured* output?

GETTING A CLOSER LOOK: RESEARCH ACTIVITIES

It has been suggested that learners gain a certain sense of confidence from carrying out mechanical, meaningful, and communicative drills. Devise a survey of perhaps ten questions to determine learners' beliefs about drills. Try to create questions that elicit what learners think they learn from drills, as well as how they feel when doing them. Administer the survey to a class. What are the results? To what extent are the results attributable to the fact that learners may not have access to other kinds of grammar practices?

MAKING COMMUNICATIVE LANGUAGE TEACHING HAPPEN: PORTFOLIO ACTIVITIES

Expand on your portfolio materials from Chapter 7 by preparing at least three structured output activities as follow-ups to structured input activities. Be sure that one activity moves from sentences to connected discourse and that another includes both written and spoken output.

CHAPTER 9

Suggestions for Testing Grammar

In this chapter we explore:

- The use of structured input formats for testing grammar
- The use of structured output formats for testing grammar
- The use of information that is an outcome of class activities as possible testing material ("being responsible for what happens in class")

SOME PRELIMINARIES: A REVIEW OF TESTING PRINCIPLES

In Chapter 5 we examined some aspects of test development that are important for this chapter as well. We briefly review each of them here.

Washback Effects

You may remember that the washback effect refers to the relationship between what happens in class and how learners are tested. Specifically, we cited Krashen and Terrell (1983), who argue that if you want acquisition to happen in the classroom, then you must have tests that promote acquisition. In other words, tests should not be divorced from how one learns something. A fill-in-the-blank test on the present tense, for example, bears little relationship to structured input and output activities in class. A student confronted with a fill-in-the-blank test will not be engaging in the kind of behaviors that occurred in class.

Four Criteria for Designing a Good Test

As indicated in Chapter 5, Carroll (1980) identifies four general criteria in testing:

- *Economy* refers to obtaining the maximum amount of information about what the learner knows or can do in as little time as possible; teachers and students should spend a minimum amount of effort on the test. In short, we want to sample well but not exhaust the possible things to be tested.

183

- *Relevance* involves the match among the course, curriculum goals, and the tests. For a test to be relevant, it should reflect not only *what* has been taught and learned but also *how* it was taught and learned.
- *Acceptability* considers to what extent learners accept the test as valid. They should not perceive themselves as victims; instead, they should participate willingly because the test appears to be a fair and reasonable way of assessing what they have learned.
- *Comparability* takes into account how groups of learners perform on a test. To achieve comparability, we would like all learners from all courses at the same level to perform roughly the same. What is more, if we gave the test again a year later to another group at the same level, their test scores should be similar to those of the group who took it the year before. Another aspect of this criterion is that two different kinds of tests that test the same knowledge or ability should yield similar results, that is, a student who does well on one kind of test should not bomb the other, and vice versa.

Just as we saw with tests of oral language ability, these criteria and considerations should also inform how we test any other aspect of language. We now turn our attention to testing grammar.

STRUCTURED INPUT FORMATS FOR TESTS

In Chapters 7 and 8 on grammar instruction, we presented guidelines for developing structured input and structured output activities. These guidelines, repeated here, help make grammar instruction consistent with the overall goals of communicative language teaching. In addition, they are informed by some general tenets of second language acquisition research. The principles are

- Present one thing at a time.
- Keep meaning in focus.
- Move from sentences to connected discourse.
- Use both oral and written input and output.
- Have the learner do something with the input, or have other learners respond to the content of the output.

These same guidelines can be utilized in the construction of test sections. The sample test section following (Section A) uses an input-based testing procedure. Learners first must attend to the verb ending in order to determine which person is being described. They then agree or disagree and state their reasons. Note that meaning is kept in focus and that learners do something with the input. The guideline "Present one thing at a time" is observed because the items are restricted to the third-person singular. But the test section covers more than just this one verb form: two tenses are being tested as well (past and present). The items can be read to learners or by them, as both oral and written language are desirable.

First match the sentence you hear with the man. Then indicate whether or not you think it is a true statement.

1. ❑ Kennedy ❑ Bush
   ❑ agree ❑ disagree
2. ❑ Kennedy ❑ Bush
   ❑ agree ❑ disagree
3. ❑ Kennedy ❑ Bush
   ❑ agree ❑ disagree
4. ❑ Kennedy ❑ Bush
   ❑ agree ❑ disagree

[Test takers hear the following items:]

1. He was a great man. **2.** He keeps strange hours. **3.** His brother wanted to be president, too. **4.** He hopes to change America.

If an instructor employs both structured input and structured output activities in classroom lessons, then Section A will be consistent with the way the forms were taught and should therefore be both relevant and acceptable to the learners. It tests the learners' ability to attach meaning through the grammar. Section A is also an economical way of sampling learners' knowledge of present- and past-tense verb forms. You do not need to test everything in one section!

Whereas Section A tests third-person singular, Section B tests the first-person plural. If both sections were part of an exam, the criterion of "relevance" would be met because learners would be tested on more than just the third-person forms. In the following test section, learners must again attend to verbal distinctions in order to determine the time frame of the sentence. Meaning is kept in focus in two ways: first, in the global context of having learners identify the frame of reference, and, second, by having the learners do something with the input (they indicate whether the item applies to them). Issues related to grading such a section are addressed later in the chapter.

Section B

Indicate whether the speaker is relating information from his childhood or information about the present. Then decide if the information applies to you.

MODEL: *(you hear)* We would go to the beach for a week after school let out.
        (you choose) childhood
        (you indicate) This does not apply to me.

1. ❑ childhood   ❑ present
   ❑ This applies to me. ❑ This does not apply to me.
2. ❑ childhood   ❑ present
   ❑ This applies to me. ❑ This does not apply to me.
3. ❑ childhood   ❑ present
   ❑ This applies to me. ❑ This does not apply to me.

[Test takers hear the following sentences:]

1. We moved around a lot.   **2.** We have two dogs.   **3.** We ate dinner promptly at 5.   **4.** We had many opportunities.   **5.** We speak when spoken to.   **6.** We read a little every night before going to bed.

Activity B from Chapter 7 (p. 143) could be used exactly as it was formulated for classroom use as a section on the test. The targeted items require learners to process the verb forms for past, present, or future markings. In the testing version (Section C), you would still want to keep one thing in focus at a time and therefore limit the items to third-person plural, for example. The choice of third-person plural is a deliberate one because Sections A and B utilize other forms. By relating the sections in this way, an instructor addresses not only Carroll's recommendation for economy and our guideline for "one thing at a time" but also a concern for *completeness*. The test should sample a bit of everything the learners were taught and not be overly limited in scope.

Section C

Listen to each sentence. Then select one of the time-related adverbials that can be added to the sentence you hear.

MODEL: *(you hear)* Terry and Pat deposited money in the bank.
   (you select from)

a. last Monday
b. right now
c. next week

[Test takers hear the following items:]

1. Terry and Pat vacationed in Hawaii.   **2.** Terry and Pat will buy a house together.   **3.** Terry and Pat are preparing their taxes. **4.** Terry and Pat adopted a baby.   **5.** Terry and Pat will face many problems.

You might question why a test would need to include input-based formats when you have already moved to output in the classroom. In other words, since instruction always moves to output in the end, why can't you simply test via output-based formats? The question is a good one. A method that emphasizes comprehensible input and structured input in the instruction cannot then ignore these in the testing. To do so runs the risk of making these instructional elements irrelevant as classroom practices in the minds of the learners. In short, the test can reinforce classroom practice or it can undermine it.

STRUCTURED OUTPUT FORMATS FOR TESTS

Output-based testing formats that follow the guidelines for structured output activities can be combined with input-based sections. An example of an output-based test format combined with input would be to add some structured output to Section B. When learners explain their selections, they need to use the very structures that are being processed in the input. And, depending on the level of the learners, they could be asked to comment on the item. Here is an example.

Section D

Indicate whether the speaker is relating information from his childhood or information about the present. Then decide if the information applies to you. Finally, explain how it does or doesn't apply and comment on it. A model is provided.

MODEL: *(you hear)* We would go to the beach for a week after school let out.
(you choose) childhood
(you indicate) This does not apply to me.
(you explain) When we were kids, we went to the mountains for vacations.
(you comment) As we got older, my brothers and sisters and I did not like the mountains because they were so isolated.

1. ❏ childhood ❏ present
   ❏ This applies to me. ❏ This does not apply to me.

_____

_____

_____

2. ❏ childhood ❏ present
   ❏ This applies to me. ❏ This does not apply to me.

_____

_____

_____

3. ❏ childhood ❏ present
   ❏ This applies to me. ❏ This does not apply to me.

_____

_____

_____

[Test takers hear the following sentences:]

1. We moved around a lot. **2.** We have two dogs. **3.** We ate dinner promptly at 5. **4.** We had many opportunities. **5.** We speak when spoken to. **6.** We read a little every night before going to bed.

As a test section, Section D meets the guidelines for developing structured input and output activities: One thing at a time (past versus present verb forms; first-person plural); meaning is kept in focus (each individual will respond differently to the output portion); a combination of sentences and connected discourse; a combination of oral input and written output; the learners do something with the input. This test section also incorporates Carroll's testing criteria: It is relevant (it follows the structured instructional pattern), economical (it samples knowledge), and acceptable (because the same activity types were used in classroom activities, learners will perceive the test as valid and reasonable).

Almost any structured output activity can be developed into a testing section. In Chapter 8 we saw the following activity, which focused on using the first-person singular object pronoun in Italian, *me*.

Activity B (from Chapter 8).   My Friends

Step 1. Write at least five statements about what your friends do for you—or to you—that makes you appreciate them.

ESEMPIO: *Me ascoltano.*

Step 2. Now write at least five statements about what your friends do to or for you that sometimes gets on your nerves.

ESEMPIO: *Non me renderono di soldi.*

With a different focus (for example, professors, pets, or roommates), this activity can become a test section. The example, Section E, focuses on family.

Section E

Step 1. Using *me,* write at least three statements about what parents (or brothers, sisters) do for you—or to you—that makes you appreciate them.

Step 2. Again using *me,* write at least three statements about what your parents (or brothers, sisters) do to or for you that sometimes gets on your nerves.

Note how, in the test section, the instructions are reduced from "Write five sentences" to "Write three sentences," reflecting Carroll's criterion of economy in testing. Many instructors feel that the number of items in a test section must be a multiple of five. Although this is the convention, there is no rule that states a test section cannot have three items. We suggest that the number of items in a section reflect how "important" that grammatical feature is. (We place the word *important* in quotes because it is a relative term. Great debates rage over which grammar features are important and which are not.)

Pause to consider . . .

how to score the output test Sections D and E. What would you give points for? What would you take points off for? If the purpose in Section E, for example, is correct use of *me*, would you score for anything else?

BEING RESPONSIBLE FOR
WHAT HAPPENS IN CLASS

189

*Being Responsible
for What Happens
in Class*

In Chapters 7 and 8, we advocated an approach to grammar instruction that is meaning-based. Grammar activities should lead students to exchange information with each other and with the instructor. In this section, we encourage "washback effects" by suggesting that the information exchanged in class is appropriate for a test. Just as comprehension checks (see Chapter 2) are ways of ensuring that learners are attending to the input, using the results of in-class activities as the basis for test sections reinforces the importance of interaction with classmates and paying attention in the classroom. Moreover, using the content of classroom interactions on tests can be viewed as an extension of one of the guidelines for creating structured output activities: "Others must respond to the content of the output."

Recall from Chapter 7 the following structured input activity.

Activity P (from Chapter 7).   Attitudes Toward the Government

Step 1. Indicate the extent to which you agree with each statement.

  5: Strongly agree
  4: Agree
  3: Somewhat in agreement
  2: Disagree
  1: Strongly disagree

The government . . .	5	4	3	2	1
1. understands us.	❏	❏	❏	❏	❏
2. helps us.	❏	❏	❏	❏	❏
3. controls us.	❏	❏	❏	❏	❏
4. ignores us.	❏	❏	❏	❏	❏
5. taxes us too much.	❏	❏	❏	❏	❏
6. doesn't represent us.	❏	❏	❏	❏	❏
7. guides us.	❏	❏	❏	❏	❏

Step 2. Share your responses with the class. Someone should tabulate the scores and calculate a class average for each item.

Step 3. Overall, does the class have a positive, negative, or mixed attitude toward the government?

We now propose to adapt this activity in two different ways as a test section. As the quoted excerpt by Krashen and Terrell (see p. 99) suggested, we should give tests that encourage learners to engage in acquisition activities. In other words, tests should "teach" learners that paying attention to input and meaning-based activities is not just for fun but is critical for acquisition. Creating test sections that depend on information exchanged in class should clearly demonstrate to the learners just how important classroom interactions are. In order to complete the test section, the learners must have participated in and attended to the interaction that leads to it. Section F encourages individual expression, whereas Section G focuses more specifically on the interaction itself. The class interaction supplies the content for both sections.

Section F

Compare and/or contrast your classmates' attitude toward the government with your own by writing at least a five-sentence paragraph using *us*. You can use the seven verbs listed to help stimulate your thinking.

MODEL: The class believes that the government understands us, but I do not agree.

| understand | control | help | tax |
| represent | guide | ignore | |

Section G

We responded to the following statements in class. Select three of the statements to which the class had strong reactions (both agreement and disagreement) and recount the information used to support the argument.

The government . . .
1. understands us.
2. helps us.
3. controls us.
4. ignores us.
5. taxes us too much.
6. doesn't represent us.
7. guides us.

MODEL: The class strongly agreed that the government helps us. The examples we gave were student loans, Social Security, and Medicare.

Pause to consider . . .

how you would score Sections F and G. Would you count the accuracy of the statements about the class opinion? Why or why not, and what are the consequences of either position? Would use of the pronoun figure into your scoring criteria? Would it be the *sole* criterion for getting the item correct?

Activity Q was also included in Chapter 7 as an example of a structured input activity. It, too, can be adapted for a test to hold learners accountable for the interactions they have had in the classroom.

Activity Q (from Chapter 7).   State of Mind

Find people in the class who answer "Yes" to the following questions. Rules: (1) You may not use anything but Spanish; (2) you may not ask a person more than one question in a row; (3) if you find someone who answers "Yes" to a question, ask for that person's signature on the line next to the question; (4) when being asked a question, listen carefully; (5) do not sign your name unless you have been asked a complete question.

1. Do you get tense when speaking in Spanish? _____
2. Do you get nervous before taking a big exam? _____
3. Do you get angry easily? _____
4. Do you get depressed during the holidays? _____
5. Do you get bored when you're not in school? _____

Note how Section H adapts Activity Q for testing purposes. The learners are focused on a specific element of the grammar at the same time they are responsible for what happened in class.

Section H

Write a sentence for each of the following that describes how you feel in that situation. Then indicate who else in the class feels the same way you do.

1. When speaking Spanish, I _____

_____. _____ also feels

    this way.

    .
    .
    .

5. When I'm not in school, I _____

_____. _____ also

    feels this way.

Similarly, if Activity N from Chapter 7 were carried out in class with a student named "Tom," then Section I would be the natural follow-up for a test.

Activity N (from Chapter 7).   Would He or Would He Not?

Step 1. Select someone from the class whom you all think you know well. That person should sit by himself during the first part of this activity.

Step 2. Write that person's name in the blank as indicated. Then complete each statement with information that you believe to be true.

Unless he had to, _____
                                 (name)

1. would never eat _____.
2. would never watch _____.
3. would never go to _____.
4. would never spend money on _____.
5. would never _____.

On the other hand, _____
                               (name)

6. would probably eat _____ without reservation.
7. would go to _____ on vacation.
8. would study _____, time permitting.
9. would gladly spend money on _____.
10. would _____.

Section I

Identify three things that you and *(Tom)* both would do and three things neither of you would do. Write in complete sentences.

> ## *Pause to consider . . .*
>
> how to write a test section for multisection courses. How would the directions lines for Section I have to be different if the test were given to twenty sections of French 101, which are taught by twelve different instructors?

So far, all of our examples of testing the content of classroom interactions have been output-based testing sections. But there is no reason why an input-based testing section could not also test information exchanged in class. For example, Activity N (from Chapter 7) was an input-based task in class. The following could be used as an input-based testing section.

Section J

We have seen in class what Harriet does, doesn't do, would do, and would never do. For each pair of sentences you hear (or read), indicate which one is true for Harriet.

1. **a.** Harriet would never watch a soap opera.
   b. Harriet watches soap operas.
2. **a.** Harriet would never eat snails.
   b. Harriet eats snails.
3. **a.** Harriet would never go to Iowa.
   b. Harriet goes to Iowa.

As you examine Section J, note how the learner must attend to the verb form as part of paying attention to the meaning. That is, the grammatical difference between *would never eat* and *eats* determines the truth-value of each sentence. There is no better way of keeping meaning in focus than by working with the truth-value of information!

> ## *Pause to consider . . .*
>
> how learners might react to test sections that examined information exchanged in class. In other words, would they find test sections of this nature acceptable? Why or why not? What would the instructor have to do to make such sections acceptable to the test takers?

Entire books have been written on language testing—both theory and practice—and we have not attempted to survey all the issues in this chapter. We focused very specifically on testing grammar so that teaching is not viewed as somehow divorced from testing. On the one hand, we adapted the kinds of activities done in class to test sections. On the other, we took certain interactive classroom activities and created test sections based on those interactions. In this approach, the learners are consistently given the opportunity to apply the content to themselves, to state their own opinions and beliefs. Instructors accomplish several things by doing this: (1) We keep meaning in focus; (2) we provide a context for using the grammar (not merely contextualizing the grammar); (3) we connect processing the language with producing it. Grammar becomes the *means* to an end; knowing the grammar rules and memorizing the forms are *not* the goal. Learners, therefore, should not view grammar only as an object of study and manipulation. Rather, they should view grammar as a way to express meaning, interact, and communicate. Because learners are motivated by tests, we can use tests to underscore what grammar is supposed to do for them.

KEY TERMS, CONCEPTS, AND ISSUES

test
washback effect
economy
  sampling
relevance
  test what and how you teach
acceptability
  test takers' perspective
comparability
  similar results
  institutional perspective
relationship of structured input
 activities to test sections
  one thing at a time
  keep meaning in focus

move from sentences to
  connected discourse
use both written and oral
  input/output
the learner must do something
  with the input
others must respond to the
  learner's output
attending to form-meaning
  relationship
completeness
learner responsibilities
  attending to input in class
  attending to interactions in class
  applying content to self

THINKING MORE ABOUT IT: DISCUSSION QUESTIONS

1. Placement tests are often multiple choice in nature because they are subsequently machine scored. How do you think a student in the classes where you teach or will be teaching would react to a multiple-choice grammar test at the end of a lesson? Do you think multiple choice is a valid way of getting at what learners know about grammar?

2. Discuss the pros and cons of using both structured input and structured output activities on a test. Refer to the concept of washback as well as some of Carroll's ideas about criteria for good tests.

GETTING A CLOSER LOOK:
RESEARCH ACTIVITIES

Collect samples of tests given by instructors of the language that you (will) teach. Examine them for input- versus output-based formats, as well as for the meaningful and communicative versus mechanical nature of the test items or sections. Prepare a brief report with examples in which you explain (a) the philosophy underlying the tests given by these instructors and (b) the extent to which you see these tests as reflecting the teaching of communicative language abilities.

MAKING COMMUNICATIVE LANGUAGE
TEACHING HAPPEN: PORTFOLIO ACTIVITIES

Create a test section that focuses on the grammar points you have been developing in your portfolio. Be prepared to defend it in terms of washback, economy, relevance, and acceptability.

CHAPTER 10

Listening Comprehension

In this chapter, we explore:

- Listening as a psycholinguistic process that consists of various levels of activity, from perception of sounds to the use of personal experience and cultural context to assign meaning to what is heard
- Listening as a communicative act, with a distinction made between collaborative and noncollaborative listening and attention to the skills and strategic responses listeners have at their disposal
- The extent to which classrooms provide for the development of listening as a skill
- The development of listening activities for outside the classroom (e.g., in the language laboratory)

LISTENING AS A PSYCHOLINGUISTIC PROCESS

Listening, like reading, has often been referred to as a "passive" or "receptive" skill. These terms stand in contrast to "active" or "productive," used to refer to speaking and writing skills. The term *passive* is an unfortunate one, for it suggests that the listener is a mere bystander during communication, a submissive individual, unable to act, who does not participate and merely accepts whatever is thrown her way. Despite the persistence of the terms *passive* and *receptive* for listening skills, scholars agree that listeners are active participants during the communicative act and that listening is a dynamic process drawing on a variety of mental processes and knowledge sources. Wolvin and Coakley (1985) divide the act of listening into three very broad sets of processes:

1. Perceiving aural stimuli
2. Attending to aural stimuli
3. Assigning meaning to aural stimuli

At each step of the way, learners are actively engaged in processing what they hear. We now examine each set of processes in turn, spending most of our time on the third.

Perception of aural stimuli refers to the physiological aspects of listening. Sound waves enter the ear canal, causing the ear drum to vibrate. These vibrations are converted into electrical impulses that trigger the release of chemicals, which in turn react with the acoustic nerve (analogous to the optic nerve in vision), which transmits a signal to the brain. Clearly, the ear drum must be a sensitive organ, sending the vibrations and electrical impulses that represent the differences between *ship* and *sheep*, *cad* and *cat*, and *talk* and *talked* correctly to the brain. Perception, then, is a necessary aspect of listening comprehension, but it cannot be equated with it.

Attending to aural stimuli involves active concentration by the listener. The listener must be focused on the aural stimuli and must select what to pay attention to and what to disregard. At any given moment, a listener could be talking on the phone with the TV or radio on, birds singing in the trees, children playing and screaming in the backyard, and cars zooming down the street. If the purpose is to carry on the phone conversation, the listener must tune out the background noises and attend only to the incoming sounds on the telephone in order to be successful. This ability suggests that we all have some internal mechanisms responsible for filtering incoming stimuli; we can (and do) perceive all the sounds around us, but we attend only to some of them. Like perception, however, attending to stimuli is a necessary aspect of listening but, by itself, not a sufficient one.

Once stimuli are attended to, they must be assigned meaning. For the present discussion, this is perhaps the most important set of processes in listening for comprehension. Assigning meaning is not a straightforward phenomenon and is perhaps trickier than perception and attention. Why is this so? *Assigning meaning to perceived and attended stimuli* is an interpretative act that involves personal, cultural, and linguistic matters interacting in complex ways. The word *run*, for example, can mean one of the following (and perhaps more):

1. A fast, forward movement involving the legs
2. Nose dripping
3. The act of seeking a political office
4. Not turning something off (e.g., He left the water running.)
5. A snag in a pair of pantyhose
6. Massive sales (e.g., We had a run on size 8 shoes. They're all gone.)
7. A trip (e.g., making a run to Chicago)
8. A race
9. Bowel problems (e.g., He has the runs.)

But the likelihood of a listener misassigning meaning to the word *run* is greatly diminished if the word is used as a noun instead of a verb; if the speaker is a truck driver rather than a political pundit; if the occurrence of the word happens as part of the development of a single topic; or if the speaker and listener share the same cultural and personal backgrounds.

However, assigning meaning is not limited to the word level. Whole sentences must be interpreted, and sometimes individual words can be assigned meaning only after the entire sentence has been heard. Richards (1983) outlines the complex nature of assigning meaning to attended aural stimuli in six steps:

1. The speech event or interactional set is determined (e.g., this is a lecture, this is a debate, this is an interrogation, this is a job interview).
2. Scripts (episodic prototypes) relevant to the situation or context are recalled (i.e., the listener brings forth a master scheme of how the interaction or set is to play out and what kind of language will be used).
3. The speaker's goals are determined by way of the situation, the script, and the position of the utterance in the flow of discourse (e.g., during an interview a listener might determine that at this point the speaker is trying to find out about his experience).
4. The propositional or referential content of the speaker's utterance is determined.
5. An illocutionary meaning is assigned to the speaker's utterance (e.g., that utterance was a compliment, that utterance was a request, that utterance was a slur).
6. The meaning is retained and acted upon, but the actual form in which it was encoded by the speaker (and received by the listener) may not be remembered (e.g., the listener may say, "thirty-nine," but not subsequently remember whether the question was "How old are you?" "What is your age?" "And your age?" "Please state your age," and, when reporting the conversation later, may say that the person asked him how old he was).

As an example of how this complex act of listening occurs, let's take an example from a negative television ad during an election campaign. We hear the first line ("So-and-so claims to be for the people"), and we determine the situation: This is a political campaign ad on TV. We then call forth from our memory similar ads ("They're going to give me reasons the other guy is bad. They're going to talk about something he's done in the past. I'll probably see a photo of the guy."), and we determine the goal ("They want me to think bad things about this guy so that I'll vote for their guy."). Then we watch the ad and hear the final question—"Does this sound like someone who should hold public office?"—and we assign referential meaning to it. Finally, we assign the question its illocutionary meaning ("Even though this is a question, they don't expect an answer since they really aren't talking to me. The question is rhetorical and is actually a statement telling me that the guy should not hold public office.").

Although speakers might share a common culture and language that direct them to assign particular meanings to particular streams of speech, this is no guarantee that they will always assign the *same* illocutionary meanings to utterances they hear in conversations. Because of personal and individual psychological makeup, what is understood as a compliment by one person might be seen as a snide remark by another. What is interpreted as a mere suggestion or opinion by someone might be interpreted as a command by someone else.

Thus, meaning assignment during listening is not a purely linguistic act or even a social act; it can also be an individual act.

Assigning meaning to aural stimuli can also involve the construction of meaning, even though something specific was not said. This is called *inference*. We "infer" whenever we project beyond the referential meaning encoded in someone's utterance. Assigning illocutionary meaning to an utterance is a type of inference, but one can also infer meaning *when no utterance was uttered*. Note the following interchange.

A: Are you free this evening?
B: What time?
A: 8:00.
B: Pick me up at 7:45.

Now compare it to an expanded version.

A: Are you free this evening? I'd like us to go out.
B: It depends when. What time do you have in mind?
A: 8:00. Is that O.K.?
B: 8:00 is fine. Pick me up at 7:45.

In the first version, both speakers are projecting beyond the concrete referents of their utterances. B knows that A is asking for a date even though A never uses the words *date* or *go out*. A knows that B has accepted in the end even though B has not said *I accept, Yes I will go out with you*, or any other such response. Such things were simply inferred.

Inference for second language learners is as important as it is for first language speakers and can take on characteristics that do not normally occur during native-to-native interactions. One additional characteristic is that inference can actually include deducing meanings of novel or unfamiliar words and phrases, that is, inferring the referential meaning of words during the act of listening. In this case, the learner fills in lexical gaps based on contextual and pragmatic cues. In the conversational exchange we just saw, B says, "Pick me up." There are a variety of ways of saying this in colloquial English: *Come by, Swing by, Buzz by*, among others. Imagine the second language learner who hears *Swing by* or *Buzz by*. She very well may not be familiar with these expressions, but does that mean she cannot complete the act of setting up the date? The learner can infer the meaning of *swing by* or *buzz by* given the situation and the script already understood by both speakers for setting up a time to get together.

Pause to consider . . .

the kind of listening involved in "channel surfing." Can you describe channel surfing in terms of perceiving, attending, assigning meaning, and inferring? Are you equally able to channel surf in your second language?

Although some people tend to equate communication with speaking, it is clear that a communicative act involves both expression and interpretation of meaning. In oral interactions, interpretation refers to listening as well as speaking, and in everyday life both native speakers and second language speakers engage in a variety of communicative situations during which they listen. Broadly speaking, there are two types of listening situations: *collaborative* and *noncollaborative*. Collaborative situations are those in which both speaker and listener work together to negotiate meaning. The listener actively collaborates in the construction of the discourse. Nodding, furrowing the brow, asking questions, commenting on what was said, adding to what was said, saying "Yeah, yeah" or "Huh!?"—all of these allow the listener to play an active role in shaping what the other speaker says and how she says it.

Noncollaborative situations are those in which the listener does not participate in the construction of discourse and is merely an observant listener. The speaker is the sole person who determines the nature of the discourse. Listening to a song is an example of noncollaborative listening, as is listening to the president's State of the Union Address.

Listening situations also fall along another dimension: *modality*, aural versus visual perception. Although it is true that listening involves aural stimuli, it is not the case that listening deals exclusively with the aural mode. In many, if not most cases, listeners *see* the other interlocutor and receive information on how to interpret messages via facial expressions, body posture, gestures, signs, slides, and other visual features. For example, students sitting in a large lecture hall listening to a professor's formal lecture might very well be attending to overhead transparencies, handouts, or other visual clues in addition to the visual cues provided by the professor. The opposite case would be a telephone conversation in which accompanying visual stimuli are absent (at least, until the time when videoconferencing becomes the staple of every household and business): The modality here is aural only.

Thus, we can say that listening situations can be categorized according to two sets of features: the presence or absence of collaboration and the presence or absence of accompanying visual stimuli. This relationship is illustrated in Figure 10.1.

Pause to consider . . .

other listening examples. Can you add other situations to each of the boxes in Figure 10.1? To do so, review what listening you have done in the last week.

	Modality	
	Aural Only	Aural + Visual
Collaborative	Telephone Walkie-Talkie	Interview Game
Noncollaborative	Radio News Voicemail	TV News Formal Lecture

FIGURE 10.1 Dimensions of a listening situation

Let us now consider listener performance. What strategies or tactics do skilled listeners use during communication? It seems intuitively obvious that strategies may change depending on the collaborative or noncollaborative nature of the situation. For collaborative situations, Rost (1990) summarizes a number of what he calls *"strategic responses* that constitute effective listener performance in collaborative discourse"* (p. 115). (Since a listener cannot interact with the speaker in a noncollaborative setting, there are no strategic responses to be discussed for the latter.) Rost lists eight skills and eleven strategic responses.

Skills

1. Recognizing indicators used by the other speaker to (a) introduce new ideas, (b) change topics, (c) provide emphasis and/or clarification, or (d) express contrary points of view
2. Maintaining continuity of context in order to assist the prediction and verification of propositions in the discourse
3. Identifying an interpersonal frame that suggests what the speaker's intent is toward the listener
4. Recognizing changes in prosody—pitch, speed, pauses—and identifying both patterns and inconsistencies in how the other speaker uses these
5. Identifying ambiguity and contradictions in what the other speaker says; identifying places where inadequate information is given
6. Distinguishing between fact and opinion; also, identifying uses of irony, metaphor, and other "nonreferential" use of language
7. Identifying needed clarifications of topics and ideas
8. Providing appropriate feedback to the other speaker

(Based on Rost, 1990, p. 115)

Strategic Responses

Skilled listeners will . . .

1. Try to identify points at which they can switch to the speaker role
2. Look for those places in the discourse where they are to participate in socially appropriate ways (i.e., recognize cues indicating they should obligatorily take a turn at speaking)

3. Provide appropriate cues to the speaker that they are following the discourse
4. Provide prompts to the speaker to continue the discourse
5. Provide cues to indicate how they align with the speaker's intent
6. Evaluate the speaker's contributions and reformulate them when they conflict with listener goals
7. Be aware of power asymmetries in the discourse and recognize when a "superior" party is enforcing interpretative rules
8. Identify a plausible speaker's intent when interpreting an utterance
9. Afford recognition to the speaker's intent in participating in unequal encounters
10. Identify parts of discourse needing repair and query those points when appropriate
11. Utilize gambits (set phrases and other linguistic patterns that promote interaction) for checking understanding when appropriate

(Based on Rost, 1990, p. 116)

What is clear from these skills and strategic responses is the role that the listener plays in *maintaining the discourse.* The listener is not a bystander but a co-constructor of the discourse. The listener provides cues about how well he understands and must signal the other speaker in various ways about how the topic is developing. Another important job of the listener is to signal nonunderstanding through global, local, and transitional queries (Rost, 1990, p. 112). A *global query* functions at the broad level of the entire discourse: "I don't understand. Could you start from the beginning and speak a little more slowly?" "Do you want me to remember all of this? Should I take notes?" A *local query* identifies a particular point in the discourse that the listener has not understood and requests clarification of that point: "What do you mean by 'strategic response'?" and "Strategic response?" (with rising intonation) both signal that the listener has not understood a specific point. *Transitional queries* indicate difficulty with a hypothesis or prediction made by the listener. "Why did she do that?" and "I don't see the problem with that" are indications that the listener has understood but cannot integrate the information with previous knowledge or with predictions already made about the topic.

In sum, we see that listening acts can vary along two major dimensions: type of collaboration and aural-visual modality. Listeners can be collaborative listeners during face-to-face interchanges and telephone conversations, or they can be noncollaborative listeners while listening to the radio. They can be engaged in aural-only situations (radio, telephone) or aural plus some kind of visual stimulus (watching TV). In addition, we see that listeners are active (not passive) participants in the act of communication. Listeners must understand when to take on the role of speaker and add to the topic. They must understand when to confirm what they've heard and support the speaker's discourse, and they must know how to signal nonunderstanding to the other speaker. It goes without saying that skilled listeners develop these abilities through communicative interaction itself and not through guided, manipulative practices. This is the focus of the remainder of this chapter, in which we examine ways to develop communicative listening skills.

Pause to consider . . .

how conscious we are of our skills and strategies. Reread Rost's lists of skills and strategic responses. Do you think we use these skills and strategies consciously or unconsciously? In other words, are these things we just do or are they things we have to think about and then do? Are you able to use these skills and strategies equally in your first and second languages?

LISTENING IN THE SECOND LANGUAGE CLASSROOM

What kinds of listening tasks do classroom learners generally engage in? Are they given opportunities to listen in a wide variety of situations? Do they have the opportunity to develop the skills and strategic responses described in the previous section? Classrooms are limited in their ability to provide learners a full range of everyday listening tasks and situations. If we take Figure 10.1., for example, and attempt to place into it typical classroom and formal listening activities, what activities can go in each box? We offer some suggestions in Figure 10.2; you should think of activities to complete the remaining boxes.

The classroom second language learner tends to be engaged in only two kinds of listening situations: collaborative aural + visual situations (classroom discussion where there is use of the blackboard, overheads, or other presentation devices) and noncollaborative aural-only situations (lab practice). Although there is increased interest in the use of video and TV in language classrooms, which represent noncollaborative aural + visual listening situations, the use of these media is far from being everyday. If we probe even further, we see that the two situations that do present themselves may not always offer learners opportunities to develop the full range of skills and strategic responses used by skilled listeners.

		Modality	
		Aural Only	Aural + Visual
Collaboration	Collaborative	???	Classroom "Discussion"
	Noncollaborative	Lab Materials	Watching a Video

FIGURE 10.2 Common listening situations in the second language classroom

Classroom	Nonclassroom
Tends to be group participation, guided by a teacher	Often only two participants
Learners interact with teacher and other learners	Learners interact with native speakers
Teacher tends to control topic development	Learners participate in topic development
Setting is always the classroom	Settings are varied
Social roles are fixed	Social roles vary
Purpose includes evaluation (either immediate or delayed)	Purpose is largely communicative (informational and/or social)

Classroom Discussions and Conversations

A comparison of classroom and nonclassroom discussions suggests that max-imal active participation of the learner as listener is limited in a number of ways. Table 10.1 lists some of the differences between listening in class and lis-tening outside of class. First, in the classroom, learners "share" the instructor with everyone else during the discussion and, given the public nature of the discourse, might be unwilling to show nonunderstanding. In the nonclassroom setting, language learners often get the chance to interact one-on-one with a native speaker, who will signal nonunderstanding, will confirm, and will read-ily take turns. The native speaker can thus provide the learner with a variety of appropriate models of listening performance. Classroom learners, however, cannot do this with each other; only the instructor can provide a model of the fullest range of skilled listener behaviors. Because instructors tend to control the topic of the discussion and also make great use of question asking, learner-listeners may not be given the opportunity to function as co-creators in the dis-course and to develop appropriate listener responses. On the other hand, roles outside the classroom vary as learners act as listeners in conversations with friends, clerks, doctors, telephone solicitors, bus drivers, and other individuals with whom they may have equal or nonequal status relationships. In the class-room, learners are in an unequal power relationship with their instructors. Finally, whereas the purpose of listening in the nonclassroom situation is either informational (receiving a message) or social (establishing and maintaining relationships), the purpose of listening in the classroom is often evaluative (the instructor keeps an eye out for who is having problems and who isn't, who is paying attention and who isn't, with the intent of providing feedback or assigning a grade).

The classroom, then, may not be an ideal place for the development of all listening skills and strategic responses. Nonetheless, it is the place where such skills and responses *can begin to develop*. Instructors can take steps toward maximizing class time for the development of listening. Here are some suggestions.

1. Use the second language to conduct business. Making announcements, describing what will be on a test, and assigning homework all push learners toward purposeful listening. Because learners have a great stake in comprehending the business at hand, they will be more likely to question, confirm, and signal nonunderstanding in order to get the message.

2. Allow learners to nominate topics and structure the discourse. They are much more likely to get involved in active participatory listening if they help control the topic. One teaching technique would be to reserve five minutes a day or ten minutes every other day during which a learner can nominate a topic. The class can decide on Monday, for example, who will nominate a topic on Wednesday, and then on Wednesday another who will nominate a topic on Friday, so that all eventually are involved in nominating topics during the term. The learner in charge can solicit opinions from classmates about what to discuss (e.g., "We would like to know about where you are from. What was it like growing up there?").

3. Be a participatory listener yourself. When learners attempt to express themselves, you need to respond as a listener, not an instructor. That is, as a listener the instructor should engage in appropriate listening performance. In this way, learners see and hear how to perform as listeners in the second language.

4. Set aside telephone time. Instructors can increase the scope of listening opportunities by encouraging biweekly phone calls. Learners must call another instructor or a native speaker and interview that person over the phone. Or, an instructor might set aside a block of time during which she receives telephone calls in the second language from her learners, who ask questions, get information, or simply "chat."

5. Provide some good listening gambits to learners. In addition to simply allowing more opportunities for collaborative listening, instructors can also point out to learners typical listening gambits for signalling nonunderstanding, confirmation, and so forth. The instructor can place signs around the room with second language equivalents of gambits such as:

I didn't catch that.

Could you speak more slowly, please?

What is _____?

Did you say _____? What's that?

I don't understand _____.

Really?

No kidding!

O.K., O.K.

Oh, I'm sorry. My mind was wandering.

Academic Listening in the Classroom

In addition to discussions and conversations, the classroom can also provide opportunities for the learner to listen in noncollaborative aural + visual-stimuli situations. Language instructors sometimes forget that academic listening is a very common type of communicative listening. If learners continue their education in the second language, they will no doubt need to attend lectures and presentations. The instructor can thus include an occasional listening situation that functions like academic listening: delivering a lecture or presentation (complete with use of blackboard, overhead, slides, and photos) and having learners take notes. Learners are then asked to do one of several things with the information they have heard:

- Summarize it in written form
- Make a visual representation of the information (charts or posters, for example, depending on the information)
- Take a test on the information
- Some combination of the above

Such opportunities provide a different type of listening situation in which the strategies required may be different from those used in more "conversational" listening. Since students may not be able to interrupt and may have to wait until an appropriate time to ask a question or receive a clarification, they are pushed to process language far beyond the sentence level.

Pause to consider . . .

the relevance of classroom listening to nonclassroom listening. Think back to the first time you listened to the second language in a nonclassroom setting. What were the characteristics of that listening situation? Did your classroom experiences prepare you for the nonclassroom experience?

LISTENING IN THE LANGUAGE LABORATORY

We now examine the use of the laboratory for developing listening abilities. It is probably fair to say that traditional language laboratory materials offer noncollaborative, aural-only types of practice. The exercises in these practices contain sentence-level, dialogue-level, or monologue-type discourse, but they are noncollaborative in nature. Typical examples are described here. (Note: When we refer to laboratory listening, we do not suggest that the learner has to sit in a laboratory booth to complete the exercises. It is increasingly common for learners to do these kinds of activities in isolation at home with a CD player or computer.)

Activity A. Sentence-Level Listening Practice

Listen to each sentence and determine whether it is true or false according to the visual clue.

Activity B. Dialogue-Level Listening Practice

Listen to Alphonse and Christine make plans for this evening. Then indicate who said what.

ALPHONSE   CHRISTINE

❏   ❏   **1.** This person wants to go out to eat.

❏   ❏   **2.** This person wants to get home early.

❏   ❏   **3.** This person offers to drive.

Activity C. Monologue-Type Practice

Listen to the speaker as he talks about Holy Week in Spain. Then answer the questions that follow.

1. What city in Spain is most famous for its celebration of Holy Week?

2. How many tourists visit that city every year for this religious event?

How do these noncollaborative situations in the laboratory compare with other nonclassroom, noncollaborative listening? First, let's recall what other noncollaborative listening situations exist. One can listen to the radio for news, weather, music, and announcements; to songs, books on tape, and other pre-recorded material; to recorded messages on phones. One can watch TV, a movie, or a play or watch-listen to a commencement speech or political debate. There are, of course, other situations, but what these all have in common is that listeners have some control over the topic. They often decide what radio station to listen to, whether or not to listen to the news, whether to listen to a murder mystery or a science fiction book on tape, and so forth. In addition, listeners approach their task with a purpose: getting the message regarding some specific news story, finding out where a sale is taking place, determining who did what to whom. We may listen for purely entertainment reasons. We listen to a certain song not for information but simply because we like the song; likewise, we may watch a particular TV show simply because we like it. Finally, in the nonclassroom setting noncollaborative listeners generally determine when they are done listening. They may change the channel, turn off the radio or TV, fast forward to a different song, or simply tune out.

In Table 10.2 the characteristics of out-of-laboratory noncollaborative listening are contrasted with those of the laboratory. In the laboratory the learner does not control topics; these are predetermined. Nor does the learner initiate and terminate listening: listening is completed when the task is completed.

TABLE 10.2 A Comparison of Noncollaborative Listening In and Out of the Laboratory

Laboratory	Nonclassroom
Topic is predetermined	Learner controls the topic
Purpose is often to practice	Learner listens for information
(same as above)	Learner listens for entertainment
Initiation and termination of listening is determined by another	Learner initiates and terminates listening

Finally, in the laboratory the learner listens as part of language-learning practice and is very often evaluated on his performance.

It is difficult to imagine learners controlling the topic or the initiation and termination of the listening act itself while in the laboratory (except, of course, when the listener chooses to walk away before finishing the lesson!). But it does seem possible that we can increase the communicative purpose of listening, that is, listening for information. Laboratory activities A, B, and C presented earlier all lack informational purpose: the learner listens in order to answer questions. But in real life, we often listen in order to report to someone or to summarize information. We listen to the weather report only to tell someone else later what the weather is going to be like or to use that information to make a decision. We listen to the news and then discuss it with friends. We listen to a speech and then report on it or summarize it for someone else. In short, listeners take information and then transform it into their own words for others. How often do learners get the opportunity to do this in the second language? It seems that the language laboratory could provide useful opportunities. Here are some possibilities for noncollaborative purposeful listening.

1. Listen to a radio broadcast, lecture, monologue, story, or some other oral text and prepare:
   a. A written summary
   b. An oral summary
   c. An outline
   d. Some combination of a, b, and c
2. Listen to a conversation or dialogue and then report it as a narrative.
3. Listen to a set of directions (instructions) and then perform a task.

Tasks 1 and 2 are straightforward and have begun to appear in laboratory materials. As one example, here is the task assigned to students in an activity based on listening to a short text about the increase in multiple births (i.e., twins, triplets, quadruplets). The selection presented here is actually the final section of the listening task.

Activity D. Synthesis

Step 1. The speaker mentioned four principal factors that have contributed to the increase in multiple births. Complete the following chart, identifying the factors and how each contributes to this increase.

Factors That Lead to Increased Multiple Births	
Factors	**How They Contribute**
1. Many women wait to have children.	1.
2.	2.
3.	3.
4.	4. This increases the chance of multiple fertilized eggs surviving in the womb.

Step 2. In a short composition, use the information from your chart to explain why there has been an increase in multiple births. You might want to use the following sentences to begin your composition: "Different factors contribute to the recent rise in multiple births. These factors are the following:"

These kinds of activities encourage learners to synthesize information (that is, distill ideas) they have listened to and report on it in their own words. The chart in Activity D requires learners to select ideas and to organize them in a coherent way. The follow-up writing activity then asks learners to pull these ideas together using connected discourse. Thus, listening is not an activity in and of itself but, rather, part of a more complex communicative activity that goes beyond listening. In a sense, *listening is a means to an end*; it is not the end itself.

The third task type (listening to a set of directions and then performing a task) is rarely found in language teaching materials. It is usually limited to the lesson on giving and receiving directions, in which learners demonstrate comprehension by starting at point A on a map and winding up at a predetermined point B. But in real life oral directions and instructions are given to listeners in a variety of situations. The following list illustrates actions that might require following oral instructions:

- Following a recipe
- Entering a contest
- Filling out forms
- Building something
- Putting something together
- Playing a game
- Analyzing some kind of data
- Using an electronic device
- Taking or administering medicine
- Playing a sport or performing an athletic activity

This is a partial list, but note how far we have gone beyond the usual giving and receiving of directions for getting somewhere. Laboratory materials can offer more of these kinds of listening opportunities. For example, the following activity could easily be performed in a lab or as a homework assignment.

Activity E.   Playing a Card Game

In this activity, you will learn how to play a card game. On the recording, one person will be giving instructions to another. Listen and pay attention to the instructions as best you can. It is helpful to have a deck of cards handy to act out the instructions as you receive them. Afterward, you will answer some questions about the rules of the game, and tomorrow in class you will need to show that you have understood the rules by actually playing the game! Listen to the recording as many times as you like. (Note: You will encounter a number of new words and phrases as you listen, but you should be able to guess these based on the context and the situation. Keep in mind that you are learning a card game. What are typical expressions and words used in playing cards that you use in your first language?)

Text of the Recording

> ROB: O.K. First, I deal out five cards.
> GERRI: O.K. Why five?
> ROB: Hold on, hold on. O.K., pick them up and organize them according to numbers. Say, fours, fives. Like this. If you have two fives, put them together, if you have . . .
> GERRI: What if I have more than two?
> ROB: Well, then put them all together. The idea is to group your cards by numbers. You done?
> GERRI: Yeah, uh huh.
> ROB: O.K. Now . . . *(The instructions continue.)*

Follow-up Questions

1. How many cards are dealt at the beginning?
    a. Five   **b.** Seven   **c.** Ten
2. Cards are supposed to be grouped. Are they grouped by number or suit?

Note that comprehension in this activity is examined in two ways. First, the learner answers some questions about the game itself, demonstrating how well he has understood its basic elements. Second, the learner is asked to play the game in class, demonstrating how well he integrated what he heard on the recording into long-term memory, a part of listening performance that is essential in everyday life.

---

*P*ause to consider . . .
_____

some other examples. Can you think of additional activities that could be used for listening outside of class?

GETTING READY TO LISTEN

Currently of special interest to language teachers is the use of "prelistening" activities. *Prelistening activities* are designed to help orient learners before they actually begin listening to something. This orientation helps maximize learners' comprehension. Recall that in listening, attention requires that we focus on aural stimuli and that we make decisions about what to attend to and what to ignore. When we attend to aural stimuli, we often have scripts in mind and make predictions about what we are going to hear. This facilitates comprehension, but we generally do this unconsciously. In second language situations, on the other hand, particularly in the beginning stages, *consciously* orienting learners before a listening task has been shown to increase comprehension.

Prelistening activities fall into three general groups that are not necessarily mutually exclusive:

1. Vocabulary preparation
2. Review of existing knowledge
3. Anticipation of content

We examine each in turn.

Vocabulary preparation is the simple task of acquainting learners with unfamiliar words and expressions that will be either useful or necessary for the listening excerpt. The goal is not to have learners memorize words and produce them but to recognize them and attach meaning to them when they hear them. Thus, most prelistening vocabulary preparation is limited to input-oriented activities. Instructors can make use of visuals, Total Physical Response, definitions, and even lists. But another way (and perhaps a better one because the vocabulary is linked with content) is to embed the new words and expressions in either a review of existing knowledge or in an anticipation of content.

Review of existing knowledge requires learners to reflect on what they already know. For example, in Activity E with the card game instructions, most learners know a great deal about card games even if they don't play cards themselves. They probably know that

There is a dealer

Cards are shuffled, dealt, shown, discarded, and so on

People sometimes bet

Players can either win or lose

Cards have numbers or faces (jack, queen, king)

Cards have suits

A review of existing knowledge explicitly calls forth some of these concepts to check what learners actually know about some topic in its most general sense. As mentioned earlier, vocabulary preparation can be combined with a review of knowledge. For example, prior to listening to the instructions on the card game, learners might be given a quiz on what they know about cards and card games, with new vocabulary and expressions glossed.

Activity F.   Before Listening

What do you already know about cards and playing cards? See if you can determine whether the following statements are true or false.

1. Card games may involve one or more persons.
2. When two or more people are involved, one person must deal.
3. A person always deals from right to left.
4. Cards are always dealt face down.

Learners might or might not know the answers to these questions, so it is irrelevant if they get them all right or all wrong when they answer. What is important is that, after completing the activity and checking their answers, they have either confirmed or developed some knowledge of cards and card playing before they begin listening *and* they have begun to bind meaning with form (in this case, related vocabulary and expressions). A review of existing knowledge can take a variety of forms and can be teacher led, textbook led, or on the recording that learners listen to. Some examples of activity types for a review of existing knowledge are listed following. Of course, any combination of activities can be used, since there is nothing wrong with variety!

- Quizzes
  True/false/"don't have a clue"
  Multiple choice
  Short answer
- Teacher-Led Discussion
  The instructor leads a discussion in which she explains and asks questions, using the blackboard and other visual devices.
- Short Reading
  Learners read a short text before listening. They then answer questions, participate in a teacher-led discussion, or perform some other task.
- Learner Brainstorming
  Either in groups or with the instructor, or a combination of the two, learners brainstorm what they know about the topic. They might create a semantic map, make lists of concepts, or trade experiences.

Some activities (like brainstorming) might need to be conducted in the first language, especially in the early stages. The role of the instructor, then, is to take the concepts expressed in the first language and transform them into the second language.

Anticipation of content directs learners to predict some of the things that a speaker might say. When we listen to a weather report while driving, for example, we expect to hear certain phrases and expressions and not others. And we expect the report to be about our local area. "Thirty percent chance of thunderstorms," "High in the low 90s this afternoon," "Grab an umbrella if you're leaving your house because . . ." are samples of expressions that we expect to hear. We do not expect to hear such things as "It's *coooold* in Moscow today" or "Next year should bring us more rain." In the card game listening activity, what would one expect to hear? What would one expect to hear if the listening activity specifically involves instructions on how to play a game? One would expect to hear the rules of the game, the objective of the game (how one wins), what a winning hand is, how to score points, and so forth. The same activities used to review existing knowledge can be used to anticipate content: Learners can be quizzed in some way; they can be taken through a teacher-led discussion (question-and-answer session); they can read a short text (say, the rules for another game and can then make a list of things they expect to be told); or they can brainstorm.

LISTENING AND CULTURE

As we said earlier, culture is not something that can be divorced from activities. Rather than discuss the teaching of culture as a separate matter, we have included, here and there, suggestions for how you might view the activities you have been reviewing and/or developing in a cultural context. Now we would like to make some points a little more salient.

Listening activities—and by extension reading activities, which are discussed in Chapter 11—are excellent devices for bringing cultural materials into the second or foreign language classroom. But what do we mean by "culture"? Language teachers typically distinguish culture with a big C from culture with a little *c*. Culture with a big C refers to those aspects and artifacts of a society that represent what we might call achievements—art, music, architecture, and so on. Culture with a little *c* refers to the everyday aspects of life within a society. In this domain we would include such things as how people greet each other, eating habits and customs, the nature of "personal space," the nature of social deference, and so on. As you think about the teaching of culture as part of your lesson planning, you may want to keep these distinctions in mind so that you're aware of which kind of "culture" you're discussing.

How can listening activities incorporate culture? Culture, like just about anything, can be viewed from the outside, that is, as an object. Thus, culture can be *the content of listening activities* that you develop or find. In this chapter, a cultural event in Spain (Holy Week, Activity C) formed the content of the listening. Learners would hear a passage about this special event and then answer some comprehension questions. However, the use of culture in such activities should not stop with a series of questions regarding what was listened to; it should also include possible inferences about the society or people related to the content. In this sense, we are talking about learners conducting a mini-*cultural analysis*. For example, in the passage on Holy Week in Spain, learners would hear about the processions, how people from all over flock to the southern cities in Spain, especially Seville, and so on. But apart from that, what does this event reveal about the people who celebrate it? And how does this compare with the observance of Holy Week in the United States? Learners might be asked to reflect on some questions that bring the cultural analysis into focus. For example:

- Can you think of any U.S. city that celebrates Holy Week this way?
- If so, what does this suggest about that city compared to others in the United States?
- If not, what kind of processions and parades are well known in the United States? What does this suggest about the beliefs or backgrounds of Americans and those of Spaniards?

Depending on level, such questions can be addressed in the first or the second language; if they are addressed in the second language, level will dictate the structuring of the task. For example, you might ask the question and "discuss" it in advanced classes, but in beginning or lower-level classes, in which students' abilities do not allow them to discuss the topic in the second language, you might use multiple-choice questions or checklists.

Another way to incorporate cultural material into listening activities is to use authentic listening texts from television or radio. Commercials, films, and so on often reveal things about cultures that are not overt. For example, some commercials in Europe and Japan contain images or information that one would never see in the United States (e.g., a commercial for a glue in which nuns attempt to reattach the penis that had fallen off a baby Jesus statue). The question that you might use to initiate a cultural discussion is this: Since you would never see this kind of commercial in the United States, what kind of cultural differences might be inferred between the United States and the country where this commercial was made?

The goal of such cultural analyses is not to make learners experts in culture; we do not believe you can teach culture in the same way you might teach the past tense. Instead, the goal should be much more modest: to help students develop *cultural sensitivity*. Cultural sensitivity means understanding that other cultures and societies have values and beliefs different from a student's own. In fact, one might even suggest that cultural sensitivity begins at home! The United States is a good place to begin to look at how culture can vary from place to place. Learning about one's own cultural values and making them salient is a good first step to take before beginning to look at other cultures.

Pause to consider . . .

the concept of examining one's own cultural values first. What kinds of classroom activities could be used to stimulate thinking about one's own culture? Here are some phrases that can be used as jumping off points: "Time is money," "You're invading my personal space," "We're a car culture." Can you think of any others?

The inclusion of cultural material, whether culture with a big *C* or culture with a little *c*, has implications for activity development. We saw earlier that a framework for listening activities would include a prelistening phase ("getting ready to listen") to prep learners before they listen in order to maximize the comprehension experience. Vocabulary and knowledge about the topic could be introduced or checked before the activity. The same would be true for listening activities in which culture is the focus. For example, returning to the Holy Week activity, concepts and knowledge that might be reviewed before listening include the following:

- What is Holy Week?
- What is Good Friday?
- What kind of religion would be most likely to have processions?
- What would you expect to find in such processions?

Not only would such work on concepts get learners in tune with the possible content of the listening passage, but it would also seed vocabulary used in the passage. The same would hold for any small *c* cultural topic. Imagine a short listening passage on how people greet each other in Japan. Here are some prelistening topics that could be covered:

- What the function of a greeting is (the nature of perfunctory greetings versus greetings that actually do something)
- What learners already think they know about the way Japanese people greet each other
- What learners know about social status in their own country and how it affects the greetings they choose

In short, because cultural topics may include new information that learners may not be able to decipher without some help, the use of prelistening activities to prepare them for what they are going to hear takes on an even greater importance than in other listening activities.

SUMMARY

In this chapter, we examined four major areas of second language listening: the psycholinguistic processes, listening as a communicative act, listening in the second language classroom, and listening in the language laboratory. We saw that listening is far from a passive skill. Indeed, the learner-listener is actively engaged in mental computations that are linguistic and nonlinguistic in nature. The listener is an active co-constructor of meaning in collaborative situations, and even in noncollaborative situations her mind is busy inferring, guessing, anticipating, and integrating meaning as she attends to the aural stimuli. We also saw that listening is not just aural but, in everyday life, is generally part of communicative situations in which visual and other stimuli are present. Thus, few are the cases where real-world listening is purely "ear only." In examining language-teaching practices, we considered the nature of listening in order to ask ourselves what range of listening practices learners get both in and out of the classroom. Our conclusion was that opportunities to listen in the second language are generally restricted to a small set of types, but that there are ways to increase both the opportunities to practice listening and the variety of situations in which listening is used. We ended with a brief examination of issues related to listening and culture.

Before we conclude, let us reflect on this chapter and Chapter 2 on working with input. In essence, aren't both chapters about the same thing? Aren't they both concerned with issues of comprehension and aural stimuli? In a certain sense this is true, but at the same time it is not. Our discussion of the role of comprehensible input in second language acquisition dealt exactly with that: *acquisition.* Comprehensible input is a factor related to the acquisition of a linguistic system—vocabulary, morphology, syntax, phonology, and other linguistic features. As such, comprehensible input is a factor external to the learner; it consists of the linguistic data that he relies on to build a linguistic system.

Listening comprehension, on the other hand, deals with skill development. It refers to what learners understand and don't understand as they interact in a communicative setting and how they signal comprehension and help to maintain the flow of discourse (in collaborative situations). Thus, listening comprehension is about factors internal to the learner.

Clearly the two concepts are related. If input is to be of any acquisitional use, it must be comprehended, which in turn suggests issues of listening. However, it is intuitively obvious that learners can make sense of and grasp the main ideas in a speech stream that contains incomprehensible input. They may thus be able to "function" in a communicative interaction but not receive the right kind of input for acquisition. This is an important distinction to keep in mind as you develop materials for language teaching.

KEY TERMS, CONCEPTS, AND ISSUES

psycholinguistic processes
  perceiving
  attending
  assigning meaning
inference
listening as communication
  collaborative versus
   noncollaborative listening
  modality
  skills
  strategic responses
  maintaining the discourse
  gambits
classroom versus nonclassroom
 listening

listening in the language laboratory
listening as a means to an end
prelistening activities
  vocabulary preparation
  review of existing knowledge
  anticipation of content
listening and culture
  big *C* versus little *c*
  cultural analysis
  cultural sensitivity
  the importance of prelistening
   activities
comprehensible input versus
 listening as communication

THINKING MORE ABOUT IT: DISCUSSION QUESTIONS

1. Make a list of all the listening situations you encountered yesterday. Compare your list to those of several classmates. How varied are the situations in which you found yourselves listening?
2. What does it mean that listening can be characterized as a linguistic, social, and individual act? Provide concrete examples of each.
3. Which is more common in classroom situations: listening in an aural-only mode or listening in an aural + visual mode? Which is more common in nonclassroom situations? Which are more frequent in classroom situations: collaborative or noncollaborative listening tasks? Which are more frequent in nonclassroom situations?

GETTING A CLOSER LOOK:
RESEARCH ACTIVITIES

Observe three classes taught by three different instructors. List and characterize the listening situations the learners are exposed to, using the scheme found in Figures 10.1 and 10.2 on pages 200 and 202. Does variety characterize the experience of the listeners?

MAKING COMMUNICATIVE LANGUAGE
TEACHING HAPPEN: PORTFOLIO ACTIVITIES

Create a set of materials that provide a diversity of listening experiences for language learners. The materials should contain both collaborative and non-collaborative activities and aural-only as well as aural + visual modalities. You should also vary the response type and provide any prelistening activities you think are necessary.

CHAPTER 11

Comprehending Written Language

In this chapter we explore:

- Reader-based factors and the contributions readers make to comprehension
- Text-based factors and the effects the language found in texts has on comprehension
- The impact that reading has on vocabulary acquisition and on making form-meaning connections
- An interactive model of reading that explains the interplay of reader- and text-based factors in reading comprehension
- An instructional framework that helps second language readers comprehend written passages

PRELIMINARY CONSIDERATIONS IN SECOND LANGUAGE READING

A number of factors may affect the relative difficulty a language learner has with reading in the second language. These factors would require that instruction be focused initially on lower-level aspects of written language. It is beyond the scope of this work to address the type of instruction required, but teachers should be aware of these factors.

Literacy in the first language is one such factor. We know that university students taking a second language are literate in their first language, but first language literacy cannot be taken for granted in community-based instructional programs. Learners in such programs may not know that print has meaning or that the symbols on the page relate to the sounds of the spoken language. Determining the literacy level of language learners is a priority in programs like these.

Another factor is difference in symbol systems. Second language reading is made more difficult if the symbols used in the learner's first and second language are not the same. Consider the differences among the Greek, Roman, and Cyrillic alphabets and the difficulty a learner would have simply identifying (recognizing) the letters. Any experienced native reader of the Roman alphabet knows that the symbols shown in Figure 11.1, although different from each other, all represent the same letter.

a a a a a a a a a

FIGURE 11.1 Variations on the letter *A*

A native reader of the Greek alphabet might think that these symbols are significant variations. Second language reading is made even more difficult when the native language writing system is not alphabetic but pictographic or logographic. It is also more difficult if one of the two languages reads left to right and the other reads right to left or if one reads top to bottom and the other reads bottom to top.

Either lack of literacy or any of the differences in symbol systems requires a period of instruction dedicated to learning the features of the written code and practicing with the code until letter recognition becomes effortless and automatic. In this chapter, we assume that such letter recognition skills have already been automatized.

HOW READERS CONTRIBUTE TO COMPREHENSION: THE FUNCTIONS OF SCHEMATA

Beginning in the late 1960s and early 1970s, research on L1 reading demonstrated that readers themselves play a role in the comprehension process. Such research was conducted under the rubric of *schema theory*.

> According to schema theories, all knowledge is packaged into units. These units are the schemata [plural of *schema*]. Embedded in these packages of knowledge is, in addition to the knowledge itself, information about how this knowledge is to be used. A schema, then, is a data structure for representing the generic concepts stored in memory.
>
> (Rumelhart, 1980, p. 34)

According to this research, what readers brought to the task of text comprehension was their schemata—the personal knowledge and experience that they relied on to represent and understand concepts. For example, two native speakers of English, one with a background in linguistics, the other with a background in art history, may both attempt to read Chomsky's latest work on linguistic theory. The one with a background in linguistics will have less difficulty reading the text than the one with a background in art history. As another example, what do you understand in the following excerpt?

The new possibility of wound-string configurations implies that the energy of a string in the Garden-hose universe comes from two sources: vibrational motion and winding energy. From the legacy of Kaluza and Klein, each depends on the geometry of the hose, that is, on the radius of its curled-up circular component, but with a distinctly stringy twist, since point particles cannot wrap themselves around dimensions.

(From Brian Greene, *The Elegant Universe*, Vintage Books, New York, pp. 239–240)

If you are the typical layperson reading this book, that paragraph probably doesn't make much sense, regardless of whether you are a native speaker of English or not. The excerpt would make more sense if you had a background in contemporary quantum theory (i.e., if you had relevant schemata) and would make even more sense if you had read what led up to that excerpt (i.e., again, if you had relevant schemata from the book from which this excerpt is drawn). There is nothing about the language of the text that is difficult for a native speaker or for an advanced learner of English as an L2 (perhaps even an intermediate learner) to understand. The problem in comprehending the text for most people is that they just don't have the background or schemata required to process the new information. Your eyes may move horizontally across the page, but your mind is not able to grasp the intended meaning of the author.

The question arises, then, about how schemata function in reading comprehension. Just what do they do? Basically, they function to constrain the interpretation of incoming information (and *constrain* is used here in a positive sense) in several ways: to disambiguate, elaborate, filter, compensate, and organize information. Examples of each follow.

To Disambiguate

One way in which schemata constrain our interpretations is to disambiguate passage information: We tend to screen out certain possibilities in a passage consistent with our background knowledge. To demonstrate, Anderson and colleagues (1976) gave two ambiguous passages to two groups of readers, physical education majors and musicians. The first passage could have been interpreted as either a prison break or a wrestling match, the second passage as either a card-playing session or a musical practice session. Segments of each passage are given here to illustrate their ambiguous qualities.

1. **Prison/Wrestling**
   Rocky slowly got up from the mat, planning his escape. . . . What bothered him most was being held, especially since the charge against him had been weak. He considered his present situation. The lock that held him was strong, but he thought he could break it.

2. **Cards/Music**
   When Jerry, Mike, and Pat arrived, Karen was sitting in her living room writing some notes. She quickly gathered the cards and stood up to greet her friends at the door. They followed her into the living room but as usual they couldn't agree on exactly what to play.

Anderson et al. showed that physical education majors consistently interpreted the Prison/Wrestling passage as a wrestling match, whereas the music majors interpreted it as a prison break. On the other hand, the music majors consistently interpreted the Cards/Music passage as being about playing music, whereas the physical education majors interpreted it as playing cards.

To Elaborate

Schemata also play an elaborative function in comprehension when we use our knowledge to make inferences; we fill in gaps either in things we did not comprehend or in things that were not in the passage. The elaborative function of schemata, for example, leads readers to indicate that information was actually present in a text when it was not, if such information could be logically inferred from the content of the text (Perkins, 1983).

Research on narrative texts has shown a definite structural pattern to elaborations. Fairy tales, for example, are organized around a highly predictable structure, a structure readily used by readers to organize and recall information. Riley (1990) found that her L2 readers were sensitive to the kinds of information present in fairy tales. In her study, subjects tended to provide endings to the various episodes in the story whether or not such endings appeared in the original. "For example, many subjects stated that the wife divorced her husband, the werewolf, in order to end the episode before recounting the [next] episode that contained the wife's marriage to the second knight" (p. 130). In the minds of the readers, a divorce from one husband logically preceded a marriage to another.

To Filter

Schemata also have a filtering function. Once a schema is activated, all incoming information is filtered through it. This function is not the same as disambiguating a text; rather, a schematic filter provides an evaluative perspective on unambiguous incoming information. This function of schemata was demonstrated in first language reading by Pichert and Anderson (1977, cited in Bransford, 1979). Two groups of readers were given the same passage about two boys and the house in which they were playing. One group was to imagine themselves as potential house buyers, the other group as thieves. The information recalled by the two groups was different, reflecting their different perspectives on the information presented in the text. For example, the house buyers recalled that the house had a leaky roof, whereas the thieves recalled that there was a color television set. The house buyers recalled the spaciousness of the dining room, whereas the thieves recalled the open drawer of sterling silver. In a certain sense, what readers get out of a passage depends on what they bring to it.

Readers need not be provided with an external perspective in order to filter information. Steffensen, Joag-Dev, and Anderson (1979) demonstrated how Indians and Americans, reading letters describing marriage ceremonies in the two cultures, interpreted information about the two ceremonies through a culturally generated schematic filter. As Steffensen and colleagues point out, "Wearing an heirloom wedding dress is a completely acceptable aspect of the pageantry of the American marriage ceremony and reflects interest in tradition that surfaces on this occasion. [A subject from India] appears to have completely

221

*How Readers
Contribute to
Comprehension: The
Functions of
Schemata*

missed this and, on the basis of the Indian emphasis on the relative financial power of the two families (which can be shown by even such a small detail as wearing an up-to-date, fashionable sari), has inferred that the dress was out of fashion" (p. 21). An unambiguous sentence about wearing Grandma's wedding dress was filtered through the Indian reader's cultural perspective on weddings.

Pause to consider . . .
---

culturally driven interpretations. Can you teach a native speaker of English to comprehend a passage the same way a native speaker of French or Dutch would? Can you teach culturally appropriate appreciation of a passage's content?

To Compensate

Another function that schemata can play in comprehension is to compensate for other knowledge sources such as underdeveloped orthographic knowledge, lexical knowledge, and syntactic knowledge. Just as the word *constrain* was not used with negative connotations earlier, the word *compensate* is not used here in a negative sense. For example, a nonnative speaker of English would not have to know anything about the morphology of the past tense to determine correctly that each of the following sentences refers to a past event. These sentences demonstrate that certain knowledge sources can compensate for linguistic knowledge. What contextual cues are available in the following three sentences indicating a past time?

1. The Louisiana Purchase in 1804 dramatically increased the size of the United States.
2. The last time I saw him, he was getting better.
3. Armstrong and Aldrin walked on the moon before anyone else.

By utilizing such contextual cues as dates, adverbials, and historical knowledge, readers could construct meaning from these sentences. The intent of the example is not, however, to discount the role of linguistic knowledge in comprehension. To rely on a small set of knowledge sources without complete recourse to linguistic knowledge may lead a reader to construct inaccurate meanings. The following example demonstrates the point. Lee (1990) showed how one reader interpreted a passage on feudalism, a sociopolitical structure, as a feud between two individuals. Note that elements of the original are clearly the basis of the reader's reconstruction. (Subjects read the passage in Spanish but recalled it in English.)

Printed Text (Translated from Spanish)
Feudalism was based on an agreement of honor between two men.
One, called a "lord" or "don," controlled a lot of land. The other, called a "vassal," promised to serve and protect the lord so that the latter would permit him to use part of his land. White the agreement was in

place, the vassal could use the land, including the buildings and peons, to make himself richer. In exchange for these rights, he gave part of his earnings to the lord and served him faithfully in time of war.

Reader's Reconstruction

. . . there were two people who feuded over land. One was rich and already had a lot of land. His name was Mr. Don. The other was a simple farmer who owned just a little land. Mr. Don wanted this other man's land because it would make him more rich. . . .

This subject's knowledge of the target language was not sufficient to correct his (mis)interpretation of the passage. Rather, he fed the incoming information through his knowledge of (or schema for) feuds in order to construct the meaning he did. Clearly, his background knowledge was compensating for his other knowledge sources. Yet if not for his background knowledge, the reader would not have been able to interpret any information from the text. This reader's reconstruction demonstrates that not only must a schema be activated for comprehension to take place, but the appropriate schema must be activated for accurate comprehension to result. This reader instantiated a schema for feuds, not feudalism. A prereading instructional practice that activated a feudalism schema would have gone a long way in helping this reader comprehend accurately.

To Organize Information

Carrell (1984a) refers to our knowledge of the overall organization of a text and its conventional constructs as *formal schemata*. Such conventional orders include chronological order in narratives and cause-effect relationships and problem-solution discourse in expository texts. Following work on first language reading, Carrell (1984a) and Riley (1990) found that second language readers are better able to comprehend stories that follow a conventional organization. Importantly, she found that even when readers do not read a text that is organized conventionally, they tend to recall it in a conventional order. In other words, formal schemata operate both to encode information (organize it coming in) as well as to structure how it is recalled (organize it going out). Carrell (1984b) and Lee and Riley (1990) investigated second language learners' formal schemata for expository texts. In both studies, second language readers who recognized and then utilized the organization of the text to organize their recalls were able to recall more than those who did not. Additionally, Lee and Riley provided a group of learners with information about the organization of the text as a prereading, advance organizer. Those who received the advance organizer recalled more than those who were not given it.

We have seen in this section how schemata constrain the interpretation of incoming information; these schemata are the readers' contributions to comprehension. Later in this chapter, we present an instructional framework that seeks to activate readers' background knowledge—knowledge appropriate to the text—in order to facilitate their comprehension. Before presenting this instructional framework, we examine how features of texts influence comprehension.

Pause to consider . . .

the negative connotations associated with the word *compensate*. Stanovich (1980) demonstrated that knowledge sources compensate for each other during native language reading. In foreign language instruction, the compensation of topic knowledge and background knowledge for underdeveloped linguistic knowledge came to be viewed by some as negative and by others as positive. On the negative side, educators feared readers would be too successful with their comprehension and ignore developing their linguistic knowledge. On the positive side, educators took advantage of topic and background knowledge to encourage language learners to read early in their learning experience. Do you understand the two sides of the issue? Where do you stand? Do you see one knowledge source compensating for another as a negative or a positive dimension of reading in a second language?

THE EFFECTS OF TEXT FEATURES ON READING COMPREHENSION

Instructional materials for reading in a second language were once tied to the grammatical structures and vocabulary being taught. It was assumed (incorrectly) that learners could not understand language they had not been taught. Research has challenged these assumptions. For example, Lee (1987b) showed that learners who had never been taught the Spanish subjunctive (either forms or functions) could understand the information being conveyed by the subjunctive forms just as well as could learners who had been taught the subjunctive. Johnson (1981) gave original and simplified versions of a passage to learners of English as a second language. The passages had been simplified by reducing the number of relative clauses and the figurative language, using higher frequency vocabulary, and simplifying the sentence structure. She showed that the learners' comprehension was not affected one way or another by these simplifications. Strother and Ulijn (1987) also presented ESL learners with an original and simplified version of a passage. They simplified passive structures, nominalizations, and particles. They, too, found no difference in comprehension across the simplified and unsimplified versions of the passage.

Although the results of the three studies converge, you should not conclude that language plays no role in second language reading comprehension. Language does have a role in reading comprehension, but instructors should not view the language of the text as the only criterion for judging a text's appropriateness. Text characteristics need to be judged and evaluated in light of the readers' characteristics. In fact, whereas many researchers have found that simplification does not affect comprehension, others have found evidence that it does; we know that the language of the text *can* make a difference. Let's look at some examples where differences in comprehension have resulted from differences in the language learners read.

How specific the words are in a text can make a difference. First and second language readers comprehend the passage better when the lexical items are transparent and specific rather than opaque and general (Bransford & Johnson, 1972; Carrell, 1983; Lee, 1986b). *Transparent* words explicitly refer to the topic; *opaque* ones do so indirectly. Note, for example, the use of *things* for *clothes* and *facilities* for *washing machines* in the following sets of sentences.

Transparent Version

The procedure is actually quite simple. First you arrange the clothes into different groups. Of course, one pile may be enough depending on how much wash there is to do. If you have to do it somewhere else due to lack of washing machines, that is the next step; otherwise, you are ready to begin.

Opaque Version

The procedure is actually quite simple. First you arrange things into different groups. Of course, one pile may be enough depending on how much there is to do. If you have to do it somewhere else due to lack of facilities, that is the next step; otherwise, you are ready to begin.

Not only does choice of lexical item affect comprehension; the way information is organized does, too. Carrell (1984b) presented the same information to learners of English as a second language but organized it in four ways: (1) as a comparison/contrast; (2) as a problem with a solution; (3) as a collection or series of descriptions; and (4) as a cause-and-effect relationship. Both comprehension and retention of information were best for more highly organized information (comparison/contrast, problem/solution, and cause/effect) than for more loosely organized information (collection of descriptions). Lee and Riley (1990) found similar results on text organization with learners of French. They also found that providing learners with information about text organization prior to reading improved their comprehension.

Discourse can be organized differently not just at the text level but also at more local levels within the text. Flick and Anderson (1980) gave first and second language readers short passages that contained explicit and implicit definitions; examples of each type of definition follow:

Explicit: Negative pressure is that type of pressure whose value is below atmospheric.

Implicit: From fluid mechanics it can be shown that as a fluid or gas passes through a venturi, its velocity increases; but its pressure decreases to some value below atmospheric. This negative pressure is greatest at the point in the throat where the fuel pick-up is located.

(Flick & Anderson, 1980, pp. 345–346)

They found that both first and second language readers comprehended explicit definitions better than they did implicit ones.

The research studies mentioned are only examples of the many investigations into the effects of text characteristics on comprehension. Even from this small sample of research, you can see that no facile conclusion can be reached.

The language of the text might or might not affect comprehension. There really are no rules that account for when text characteristics will prevent readers from making their contributions to the construction of meaning.

Pause to consider . . .

text selection for nonnative readers. After reviewing a considerable amount of research, Swaffar, Arens, and Byrnes (1991, pp. 137–139) proposed the following as key considerations in selecting materials for L2 readers:

Select topics familiar to students.
Select topics of interest to students.
Select texts with overt development of ideas.
Select texts with greater structural organization.
Select texts with a recognizable agent or concrete subject.
Select texts that have little extraneous prose.
Select texts that have unambiguous intents.
Select texts of appropriate length.

Given what you have just read about both reader contributions to comprehension and the language of texts, how would you implement these recommendations? Are these recommendations absolutes or are they related to other factors? When would text length be an issue? How would you determine "interest"?

INTERACTIVE MODELS OF READING

The research on reader contributions and text effects demonstrate that comprehension involves both reader-based and text-based factors. The two sets of factors are not easily isolated because they tend to interact. Perhaps the clearest demonstration of how the two interact can be found in an experiment conducted by Mohammed and Swales (1984). They asked four groups of subjects to read an instruction booklet for an alarm clock and then use the instructions to set the time and alarm on the clock. Their subjects were native and nonnative readers of English who had either science or humanities backgrounds. The researchers found that subjects with science backgrounds completed the two tasks more quickly than the others. Among the slowest to finish were two native readers with humanities backgrounds. Two nonnative readers—one with a science background and the other, who had a low level of second language proficiency, with a humanities background—did not complete the tasks. Mohammed and Swales concluded that a particular level of language proficiency was required in order to understand the technical directions; yet, once that level was attained, background knowledge and appropriate schemata were better predictors of success than was language proficiency. Just as one cannot read in a second language without some knowledge of that language, one cannot comprehend much unless one can bring more to the task of reading than just linguistic knowledge.

Schema-theoretic research led to new, *interactive* models for the reading process. Rumelhart (1977) proposed an interactive model of processing consisting of several knowledge sources representing different levels of linguistic representation (feature, letter, letter cluster, lexical, syntactic, and semantic knowledges). Interactive models of reading posit that the components of the model, namely, the knowledge sources, all act simultaneously and in parallel on the incoming written input. For example, semantic knowledge can be used to decide which letters comprise a word at the same time that letters in words may trigger semantic knowledge to be used. In a passage on medical care, you would expect certain words, such as *doctor* and *nurse,* to appear. When you arrive at these words in the passage, your brain does not necessarily need to analyze each letter and letter cluster to determine their meanings. In a certain sense, the brain is "ready" for these words and might need only the *d-o* of *doctor* or the *n-u-r* of *nurse* to access their meanings.

Interactive models fundamentally redefined the relationship among knowledge sources. Figure 11.2 is a graphic representation of a prototypical interactive model for reading. Note that in the interactive model, each knowledge source is connected to each of the others. Each can influence the others, singly or in combination, so that semantic knowledge can aid feature analysis or syntactic knowledge can aid letter analysis.

What follows is a very brief description of the elements of this model. *Feature analysis* refers to the act of recognizing a loop in a letter and the direction of that loop (*p*), whereas *letter analysis* is recognizing that the loops make a specific letter (*p* versus *d* versus *b*). Certain letters do and do not cluster in particular languages, and the clusters syllabify in particular ways. *Letter cluster analysis* thus tells us that the letters *th* cluster in English as in *the* and *ar-thri-tis.* *Syntactic knowledge* identifies the order of words in a language (for example, knowing that subjects often precede verbs so that the agent of an action is correctly identified: "John hit Charlie" is not the same as "Charlie hit John"). The same words ordered in different ways can produce different meanings, as in "plan to fail" versus "fail to plan." It is our syntactic knowledge that identifies the meaning in the order of the words. *Lexical knowledge* concerns individual

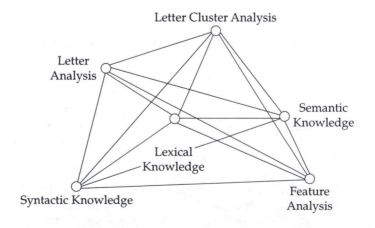

FIGURE 11.2 Interactive model of reading

word properties and meanings, so that the word *work* is identified rather than similar words such as *word* and *fork*. *Semantic knowledge* governs meaning at all levels: words, phrases, clauses, sentences, paragraphs. For example, our semantic knowledge tells us that the differences between the following two sentences are probably minimal if the attraction is mutual, or maximal if the attraction is unidirectional: "Pat loves Chris" versus "Chris loves Pat."

According to interactive models of reading, comprehension is built up or constructed from knowledge sources interacting with each other on the input from the written page. *Comprehension,* by definition, is the process of relating new or incoming information to information already stored in memory. Readers make connections between the new information on the printed page and their existing knowledge. They must allow the new information to enter and become a part of their knowledge store. "To say that one has comprehended a text is to say that she has found a mental 'home' for the information in the text, or else that she has modified an existing mental home in order to accommodate that new information" (Anderson & Pearson, 1984, p. 255).

Once interactive models of mental processes began to guide research and the interpretation of experimental results, reading was referred to as an *interactive process.* Educators quickly adopted the terminology to refer to readers and texts, who were the people and objects of reading. Educators began to refer to reading as the *interaction* between a reader and a text, so that we now talk about *interactive* approaches to teaching reading. McNeil (1984) provides a useful example of such an approach: the process of reading involves "actively constructing meaning among the parts of the text and between the text and personal experience. The text itself is [but] a blueprint for meaning" (p. 5). The blueprint metaphor is quite appropriate, for it originated in the construction field. Someone must take a blueprint and use it to make a building. In a sense, the blueprint guides the construction of the building, but it is not the building. Similarly, the text guides comprehension, but it is not comprehension. The reader takes the text and gives it meaning.

Pause to consider . . .

how the mind works—and when it doesn't work. Have you ever found yourself at the bottom of the page of what you have been reading but are unable to remember how you got there? What does that say to you about what comprehension is and isn't?

READING AND LANGUAGE DEVELOPMENT

Reading in a second language has both an informational outcome and potential linguistic outcomes. The informational outcome is, obviously, that the reader learns about the content of the passage. The potential linguistic outcomes are that the reader may acquire new vocabulary and that he or she may make form-meaning connections. Both outcomes have been verified by empirical research, which allows us to assert that written language serves as input for language acquisition. Krashen (1993) refers to the linguistic outcomes of reading as "the power of reading."

Pulido (2000) and Rott (1999) have shown with Spanish and German, respectively, that second language readers learn new words from reading them in context. Leow (1997; 1998) and Shook (1994) have shown that learners of Spanish can gain greater knowledge of grammatical forms they know only slightly from reading these forms in context. Leow has investigated the present perfect and affirmative commands, whereas Shook has investigated present perfect and relative clauses. Lee (2002) and Leeser (2003) have found that second language learners of Spanish who knew nothing about future tense morphology can begin to acquire it as a result of comprehending passages that contained this tense. These linguistic outcomes merely happen; that is, they happen incidentally as a byproduct of reading, not as the intended outcome of instruction. The arguments to incorporate reading into beginning-level language courses can now be made not just in the service of cultural goals but also in the service of acquisitional goals.

A FRAMEWORK FOR HELPING L2 LEARNERS COMPREHEND WRITTEN LANGUAGE

Because language learners do not have the verbal virtuosity of native readers, instructors need strategies to facilitate the reading comprehension process. The purpose of providing reading instruction is to build bridges between the reader and the information contained in the text. The framework presented in this chapter guides learners' interactions with a text in order to maximize their comprehension. There are three essential phases to the instructional framework: preparation (prereading), guided interaction (during reading), and assimilation (postreading). Although we do present each phase separately, they should be conceived of as a whole. Each phase of a lesson is interdependent with the other phases because they build on one another.

Preparation: *Activating Appropriate Schemata*

The linguistic demands on reading in a second language can inhibit learners' background knowledge from being activated to its fullest extent (Carrell, 1983; Hudson, 1982). Second language learners need help bringing their knowledge to bear on the process of comprehension. The initial phase of the instructional framework, therefore, must be to activate learners' background knowledge and direct it toward the information in the passage. In other words, schemata must be *activated* and must be *appropriate* to the passage being read. Activating the reader's knowledge of feudalism, for example, would have steered him toward an appropriate interpretation of the passage on pages 221–222.

What knowledge needs to be activated so that readers will comprehend the information? The answer to this question depends on the text and what it says, as well as on the readers and what they know. As the research of Mohammed and Swales (1984) indicates, the needs of a group of engineering majors reading technical instructions are different from those of a group of humanities majors reading the very same text.

Many techniques serve to activate knowledge relevant to a particular text, including brainstorming; previewing titles, headings, and illustrations; using world knowledge; taking a pretest; and scanning for specific information. We now describe each of these techniques.

Brainstorming

Brainstorming is synonymous with idea generation, or putting ideas "out on the table" but not criticizing or commenting on them in any way. The technique allows for the maximum of perspectives on a topic to emerge; it provides the instructor and readers a broad information base to begin bridging the gap between the readers and a text. Brainstorming takes place before readers are given a text. You ask them what they know about the topic of the text, recording everything they tell you (on the board or an overhead transparency), whether or not the information supplied is relevant to the particular text. Note the following examples, designed to precede a reading about weddings.

Activity A.   Brainstorming with the Whole Class

Step 1. As a class, generate a list of all the ideas you associate with weddings. Come up with as many different ideas as possible in five minutes.

Brainstorming can also be carried out in groups or pairs. If groups are given the specific task of listing five things they know about a topic, then the potential for more diverse responses is there. Also, such task-oriented group work provides a mechanism for maximizing the participation of each individual.

Activity B. Brainstorming in Pairs

Step 1. Working with a partner, list five things you associate with weddings. Try to come up with five very different things. You have two minutes.

1.
2.
3.
4.
5.

Step 2. Share your list with the rest of class and listen as they share theirs. Write down any ideas you did not think of.
(*Option for Step 2:* The instructor creates a master list of ideas on the board or overhead transparency.)

Pause to consider . . .

why time limits should be imposed on brainstorming. What kind of classroom dynamic is generated when time limits are imposed and adhered to during activities? What might the interaction between instructor and learners, and learner and learner, be like if there were no stated time limit?

Once ideas have been generated, the readers need to verify whether or not the information is relevant to the text at hand. Brainstorming must be followed up by a task that has readers focusing on a particular text, since *appropriate* knowledge must be activated. They must examine what they collectively know in order to decide what is relevant (and thus appropriate) to the text at hand. The common follow-up to brainstorming is having readers quickly skim a text for the sole purpose of noting whether or not the ideas they generated are present in the text. They either confirm an idea's presence or reject the idea as being irrelevant. Although this task might seem to be guided interaction, skimming the text with this very limited purpose is not really reading the text. The readers are not extracting what the author *has said* about that information; they only learn if the information is *present*.

Activity A.   Continuation . . .

Step 2. As rapidly as possible, skim the text to determine whether or not the ideas on the board *(or overhead)* are actually in the reading. All you have to do is say whether or not the information is there; you do not have to know (not yet anyway) what the author says about that information. You have five minutes.

Step 3. Share what you found with the rest of the class. As you do, erase from the board all those ideas that are *not* in the text. Do you all agree?

Previewing Titles, Headings, and Illustrations

Most texts carry a title and subtitle that are sometimes, although not always, indicative of the content. Sometimes, headings mark the different ideas included in a text, and informative illustrations and photographs describe some of its contents. You can exploit each of these sources of information as a means to activate appropriate schema, as in Activity C.

Activity C.   Titles, Subtitles, and Headings

Step 1. Read the title and subtitle of the passage. Based only on this information, list three ideas you would expect to find in this reading.

1.
2.
3.

Step 2. Share your ideas with two or three classmates. Did you come up with similar information? Did your classmates think of something you would like to add to your list?

Step 3. Now read the section headings. In which sections do you think you will find the ideas you and your classmates thought of?

Step 4. Quickly skim those sections to determine whether or not the information is there. Report back to the class what you found (or didn't find).

You can work with illustrations and photographs in a variety of ways. They can be the basis of an initial brainstorming task, or they can be used to confirm or reject ideas generated from a brainstorming task. In the following activity, the illustrations are used as the very first device to activate appropriate schema.

Activity D. Illustrations and Photographs

Step 1. Working with a partner, describe what you see in each of the photographs that accompany the article. Be as detailed in your description as possible.

Step 2. Based on these photographs, list at least three pieces of information you would expect to find in the article.

1.
2.
3.

Step 3. Share your list with your classmates. Did they think of something you would like to add to your list?

Step 4. Quickly skim the article to determine whether or not these ideas are going to be treated by the author. Report back to the class what you find.

---

*P**ause to consider** . . .*

the purpose of reporting back to the class. Why is reporting back to the class an appropriate way to bring closure to brainstorming-oriented activities? What would the activities be like without such a task?

Using World Knowledge

Topic knowledge is but one type of schema; other schemata come into play that we can classify as *world knowledge*. For example, an article about liposuction that appeared in the *New England Journal of Medicine, Newsweek, Cosmopolitan,* or *Seventeen* would be approached and interpreted differently because we have a different set of expectations based on the type of magazine we are reading. The magazines are directed at different audiences; the tone of the authors, as well as their credentials, would be very different. The source of the text directly affects how readers should interpret the content; it determines which schema is appropriate. Whereas language learners probably have little knowledge of the various magazines and newspapers from the target culture, they can be guided to make associations with magazines and newspapers from their own culture. The following example illustrates this point.

Activity E. World Knowledge

Step 1. Read the title and subtitle. Then look at the pictures and read the captions. Based solely on this information, if this article were to be published in an American magazine or newspaper, which would it be?

a. *Time*
b. *Ladies' Home Journal*
c. *The National Enquirer*
d. *The New Republic*
e. _____ (some other one?)

Step 2. Working with a partner, compare the reasons for your choices. Were you thinking along the same lines?

World knowledge can be exploited in other ways as well. We are all probably very experienced at filling out forms in our native language. With this experience, we have certain expectations for the types of information requested on forms. That knowledge can facilitate second language readers' comprehension of forms in the target language. For example, we know we have to sign most forms we fill out. That knowledge would lead us to search for the place to sign whether or not we knew the target language words for "Signature" or "Sign here."

Pause to consider . . .

some common types of documents and forms that language learners could easily figure out on the basis of world knowledge. Do you have personal experiences you can relate?

Taking a Pretest

In research settings, a common technique for measuring how much a subject has learned from an experimental treatment is to administer a test both prior to and after the treatment. In an instructional setting, the pretest technique can be used to activate appropriate schemata. You could write a ten-item quiz on the content of the reading, administer the quiz, and then discuss it as a pre-reading activity. Critically, you would *not* correct the learners' answers, since the point of reading the article is to learn the answers. The instructor would simply find out who believed what about the topic. The quiz serves to activate appropriate knowledge that readers subsequently apply to the text.

Activity F. Quiz

Step 1. To the best of your ability, answer each of the following questions. Leave no question unanswered. If you are uncertain, then make as good a guess as you can.

Step 2. Compare your answers with a partner [or *group* or *whole class*]. Did you have the same answers? Which answers are you sure of? Which ones are you unsure of?

Scanning for Specific Information

Passages vary so much from one to another that you might decide a particular passage does not need an extensive preparation. It might be appropriate simply to have readers scan the text for specific information that will activate an appropriate schema. For example, a certain text might contain a series of numbers that will clue the learners about the content. You could then direct them to find the numbers and determine what they refer to. Also, there might be two or three concepts that are crucial to understand in order to comprehend the text as a whole. Learners could be directed to find these terms in the text and then define them, thereby activating appropriate schemata.

Activity G. Scanning

Step 1. Find the following three words in the text and underline the sentences in which you find them.

  a. *feudalism*
  b. *stewardship*
  c. *tithes*

Step 2. Working with two or three classmates, either write a definition of the words or list as many things as you can think of that you associate with each.

Step 3. Share your work with the rest of the class. Are you all sure what these words mean?

Although learners can be taught to deduce the meanings of words from context, identify cognates, or simply skip over words they do not know, their comprehension of a text may depend on such an unknown word. When an unknown word is a key to understanding, we would encourage instructors to preview that word in an activity such as Activity G. The consequences for the learner are as obvious as misinterpreting *feudalism* as *feud*.

Pause to consider . . .

reading as both a private and a social act. We have included paired and group work as part of the prereading activities because we believe reading need not be a solitary, private act but can and should also be a social, public one. Before reading further, do you think that the "Guided Interaction" phase of a reading lesson should be private or social?

Guided Interaction

If activating appropriate schema can be thought of as building a bridge between a reader and a text, then *guided interaction* is making a plan for crossing the bridge—and then crossing it. Second language readers, who tend to read word for word when left to their own devices, need to be directed in how to read in another language. The instructor's function is to provide that direction. You can think of the guided interaction phase of the lesson framework as the readers' *exploration* of the content. But these explorers are not going into uncharted waters or virgin territory. You will provide them a map or a route to follow. What is the best way to divide a long passage into manageable segments? On what information should the reader focus within those segments? The passage might be short but dense. Where are the appropriate points to stop the readers to make sure they have understood before they continue?

The guided interaction phase of the reading lesson consists of a combination of two types of tasks, namely, *management strategies* and *comprehension checks*. Management strategies suggest to the readers ways in which to divide a passage, to break it into sensible parts. Comprehension checks during the guided interaction phase of the lesson allow readers to monitor their comprehension in an ongoing way rather than read from start to finish only to find they did not understand. It is better to know immediately that you have not understood something than to arrive at the end of a reading and realize you missed something, if not everything, along the way. Management strategies and comprehension checks can be paired in the following ways.

Management Strategies	**Comprehension Checks**
1. Read one section at a time of a passage with headings.	Write a one-sentence summary of the section. Select key words from the section. List main ideas. Answer questions.
2. Read one section at a time of a passage with no headings.	All of the above. Write a heading that specifies the content.

What kinds of questions will guide readers into the text and not simply encourage them to search for matching wording? The following example provides an answer to this question.

Let's say that the class has been asked to read a three-page article that describes and explains nine different behaviors characterizing the social organization of a herd of elephants. Traditionally, such a reading would be followed by a set of comprehension questions presented in the same order in which the information appears in the passage. Such a set of traditional comprehension questions for the passage about elephants follows.

Traditional Comprehension Questions

1. What is the theme of this article?
2. Based on the tone, is the article in favor of or against elephants?
3. Is the fight between males for the leadership of the herd a fight to the death?
4. When do baby elephants learn to use their trunks?
5. What do male elephants use their trunks for? Female elephants?
6. What is a matriarchy?
7. To what does the phrase *steps according to age* refer?
8. Are elephants violent or peaceful animals?
9. How is the care of young elephants shared among all members of the herd?
10. Is the organization of the herd democratic?
11. What is a herd of elephants made up of?
12. Do the males remain in the herd in which they are born for their entire lives? Do the females?

13. Which of the behaviors described in the article are instinctive and which are learned?
14. What information in the article supports the idea that elephants are intelligent, difficult, active, powerful, and fun loving?
15. On what is the social organization of a herd of elephants based?

These comprehension questions can easily be transformed into task-based classroom activities, as in Activity H. Specific questions from the list provided are indicated in parentheses. As you read Activity H, ask yourself which is better for the language learner, traditional comprehension questions or a task-oriented guided interaction?

Activity H. Guided Interaction

Step 1. Since this is a relatively long reading, it would be best to read it section by section. After reading each section fairly quickly, pause to collect your thoughts by writing a sentence that captures the main idea of the section. Compare your sentences with those of a classmate. Do you agree on the main ideas?

Step 2. Go back and reread each section, paying more attention to the details. Using a highlighter, identify key words or phrases that will help you remember what you have read. At the end of each section, look at what you have highlighted. Does it spark your memory? Compare the words and phrases you have highlighted with those of your classmates. Have you chosen different words?

Step 3. Based on what you have read, check off the statements that are true.

❏ From the tone of the article, it is evident that the author is pro-elephant. (Question 2)
❏ Even though elephants are normally quite peaceful, they are capable of tremendous violence. (Question 8)
❏ An elephant herd is a democratic unit. (Question 10)
❏ Elephants and humans share similar preoccupations with their young. (Question 9)

Step 4. Complete the following statements:

1. A herd of elephants is composed of . . . (Question 11)
   a. males and females in more or less equal proportions.
   b. more males than females.
   c. one male and various females, like a harem.
2. The care of the young is . . . (Question 9)
   a. shared equally among males and females.
   b. the responsibility of the males.
   c. the responsibility of the females.
3. Of the young that are born in a herd . . . (Question 12)
   a. the males and females are members of the same herd for all their lives.
   b. the males and females form subgroups, which eventually leave the herd.
   c. the males leave the herd but the females remain.
   d. the females leave the herd but the males remain.

Step 5. Working with two or three classmates, make a list of all the behaviors described in the article. Then share your list with the rest of the class, adding to your list whatever behaviors you might have missed. Finally, as a class, indicate whether each behavior is instinctive or learned. (Question 13)

Step 6. According to the introductory paragraphs, elephants are intelligent, difficult, active, powerful, and fun-loving animals. As a class, identify the information in the article that supports the idea that elephants really are as they are described. (Question 14)

Pause to consider . . .

the pros and cons of having learners read in class. Some instructors believe that reading is an activity learners should do at home, not in class. Is reading instruction so different from other aspects of language instruction? In what ways is the guided interaction no different from other kinds of in-class activities?

Assimilation

If the preparation phase was to build a bridge between the readers and the text and the guided interaction phase was to lead readers across the bridge, then the assimilation phase is the building inspection. You want to be sure that all the pieces are in place and that the experience of crossing the bridge will be memorable.

Most lesson frameworks for reading end with the guided interaction phase. Once comprehension is checked and verified as accurate, the reading lesson is over. However, we advocate continuing the lesson based on the content of the reading. For, after all, why do we read? The answer to this question is varied. We read to pass the time in the dentist's waiting room and to focus our attention on something other than the sound of a drill. We read to keep abreast of the latest world events. We read to fall asleep at night. But those purposes do not reflect reading in an academic setting. Why do we do that? Reading in an academic setting is equated with reading to learn, which means that the content of what we read is important. We read to get the information and do something with it. At times, all we do with the information is give it back to the professor on a test; at other times we discuss it; and sometimes we write papers about it. The purpose, then, of the assimilation phase is to encourage second language readers to learn from what they have read. To accomplish this goal, we present tasks and activities that are study-skills-oriented: ways to organize information in order to learn that information.

Some common techniques that can be considered study-skills-oriented are

- To associate a person's name with places and/or events
- To identify main ideas and the key words associated with those ideas
- To write a test based on content

- To write questions for the passage as a whole or the various subsections of a passage
- To outline a passage
- To classify information as main idea, supporting information, and details
- To identify the themes treated in a passage
- To create a poster of the contents of a passage
- To write a summary
- To establish cause-effect relationships, problem/solutions, advantages/disadvantages
- To draw a semantic map or a Venn diagram of the content
- To fill in a chart or table

The assimilation phase overtly focuses the language learners' reading experience on information. As the instructor, you must determine what information you want them to learn, which is based on the reasons you selected the text. In the assimilation phase, the readers are given a task or series of tasks in which they organize the information in the text. By carrying out an organizing task, the readers internalize the content of the reading, thereby ensuring that they are reading to learn.

Activity I. Assimilation

Step 1. Review what you did in the preparation and guided interaction activities. Then, complete the following semantic map without rereading the article (if you can).

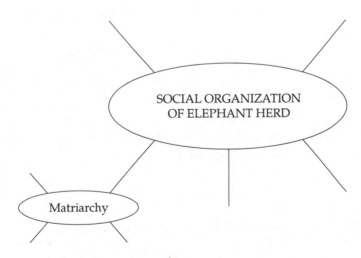

Step 2. You have three options for working with the semantic map.

Option 1. Using only the semantic map, write a summary of the article you read.

Option 2. Using only the semantic map, write a short quiz on the content of the article. Try not to be too detail-oriented with your questions. After all, you should write a quiz that you think is fair. You should also write a quiz that you would be willing to take!

Option 3. Using only the semantic map to guide you, write three essay questions covering the content of the entire article. As you write the questions, think about keeping the answers to two or three paragraphs. Remember, the questions you write just might be the ones your instructor uses on the exam!

Pause to consider . . .

the thought processes a learner would have to use in order to write test questions. How does writing a test or writing test questions get readers to assimilate the content of what they have read? What would you do with the questions the learners submitted to you? Would you use them on a test? Would you edit them and give them back to the whole class on a handout?

Through task-based activities, students interact with the content of a text a number of times; they read and reread. But each time they do, they are engaged in another activity as they complete another task. They are given something new to think about and do each time they read. Each act of reading has a purpose: the readers' search for meaning.

PERSONALIZING THE CONTENT OF A TEXT

An important aspect of reading, often not taken into account in early stage second language instruction, is an exploration of what Grellet calls the communicative function of a text. Outside of classroom settings, authors frequently expect readers to respond to the content of the article. As Grellet argues,

> Exercises must be meaningful and correspond as often as possible to what one is expected to do with the text. We rarely answer questions after reading a text, but we may have to
>
> • Write an answer to a letter
> • Use the text to do something (e.g., follow directions, make a choice, solve a problem)
> • Compare the information to some previous knowledge
>
> (Grellet, 1981, p. 9)

Each of Grellet's examples can be exploited in the language classroom. Exploring the communicative function of a text can also be thought of as *personalizing its content*. Once readers gain information from a text, can they then relate to it personally and, therefore, more meaningfully? Can they apply the content to themselves, to their experiences, to the world as they know it? The following activity exemplifies how the content of an article on animals' sixth sense can be related to the readers' lives. To use Grellet's terms, the readers will compare the content of the article to previous knowledge.

Apply what you learned about animals' sense of direction to your own experiences by describing the sense of direction of various members of your family. Use the words and phrases listed that you think are appropriate. A model is provided.

MODEL: My father has the sense of direction of a turtle because it is a mystery how he always knows how and where to go when we visit a city for the first time. He never needs a map.

Family Member	Animal	Category
Mother	Bird	Always knows where north is
Father	Reptile	When given directions, memorizes them immediately
Sister	Locust	Always gets lost when visiting a city for the first time
Brother	Butterfly	Needs a detailed map to find someone's house for the first time
Grandfather	Bee	
Grandmother	Turtle	

The following activity demonstrates how learners can personalize the content of the reading about elephant behavior. In this activity, they relate the reading to the world as they know it.

Activity K. Communicative Function of a Text

Step 1. Working with two or three classmates, put the number that corresponds to your own opinions next to each of the following sentences.

We believe that for the majority of people our age,
  1 = It is important . . .
  2 = It will be important some day . . .
  3 = It is not very important . . .

  a. _____ to have a leadership role in whatever group one is associated with.
  b. _____ to live in a safe and protected area.
  c. _____ to lead an active social life.
  d. _____ to count on child care while at work.
  e. _____ to have various opportunities to find companionship.
  f. _____ to make friends.
  g. _____ to advance professionally.
  h. _____ to have economic security in old age.
  i. _____ to have a place to live in old age.

Step 2. Compare your answers with those of the rest of the class by indicating how many people responded to each item with a 1, a 2, or a 3.

Step 3. Which items were most important to the majority of the class? Which were not important? Does the class agree on what to look for in life?

Step 4. Go back over the sentences, but this time indicate with the letter *E* those statements that can apply to elephants. Then explain what information from the article supports your choices. In what ways are humans and elephants similar?

Pause to consider . . .

the contribution of the content of readings to interactional activities. Activities J and K could also be done without having read an article about anything. In this case, references to the articles would have to be eliminated. Go back through Activities J and K, locating references to the articles. If you were to eliminate those references, would the activities still be worth doing? In other words, are they good activities? What does adding content do for the activities?

READING AND CULTURE

In Chapter 10, we suggested the use of listening activities to help language learners develop cultural sensitivity. Reading is another comprehension phenomenon that can be used to help learners develop cultural sensitivity.

Written texts can deal with culture in a variety of ways. Some texts, of course, explicitly describe cultural differences or cultural phenomena. Every experienced teacher has certain favorite readings on French wine, Spanish bullfights, or German cinema. Some texts might even speak to the kinds of little *c* cultural values we touched upon in Chapter 10. In the following text, a Quebecois celebrity is commenting on the differences between how Quebecois and French people react to restaurants that disappoint them.

> *Si nous mangeons parfois mal dans certains restaurants du Québec, c'est que nous n'avons pas le courage de rouspéter. Les Français gueulent, et ils ont raison. Tant que nous resterons des mauviettes, nous aurons la cuisine que nous méritons. Vous payez votre repas, faites en sorte d'en avoir pour votre argent. C'est d'ailleurs très souvent un service à rendre au propriétaire de l'établissement qui ne sait pas toujours ce qui se passe dans ses cuisines. La phrase: «Je me tais et préfère ne pas revenir» est à bannir de notre vocabulaire.*

If we often eat poorly in certain restaurants in Quebec, it's that we don't have the courage to protest. The French (on the other hand) gripe, and they are right to. As long as we remain wimps, we will get the food that we deserve. You pay for your meal and pretend to get your money's worth. Moreover, it's often a service we give to a restaurant owner who still does not know what's going on with his dishes. The phrase "I just keep quiet and prefer not to return" should be banished from our speech.

In such a text, the author literally points to differences in cultural values that lead to different behaviors, in this case, the need to not make a scene versus the need to let one's dissatisfaction be known.

Often, however, culture is *embedded in the language of the text.* For example, the author in Quebecois French uses the word *mauviettes,* which is translated as "wimps." But *mauviettes* literally means "skylarks." The natural questions are, What words do we use to represent this concept in English, and why do French speakers use *skylarks?* Does French in general use animals to represent traits more than English does? If so why? What kinds of words does English use to represent traits? How does the social context within our own culture influence us to use one word or another?

Such "microanalyses" of a written text may or may not be appropriate for all levels of language learning, but we can see that often there is cultural information in written texts that goes unnoticed unless we point it out. One possible use of written texts in class is to include another phase of reading after personalization that we might call "Language in the Text." In such a phase, we might pull out just one word or phrase that serves as a point of departure for noting cultural differences and then develop an activity to go with it. The type of activity, again, depends on the level of the learner. The lower the level of speaking proficiency, the greater the need to *not* rely on open-ended questions and activities.

---

*P*ause to consider . . .

how culture is embedded in language and may show up in written texts (or listening texts, for that matter). Examine this chapter for language. Do you see any use of English that reveals something cultural about our academic society? Do you see anything that reveals something about American culture as opposed to the culture of the language you teach?

SUMMARY

In this chapter we have explored what it means to comprehend written language, focusing in particular on what is involved in comprehending a second language. Under the rubric of schema theory, a great deal of research was carried out on the contributions that individual readers make to comprehension. We presented five functions of schema: to disambiguate, elaborate, filter, compensate, and organize information. We then examined the effects of text characteristics on comprehension, demonstrating that language does affect comprehension in a variety of ways: lexical choice, the organization of information, and level of language proficiency. We presented an interactive model of reading, one in which a variety of knowledge sources comes into play. An important feature of interactive models is that the knowledge sources do not operate sequentially but simultaneously, that each knowledge source can influence the other.

We then proposed and described an instructional approach to reading that comprises a lesson framework to surround the text and activities to go beyond the text. The approach reflects what is known about how the mind processes information. Reading is a mental activity during which textual elements are taken in and acted on by linguistic processes mediated by the individual reader's characteristics. The approach also reflects what we know learners do with texts when left to their own devices. They read word for word, translating on the page and in their heads; such practices should be avoided. Finally, the approach emphasizes the communicative function of texts. In developing this approach, we have shown how research on the interactive nature of reading can be transferred to the second language classroom. In effect, our approach promotes reading instruction as the *interaction* between a reader and a text.

KEY TERMS, CONCEPTS, AND ISSUES

symbol systems
schema theory
readers' contribution
 to comprehension
functions of schemata
  disambiguate
  elaborate
  filter
  compensate
  organize information
effects of text features
 on comprehension
  choice of vocabulary
  organization of information
interactive models of reading
interaction of reader contributions
 and text characteristics
  knowledge sources
  interaction of knowledge sources
  comprehension
  blueprint metaphor for texts
reading and language development
  vocabulary acquisition
   from reading
  form-meaning connections
   from reading

instructional framework for
 reading lessons
  preparation (activating
   appropriate schemata)
   brainstorming
   previewing titles, headings,
    and illustrations
   using world knowledge
   taking a pretest
   scanning for specific information
  guided interaction
   management strategies
   comprehension checks
  assimilation
   various techniques
   reading to learn
  personalizing the content
  reading and culture
   culture embedded in language

THINKING MORE ABOUT IT:
DISCUSSION QUESTIONS

1. Following is part of a letter (from the study mentioned on pp. 220–221) describing an American wedding, followed by recalls of the same information by an Indian and an American (Steffensen, Joag-Dev, & Anderson,

243

*Making
Communicative
Language Teaching
Happen: Portfolio
Activities*

1979, pp. 20–21). Each recall reveals a schema functioning in different ways. What are they?

PASSAGE FRAGMENT: AMERICAN WEDDING
Did you know that Pam was going to wear her grandmother's wedding dress? That gave her something that was old, and borrowed, too. It was made of lace over satin, with very large puff sleeves and looked absolutely charming on her. The front was decorated with seed pearls.

INDIAN RECALL
She was looking alright except that the dress was too old and out of fashion.

AMERICAN RECALL
Pam's mother wants Pam to carry on the tradition of wearing the family wedding gown.

McNeil (1984) has likened schemata to blueprints that readers use to construct comprehension. Do you think a blueprint metaphor is appropriate? What other metaphors might you use to describe the functions of schemata in reading comprehension?

2. Review the eight considerations Swaffar, Arens, and Byrnes (1991) set out for the selection of texts (see the Pause to consider . . . on p. 225). Keeping these considerations in mind, find two texts that you would use to teach a second-semester class. Present and explain your thinking to the class.

GETTING A CLOSER LOOK: RESEARCH ACTIVITIES

Prepare two lessons using the same reading passage. One lesson should be traditional in approach, with the passage accompanied by a set of comprehension questions. The other lesson should be based on the three-phase lesson framework. Ask two instructors to carry out the lessons and observe both classes. Based on your observations, which lesson provides the learners with the better reading experience?

MAKING COMMUNICATIVE LANGUAGE TEACHING HAPPEN: PORTFOLIO ACTIVITIES

Prepare a reading lesson for the class you are currently teaching. If you are not teaching, then direct your lesson to first-semester learners. You should have a three-phase instructional framework and at least one activity that explores the communicative function of the text.

CHAPTER 12

Writing and Composing in a Second Language

In this chapter we explore:

- The communicative dimensions of writing and the notion that written language is not merely spoken language put down on paper
- The decision-making processes involved in writing (e.g., defining the rhetorical problem, planning, transcribing, revising) and the ways in which these processes interact with each other
- Language practices that use writing
- Composing activities that help second language learners become second language writers

FUNDAMENTAL CONSIDERATIONS: WHAT IS WRITING?

We need to examine several fundamental considerations before we discuss what it means to write and compose in a second language. The first has to do with the nature of writing itself. We generally think of writing as an act of communication—that is, it involves the expression, interpretation, and negotiation of meaning, just as speaking does. Thus, writers have a purpose in writing—to express their meaning—and they have an audience in mind, even though they are not face to face with their audience members. We discuss purpose and audience in greater depth later in this chapter; they are as important for L2 writers as they are for L1 writers.

In L2 classes, "writing" is sometimes given a different meaning; it is used to refer to exercises that call on learners to produce language that displays their knowledge about the language they are learning. We call these exercises *language practices that use writing;* they are different from activities in which writing is used to communicate. For example, writing a letter to the editor of the *San Francisco Chronicle* is a communicative act, whereas doing a dictation exercise in class is not. The former involves expression of meaning ("I have a reaction to something I read in the newspaper") within a given context ("This is a newspaper; it prints

244

'Letters to the Editor'; even though my letter is addressed to the editor, I'm really writing to everyone who reads the paper."). The dictation exercise does not involve expression of meaning. Its purpose is to demonstrate that language learners can hear sounds and words, can spell correctly, and so on—in short, to display knowledge about the language they are learning. Our concern in this chapter is with *writing as communication*—how learners put thoughts down on paper and develop them into some kind of coherent text.

Another fundamental consideration is that classroom learners engaged in writing wear two hats: They are second language learners, and they are also second language writers (see Williams, in press). Spoken language and written language are very different, each with its own conventions. Written language is not just conversational language put down on paper. Consider the extreme case of written Arabic, which is a different language from spoken Arabic. Or take another look at the following sentences from a U.S. newspaper; as we pointed out in Chapter 6, no one would say these sentences in a conversation, but someone wrote them:

> COLUMBUS, Ohio—Proponents of the intelligent-design movement, which challenges Darwin's primacy in the science classroom, argued on Monday for equal footing in the state's new teaching curriculum, while critics warned that speculative theories of some ultimate agent underpinning evolution were the antithesis of true science. . . . [Professor Lawrence] Krauss argued that while much remained to be discovered about natural selection, Darwin's theory had only grown in strength through decades of experimentation and discovery that intelligent design had not been subjected to.
>
> > (From the New York Times News Service as published in the *Chicago Tribune,* March 12, 2002, p. 10)

Second language learners are still in the process of acquiring the linguistic systems that allow people to generate such sentences. Thus, learners with quite good speaking abilities in the second language may still need to acquire the properties of formal written language.

A third fundamental consideration is that reading, which exposes learners to formal written language, is the best source of input for second language writers. Through reading (i.e., interpreting messages written in formal discourse), second language writers find the type of language they need for their writing. Research on both first and second language learners has shown that someone who is a good writer is usually also a good reader.

Finally, instructors need to keep in mind the fact that writing is a skill that improves with practice. We learn to write by writing (with help from reading). If we want second language learners to become second language writers, we must provide them with writing practice.

WRITING AS COMMUNICATION

Writing, then, can be defined as a communicative act. How does writing fit into the more general definition of communication—the expression, interpretation, and negotiation of meaning—discussed previously in this book? Consider the differences between the following two grocery lists of identical items.

A	B
milk—me	1 gal skim milk
milk—kids	3 gals whole milk
bananas	bananas (only if on sale)
cereal	Cheerios (regular)

List A would be sufficiently specific if the writer and shopper were the same person but would not be so if they were different people. The elaborations and descriptions in List B would allow someone other than the writer to go to the grocery store and buy the needed items. The writer of List B thought about what information the list would have to communicate to the reader-shopper. Readers technically cannot negotiate meaning, since they don't usually have access to the writer to ask questions. The writer of List B anticipated the reader's questions and considered what to put down on paper to make the communication successful. We can see from this exercise that even in something as simple as a grocery list, writing is a communicative act. Meaning is being expressed—that is, there is a purpose to the writing—and the writer is thinking about how meaning will be interpreted and negotiated—that is, the writer is sensitive to audience.

Let's consider a somewhat more literary example than a grocery list: a seventh grader's book report. The seventh grader and the teacher-reader are both aware that the writer's purpose is to convince the teacher-reader that the writer actually read the book. How does the writer accomplish his goal? He summarizes the plot and refers to material at the beginning, middle, and end of the book. This strategy works because the teacher-reader has only one goal in mind—that is, to determine whether the writer read the book in question. Like the grocery list writer, the seventh grader writes with purpose and is sensitive to his audience.

Let's take one more example. Consider the literary critic who is writing a review of a book for a daily newspaper. Among the questions the reviewer must ask herself are these: "What knowledge do my readers have of this genre of literature?" "How interested will they be in information about the writer or in my comments about the writing style?" "What standards should I use in evaluating the book?" As the reviewer asks herself these and other questions, she is considering how most successfully to communicate her meaning—that is, how to write a review that makes sense to the people who purchase the newspaper.

From these examples we can make some observations about writing as communication. First, writers have a purpose, and they have an audience in mind for whom they are writing. Second, just as any communication is, writing is context specific. Speakers know that slang is appropriate in one context and not another, and writers know (or ought to know) that a text they produce is appropriate or inappropriate for the context in which they find themselves. Recall that context is determined by setting or place and the people involved in the communication. For writing, the setting or place is where the text will be read, and the people, of course, are the writer and the eventual readers. If the seventh grader fails to take into consideration the teacher-reader and produces a book report that does not provide information about the plot of the book, that student may inadvertently communicate to the teacher that the book never got read! In short, writing is as context-sensitive as speaking. In the next section, we review what writers do when they consider context.

Pause to consider . . .

cultural differences. How do you teach L2 writers about cultural norms? For example, American writers often write as authority figures offering a critical perspective, whereas the approach of the Asian writer is more often to offer a humble opinion not meant to offend anyone. Can you think of other cultural differences that would affect teaching L2 writing?

WRITING PROCESSES

When writers think about the context of their work, they are trying to *define the rhetorical problem.* The rhetorical problem includes all aspects of the writing situation, including the purpose of the piece of writing, the likely audience, the topic, the writer's knowledge of the topic, and the writer's own goals in writing. Good writers take all these and other aspects into consideration when they sit down to write, whereas poor writers may reduce the rhetorical problem to just "getting the assignment done."

Consider the literary critic, for example. How would her writing be different if she were reviewing a book for *People* magazine versus the *New York Times Book Review?* She would define the rhetorical problem one way for *People* and another way for the *Times Book Review;* she would most likely choose different words, write in a different style, include different content, and make other decisions depending on which publication's audience she was addressing. Even within one audience, readers might have different reasons for reading the review. One might be a casual reader hoping someone will suggest a good book to take on vacation; another may be an English professor looking for material for a new course on popular fiction. All these considerations are part of the rhetorical problem—the context for writing—and good writers make thoughtful decisions about them.

Defining the rhetorical problem is one process writers engage in as they consider what they are going to write. Several other processes are involved once the writer is ready to put thought into print. The first is planning, along with the subprocesses associated with it: generating ideas, organizing ideas, and setting goals. Writers already possess knowledge, and they have access to additional knowledge externally (e.g., books, Internet, and so on); through planning they make decisions about the knowledge needed for the specific rhetorical problem at hand. For some writers the two subprocesses of generating and organizing ideas are engaged simultaneously, whereas for others these two subprocesses take place at distinct moments. At some point, ideas must move from being unconnected and fragmented to categorized, ordered, and hierarchized. Goal setting, as defined by Flower and Hayes (1981), is something a writer does for him- or herself. Goal setting may involve content ("I have to get a definition of communication worked into this essay") as well as procedures ("Should I start with a definition and then give an example, or provide an example and then logically extract the definition?"). When a writing assignment or task calls for a minimum or maximum number of words, then a writer must count the words (a procedural decision). If the maximum number of words has been exceeded, then the writer must make reductions (a content-related decision).

At some point in the writing process, writers make their thoughts visible to others; this physical process has been called *translating thought to print* (Flower & Hayes, 1981), or *transcribing* (Dvorak, 1986); we prefer the latter term. When writers engage in this physical process, they must allocate their attentional resources and choose their focus. A writer concerned with spelling, grammar, and the formal features of transcribing may find that the more creative processes involved in planning suffer. It may be difficult to generate and organize ideas if the writer is very concerned with the form the ideas take.

Reviewing is a process that includes the subprocesses *revising* and *evaluating*. Reviewing may be a consciously planned activity ("I'll finish this section and then see where I am with this") or more spontaneous and unplanned ("This part isn't quite right"). Writers might review what they have written with the idea of revising it (reorganizing the ideas) or evaluating it in order to plan what should come next (generating more ideas). Some writers seem to find self-review difficult, and they often ask others to give them feedback on their writing. They cannot discern the problems for themselves, but they can see them when someone else points them out.

This brief description of writing processes gives some idea of how dynamic and complex writing is, whether writers are writing in their first language or their second. Second language writers have much more to think about than the grammar and lexicon of the second language.

LANGUAGE PRACTICES THAT USE WRITING

What happens when instructors give second language learners practices that make use of writing rather than practices that treat writing as a communicative act? What kinds of decisions do writers have to make? How do they define the rhetorical problem, including their purpose in writing? What planning do they have to do? In this section we examine some language practices that use writing, and in the next section we look at some composition-oriented practices that are more likely to lead to purposeful writing.

Language practices that use writing, or transcription-oriented practices, as Dvorak (1986) notes, involve writing that focuses primarily on the conventions of language form, namely, grammatical or lexical structure. These activities focus learners' attention on the subcomponents of writing, emphasizing the processes of putting ideas into visible language.

Activity A is typical of the writing practices included in textbooks; students are provided a list of words they must use to write a paragraph. As you read the activity, consider the act of writing according to the processes described in the previous section. What is the rhetorical problem? What are the relative contributions of the writing processes of planning, transcribing, and reviewing?

Activity A.   Families

Use at least ten of the following words to write a short composition about families. Underline each word used from the list in your composition.

parents	education	neighborhood
grandparents	goals	house
siblings	vacations	friends
occupations	weekends	dinner
chores	weekdays	mornings

The rhetorical problem defined for the writers is to produce a text with ten targeted lexical items. Goal setting during writing may take place in a purely quantitative way. That is, writers' concern will be not so much what they write but whether they have used particular lexical items. This is the case because their knowledge of the topic and audience includes not only what they know about families but what they know about *this type of assignment.* Specifically, the grade will most likely reflect whether or not they include ten targeted words and not what they say about families. Generating ideas will most likely focus on counting to ten. Planning can be minimal, since content is not as important as form. Although instructors may think the word list will stimulate the learners to think about content, the list really functions to *restrict* them.

Whereas Activity A focuses the writers on lexical items, Activity B focuses them on sentence structure, namely, word order. Each column contains a different part of speech (adverbs, nouns and pronouns, verbs) that the writers must use to build sentences. How will second language writers approach the task? What is the rhetorical problem? What writing processes will predominate? What goals will they set?

Activity B.   Your Family

Write a composition about your family, using the elements in the three columns as a guide.

A	B	C
frequently	I	visit
from time to time	father	call
hardly ever	mother	talk
whenever	siblings	see
always	we	listen
never	they	value

Our analysis of Activity B is similar to that of Activity A. The rhetorical problem the writers will establish for themselves will be to use the elements of the three columns, thereby focusing on form over content. Generating ideas will involve a process of elimination—that is, checking off a word once it has been used. Planning processes will involve constructing and ordering individual sentences. Reviewing will most likely focus not on what was written or how it was phrased but on which items in the lists were used.

Pause to consider . . .

the following change to the direction line of Activity B: "The words in the three columns serve only as a guide; you may add whatever you like to these lists." Does the change in wording change the rhetorical problem? Will it change the writing processes involved? Does this alteration to the direction line change this activity from a language practice to a writing practice?

The list to which writers respond can also be a list of questions, not just words and phrases. In Activity C, writers are to build a short composition prompted by a series of questions. Some might wonder why Activity C is included under the heading of language practices when it seems the most "composition-like" of the activities presented thus far. As you read it over, consider the rhetorical problem writers define for themselves, what they know about the audience, and what writing processes will be engaged. Consider also the Kinginger (1990) and Brooks (1990) research we presented in Chapter 6 to demonstrate how learners take seemingly communicative activities and turn them into drill-like practices.

Activity C.   Compare and Contrast

Write a short composition contrasting today's family with the family of three generations ago. Use your answers to the following questions as a guide to writing.

1. How big are families now? How big were they then?
2. How long do people expect to live now compared to then?
3. Is the woman's place still in the home?
4. Do people have more economic opportunities now?
5. Do people have more educational opportunities now?

What is the rhetorical problem for the language learner: to write a composition or to answer the questions? Learners will most likely underestimate and underspecify the rhetorical problem in order to answer the questions. What knowledge of the audience will learners rely on? In other words, what will they think the instructor wants? Learners will most likely see that this composition requires the use of imperfect aspect to describe the past and thereby focus on form. What planning will take place? The writers' plan—generating and organizing ideas—will probably be no more elaborate than to answer the questions in the order presented. What will they review? They might review the verb forms; they might not. They will probably review their work to determine that they answered the five questions.

> *Pause to consider . . .*
>
> possible variations on Activity C. Some instructors find that when prompt
> questions are written in the target language, learners simply answer using
> the words and wording of the questions. Are prompt questions an effective
> device for eliciting a thoughtful composition? Do they contribute to the
> tendency among learners to underspecify the rhetorical problem? Would
> writers reconceptualize the rhetorical problem if an instructor said no more
> than "Write a composition comparing and contrasting today's family with
> that of three generations past?" What would you infer about a writer who
> asked, "How many words do you want?"

Writing is a decision-making process, and even language practices that use
writing require learners to make decisions. The kinds of decisions they make,
however, do not lead them to improve as writers. As the scenarios presented
here suggest, learners are probably more aware than are some teachers that certain activities happen to ask them to respond in writing rather than to respond
orally. How different would Activity A really be, from a learning perspective,
if it had the following direction line?

Talk about your family with a partner. Use at least ten words from the
following list. Then switch roles and listen as your partner talks about
her family using at least ten words from the list.

The direction lines for Activities B and C could also be recast toward oral language use rather than written language use. Recasting the directions toward
oral language use underscores the language practice—versus the writing
practice—nature of the activities. Completing Activities A, B, and C probably
will not make second language learners better second language writers.

COMPOSITION-ORIENTED ACTIVITIES

We propose quite a different approach to second language writing, one that
engages writers in making good decisions that will improve their writing. In
such an approach, writing activities must help determine writers' conceptualization of the rhetorical problem and engage higher-level planning and reviewing processes. Let's examine a series of activities that engage second language
writers in a variety of cognitive processes all leading toward writing a composition. Even though transcription-oriented activities are more common than
compositions in beginning language instruction, the following composition
activities were designed with first-year language learners in mind. Activities D
through F can be considered prewriting exercises and Activity G the writing
phase. In each of the prewriting exercises, the learners are given options to consider. These options require them to make choices, to consciously decide on the
direction their composition will take. As you read these activities, note beside
each step what writing processes are engaged.

Activity D. Generating Content

Step 1. To each group of three or four students, the instructor will assign one of the following topics:

a. Family life at the turn of the century
b. Family life today

Each group will have ten minutes to make a list of as many ideas as possible relating its topic to each of the following:

1. Family size
2. Economic opportunities
3. Educational opportunities
4. Male and female roles
5. Society

Step 2. Report to the rest of the class the ideas your group has generated. Create a master list on the board of the ideas generated on each topic. Are there any other ideas you can think of to add to the lists?

Step 3. Each member of the class should copy the lists from the board to use later in writing.

Instructors may also want learners to use resource materials available in the classroom (books, magazines, the Internet, and so on) as a source of content for such activities. Reading in the second language not only provides learners with a source of input for formal written discourse, as noted earlier in this chapter; it also provides the content they need to write compositions that go beyond their own personal experiences.

Activity E. Selecting an Audience and a Purpose

Step 1. Keeping in mind the ideas the class generated in Activity D, think about an audience for your writing. Select an audience from the following list or propose one yourself.

a. High school students you are addressing as part of a college recruitment program
b. Readers of the school newspaper
c. Members of a businesswomen's organization
d. Members of a church council
e. Panhellenic council that governs fraternities and sororities on campus
f. Other suggestions _____

Step 2. Select one of the two topics. Then form groups of three with others working with the same topic and list your audience's characteristics. Report your list to the rest of the class. Try to help other groups by proposing characteristics they may not have considered. Take down any suggestions your classmates offer you.

Activity F. Planning and Organizing

Step 1. Now that you have an audience, what will you say to them? Working in the same groups as in Activity E, examine the lists of ideas you prepared for Activity D and indicate what information you might include in your composition.

Step 2. Working individually, prepare an outline of the composition. Once each of you has an outline, present them to each other. Have your partners thought of some things you didn't?

Step 3. *(Option)* Present your outline to someone who selected a different audience and listen to them present theirs. Can you offer any ideas or suggestions?

Activities D, E, and F engage learners in thoughtful consideration of the rhetorical problem; learners are discouraged from underestimating the rhetorical problem and reducing it to just "completing the assignment." Activities D and F focus specifically on planning and highlight the decisions needed to generate and organize ideas.

Pause to consider . . .

---

the nature of the interaction encouraged in Activities D through F. In Chapter 3, we advocated the use of oral activities that allow for the expression, interpretation, and negotiation of meaning. Although Activities D through F are writing-oriented, will they also promote language development in the learners? Why or why not?

Once a certain amount of preparatory work has been undertaken, writing the composition should begin. Whereas Activities D through F set the stage, Activity G is about transcribing, putting thought to paper or screen, and reviewing. Note the function of the questions in Activity G.

Activity G. Composing

Step 1. Take your outline and list of ideas and keep them handy as you write a composition directed at the audience you selected. *Suggestion:* Write a draft of the work and let it sit for two days. Do not think about it or read it. At the end of two days, pick it up and read it. As you do, answer the following questions.

    a. Content: Are these still the ideas you want to include?
    b. Organization: Does the order in which the ideas are presented help you get your message across to the audience?

If you answer "No" to either question, rewrite some of your composition.

Step 2. Once you think your composition is good enough to hand in, review the language you used.

    a. Verbs: Are the forms, spelling, and accents correct?
    b. Adjectives: What noun do they go with? Do the adjectives agree?
    c. [*Other elements of the language on which you wish learners to focus*]

Activities D through G help writers become conscious of the elements of good writing. Not only will the composition—the product of writing—in Activity G be better than the one generated in Activity C, but the way the writers write (the process through which they generate the product) will be qualitatively different. Activities D through G are structured to engage writing processes and to shape the decisions learners make about their writing.

Pause to consider . . .

writing as a social, rather than private, act. In what ways have we construed writing as a social act?

SUMMARY

In this chapter we first examined some fundamental considerations about writing: that writing is a communicative act, that is, it involves the expression, interpretation, and negotiation of meaning; that written language is different from spoken language and that second language writers need to learn the properties of written discourse in the second language; that reading in the second language is the best source of input for second language writers; and that writing is a skill that improves with practice.

Language practices are not the same as writing practices. Language practices may require written answers, but these practices do not lead to writing improvement. Second language learners must write in order to become better writers. The types of activities that promote writing development are those that involve decision-making writing processes: defining the rhetorical problem (purpose and audience), planning (generating ideas, organizing ideas, setting goals), and reviewing (evaluating and revising). We presented activities in this chapter that worked specifically with these processes and offered writers different options. As formulated, these activities required learners to work together through several sets of processes. Learners were directed, as writers, to make decisions about writing. We also advocated the use of readings to provide examples of formal written discourse and the content for compositions. Whereas language curricula tend to have composition classes at a later point in the curriculum, we advocated including composition activities in beginning stage classes, too.

KEY TERMS, CONCEPTS, AND ISSUES

writing as communication
written language ≠ spoken
  language
reading as input
writing as skill

second language writers are second
  language learners
writing
  transcription and language practice
  composition and writing practice

255

*Making
Communicative
Language Teaching
Happen: Portfolio
Activities*

writing as decision making
  rhetorical problem
  purpose
  audience
writing processes
  planning
    generating
    organizing
    goal setting
  transcribing
  reviewing
    evaluating
    revising

language practices that
  use writing
composition-oriented practices
  decision-making approach to
    L2 writing
activities structured around
  writing processes

THINKING MORE ABOUT IT:
DISCUSSION QUESTIONS

1. We used the example of two grocery lists in this chapter to show how writers, when they define the rhetorical problem, are sensitive to audience and purpose. Now, imagine that you are too ill to go to the grocery store yourself and someone has to go for you. Write two grocery lists that include the following items: sandwich meat, lettuce, cookies, yogurt, ice cream, and paper towels. One list is for your neighbor's sixteen-year-old son and the other for your elderly grandmother.
2. Activities D, E, and F are designed for in-class use. List the pros and cons of doing these activities in class rather than assigning them to learners to do by themselves as homework. Then list the things the instructor would do during a class session in which learners worked on Activities D, E, and F.

GETTING A CLOSER LOOK:
RESEARCH ACTIVITIES

Record two volunteers carring out Activity C and another two carrying out Activities D, E, and F. Then analyze the two interactions in terms of the writing processes explained in this chapter. Compare and contrast the two interactions for the way the learners make decisions.

MAKING COMMUNICATIVE LANGUAGE
TEACHING HAPPEN: PORTFOLIO ACTIVITIES

Using Activities D–G as a guide, create composition activities for a chapter in a textbook that does not include composition. Begin by making a list of the ideas, themes, and topics covered in the chapter and use those as suggested composition topics. Be sure that you suggest different audiences and that your materials always get the learners to make decisions.

Issues in Testing Comprehension and in Evaluating Writing

In this chapter, we explore:

- Issues related to testing listening, namely, tasks and language of assessment
- Issues related to testing reading, building on the ideas from testing listening but also exploring the difference between testing for content (product) and testi ng for skill (process)
- Issues in evaluating written work, including responding to form, to content, to drafts and the difference between analytical and holistic scoring

ONE ISSUE FOR ALL TESTS: PURPOSE

Bachman (1990) reminds us that not all tests are created for the same purpose. Within an educational setting, tests serve a variety of purposes. For example, a classroom test can indicate progress and achievement. Tests can also be diagnostic, indicating strengths and weaknesses. Entrance tests discriminate among applicants; placement tests direct learners to particular courses. Each of these tests might include an examination of listening or reading comprehension but approach it in different ways. For example, whereas a placement test might have all the items written in the test taker's native language, a classroom test might have them in the target language, particularly if all classroom instruction is carried out in the target language. Placement tests and entrance tests might favor the use of a single task type (such as multiple choice) due to its ease of scoring, whereas a classroom test or diagnostic test might use a combination of task types (multiple choice, open-ended, cloze procedures).

The point in this brief introduction is to remind ourselves that the shape of a test is always context-dependent, and that purpose is one of the major determinants of the context. What a test looks like, then, is a direct function of what that test is supposed to do and for whom it is supposed to do it.

> ***Pause to consider . . .***
>
> the nature of testing in large universities. If you are or have been a graduate teaching assistant in a large university, you may have given departmental tests. That is, as an instructor you were not free to give your own test to your class but had to administer the tests developed for all sections of Spanish, French, or German first semester, let's say. Why do you think departments give such tests rather than allow individual instructors to develop their own? Is there another purpose to tests other than what we have just seen?

TESTING LISTENING COMPREHENSION

It would seem redundant to say that a test of listening comprehension must test listening comprehension, but it is nonetheless important. Why? In some formal testing situations, aural testing of vocabulary or grammar has been equated with listening comprehension. Just a few years ago it was not uncommon to find the following as a standard listening section on a foreign language exam in the United States.

Section 1.   Oral Questions

Listen to each question carefully and then answer in a complete sentence.

1. Did you call your mother last night?
2. Did you eat eggs for breakfast this morning?
3. What time did you get up today?
4. Where did you go last night?
5. Did you arrive at class on time today?

Exam sections such as this one (used to test past tense) cannot be classified as "listening comprehension" as that concept was developed in Chapter 10. Although it is true that the test takers are listening to sentences that they must then respond to, the section itself bears little resemblance to the kind of listening that happens in real life. And because the section asks for written responses in complete sentences, the nature of performance in listening is severely compromised. What, then, should a listening test look like?

A good listening test considers at least the following three factors:

1. Content (topic domain)
2. Task (how the learner is asked to demonstrate comprehension)
3. Language of assessment

Content

For content, we can develop a listening test that is topic specific (listening to a description of someone's family) or not (listening to a news report). Whether or not to restrict the content of a listening test is determined by the purpose of the test. In certain professions, for example, a listening test that is content

258

CHAPTER 13
*Issues in Testing
Comprehension and
in Evaluating
Writing*

specific might be preferred but not necessary. Can the doctor understand the patient's description of her symptoms? Can the counterperson at the social services office understand the routine requests of clients? In other professions, specificity of content in listening tests will not be appropriate. We would expect, for example, that a U.N. interpreter could successfully comprehend a wide variety of topic domains in the second language. In these situations, the nature of test content is dictated or suggested by the nature of the profession or job.

In the typical second language classroom, however, it is clear that professional concerns rarely can be considered for the purposes of testing. In a given classroom, an instructor may have a wide array of future professionals engaged in language learning, and testing cannot be tailored to each individual in any practical manner. Listening tests can nevertheless still be either content specific or broad in content, depending on the purpose of the test. If the listening test is part of a quiz or lesson test, then content can be restricted as in the following example, which might be used on a test that focuses on family and family relationships.

Section 2.   Families and Relationships

You will hear two people talk about their families. Select one of the two speakers and, after listening, draw his or her family tree using all the information you can. The connection of lines should demonstrate family relationships, and each face should have a name under it.

If the listening test is part of an exit exam or placement test, then a wider variety of topic domains might be sampled. Or, the test might utilize a short section from a movie or some other speech sample that does not focus on any one topic domain.

Tasks

The task that a learner is asked to perform to demonstrate comprehension can fall into one of two categories: tasks that require a linguistic response and those that require a nonlinguistic response. Samples of each are listed in Table 13.1.

TABLE 13.1 Sample Linguistic and Nonlinguistic Tasks for Assessing Listening Comprehension

Linguistic	Nonlinguistic
Creating an outline	Making a graph
Filling in a chart	Creating a drawing
Labeling things in a visual display	Selecting a visual
Making a table	Indicating something on a visual with numbers, arrows, circles, etc.
Creating a quiz	Filling in missing parts in a drawing
Answering questions	Arranging items or objects
Summarizing in written or oral form	Performing a physical task (e.g., cooking something, acting something out)

A *linguistic response* is any kind of response that requires the use of language on the part of the learner to demonstrate comprehension. That is, comprehension can only be assessed based on the language that the learner *produces*. This language can be words (labeling things, filling in blanks), phrases (outlines, tables, answering questions), sentences (answering questions, writing summary statements), and connected discourse (summarizing in paragraph form). *Nonlinguistic responses* are those that do not require the production of language for comprehension to be assessed: the learner indicates comprehension visually, not verbally. In the family tree example, the learner demonstrated comprehension nonlinguistically by drawing the family tree. Here are other tasks that could be used with the same test stimuli (the description of the family) to assess comprehension.

Sample Linguistic Tasks

1. The learner answers a number of questions about the various family members.
2. The learner is asked to write a brief paragraph in which he describes the family.
3. The learner is given a list of names and is asked to write next to each the relationship of that person to the speaker.

Sample Nonlinguistic Tasks

1. The learner receives names and faces as cut-outs and must place them into the family tree; the lines that represent the tree are already drawn in.
2. The learner receives the family tree with missing members and must add faces for those who are missing.
3. The learner receives four different family trees with only slight variations among them and must select the family tree that best represents the description he heard.

If an instructor teaches more than one class, she might have learners help her create quizzes for another class. For example, after listening, learners could create five true/false statements about the family, five multiple-choice statements, or a column-matching activity (names on one side, relationships on the other in mixed order). The instructor could then grade each quiz (and the answer key that each learner provides) that night and use one or a combination of them in another class the next day.

Selection of task depends mostly on the level of the learners and the point at which the quiz or test is administered. Can the learners handle a summary? Would a word-level linguistic task be the best demonstration of their comprehension? These are the types of questions that an instructor must ask in developing listening quizzes and tests.

Language of Assessment

The *language of assessment* may seem an odd point to bring up. After all, isn't it obvious that learners are listening to something in the second language? The issue of language of assessment is not about the stimulus, however; it refers to the language used by learners when the task requires a linguistic response. Some instructors claim that everything should be done in the second

260

CHAPTER 13
Issues in Testing
Comprehension and
in Evaluating
Writing

language and that use of the native language in testing situations goes against this philosophy. However, research in second language reading (Lee, 1986a; Wolf, 1993b) demonstrates that language of assessment is a significant variable when testing reading comprehension. In Lee's and Wolf's studies, comprehension scores were significantly higher for those subjects who were allowed to respond in English (their first language) compared with those who took the test in Spanish (their language of study). Thus, learners' demonstration of comprehension was impeded when they had to write their answers in Spanish. We would expect the same to be true for listening comprehension as well.

What this means for instructors, then, is that if the actual test (including instructions and test items) is presented in the second language and if learners also have to *perform* in the second language (write answers, summarize, and so forth), then the test results are confounded by performance variables. An instructor needs to be aware of this problem and make judicious decisions based on the purpose of the test and comparison to real-life listening situations. For example, in everyday situations one engages in collaborative listening in the second language, and comprehension is demonstrated as learners use strategic responses as part of their communicative responsibilities. But when one listens to a weather report or news, watches a TV program, or engages in other noncollaborative listening situations, there may be no obligation on the part of the learner to demonstrate immediate comprehension by performing in the second language in some way.

TESTING READING COMPREHENSION

As with the testing of listening comprehension, several factors should be taken into consideration when reading comprehension is being tested. These factors include the type of task, the language of assessment, and the construction of individual test items.

Task Type and Language of Assessment

Wolf (1993a) reviews and interprets selected literature on testing second language reading comprehension. The result is a series of recommendations concerning test item construction. Wolf's discussion focuses on the effects on learners' responses of task type and the language of assessment. Research directly comparing task types clearly demonstrates that the task influences the outcome (Shohamy, 1984; Lee, 1987b; Wolf, 1993b): some tasks allow learners to demonstrate their comprehension better than other tasks do. Some might reduce these findings to saying that multiple-choice questions are easier than open-ended questions because the test taker simply selects among options in one but actually has to produce something in the other. Nevertheless, we cannot dismiss the fact that the format of a test may determine the decisions we make about the test taker.

As we discussed previously, research on the language of assessment examines the use of reading test items written in the test takers' native or target language. The results consistently show that language learners perform better on items and tasks written in their native language (Hock & Poh, 1979; Shohamy, 1984; Lee, 1986a, 1987b; Wolf, 1993b). These results hold for beginning as well as advanced foreign language learners; surprisingly, they also hold for language learners who are completing high school in which the medium of instruction is the target language. The application of these results to classroom testing can be summarized as "biasing for the best." In other words, what does the test giver want to test: what the readers know or understand or what they do *not* know or understand?

Pause to consider . . .

the relevance of the curriculum to testing. The research mentioned was carried out without consideration given to the curricula in which the learners were enrolled. If all instruction is carried out in the target language, should the test then be given in the learners' native language just because research has shown that their scores will probably be higher?

Item Construction

A test is only as good as the individual items on it. If a test item can be answered correctly without the test taker reading the passage, then the item is not passage-dependent and, thus, not a good test item (Johns, 1978; Perkins & Jones, 1985). If test items encourage test takers to read only sections of a passage or to do only a surface reading of the passage, then the items are not good ones (Cohen, 1984). If items test only isolated facts or details, they can be answered based on understanding only words and phrases and not the entire passage; such items are not good ones (Swaffar & Wälterman, 1988). Based on her review of the research, Wolf (1993a) has developed guidelines for constructing individual test items. She recommends

> (1) that all items be passage dependent; (2) that items test information from different levels of the passage, that is, main ideas as well as details; (3) that all distractors be plausible; (4) that items paraphrase information in the passage so that learners cannot match words and phrases from the item to the passage; and (5) that test takers not be allowed to refer to the passage while performing the comprehension tasks, thereby discouraging surface reading of the passage. (p. 327)

Pause to consider . . .

withholding the passage during testing. How does the idea strike you? How will the idea strike the test takers? Can you suggest other ways to achieve the goal of avoiding surface readings?

262

CHAPTER 13
Issues in Testing
Comprehension and
in Evaluating
Writing

FROM CLASSROOM ACTIVITIES TO READING TESTS

Processes and Products

Comprehension can be defined as the process of relating new or incoming information to information already stored in memory. All attempts to test and evaluate comprehension are problematic because the process is internal to the reader (it happens in the mind), but tests require external manifestation of mental processes. Some argue that "testing comprehension" is an oxymoron: Eliciting external manifestations of mental processes in a classroom testing situation is simply not possible. Others argue that testing reading comprehension is a matter of testing what a reader learned from the text. In other words, testing assesses the accuracy of the *result* of relating incoming information to information already stored in memory. Thus, although comprehension is a process, the process yields a product. This view holds that what is important in testing is not *how* a reader comprehends but *what* is comprehended. This debate will not be easily resolved.

Throughout this book, we have advocated that tests reflect classroom activities. We now examine testing reading comprehension from two perspectives, both consistent with this position. The first focuses on content—a product-oriented approach. The second focuses on applying skills learned to a new reading situation—a process-oriented approach. There are advantages to both approaches.

Pause to consider . . .

how issues in the testing of reading and the testing of listening overlap. In what way is the process versus product issue equally applicable to listening?

Focus on Content

Krashen and Terrell (1983) recommend constructing tests that encourage learners to engage in acquisition activities, either during class activities or while studying. Their recommendation lies at the heart of the *washback effect* from testing to instruction; it can be applied to reading tests as well as to other kinds of testing. Our position is that reading tests should be constructed to encourage learners to read more. The more language learners read, the better readers they become and the more language they acquire. The test sections following are derived from classroom activities, thereby demonstrating to learners that they are responsible for the class assignments and that they must read and reread the assigned texts in order to prepare for the test.

When writing a test that focuses on content, you will want to focus on the guided interaction phase, the assimilation phase, and the communicative functions of texts; Activities H, I, and K, respectively, illustrated these three aspects of reading in Chapter 11. We display each activity again for your convenience, followed by a test version of the same activity.

Activity H.   Guided Interaction

Step 1. Since this is a relatively long reading, it would be best to read it section by section. After reading each section fairly quickly, pause to collect your thoughts by writing a sentence that captures the main idea of the section. Compare your sentences with those of a classmate. Do you agree on the main ideas?

Step 2. Go back and reread each section, paying more attention to the details. Using a highlighter, identify key words or phrases that will help you remember what you have read. At the end of each section, look at what you have highlighted. Does it spark your memory? Compare the words and phrases you have highlighted with those of your classmates. Have you chosen different words?

Step 3. Based on what you have read, check off the statements that are true.

- ❏ From the tone of the article, it is evident that the author is pro-elephant.
- ❏ Even though elephants are normally quite peaceful, they are capable of tremendous violence.
- ❏ An elephant herd is a democratic unit.
- ❏ Elephants and humans share similar preoccupations with their young.

Step 4. Complete the following statements.

1. A herd of elephants is composed of . . .
   a. males and females in more or less equal proportions.
   b. more males than females.
   c. one male and various females, like a harem.
2. The care of the young is . . .
   a. shared equally among males and females.
   b. the responsibility of the males.
   c. the responsibility of the females.
3. Of the young that are born in a herd . . .
   a. the males and females are members of the same herd for all their lives.
   b. the males and females form subgroups, which eventually leave the herd.
   c. the males leave the herd but the females remain.
   d. the females leave the herd but the males remain.

Step 5. Working with two or three classmates, make a list of all the behaviors described in the article. Then share your list with the rest of the class, adding to your list whatever behaviors you might have missed. Finally, as a class, indicate if each behavior is instinctive or learned.

Step 6. According to the introductory paragraphs, elephants are intelligent, difficult, active, powerful, and fun-loving animals. As a class, identify the information in the article that supports the idea that elephants really are as they are described.

264

*CHAPTER 13
Issues in Testing
Comprehension and
in Evaluating
Writing*

Section A   (Based on Activity H, Steps 3 and 4)

Based on your reading of "The Secret Code of Elephants," comment on three of the following ideas. Be sure to cite specific information from the passage that supports your statements.

a. Tone of the article
b. Organization of the herd (leadership and makeup)
c. Care of the young
d. Violence among elephants
e. Allegiance to the herd as the young grow older

Section B   (Based on Activity H, Steps 5 and 6)

1. We often hear that animal behavior is instinctive, that animals survive in the wild because they have the instincts to survive. How true is this statement for elephants? Refer to specific information from the article when answering.
2. According to the authors, elephants are intelligent, difficult, active, powerful, and fun-loving animals. Do you agree or disagree with the authors? Be sure to cite specific information from the article to support your opinion.

Test Sections A and B parallel the in-class guided interaction activities. The test requires learners to produce evidence of their comprehension of the passage; in each case, learners must cite specifics from the passage to support their views. Another option for testing the content of the passages is to use an assimilation activity. Activity I from Chapter 11, is reproduced here, followed by Sections C and D incorporating its content.

Activity I.   Assimilation

Step 1. Review what you did in the preparation and guided interaction activities. Then, complete the following semantic map without rereading the article (if you can).

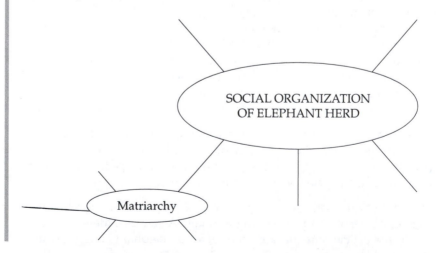

Step 2. You have three options for working with the semantic map.

> **Option 1.** Using only the semantic map, write a summary of the article you read.
>
> **Option 2.** Using only the semantic map, write a short quiz on the content of the article. Try not to be too detail-oriented with your questions. After all, you should write a quiz that you think is fair. You should also write a quiz that you would be willing to take!
>
> **Option 3.** Using only the semantic map to guide you, write three essay questions covering the content of the entire article. As you write the questions, think about keeping the answers to two or three paragraphs. Remember, the questions you write just might be the ones your instructor uses on the exam!

Section C   (Based on Activity I, Steps 1 and 2)

1. Draw a semantic map of the article using the social organization of the herd as the central organizing concept.
2. Use the map to summarize the article.

Section D   (Based on Activity I, Step 2 options)

1. Take the quiz you wrote in class.
2. Answer the essay questions you wrote in class.

Recall that in Activity K in Chapter 11, learners are asked to personalize the content of the reading about the secret code of elephants, relating it to the world as they know it. Test Section E builds from this activity and demonstrates that both comprehension of the passage and class participation are important.

Activity K.   Communicative Function of a Text

Step 1. Working with two or three classmates, put the number that corresponds to your own opinions next to each of the following sentences.

We believe that for the majority of people our age,

1 = It is important . . .
2 = It will be important some day . . .
3 = It is not very important . . .

> **a.** _____ to have a leadership role in whatever group one is associated with.
> **b.** _____ to live in a safe and protected area.
> **c.** _____ to lead an active social life.
> **d.** _____ to count on child care while at work.
> **e.** _____ to have various opportunities to find companionship.
> **f.** _____ to make friends.
> **g.** _____ to advance professionally.
> **h.** _____ to have economic security in old age.
> **i.** _____ to have a place to live in old age.

266

CHAPTER 13
Issues in Testing
Comprehension and
in Evaluating
Writing

Step 2. Compare your answers with those of the rest of the class by indicating how many people responded to each item with a "1," a "2," or a "3."

Step 3. Which items were most important to the majority of the class? Which were not important? Does the class agree on what to look for in life?

Step 4. Go back over the sentences, but this time indicate with the letter *E* those statements that can apply to elephants. Then explain what information from the article supports your choices. In what ways are humans and elephants similar?

Section E   (Based on Activity K)

1. Indicate which of the following items were important to the class.

   a. _____ To have a leadership role in whatever group one is associated with.
   b. _____ To live in a safe and protected area.
   c. _____ To lead an active social life.
   d. _____ To count on child care while at work.
   e. _____ To have various opportunities to find companionship.
   f. _____ To make friends.
   g. _____ To advance professionally.
   h. _____ To have economic security in old age.
   i. _____ To have a place to live in old age.

2. The class discussed ways in which elephant and human behaviors are similar. First, summarize both sides of the discussion. Then, state which side you agree with, using specific passage information to support your point of view.

Pause to consider . . .

how many test sections are needed to evaluate reading. On a midterm or final exam, what percentage of the test should be dedicated to reading? How many reading test sections should there be?

Focus on Skills Application

The alternative to testing content is to test the application of reading skills to a new reading. The teaching-testing philosophy behind this practice is that the assigned class readings are themselves not important. The act of reading and the accumulation of reading skills should instead be the focus.

To focus on the application of reading skills, construct a series of test sections whose structure mirrors that of class activities: preparation, guided interaction, assimilation, and the communicative functions of texts. Section F is an example of how to adapt the preparation-oriented in-class formats from Chapter 11, Activities A and G, for a test. (The adaptation of guided interaction, assimilation, and communicative function activities to testing formats was demonstrated in the previous section.)

Activity A.   Brainstorming with the Whole Class

Step 1.   As a class, generate a list of all the ideas you associate with weddings. Come up with as many different ideas as possible in five minutes.

Step 2.   As rapidly as possible, skim the text to determine whether or not the ideas on the board *(or overhead)* are actually in the reading. All you have to do is say whether or not the information is there; you do not have to know (not yet anyway) what the author says about that information. You have five minutes.

Step 3.   Share what you found with the rest of the class. As you do, erase from the board all those ideas that are *not* in the text. Do you all agree?

Activity G.   Scanning

Step 1.   Find the following three words in the text and underline the sentences in which you find them.
   a. *feudalism*   **b.** *stewardship*   **c.** *tithes*

Step 2.   Working with two or three classmates, either write a definition of each of the words or list as many things as you can think of that you associate with each.

Step 3.   Share your work with the rest of the class. Are you all sure what these words mean?

Section F   (Based on Activities A and G)

1. Find the following three words in the text and underline the sentences in which you find them.
   a. *feudalism*   **b.** *stewardship*   **c.** *tithes*
   Then write a definition of each of the words.
2. Now, skim the passage to determine whether or not the following topics are covered in the reading.

YES	NO	
❏	❏	**1.** Inheritance laws for titles and property
❏	❏	**2.** Women's rights
❏	❏	**3.** The effects of war on the economy

> *Pause to consider . . .*
>
> the appropriate text for a testing situation. Review page 225 containing the guidelines suggested by Swaffar and her colleagues (1991) for selecting texts and other teaching materials. Which of these apply to testing as well?

In Chapter 12, we distinguished between transcription-oriented practices and composition activities in teaching writing in a second language. The evaluation of transcription-oriented practices is a fairly simple, straightforward issue: You grade according to the intent of the practice. If the writers were directed, as in Chapter 12's Activity A (on page 249), to include ten targeted words in a short composition, the grade should reflect the presence or absence of these words. If, as in Activity B (on page 249), the focus of the activity is sentence structure and word order, the grading should reflect only those elements. Composition activities, however, engage qualitatively different thinking processes and yield a qualitatively different product than do the transcription-oriented Activities A and B. We focus our discussion here on issues concerning the evaluation of compositions.

Responding to Form

Responding to form, otherwise known as "error correction" or "corrective feedback," is perhaps the most debated issue in language instruction. It goes far beyond composition. The underlying question is whether corrective feedback is effective: In the case of composition, does corrective feedback improve learners' writing? The answer is Yes and No. Some research supports the idea that responding to form brings about changes in learners' writing (see, e.g., Lalande, 1982), whereas other research does not (see Semke, 1984). Still, other research (Robb, Ross, & Shortreed, 1986) suggests a middle ground. Let's review these studies.

Lalande (1982) compared two methods of treating errors in the writing of second-year university learners of German. In the first method, instructors corrected errors and learners rewrote their compositions incorporating the corrections. In the second method, instructors coded the errors (for example, using *Nag* to indicate noun-adjective-agreement errors and *T* to indicate an error in tense selection). Learners then had to rewrite their compositions addressing these errors. Additionally, learners in the second method had to track the number and types of errors they made on each composition. Lalande found that learners in the second method improved their linguistic accuracy in writing more than did learners in the first method, although only to a small extent.

Semke (1984) compared several methods of providing feedback to first-year university learners of German. Instructors used one of the following methods:

- Commenting on the content
- Correcting errors
- Commenting on the content and correcting errors
- Coding errors for learners to then self-correct

At the end of the quarter, learners who received comments on content only were superior to all other groups. Not only did they write more (they produced longer works), they also wrote more accurately (with fewer grammatical errors) than did the other groups.

Robb, Ross, and Shortreed (1986) expanded considerably on the designs of Lalande and Semke. They tracked learners over a year-long period, used multiple methods of feedback, and scored the compositions along a variety of lines. The methods used were

- Correcting errors
- Coding errors
- Highlighting errors but not correcting or coding them
- Indicating in the margin the number of errors made

They found that writing improved less as a result of feedback on errors than as a result of having additional opportunities to write. Labor-intensive methods of providing feedback, such as correcting and coding errors, did not produce results commensurate with the instructor's investment of time. Moreover, when instructors respond to form, so do learners. That is, since instructors were indicating surface errors, rather than errors in meaning, learners responded by focusing their attention on changing the surface features, not their meanings.

Pause to consider . . .

the parallel between this line of research on writing and the research insights presented in Chapter 1. Can you draw a parallel between stages of language development and the improvement in linguistic accuracy that results from having more opportunities to write?

Responding to Content

Writing involves not only form but content. Feedback on compositions should include responding to the content (the intended meanings) whether or not one responds to form. The type of instructor response should encourage writers to express themselves better. The instructor, acting on behalf of the intended audience, will in effect negotiate written meaning with the writer. This concept is essential for formulating a coherent approach to teaching and evaluating writing. Yet, as research shows, we must carefully construct our responses to content.

Zamel (1985) examined the comments, reactions, and markings that appeared on compositions assigned and evaluated by fifteen instructors teaching their own university-level ESL classes. She found that, by and large, instructors

- Make vague comments about abstract rules and principles that learners are unable to interpret
- Correct on a clause-by-clause basis without considering the text as a whole
- Respond to some problems but not others so that their reactions appear arbitrary and idiosyncratic
- Tend to give conflicting signals about what to improve when providing overall comments and suggestions
- Tend not to review their feedback when reviewing a revised composition and so accept revisions that address surface-level language errors

270

CHAPTER 13
Issues in Testing
Comprehension and
in Evaluating
Writing

Overall, Zamel found that the instructors were poor communicators who faulted their students for being imprecise and vague but were themselves no better at communicating their responses.

Pause to consider . . .

your own writing experiences. Which of your instructors provided you the type or feedback that made you a better writer? Which provided feedback that was confusing or even contradictory? What type of feedback would/do you give learners?

Responding to Drafts

As Zamel found, even instructors who responded to content accepted revisions of the work with only changes in surface errors. This practice is questionable on two levels. First, we have seen repeatedly that learners "read" their instructors. If the instructor accepts rewrites that only address grammatical errors, then learners will most likely interpret the intent of the writing to be correct form production. On the other hand, learners may not know how to address content-related issues in their rewrites. Their practice of correcting only the grammatical errors is a call to the instructor to teach them how to address other issues. Colomb and colleagues (1991) recommend that instructors respond only to the content of a draft and not to formal errors, even though learners find it easier to focus on their formal errors than they find it to work on their expression of meaning. But the issue is also one of instructor effort. Why respond to formal errors before the writer has produced the "final" version that includes all the content? Here is an example. The following two samples of writing are a second language learner's draft and a rewrite of a definition of the term *meaningful*. As you read them, consider the ways in which an instructor would waste time responding to the formal errors in the draft.

Draft
If activity "meaningful" then learner required to interpret/ comprehend the language so to complete the activity. If activity "meaning bearing," not only meaningful, but it must require a personal/affective response by learner.

Rewrite
Both *meaningful* and *meaning bearing* are terms to categorize activities. Meaningful activity require learner comprehend/interpret item language in order to carry out the activity. Meaning-bearing activity meet criteria for meaningful but also require learner provide some type of evaluative response to item. Examples of evaluative responses are personal and affective responses, assessments of the information, etc.

Pause to consider . . .

the kind of response to the content of the draft that would focus the writer on addressing the meaning. What would you say to a second language learner who wrote the draft of the definition in order to focus the writer on content and meaning?

Holistic versus Analytical Scoring

We first introduced holistic and analytical scoring with reference to oral testing (Chapter 5). A discussion of these two types of scoring criteria is also relevant to evaluating writing. Whether you use holistic or analytical scoring procedures, you are applying criteria in order to evaluate a composition. Holistic scoring results in an overall assessment of the work, reflected in a single score, rating, or grade based on descriptions of performance at a variety of levels. The rater evaluates the "fit" between the composition and the description. Examples of holistic descriptions are the ACTFL Proficiency Guidelines and the TOEFL Test of Written English. The TOEFL Test of Written English has six levels. The following description corresponds to Level 4; writing samples that "fit" this description would be rated "4."

- Is adequately organized and developed
- Uses some details to support thesis or illustrate an idea
- Demonstrates adequate, but possibly inconsistent, facility with syntax and usage
- May contain some errors that occasionally obscure meaning

Analytical scoring is analogous to componential scoring, which was discussed in Chapter 5. Each component of the composition is evaluated (scored, rated, or graded); the component scores are typically added together to yield a final evaluation. Whereas holistic-level descriptions collapse a number of categories into one level, the analytical criteria expand the descriptions of each category. Lee and Paulson (1992) developed the analytical scoring criteria listed in Table 13.2. As you read them, note that the categories are not weighted equally. The weightings should reflect the importance of the category. One way to determine importance is to consider how it was treated during instruction.

Whether you select holistic or analytical scoring criteria, you must ensure that (1) writers are both aware and knowledgeable of the criteria, and (2) the criteria are applied consistently to all writers. When learners know how they will be evaluated, they can write with the criteria in mind. For example, if writers do not know that vocabulary use will be assessed, they may not review their use of vocabulary. Some educators recommend teaching learners how to apply the evaluation criteria to their own and to their peers' compositions as a means of familiarizing them with the criteria. Consistent application of criteria is a fundamental consideration in all testing situations. You are already familiar with the term *inter-rater reliability* (from Chapter 5) to describe a situation in which two different raters agree on an evaluation. An issue that arises in composition grading is that of *intra-rater reliability,* in

TABLE 13.2 Evaluation Criteria for Compositions

Content (Information Conveyed)	Points
• Minimal information; information lacks substance (is superficial); inappropriate or irrelevant information; or not enough information to evaluate	19
• Limited information; ideas present but not developed; lack of supporting detail or evidence	22
• Adequate information; some development of ideas; some ideas lack supporting detail or evidence	25
• Very complete information; no more can be said; thorough; relevant; on target	30

Organization	
• Series of separate sentences with no transitions; disconnected ideas; no apparent order to the content; or not enough to evaluate	16
• Limited order to the content; lacks logical sequencing of ideas; ineffective ordering; very choppy; disjointed	18
• An apparent order to the content is intended; somewhat choppy; loosely organized but main points do stand out although sequencing of ideas is not complete	22
• Logically and effectively ordered; main points and details are connected; fluent; not choppy whatsoever	25

Vocabulary	
• Inadequate; repetitive; incorrect use or nonuse of words studied; literal translations; abundance of invented words; or not enough to evaluate	16
• Erroneous word use or choice leads to confused or obscured meaning; some literal translations and invented words; limited use of words studied	18
• Adequate but not impressive; some erroneous word usage or choice, but meaning is not confused or obscured; some use of words studied	22
• Broad; impressive; precise and effective word use and choice; extensive use of words studied	25

Language	
• One or more errors in use and form of the grammar presented in lesson; frequent errors in subject/verb agreement; non-Spanish sentence structure; erroneous use of language makes the work mostly incomprehensible; no evidence of having edited the work for language; or not enough to evaluate	13
• No errors in the grammar presented in lesson; some errors in subject/verb agreement; some errors in adjective/noun agreement; erroneous use of language often impedes comprehensibility; work was poorly edited for language	15
• No errors in the grammar presented in lesson; occasional errors in subject/verb or adjective/noun agreement; erroneous use of language does not impede comprehensibility; some editing for language evident but not complete	17
• No errors in the grammar presented in lesson; very few errors in subject/verb or adjective/noun agreement; work was well edited for language	20

Total points _____ /100

Source: Lee and Paulson (1992), p. 33

which the same rater applies the criteria consistently across all the compositions he or she evaluates. When raters are tired, they may not make the same judgments that they do when they are alert. After evaluating fifteen compositions without resting, level distinctions can become blurred.

Pause to consider . . .

other categories for analytical criteria. Among them are

> Thought organization
> Quality of arguments/explanations
> Surface features/mechanics (handwriting and spelling)
> Communicative quality (ease of reading)
> Expression
> Cohesiveness
> Comprehensibility
> Stylistic techniques

On what basis do you choose one category over another? What weighting would you give to the category?

SUMMARY

In this chapter, we discussed a number of issues in the testing of listening and reading and the evaluation of writing. These issues can be added to the list of considerations we presented in earlier chapters. We began by considering that different tests have different purposes. Thus, any decision about the test (from task types to evaluation criteria) must be made in the appropriate context. As we have done in previous chapters on testing, we adapted classroom activities as test sections, underscoring our position that instructors should test what and how they teach. After a brief discussion of listening, we presented two approaches to testing reading: one that focused on content and another that focused on the application of skills. Focusing testing on content would lead the learners to read and reread, to go beyond a surface reading of the assigned passages. Focusing testing on applying skills would lead the learners to appreciate the instructional framework (the *how* of reading) rather than the content (the *what* of reading). Either approach to testing is consistent with the type of instruction advocated in Chapter 11. We then presented several issues in evaluating writing, including research on the effects of feedback provided to learners, whether and when to respond to form and/or content, and the use of holistic versus analytical criteria. Like teaching, testing involves making decisions. Decisions about tests, however, seem to have greater emotional consequences for learners. Although you might be able to motivate learners with tests and thus reinforce your classroom practices, you could also unmotivate them and undermine your classroom practices. Whatever decisions you make about testing, you must be able to justify them not only to yourself but to the learners.

KEY TERMS, CONCEPTS, AND ISSUES

purpose of tests
testing listening comprehension
  content
  specificity
  task
  linguistic versus nonlinguistic
   response
  language of assessment
testing reading comprehension
  task type
  language of assessment
  bias for the best
  curricular considerations
item construction (guidelines)
  passage dependency
  levels of information
   main idea versus detail
  plausibility of distractors
  paraphrasing
  discouraging surface readings
process versus product
  mental processes
  external manifestations

focus on content
  washback effects
focus on skills application
evaluating writing
  responding to form
   various treatment methods
   effectiveness
   labor-intensive feedback
  responding to content
   negotiation of meaning
  responding to drafts
   form versus meaning
  holistic scoring
   level descriptions
  analytical scoring
   categories
   weights
intra-rater reliability versus inter-
  rater reliability
writer's knowledge of criteria

THINKING MORE ABOUT IT: DISCUSSION QUESTIONS

1. Review the issues in testing listening and reading. Then, make a chart or table in which you list in one column the issues that they share. In another column, list the issues that may be different. If you can think of any issues not mentioned in this chapter, add them to the table.
2. In this chapter, we mentioned "biasing for the best" in testing. What are the pros of biasing for the best? What are the cons? Discuss this with your classmates.
3. Examine the Lee and Paulson (1992) analytical scoring criteria presented in this chapter for evaluation of writing. List the three most important characteristics of these criteria. Then, either justify or suggest changes in (a) the categories represented and (b) the weighting of the components. On what principles do you base any changes? What factors seem to come up?

GETTING A CLOSER LOOK: RESEARCH ACTIVITIES

Select three student compositions that you think are clearly three different grades. Then select a fourth that you think deserves the same grade as one of the other three. Make ten copies of each and hand them to ten different instructors along with a copy of Lee and Paulson's analytic scoring criteria. Then collect all the compositions and their grades. What is the inter-rater reliability? Report any problems or suggest what might need to happen (e.g., adjust the criteria, conduct a pregrading workshop on using the criteria, and so on).

MAKING COMMUNICATIVE LANGUAGE TEACHING HAPPEN: PORTFOLIO ACTIVITIES

Select either listening or reading as your domain, or if you prefer you may work with both. Develop two versions of the same test, one for placement and one for in-class testing. (If you do both listening and reading, you will have four versions in the end: two versions for the reading test and two versions for the listening test.) Review Wolf's (1993a) suggestions for developing appropriate test items as you work.

Sample Processing Instruction Lesson on the French Causative

THE **FAIRE CAUSATIF:** *AN INTRODUCTION*

We often ask or get people to do things for us by telling them to do something.

Paul says, "John, would you mind doing the dishes?"

If you and I were to describe what is happening we might say:

"Paul gets John to do the dishes."

or

"Paul makes John do the dishes."

This is called a *causative* construction (because someone is causing a behavior in someone else.) French has a similar structure using the verb *faire*. Let's repeat our examples from above.

Paul says, *"Jean, pourrais-tu faire la vaisselle?"*

We say, *"Paul fait faire la vaisselle à Jean."*

How would we describe the following scenario?

Wynne says, *"Sara, pourrais-tu promener le chien?"*

We would describe Wynne getting Sara to do it like this:

We say, *"Wynne fait promener le chien à Sara."*

Note. From "Processing Instruction and the French Causative: Another Replication," by B. VanPatten and W. Wong, in *Processing Instruction: Theory, Research, and Commentary*, ed. by B. VanPatten, 2003. Mahwah, NJ: Erlbaum. Adapted with permission.

Often we don't mention who we get to do something; we might simply say we have something done.

"*Paul fait nettoyer la chambre.*"

In this case, Paul has the room cleaned, but we don't know how or by whom.

One of the problems the *faire causatif* presents is in listening comprehension. Second language learners of French often misinterpret what they hear because the word order is different from English. For example, it is not uncommon for learners of French to make the following mistake:

They hear, "*Jean fait faire la vaisselle à Paul.*"
They incorrectly think, "John is doing the dishes for Paul."

or

They hear, "*Marc fait couper les cheveux.*"
They incorrectly think, "Marc cuts hair."

In the activities that follow, we will practice hearing and interpreting the *faire causatif.*

Activité A   Listen to each sentence. Then indicate who is performing the action by answering each question.

1. Who cleans the room? _____
2. Who packs the bags? _____
3. Who watches the movie? _____
4. Who sings? _____
5. Who does the chores? _____
6. Who looks for the dog? _____
7. Who watches the show? _____
8. Who reads the instructions? _____

Activity A Teacher's Script Read each sentence ONCE. After each sentence, ask for an answer. Do not wait until the end to review answers. Students do not repeat or otherwise produce the structure.

1. *Claude fait nettoyer la chambre à Richard.*
2. *Marc fait les valises pour Jean.*
3. *Sandra fait voir le film à Pierre.*
4. *Louis fait chanter une chanson de noël à Suzanne.*
5. *Simon fait les devoirs au lieu d'Henri.*
6. *Louise fait chercher le chien à Diane.*
7. *Ma mère fait regarder le spectacle à mon père.*
8. *Sally fait lire les instructions à Jean Luc.*

Activité B   Listen to each sentence. Then indicate what it means in English.

1. a. Lucie paints the walls.   b. Lucie has the walls painted.
2. a. Robert builds a house.   b. Robert has a house built.

3. a. Marie does chores.   b. Marie has the chores done.
4. a. Donnie is making the cake.   b. Donnie is having the cake made.
5. a. Sabine corrects the mistakes.   b. Sabine has the mistakes corrected.
6. a. George washes the dishes.   b. George has the dishes washed.

Activity B Teacher's Script Read each sentence ONCE. Review the answer after each question; do not wait until the end to review answers. Students do not repeat or otherwise produce the structure.

1. *Lucie fait peindre les murailles.*
2. *Robert fait construire une maison.*
3. *Marie fait les devoirs.*
4. *Donnie fait préparer le gâteau.*
5. *Sabine fait corriger les fautes.*
6. *Georges fait la vaisselle.*

Activité C Read each sentence. Then decide whether or not it is typical of a parent-child relationship. Imagine the child is ten years old.

Un parent…

	C'EST TYPIQUE	CE N'EST PAS TYPIQUE
1. *fait faire les devoirs à son enfant.*	❏	❏
2. *fait étudier la musique à son enfant.*	❏	❏
3. *fait faire de l'exercice à son enfant.*	❏	❏
4. *fait nettoyer la salle de bain à son enfant.*	❏	❏
5. *fait garder la sœur de 5 ans à son enfant.*	❏	❏
6. *fait se laver les mains à son enfant.*	❏	❏
7. *fait regarder les nouvelles à son enfant.*	❏	❏

Now, repeat the above but this time imagine that the child is eighteen and still lives at home. Do any answers change?

Un parent…

	C'EST TYPIQUE	CE N'EST PAS TYPIQUE
1. *fait faire les devoirs à son enfant.*	❏	❏
2. *fait étudier la musique à son enfant.*	❏	❏
3. *fait faire de l'exercice à son enfant.*	❏	❏
4. *fait nettoyer la salle de bain à son enfant.*	❏	❏
5. *fait garder la sœur de 5 ans à son enfant.*	❏	❏
6. *fait se laver les mains à son enfant.*	❏	❏
7. *fait regarder les nouvelles à son enfant.*	❏	❏

Activity C Teacher's Note When reviewing the activity as a group, you read the item out loud and students respond only with *C'est typique* or *Ce n'est pas typique.*

EXAMPLE: *"Numéro 1. Un parent fait faire les devoirs à un enfant de dix ans Comment réponds-tu, Robert?"*
"Ah, c'est typique."
"Bon, et les autres?"
(Students respond.)
Students do not repeat or otherwise produce the structure.

Activité D   In this activity you will compare and contrast what someone gets a child to do with what someone gets a dog to do. For each item, indicate whether it refers to the small child *(à l'enfant)*, the dog *(au chien)*, or possibly both *(à tous les deux)*.

Un adulte…

1. *fait chercher l'os à/au* _____.
2. *fait faire la vaisselle à/au* _____.
3. *fait manger les restes à/au* _____.
4. *fait jouer du piano à/au* _____.
5. *fait faire une promenade à/au* _____.
6. *fait faire son lit à/au* _____.
7. *fait garde la maison à/au* _____.
8. *fait boire de l'eau à/au* _____.

Does everyone in class agree?

Activity D Teacher's Note   Conduct as in Activity C.

EXAMPLE: *"O.K. On va voir. Numéro 1. Un adulte fait chercher l'os à qui? Sharon?"*
"Au chien."
"O.K. Tout le monde est d'accord?"
(Students respond.)
"Et qu'est-ce qu'un adulte fait chercher à son enfant?"
(Students may volunteer things like their books, a toy, etc.; students do not say or repeat the verbs. They just provide nouns and so on.)

Activité E   In this activity you will hear a series of sentences about what a university does and does not make a typical student do. Indicate whether you like the obligation or not.

	ÇA ME PLAÎT	ÇA NE ME PLAÎT PAS
1.	❏	❏
2.	❏	❏
3.	❏	❏
4.	❏	❏
5.	❏	❏

Which items did you and your classmates indicate that you liked? That you didn't like?

Activity E Teacher's Script Read each statement once. Repeat only if a student asks for it. After reading all statements, go back and review with the class to see how students responded. Follow examples from previous activities. Students do not repeat or otherwise produce the structure.

1. *L'université fait suivre un cours de langue étrangère à l'étudiant.*
2. *L'université ne fait pas suivre un cours de philosophie à l'étudiant.*
3. *L'université fait décider sa carrière à l'étudiant trop tôt.*
4. *L'université fait terminer les études dans quatre ans à l'étudiant.*
5. *L'université ne fait pas faire de la recherche originale à l'étudiant.*

THE FAIRE CAUSATIF *WITH OBJECT PRONOUNS*

The *faire causatif* can be used with object pronouns if the parties involved are understood or already known.

Mon professeur nous *fait aller au laboratoire une fois par semaine.*

Mon ami me *fait passer l'aspirateur à cause de ses allergies.*

Où est Jean-Paul?

À la bibliothèque. Je lui *fais rendre un livre.*

Après avoir practiquér le faire causatif avec les élèves, Mme Duval leur *fait écrire un exercice.*

Remember there can be a problem in correctly interpreting such sentences when you hear them. Do not mistake the first noun or person you hear as the person who performs the action mentioned.

Mon ami me *fait passer l'aspirateur à cause de ses allergies.*
    Who vacuums? I do, not my friend.

Robert nous *fait rendre un livre à la bibliothèque.*
    Who returns the book? We do, not Robert.

In the activities that follow, you will continue to practice hearing and interpreting the *faire causatif.*

Activité F   Listen to the sentences and indicate the most likely scenario.

1. a. We watch TV.   b. Jack watches TV.
2. a. He buys a gift for me.   b. I buy the gift.
3. a. We write the paper.   b. She writes the paper for us.
4. a. I vacuum for my friend.   b. My friend vacuums.
5. a. He ask for directions.   b. His friend asks for directions.
6. a. She does the dishes.   b. Her mom does the dishes.
7. a. We draw the horse.   b. He draws the horse.
8. a. He tells the truth.   b. We tell the truth.

Activity F Teacher's Script Read each sentence ONCE. After each sentence, ask for an answer. Do not wait until the end to review answers. Students do not repeat or otherwise produce the structure.

1. *Nous faisons regarder la télé à Jacques.*
2. *Il me fait acheter un cadeau.*
3. *Elle nous fait écrire le travail.*
4. *Je fais passer l'aspirateur à mon ami.*
5. *Il lui fait demander des directions.*
6. *Elle fait la vaisselle pour sa mère.*
7. *Nous lui faisons dessiner le cheval.*
8. *Il nous fait dire la vérité au professeur.*

Activité G Listen as your instructor makes a statement about what the university makes him or her do. Decide whether it is true or false.

	C'EST VRAI	C'EST FAUX
1.	❏	❏
2.	❏	❏
3.	❏	❏
4.	❏	❏
5.	❏	❏

Activity G Teacher's Script Conduct like activities C–E. Students do not repeat or otherwise produce the structure.

1. *L'université me fait donner trois cours chaque semestre.*
2. *L'université me fait limiter la quantité de bonnes notes dans chaque cours.*
3. *L'université me fait récupérer l'heure si je manque un cours.*
4. *L'université me fait remettre les notes à une date spécifique.*
5. *L'université me fait payer pour les photocopies.*

Activité H Finish the four statements in your own way to indicate something that your instructor gets you and your classmates to do regularly or occasionally. Then compare with the class. Did you all write similar things?

Le professeur…

1. *nous fait écrire* _____
2. *nous fait lire* _____
3. *nous fait travailler* _____
4. *nous fait regarder* _____

Activity H Teacher's Note Allow students 4–5 minutes to complete the sentences. Then call on one student to read Item 1 aloud. Survey the class to see who wrote something similar or different. Go back to the first student and have him or her read Item 2. Repeat until all items are reviewed.

References

American Council on the Teaching of Foreign Languages. (1986). *ACTFL Proficiency Guidelines.* Hastings-on-Hudson, NY: American Council on the Teaching of Foreign Languages.

American heritage dictionary of the English language. (1993). New York: American Heritage Publishers and Houghton Mifflin.

Anderson, R. C., Pichert, J., Goetz, E., Schallert, D. L., Stevens, K., & Trollip, S. (1976). Instantiation of general terms. *Journal of Verbal Learning and Verbal Behavior, 15,* 667–679.

Anderson, R. C., & Pearson, P. D. (1984). A schema-theoretic view of basic processes in reading comprehension. In P. D. Pearson (Ed.), *Handbook of reading research* (pp. 255–292). New York: Longman.

Bachman, L. F. (1990). *Fundamental considerations in language testing.* Oxford: Oxford University Press.

Bachman, L. F., & Palmer, A. S. (1983). *Oral interview test of communicative proficiency in English.* Urbana, IL: Photo-offset.

Barnett, M. A. (1989). *More than meets the eye: Foreign language reading theory and practice.* Englewood Cliffs, NJ: Prentice-Hall.

Benati, A. (2001). A comparative study of the effects of processing instruction and output-based instruction on the acquisition of the Italian future tense. *Language Teaching Research, 5,* 95–127.

Benati, A. (2003). The effects of structured input activities and explicit information on the acquisition of the Italian future tense. In B. VanPatten (Ed.), *Processing instruction: Theory, research, and commentary.* Mahwah, NJ: Erlbaum.

Bernhardt, E. B. (1986). Reading in the foreign language. In B. H. Wing (Ed.), *Listening, reading and writing: Analysis and application* (pp. 93–115). Middlebury, VT: The Northeast Conference on the Teaching of Languages.

Bernhardt, E. B. (1991). *Reading development in a second language.* Norwood, NJ: Ablex.

Binkowski, D. D. (1992). *The effects of attentional focus, presentation mode and language experience on second language learners' sentence processing.* Unpublished doctoral dissertation, University of Illinois, Urbana-Champaign.

Birdsong, D. (1999). Whys and why nots of the critical period hypothesis for second language learning. In D. Birdsong (Ed.), *Second language acquisition and the critical period hypothesis* (pp. 1–22). Mahwah, NJ: Erlbaum.

Block, E. (1986). The comprehension strategies of second language readers. *TESOL Quarterly, 20,* 463–494.

Brandsdorfer, R. L. (1991). *Communicative value and linguistic knowledge in second language oral input processing.* Unpublished doctoral dissertation, University of Illinois, Urbana-Champaign.

Bransford, J. D. (1979). *Human cognition: Learning, understanding and remembering.* Belmont, CA: Wadsworth.

Bransford, J. D., & Johnson, M. K. (1972). Contextual prerequisites for understanding: Some investigations of comprehension and recall. *Journal of Verbal Learning and Verbal Behavior, 11,* 717–726.

Breen, M. (1985). The social context for language learning—a neglected situation? *Studies in Second Language Acquisition, 7,* 135–158.

Bretz, M. L., Dvorak, T., & Kirschner, C. (1983). *Pasajes: Actividades.* New York: Random House.

Brooks, F. B. (1993). Some problems and caveats in "communicative" discourse: Toward a conceptualization of the foreign language classroom. *Foreign Language Annals, 26*(2), 233–242.

Brooks, F. B. (1990). Foreign language learning: A social interaction perspective. In B. VanPatten & J. F. Lee (Eds.), *Second language acquisition—foreign language learning.* Clevedon, UK: Multilingual Matters.

Brooks, N. (1964). *Language and language learning: Theory and practice* (2nd ed.). New York: Harcourt Brace & World.

Brown, R. (1977). "Introduction." In C. Snow and C. Ferguson (Eds.), *Talking to children* (pp. 1–27). New York: Cambridge University Press.

Buck, M. (2000). *Procesamiento del lenguaje y adquisición de una Segunda lengua. Un estudio de la adquisición de un punto gramatical en inglés por hispanohablantes.* Unpublished doctoral thesis, Universidad Nacional Autónoma de México.

Bybee, J. L. (1991). Natural morphology: The organization of paradigms and language acquisition. In T. Huebner & C. Ferguson (Eds.), *Crosscurrents in SLA and linguistic theories* (pp. 67–92). Amsterdam: John Benjamins.

Byrnes, H. (1991). Reflections on the development of cross-cultural communicative competence in the foreign language classroom. In B. F. Freed (Ed.), *Foreign language acquisition and the classroom* (pp. 205–218). Lexington, MA: D. C. Heath.

Cadierno-López, T. (1992). *Explicit instruction in grammar: A comparison of input-based and output-based instruction in second language acquisition.* Unpublished doctoral dissertation, University of Illinois, Urbana-Champaign.

Cadierno, T. (1995). Formal instruction from a processing perspective: An investigation into the Spanish past tense. *The Modern Language Journal, 79,* 179–193.

Canale, M., & Swain, M. (1980). Theoretical bases of communicative approaches to second language teaching and testing. *Applied Linguistics, 1,* 1–47.

Carrell, P. L. (1983). Three components of background knowledge in reading comprehension. *Language Learning, 33,* 183–207.

Carrell, P. L. (1984a). Evidence of a formal schema in second language comprehension. *Language Learning, 34,* 87–112.

Carrell, P. L. (1984b). The effects of rhetorical organization on ESL readers. *TESOL Quarterly, 18,* 441–469.

Carroll, J. B. (1980). *Testing communicative performance.* London: Pergamon.

Carroll, S. E. (1999). Putting "input" in its proper place. *Second Language Research, 15,* 337–388.

Carroll, S. E. (2001). *Input and evidence: The raw material of second language acquisition.* Philadelphia: John Benjamins.

Chastain, K. (1970). A methodological study comparing the audiolingual habit theory and the cognitive code-learning theory—A continuation. *The Modern Language Journal, 54,* 257–266.

Cohen, A. D. (1984). On taking tests: What the students report. *Language Testing, 1*(1), 70–81.

Cheng, A. (1995). *Grammar instruction and input processing: The acquisition of Spanish* ser *and* estar. Unpublished doctoral dissertation, University of Illinois, Urbana-Champaign.

Colomb, G., Kinahan, F., McEnerney, L., & Williams, J. (1991). *Little red schoolhouse.* Urbana, IL: Programs in Professional Writing.

Corder, S. P. (1981). *Error analysis and interlanguage.* Oxford: Oxford University Press. (Reprinted from Corder, S. P. (1967). The significance of learners' errors. *International Review of Applied Linguistics, 5,* 161–170.)

Crookes, G., & Gass, S. M. (1993a). *Tasks and language learning: Integrating theory and practice.* Clevedon, UK: Multilingual Matters.

Crookes, G., & Gass, S. M. (1993b). *Tasks in a pedagogical context: Integrating theory and practice.* Clevedon, UK: Multilingual Matters.

DeKeyser, R. M., & Sokalski, K. J. (1996). The differential role of comprehension and production practice. *Language Learning, 46,* 613–642.

Doughty, C. (1991). Second language instruction does make a difference: Evidence from an empirical study of SL relativization. *Studies in Second Language Acquisition, 13,* 431–470.

Doughty, C., & Pica, T. (1986). "Information gap" tasks: Do they facilitate second language acquisition? *TESOL Quarterly, 20,* 305–325.

Doughty, C., & Williams, J. (Eds.). (1998). *Focus on form in classroom second language acquisition.* Cambridge: Cambridge University Press.

Dubin, F., Esky, D. E., & Grabe, W. (Eds.). (1986). *Teaching second language reading for academic purposes.* Reading, MA: Addison-Wesley.

Dvorak, T. R. (1986). Writing in a foreign language. In B. H. Wing (Ed.), *Listening, reading and writing: Analysis and application* (pp. 145–163). Middlebury, VT: Northeast Conference on the Teaching of Foreign Languages.

Ellis, R. (1984). *Classroom second language development.* London: Pergamon.

Ellis, R. (1986). *Understanding second language acquisition.* Oxford: Oxford University Press.

Ellis, R. (1989). Are classroom and naturalistic acquisition the same? A study of the classroom acquisition of German word order rules. *Studies in Second Language Acquisition, 11,* 305–328.

Ellis, R. (1994). *The study of second language acquisition.* Oxford: Oxford University Press.

Farley, A. P. (2001a). The effects of processing instruction and meaning-based output instruction. *Spanish Applied Linguistics, 5,* 57–94.

Farley, A. P. (2001b). Authentic processing instruction and the Spanish subjunctive. *Hispania, 84,* 289–299.

Farley, A. P. (2003). Processing instruction and the Spanish subjunctive: Is explicit information needed? In B. VanPatten (Ed.), *Processing instruction: Theory, research, and commentary.* Mahwah, NJ: Erlbaum.

Farley, A. P. (in press). *Structured input.* New York: McGraw-Hill.

Finkel, D., & Monk, G. S. (1983). Teachers and learning groups: Dissolution of the Atlas complex. In C. Bouton & R. Y. Garth (Eds.), *Learning in groups* (pp. 83–97). San Francisco: Jossey-Bass.

Flick, W. C., & Anderson, J. I. (1980). Rhetorical difficulty in scientific English: A study in reading comprehension. *TESOL Quarterly, 14,* 345–351.

Flower, L., & Hayes, J. R. (1981). A cognitive process theory of writing. *College Composition and Communication, 32,* 365–387.

Freed, B. F. (Ed.). (1991). *Foreign language acquisition research and the classroom.* Lexington, MA: D. C. Heath.

Garrett, N. (1986). The problem with grammar: What kind can the language learner use? *The Modern Language Journal, 70,* 133–148.

Gass, S. M. (1997). *Input, interaction, and the second language learner.* Mahwah, NJ: Erlbaum.

Gass, S. M., & Selinker, L. (1983/1992). *Language transfer in language learning* (2nd ed.). (1st edition published 1983). Philadelphia: John Benjamins.

Gass, S. M., & Selinker, L. (2001). *Second language acquisition: An introductory course.* Mahwah, NJ: Erlbaum.

Grellet, F. (1981). *Developing reading skills. A practical guide to reading comprehension exercises.* Cambridge: Cambridge University Press.

Harley, B., & Wang, W. (1997). The critical period hypothesis: Where are we now? In A. M. B. de Groot & J. F. Kroll (Eds.), *Tutorials in bilingualism: Psycholinguistic perspectives* (pp. 19–51). Mahwah, NJ: Erlbaum.

Hatch, E. M. (1978a). Discourse analysis and second language acquisition. In E. Hatch (Ed.), *Second language acquisition: A book of readings* (pp. 402–435). Rowley, MA: Newbury House.

Hatch, E. M. (Ed.). (1978b). *Second language acquisition: A book of readings.* Rowley, MA: Newbury House.

Hatch, E. M. (1983). Simplified input and second language acquisition. In R. W. Andersen (Ed.), *Pidginization and creolization as language acquisition* (pp. 64–86). Cambridge, MA: Newbury House.

Hedge, T. (1988). *Writing.* Oxford: Oxford University Press.

Hendrickson, J. M. (1978). Error correction in foreign language teaching: Recent theory, research, and practice. *The Modern Language Journal, 62,* 387–398.

Henning, G. (1987). *A guide to language testing: Development, evaluation, research.* Cambridge, MA: Newbury House.

Hock, S. T., & Po, C. L. (1979). The performance of a group of Malay-Medium students in an English reading comprehension test. *RELC Journal, 10,* 81–89.

Hosenfeld, C. (1977). A preliminary investigation of the strategies of successful and non-successful readers. *System, 5,* 110–123.

Hosenfeld, C. (1984). Case studies of ninth-grade readers. In J. C. Alderson & A. H. Urquhart (Eds.), *Reading in a foreign language* (pp. 231–244). London: Longman.

Hudson, T. (1982). The effects of induced schemata on the "short circuit" in L2 reading: Nondecoding factors in L2 reading performance. *Language Learning, 32*(1), 1–29.

Jacobs, H. J., Zingraf, S. A., Wormuth, D. R., Hartfiel, V. F., & Hughey, J. B. (1981). *Testing ESL composition: A practical approach.* Rowley, MA: Newbury House.

Johns, J. (1978). Do comprehension items really test reading? Sometimes! *Journal of Reading, 21,* 615–619.

Johnson, P. (1981). Effects on reading comprehension of language complexity and cultural background. *TESOL Quarterly, 15,* 169–181.

Kaplan, M. A. (1987). Developmental patterns of past-tense acquisition among foreign language learners of French. In B. VanPatten, T. R. Dvorak, & J. F. Lee (Eds.), *Foreign language learning: A research perspective* (pp. 52–60). Cambridge, MA: Newbury House.

Kinginger, C. (1990). *Task variation and classroom learner discourse.* Unpublished doctoral dissertation, University of Illinois, Urbana-Champaign.

Knorre, M., Dorwick, T., VanPatten, B., & Villareal, H. (1989). *Puntos de partida: An invitation to Spanish.* New York: Random House.

Kramsch, C. J. (1991). The order of discourse in language teaching. In B. F. Freed (Ed.), *Foreign language acquisition and the classroom* (pp. 191–204). Lexington, MA: D. C. Heath.

Krashen, S. D. (1982). *Principles and practice in second language acquisition.* New York: Pergamon.

Krashen, S. D. (1984). *Writing: Research, theory and applications.* Oxford: Pergamon.

Krashen, S. D. (1993). *The power of reading.* Englewood, CO: Libraries Unlimited.

Krashen, S. D., & Terrell, T. D. (1983). *The natural approach.* New York: Pergamon.

Kroll, B. (Ed.). (1990). *Second language writing: Research insights for the classroom.* Cambridge: Cambridge University Press.

Lado, R. (1957). *Linguistics across cultures.* Ann Arbor: University of Michigan Press.

Lalande, J. F. (1982). Reducing composition errors: An experiment. *The Modern Language Journal, 66,* 140–149.

Lamendella, J. (1977). General principles of neurofunctional organization and their manifestation in primary and secondary language acquisition. *Language Learning, 27,* 155–196.

Larsen-Freeman, D. (1985). State of the art on input in second language acquisition. In S. M. Gass & C. G. Madden (Eds.), *Input in second language acquisition* (pp. 433–444). Rowley, MA: Newbury House.

Larsen-Freeman, D., & Long, M. H. (1991). *An introduction to second language acquisition research.* New York: Longman.

Lee, J. F. (1986a). On the use of the recall task to measure L2 reading comprehension. *Studies in Second Language Acquisition, 8,* 201–211.

Lee, J. F. (1986b). Background knowledge and L2 reading. *The Modern Language Journal, 70,* 350–354.

Lee, J. F. (1987a). Morphological factors influencing pronominal reference assignment by learners of Spanish. In T. Morgan, J. F. Lee, & B. VanPatten (Eds.), *Language and language use: Studies in Spanish* (pp. 221–232). Lanham, MD: University Press of America.

Lee, J. F. (1987b). The Spanish subjunctive: An information-processing perspective. *The Modern Language Journal, 71,* 50–57.

Lee, J. F. (1989). Teaching and testing an expository text. In D. Koike & A. Simoes (Eds.), *Proceedings of the conference on Portuguese language: Teaching and testing* (pp. 92–107). Austin, TX: University of Texas at Austin.

Lee, J. F. (1990). Constructive processes evidenced by early stage non-native readers of Spanish in comprehending an expository text. *Hispanic Linguistics, 4*(1), 129–148.

Lee, J. F. (2000). *Tasks and communicating in language classrooms.* New York: McGraw-Hill.

Lee, J. F. (2002). Processing Spanish future tense morphology incidentally while reading in a second language. *Studies in Second Language Acquisition, 24,* 55–80.

Lee, J. F., Cadierno, T., Glass, W. R., & VanPatten, B. (1997). The effects of lexical and grammatical cues on processing past temporal reference in second language input. *Applied Language Learning, 8,* 1–23.

Lee, J. F., & Paulson, D. L. (1992). Writing and compositions. In B. VanPatten (Ed.), *Instructor's manual and test bank for ¿Sabías que… ? Beginning Spanish* (pp. 30–34). New York: McGraw-Hill.

Lee, J. F., & Riley, G. L. (1990). The effect of prereading, rhetorically-oriented frameworks on the recall of two structurally different expository texts. *Studies in Second Language Acquisition, 12,* 25–41.

Leemann Guthrie, E. (1984). Intake, communication, and second language teaching. In S. J. Savignon & M. S. Berns (Eds.), *Initiatives in communicative language teaching* (pp. 35–54). Reading, MA: Addison-Wesley.

Leeser, M. (2003). *The effects of mode, pausing, and topic familiarity on L2 learners' comprehension and input processing.* Unpublished doctoral dissertation, University of Illinois, Urbana-Champaign.

Leow, R. (1997). The effects of input enhancement and text length on adult L2 readers' comprehension and intake in second language acquisition. *Applied Language Learning, 8,* 151–182.

Leow, R. (1998). The effects of amount and type of exposure on adult learners' L2 development in SLA. *The Modern Language Journal, 82,* 49–68.

Lightbown, P. (1983). Exploring relationships between developmental and instructional sequences in L2 acquisition. In H. Seliger & M. Long (Eds.), *Classroom-oriented research in second language acquisition* (pp. 217–243). Rowley, MA: Newbury House.

Lightbown, P., & Spada, N. (1993). *How languages are learned.* Oxford: Oxford University Press.

Lightbown, P. M., & Spada, N. (1999). *How languages are learned* (Rev. ed.). Oxford: Oxford University Press.

Liskin-Gasparro, J. E. (1982). *ETS oral proficiency testing manual.* Princeton, NJ: Educational Testing Service.

LoCoco, V. L. (1975). An analysis of Spanish and German learners' errors. *Working Papers on Bilingualism, 7,* 96–124.

LoCoco, V. (1976). A comparison of three methods for the collection of L2 data: Free composition, translation, and picture description. *Working Papers in Bilingualism, 8,* 59–86.

LoCoco, V. L. (1987). Learner comprehension of oral and written sentences in German and Spanish: The importance of word order. In B. VanPatten, T. Dvorak, & J. F. Lee (Eds.), *Foreign language learning: A research perspective* (pp. 119–131). Cambridge, MA: Newbury House.

Long, M. H. (1983). Does second language instruction make a difference? A review of research. *TESOL Quarterly, 17*(3), 359–382.

Long, M. H. (1990). The least a second language acquisition theory needs to explain. *TESOL Quarterly, 24*(4), 649–665.

Lowe, P., Jr. (1982). *Manual for LS oral interview workshop.* Washington, DC: DLI/FS Joint Oral Interview Transfer Project.

Lowe, P., Jr. (1988). The unassimilated history. In P. Lowe & C. W. Stansfield (Eds.), *Second language proficiency assessment: Current issues* (pp. 11–51). Englewood Cliffs, NJ: Prentice-Hall.

Madsen, H. S. (1983). *Techniques in testing.* Oxford: Oxford University Press.

Mangubhai, F. (1991). The processing behaviors of adult second language learners and their relationship to second language proficiency. *Applied Linguistics, 12*(3), 268–298.

McNeil, J. D. (1984). *Reading comprehension: New directions for classroom practice.* Glenview, IL: Scott Foresman.

Mohammed, M. A. H., & Swales, J. M. (1984). Factors affecting the successful reading of technical instructions. *Reading in a Foreign Language, 2,* 206–217.

Musumeci, D. (1990). *Il carciofo: Strategie di lettura e proposte di attività.* New York: McGraw-Hill.

Musumeci, D. (1997). *Breaking tradition.* New York: McGraw-Hill.

Muyskens, J. A., Omaggio, A. C., & Convert-Chalmers, C. (1990). *Rendez-vous: An invitation to French.* New York: McGraw-Hill.

Newsweek. August 2, 1993. Volume CXIII (p. 4). New York: Newsweek, Inc.

Nunan, D. (1989). *Designing tasks for the communicative classroom.* Cambridge: Cambridge University Press.

Omaggio, A. C. (1986). *Language teaching in context: Proficiency-oriented instruction.* Boston, MA: Heinle & Heinle.

Omaggio Hadley, A. (1993). *Language teaching in context.* Boston, MA: Heinle & Heinle.

Paulson, D. L. (1993). *The effects of task focus and L2 grammatical knowledge on writing in Spanish as a second language.* Unpublished doctoral dissertation, University of Illinois, Urbana-Champaign.

Paulston, C. B. (1972). Structural pattern drills: A classification. In H. Allen & R. Campell (Eds.), *Teaching English as a second language* (pp. 129–138). New York: McGraw-Hill.

Perkins, K. L. (1983). Semantic constructivity in ESL reading comprehension. *TESOL Quarterly, 17*(1), 19–27.

Perkins, K. L., & Jones, B. (1985). Measuring passage contribution in ESL reading comprehension. *TESOL Quarterly, 19*, 137–153.

Peters, A. M. (1985). Language segmentation: Operating principles for the perception and analysis of language. In D. I. Slobin (Ed.), *The cross-linguistic study of language acquisition* (Vol. 2, pp. 1029–1067). Hillsdale, NJ: Erlbaum.

Philips, J. K. (1984). Practical implications of recent research in reading. *Foreign Language Annals, 17*(4), 285–296.

Pica, T. (1983). Adult acquisition of English as a second language under different conditions of exposure. *Language Learning, 33*(4), 465–497.

Pichert, J. W., & Anderson, R. C. (1977). Taking different perspectives on a story. *Journal of Education Psychology, 69*, 309–315.

Pienemann, M. (1998). *Language processing and second language development.* Philadelphia: John Benjamins.

Politzer, R. L. (1965). *Foreign language learning: A linguistic introduction.* Englewood Cliffs, NJ: Prentice-Hall.

Porter, P. (1986). How learners talk to each other: Input and interaction in task-centered discussions. In R. Day (Ed.), *Talking to learn* (pp. 200–224). Rowley, MA: Newbury House.

Prince, E. (1990). *Write soon! A beginning text for ESL writers.* New York: Maxwell Macmillan.

Pulido, D. (2000). *The impact of background knowledge and L2 verbal ability on incidental vocabulary acquisition through reading for adult learners of Spanish as a foreign language.* Unpublished doctoral dissertation, University of Illinois, Urbana-Champaign.

Raimes, A. (1983). *Techniques in teaching writing.* Oxford: Oxford University Press.

Reves, T. (1982). *What makes a good language learner?* Unpublished doctoral dissertation, Hebrew University, Jerusalem.

Richards, J. C. (1983). Listening comprehension: Approach, design, procedure. *TESOL Quarterly, 17*(2), 219–240.

Richards, J. C., & Rodgers, T. S. (1986). *Approaches and methods in language teaching.* Cambridge: Cambridge University Press.

Riley, G. L. (1990). *Effects of story grammar on reading comprehension of L2 readers of French.* Unpublished doctoral dissertation, University of Illinois, Urbana-Champaign.

Rivers, W. M. (1983). *Communicating naturally in a second language: Theory and practice in language teaching.* Cambridge: Cambridge University Press.

Robb, T., Ross, S., & Shortreed, I. (1986). Salience of feedback on error and its effect on EFL writing quality. *TESOL Quarterly, 20*, 83–95.

Rooks, G. (1981). *Nonstop discussion book.* Cambridge, MA: Newbury House.

Rooks, G. K., Scholberg, D., & Scholberg, K. (1982). *Conversar sin parar.* Cambridge, MA: Newbury House.

Rost, M. (1990). *Listening in language learning.* New York: Longman.

Rott, S. (1999). The effect of exposure frequency on intermediate language learners' incidental vocabulary acquisition and retention through reading. *Studies in Second Language Acquisition, 21*, 589–619.

Rott, S. (2000). Relationships between the process of reading, word inferencing, and incidental word acquisition. In J. F. Lee and A. Valdman (Eds.), *Form and meaning: Multiple perspectives* (pp. 255–282). Boston, MA: Heinle & Heinle.

Rulon, K., & McCreary, J. (1986). Negotiation of content: Teacher fronted and small-group interactions. In R. Day (Ed.), *Talking to learn* (pp. 182–199). Cambridge, MA: Newbury House.

Rumelhart, D. (1977). Toward an interactive model of reading. In S. Dornic (Ed.), *Attention and performance*, 4 (pp. 573–603). New York: Academic Press.

Rumelhart, D. (1980). Schemata: The building blocks of cognition. In R. Spiro, B. Bruce, & W. Brewer (Eds.), *Theoretical issues in reading comprehension* (pp. 33–35). Hillsdale, NJ: Erlbaum.

Salaberry, M. R. (1997). The role of input and output practice in second language acquisition. *Canadian Modern Language Review, 53*, 422–451.

Sanz, C., & Morgan-Short, K. (2003). Positive evidence vs. explicit rule presentation and explicit negative feedback: A computer-assisted study. *Language Learning, 53*.

Sanz, C., & VanPatten, B. (1998). On input processing, processing instruction, and the nature of replication tasks: A response to M. Rafael Salaberry. *Canadian Modern Language Review, 54*, 263–273.

Sato, C. (1986). Conversation and interlanguage development: Rethinking the connection. In R. Day (Ed.), *"Talking to learn": Conversation in second language acquisition* (pp. 23–45). Cambridge, MA: Newbury House.

Savignon, S. J. (1972). *Communicative competence: An experiment in foreign language teaching.* Philadelphia, PA: Center for Curriculum Development.

Savignon, S. J. (1998). *Communicative competence: Theory and classroom practice* (2nd ed.). New York: McGraw-Hill.

Savignon, S. J., & Berns, M. S. (1984). *Initiatives in communicative language teaching.* Reading, MA: Addison-Wesley.

Savignon, S. J., & Berns, M. S. (1987). *Initiatives in communicative language teaching II.* Reading, MA: Addison-Wesley.

Schmidt, R. (1992). Psychological mechanisms underlying second language fluency. *Studies in Second Language Acquisition, 14*(4), 357–386.

Schmidt, R. (Ed.). (1995). *Attention and awareness in foreign language learning.* Honolulu: University of Hawaii.

Scott, V., & Randall, S. (1992). Can students apply grammar rules faster by reading textbook explanations? *Foreign Language Annals, 25*(4), 357–367.

Seelye, H. N. (1993). *Teaching culture: Strategies for intercultural communication.* Lincolnwood, IL: National Textbook Company.

Semke, H. (1984). Effects of the red pen. *Foreign Language Annals, 17*, 195–202.

Sharwood Smith, M. (1993). Input enhancement in instructed SLA: Theoretical bases. *Studies in Second Language Acquisition, 15*(2), 165–179.

Shohamy, E. (1984). Does the testing method make a difference? The case of reading comprehension. *Language Testing, 1*, 147–170.

Shohamy, E. (1987). Reactions to Lyle Bachman's paper "Problems in examining the validity of the ACTFL Oral Proficiency Interview." In A. Valdman (Ed.), *Proceedings of the symposium on the evaluation of foreign language proficiency* (pp. 51–54). Bloomington, IN: Indiana University.

Shohamy, E. (1993). The power of tests: The impact of language tests on teaching and learning. *NFLC occasional papers* (June).

Shohamy, E., Reves, T., & Bejerano, Y. (1986). Introducing a new comprehensive test of oral proficiency. *English Language Teaching Journal, 40*, 212–222.

Shook, D. (1994). FL/L2 reading, grammatical information, and the input-to-intake phenomenon. *Applied Language Learning, 5*, 57–93.

Snow, C. (1978). Mothers' speech to children learning languages. In L. Bloom (Ed.), *Readings in language development* (pp. 489–506). New York: Wiley & Sons.

Stanovich, K. (1980). Toward an interactive-compensatory model of individual differences in the development of reading fluency. *Reading Research Quarterly, 16*, 32–71.

Steffensen, M., Joag-Dev, C., & Anderson, R. C. (1979). A cross-cultural perspective on reading comprehension. *Reading Research Quarterly, 15*, 10–29.

Strother, J. B., & Ulijn, J. M. (1987). Does syntactic rewriting affect English for science and technology text comprehension? In J. Devine, P. L. Carrell, & D. E. Eskey (Eds.), *Research in reading in English as a second language* (pp. 89–100). Washington, DC: TESOL.

Swaffar, J., Arens, K., & Byrnes, H. (1991). *Reading for meaning: An integrated approach to language learning.* Englewood Cliffs, NJ: Prentice-Hall.

Swaffar, J., Kern, R., & Young, D. J. (1989). Reading as a classroom activity: Theory and techniques. In D. Koike & A. Simoes (Eds.), *Proceedings of the conference on Portuguese language: Teaching and testing* (pp. 61–91). Austin, TX: University of Texas at Austin.

Swaffar, J., & Wälterman, D. (1988). Pattern questions for student conceptual processing. *Die Unterrichtspraxis, 21,* 60–67.

Swain, M. (1985). Communicative competence: Some roles of comprehensible input and comprehensible output in its development. In S. M. Gass & C. Madden (Eds.), *Input in second language acquisition* (pp. 235–253). Rowley, MA: Newbury House.

Tarone, E. (1984). Teaching strategic competence in the foreign language classroom. In S. J. Savignon & M. S. Berns (Eds.), *Initiatives in communicative language teaching* (pp. 127–136). Reading, MA: Addison-Wesley.

Terrell, T. D. (1986). Acquisition in the natural approach: The binding/access framework. *The Modern Language Journal, 70,* 213–227.

Terrell, T. D. (1991). The role of grammar instruction in a communicative approach. *The Modern Language Journal, 75,* 52–63.

Terrell, T. D., Andrade, M., Egasse, J., & Muñoz, E.M. (1990). *Dos mundos: A communicative approach.* New York: McGraw-Hill.

Terrell, T. D., Baycroft, B., & Perrone, C. (1987). The subjunctive in Spanish interlanguage: Accuracy and comprehensibility. In B. VanPatten, T. R. Dvorak, & J. F. Lee (Eds.), *Foreign language learning: A research perspective* (pp. 19–32). Cambridge, MA: Newbury House.

Terrell, T. D., Rogers, M. B., Barnes, B. K., & Wolff-Hessini, M. (1993). *Deux mondes: A communicative approach.* New York: McGraw-Hill.

Terrell, T. D., Tschirner, E., Nikolai, B., & Genzmer, H. (1992). *Kontakte: A communicative approach.* New York: McGraw-Hill.

Valdman, A. (1987). The problem of the target model in proficiency-oriented foreign language instruction. In A. Valdman (Ed.), *Proceedings of the symposium on the evaluation of foreign language proficiency* (pp. 133–150). Bloomington, IN: Indiana University.

van Lier, L. (1988). *The classroom and the language learner: Ethnography and second language classroom research.* London: Longman.

VanPatten, B. (1984a). Morphemes and processing strategies. In F. Eckman, L. Bell, & D. Nelson (Eds.). *Universals of second language acquisition* (pp. 88–98). Rowley, MA: Newbury House.

VanPatten, B. (1984b). Learners' comprehension of clitic pronouns: More evidence for a word order strategy. *Hispanic Linguistics* 1(1), 88–98.

VanPatten, B. (1985a). The acquisition of *ser* and *estar* by adult classroom learners: A preliminary investigation of transitional stages of competence. *Hispania, 68,* 399–406.

VanPatten, B. (1985b). Communicative value and information processing in second language acquisition. In P. Larson, E. Judd, & D. S. Messerschmitt (Eds.), *On TESOL: A brave new world for TESOL* (pp. 89–100). Washington, DC: TESOL.

VanPatten, B. (1986). Second language acquisition research and the learning/teaching of Spanish: Some research findings and implications. *Hispania, 69,* 202–216.

VanPatten, B. (1987). Classroom learners' acquisition of *ser* and *estar:* Accounting for developmental patterns. In B. VanPatten, T. R. Dvorak, & J. F. Lee (Eds.), *Foreign language learning: A research perspective* (pp. 61–75). Cambridge, MA: Newbury House.

VanPatten, B. (1988). How juries get hung: Problems with the evidence for a focus on form. *Language Learning, 38,* 243–260.

VanPatten, B. (1990). Attending to form and content in the input. *Studies in Second Language Acquisition, 12,* 287–301.

VanPatten, B. (1991). The foreign language classroom as a place to communicate. In B. F. Freed (Ed.), *Foreign language acquisition research and the classroom* (pp. 54–73). Boston, MA: D. C. Heath.

VanPatten, B. (1992a). Second language acquisition research and foreign language teaching: Part I. *ADFL Bulletin, 23,* 23–27.

VanPatten, B. (1992b). Second language acquisition research and foreign language teaching: Part II. *ADFL Bulletin, 23,* 52–56.

VanPatten, B. (1993). Grammar teaching for the acquisition-rich classroom. *Foreign Language Annals, 26,* 435–450.

VanPatten, B. (1994). Cognitive aspects of input processing in second language acquisition. In P. Hashemipour, R. Maldonado, & M. van Naerssen (Eds.), *Festschrift in honor of Tracy D. Terrell* (pp. 170–183). New York: McGraw-Hill.

VanPatten, B. (1996). *Input processing and grammar instruction.* Norwood, NJ: Ablex.

VanPatten, B. (2000a). Processing instruction as form-meaning connections: Issues in theory and research. In J. F. Lee & A. Valdman (Eds.), *Form and meaning: Multiple perspectives* (pp. 43–68). Boston: Heinle & Heinle.

VanPatten, B. (2000b). Thirty years of input, or "intake," the neglected sibling. In B. Swierzbin, F. Morris, M. E. Anderson, C. A. Klee, & E. Tarone (Eds.), *Social and cognitive factors in second language acquisition: Selected proceedings of the 1999 second language research forum* (pp. 287–311). Somerville, MA: Cascadilla.

VanPatten, B. (2002). Processing instruction: An update. *Language Learning, 52,* 755–803.

VanPatten, B. (2003a). *From input to output: A teacher's guide to second language acquisition.* New York: McGraw-Hill.

VanPatten, B. (2003b). Input processing in SLA. In B. VanPatten (Ed.), *Processing instruction: Theory, research, and commentary.* Mahwah, NJ: Erlbaum.

VanPatten, B., & Cadierno, T. (1993). Explicit instruction and input processing. *Studies in Second Language Acquisition, 15,* 225–244.

VanPatten, B., & Fernández, C. (2003). The long-term effects of processing instruction. In B. VanPatten (Ed.), *Processing instruction: Theory, research, and commentary.* Mahwah, NJ: Erlbaum.

VanPatten, B., & Lee, J. F. (Eds.). (1990). *Second language acquisition—foreign language learning: Perspectives on research and practice.* Clevedon, UK: Multilingual Matters.

VanPatten, B., Lee, J. F., Ballman, T., & Dvorak, T. R. (1992). ¿Sabías que… ? *Beginning Spanish.* New York: McGraw-Hill.

VanPatten, B., & Mandell, P. (1999). How type of structure influences the ways in which L2 learners render grammaticality judgments. Paper presented at the annual meeting of the AAAL, Stamford, Connecticut, 1999.

VanPatten, B., & Oikennon, S. (1996). Explanation vs. structured input in processing instruction. *Studies in Second Language Acquisition, 18,* 495–510.

VanPatten, B., & Sanz, C. (1995). From input to output: Processing instruction and communicative tasks. In F. Eckman, D. Highland, P. W. Lee, J. Mileham, & R. R. Weber (Eds.), *Second language acquisition theory and pedagogy* (pp. 169–186). Mahwah, NJ: Erlbaum.

VanPatten, B., & Wong, W. (2003). Processing instruction and the French causative: A replication. In B. VanPatten (Ed.), *Processing instruction: Theory, research, and commentary.* Mahwah, NJ: Erlbaum.

Weiss, C. H. (1972). *Evaluation research: Methods for assessing program effectiveness.* Englewood Cliffs, NJ: Prentice-Hall.

White, L. (1977). Error analysis and error correction in adult learners of English as a second language. *Working Papers in Bilingualism, 13,* 42–58.

White, L. (2000). Second language acquisition: From initial to final state. In J. Archibald (Ed.), *Second language acquisition and linguistic theory* (pp. 130–155). Oxford: Blackwell.

Wildner-Bassett, M. E. (1990). Coexisting discourse worlds: The development of pragmatic competence inside and outside the classroom. In B. VanPatten & J. F. Lee (Eds.), *Second language acquisition—foreign language learning* (pp. 140–152). Clevedon, UK: Multilingual Matters.

Williams, J. (in press). *From thought to paper: Writing in a second language.* New York: McGraw-Hill.

Wing, B. H. (1987). The linguistic and communicative functions of foreign language teacher talk. In B. VanPatten, T. R. Dvorak, & J. F. Lee (Eds.), *Foreign language learning: A research perspective* (pp. 158–173). Cambridge, MA: Newbury House.

Winitz, H. (Ed.). (1981). *The comprehension approach to foreign language instruction.* Rowley, MA: Newbury House.

Wolf, D. F. (1993a). Issues in reading comprehension assessment: Implications for the development of research instruments and classroom tests. *Foreign Language Annals, 26*(3), 322–331.

Wolf, D. F. (1993b). A comparison of assessment tasks used to measure foreign language reading comprehension. *The Modern Language Journal, 77*(4), 473–488.

Wolvin, A. D., & Coakley, C. G. (1985). *Listening,* 2nd ed. Dubuque, IA: William C. Brown Publishers.

Wong, W. (2003). Processing instruction in French: The roles of explicit information and structured input. In B. VanPatten (Ed.), *Processing instruction: Theory, research, and commentary.* Mahwah, NJ: Erlbaum.

Zamel, V. (1985). Responding to student writing. *TESOL Quarterly, 19,* 79–101.

Index

orders of acquisition, 20, 84, 122–123, 129–130
organization
  of discourse and reading comprehension, 229, 222–224, 236–237, 241–242
  in writing, 247–248, 250, 252, 272
orthographic knowledge, 221
output
  classroom activities and, 90, 134, 165, 172–175, 181, 186, 188–192
  defined, 168–169
  form-focused, 10, 13, 131, 133, 168
  from input to, 90, 132–133, 169, 181
  oral and written, 173–174, 184, 188
  processing, 18, 90, 132–133, 168, 193
  structured, 3, 13, 165, 168, 172–175, 178, 181
  tests, 152, 188–192
  traditional approaches to, 10, 132–133, 170, 234
  vocabulary and, 168, 179–180
overgeneralizations, 129–130
overlearning, 129–130

paired interaction, 12–13, 49, 57, 60, 72, 233
Palmer, A. S., 111, 113
paradigms, 126–127, 154, 177–179, 181
paraphrasing, 261
particles, defined, 17
passage-dependent test items, 261
passive skills, 196, 214
pattern practices, 170–171
Paulson, D. L., 271–272, 274
Paulston, C. B., 54, 121, 170
Pearson, P. D., 227
perception of aural stimuli, 195–196, 214
Perkins, K. L., 220, 261
Perrone, C., 130
phonology, 17–18, 169
photographs, and reading comprehension, 230
Pica, T., 129
Pichert, J. W., 220
Pienemann, M., 22, 168
picture file, 42
placement tests, 256, 258
planned discourse, 130–131
planning, in writing, 244, 247–251
Poh, C. L., 261
Porter, P., 58
posttest, 154
pragmatic competence, 17, 111–113
pragmatics, defined, 17
predictions, 209, 214, 220
prelistening activities, 209–214
prereading activities, 222, 228, 233, 267
pretest, 229, 232
probes, 105–106, 108
procedures, in writing, 247
Processability Theory (Pienemann), 22–23
processes, and testing, 262, 266–267
processing instruction, 3, 124, 137, 139, 142–151, 165
processing strategies
  adjective agreement and, 143–144
  of learners, 21, 69, 138–141, 152, 165

structured input activities and, 124, 137, 142–145, 151–152, 158–159, 165
  verb morphology and, 126–127, 142–143
production strategies, 168–169
productive skills, 200
proficiency goals, 74–75, 77
  ACTFL guidelines for, 104–106, 271
  classhour goals, 74, 77, 85–86, 88–89
  communicative goals, 74, 76–77, 113
  grammatical goals, 82, 84
  lesson goals, 74–77, 85–85, 95
  Oral Proficiency Interview (OPI), 104–106, 108–109, 111, 113
  subgoals, 74, 77, 79–82, 84–86, 88–89, 95
  work outside of class and, 74, 91–94
Proficiency Guidelines, 104–106, 109, 271
proficiency tests, 104–111
prompt questions, 250
propositional content, 197
prototypes, episodic, 197
psycho-linguistic processes, 58, 195–198, 214
psycho-social purpose of communication, 53–54
Pulido, D., 228

queries, types of, 200–201
question(s)
  open-ended, 70–71, 241, 260
  oral, 98
  prompt, 250
question-and-answer model of conversation, 14, 22
quizzes, vs. tests, 100

Randall, S., 94
rating scales, componential, 98, 111, 113, 271
reader
  background knowledge of, 218, 222–223, 225, 228–229
  contribution to comprehension, 217–226, 241–242
  personalizing content, 223, 238–239, 265
reading
  communicative function of, 238–239, 241–242, 262, 265–266
  culture and, 220–221, 240–241
  defined, 245
  interactive model of, 217, 225–228, 241–242
  language development and, 227
  as private and social act, 233
  surface, 261, 273
  for writing, 251–254
reading comprehension
  assimilation and, 228, 236–237, 262, 264–266
  brainstorming and, 229, 230, 267
  comprehension checks for, 233–234
  defined, 3–4, 227, 262
  and formal schemata, 222
  guided interaction and, 233–235, 262–264, 267
  headings and, 229
  illustrations and, 229–230

instructional framework for, 217, 222, 227–238, 2241–242, 273
  management strategies for, 233–234
  organization of discourse and, 219, 222–224, 241–242
  photographs and, 230
  prereading and, 222, 228, 233, 267
  readers' background knowledge and, 218, 222–223, 225, 228–229, 231
  readers' contribution to, 217–222, 241–242
  scanning for specific information and, 229, 232–233, 267
  schemata, activating, 218–219, 221–222, 226, 227–233
  tests of, 4, 256, 260–267
  text features and, 217, 222–224, 241–242
  titles and, 229–230
  vocabulary and, 228
  world knowledge and, 218, 229, 231–232, 238
receptive role, 6–8, 10–12, 22, 68, 69
receptive skills, 195, 200
referential meaning, 138–139, 159, 197–198
referentially-oriented activities, 159
reflexive verbs, 76–77
relevance, in testing, 98–100, 177, 184, 188, 260
reliability
  inter-rater, 106, 113, 271, 273
  intra-rater, 271, 273
reporting back, 231
reporting test, 107–108
research
  on communicative language ability, 49, 51
  on grammar acquisition, 105, 107, 125–126, 129–130
  on input processing, 141, 145–152, 170
  interactional patterns, 58, 119
  on limited effects of explicit instruction, 116, 120, 123–125, 129–130
  on processing instruction, 145–152
  on structured input activities, 124–125, 132, 137, 145–152
  on text characteristics, 223–224
resource, instructor as, 68, 69
response, strategic, 199–201, 214, 260
responsibility for learning
  instructor and, 68
  learner and, 40, 68–69, 188–192, 262
responsibility for testing, 100, 104–105
restructuring, 18, 126–127, 132, 141
Reves, T., 107, 109
review
  of existing knowledge, 210, 213
  in writing, 244, 248–251, 254
revising, in writing, 244, 248, 254
rhetorical problem, 244, 247, 250–252
Richards, J. C., 197
Riley, G. L., 220, 222, 224
Robb, T., 268–269
role(s)
  authoritative, 6–8, 10–12, 22, 67–68, 71
  changing, 6–7, 10–11, 61, 70, 72